TRANSFORMING LEGAL EDUCATION

Transforming Legal Education
Learning and Teaching the Law in the
Early Twenty-first Century

PAUL MAHARG
University of Strathclyde, UK

ASHGATE

Published by
Ashgate Publishing Limited
Gower House
Croft Road
Aldershot
Hampshire GU11 3HR
England

Ashgate Publishing Company
Suite 420
101 Cherry Street
Burlington, VT 05401-4405
USA

Ashgate website: http://www.ashgate.com

British Library Cataloguing in Publication Data
Maharg, Paul
   Transforming legal education : learning and teaching the
   law in the early twenty-first century
   1. Law - Study and teaching (Higher) 2. Interdisciplinary
   approach in education
   I. Title
   340'.0711

Library of Congress Cataloging-in-Publication Data
Maharg, Paul.
   Transforming legal education : learning and teaching the law in the early twenty-first century / by Paul Maharg.
      p. cm.
   Includes bibliographical references and index.
   ISBN: 978-0-7546-4970-0
   1. Law--Study and teaching--Great Britain. 2. Law--Study and teaching--United States. I. Title.

   K100.M34 2007
   340.071'141--dc22

2007017571

ISBN: 978-0-7546-4970-0

Printed and bound in Great Britain by MPG Books Ltd, Bodmin, Cornwall.

Contents

List of Figures

Preface

A thought experiment: if you were to design a completely new law school, what would it look like? How would you design the curriculum? How would staff teach? What would students learn? I was a mature student studying law, after taking undergraduate and postgraduate degrees in the Arts, and a postgraduate Diploma in Education. I had spent seven years teaching at many levels, from PhD to adult functional illiterate. Paulo Freire's *Pedagogy of the Oppressed* was well-thumbed and annotated, so perhaps it was naïve of me to think that I could sit and listen to whole lecture courses on Scots law without questioning the general method and approach. As my mind wandered, I constructed a new law school, which was of course student-centred. Its shape and purpose changed, as I moved through the course and learned more about the intellectual structure of the discipline of law, as well as its history, politics, economics and general culture. Later, when I taught law and learned much more about the problems of teaching our difficult discipline, the ideal became clearer in outline and purpose. Staff appointments became like fantasy football league: there was even a faculty position for Freire …

This is a book about legal education and its place in the academy, the profession, and society. It is not a history of legal education, though it explores historical episodes; it does not attempt an overview of theory and practice as did the excellent Le Brun and Johnstone (1994); nor is it a pro- or prescriptive set of guidelines, though it explores theory and practice. Rather, it is a critical inquiry into the identity and possibilities of legal education, and an exploration of alternatives to our current theories and practices of teaching and learning the law. Above all, it is about the transformation of legal learning in the early twenty-first century – an invitation to explore what transformation might mean, and how in some measure it might be accomplished.

The book is personal, but it is also the work of many others since the early 1990s. One of the first I must thank is Linda Flower, Carnegie-Mellon University, for her personal encouragement. Her contribution to the research paradigm of her own disciplinary community as well as to the wider social community over the years has been inspirational. To my colleagues in the GGSL I owe many debts: to Alan Paterson's generosity and vision for the GGSL which has been the foundation of much of latter third of this book; to Leo Martin, solicitor and my co-director in the Diploma in Legal Practice for helping to maintain sanity, and for his unstoppable confidence in transactional learning; to Charles Hennessy, solicitor and Voltaire of the discussion forum, for his resourceful writing and his mordant wit at dark moments; to John Sturrock QC for his leading work on the Foundation Course and multimedia; to Scott Slorach, College of Law, for his formidable curriculum planning work and conversations about IT; to Scott

Walker, whose patience with my early gauche ideas on virtual communities was as boundless as his knowledge of IT, and without whose practical intelligence Ardcalloch would have remained the pleasant thought of an idle afternoon spent on Inchcailleach Isle, Loch Lomond.

Conversations with Abdul Paliwala, University of Warwick, over the past 14 years have stimulated and inspired all of us engaged with technology and legal education. John Mayer, CALI, has been ever-enthusiastic about simulated learning and astonishingly well-connected on most aspects of technology and legal education. From valuable conversations with Peter Martin, Legal Information Institute, Cornell, we learned much on the subject of our video projects that made us re-think our work. Richard Susskind's enthusiasm and encyclopaedic knowledge of practical initiatives in legal practice and technology has been most helpful to us.

To Julian Webb, University of Warwick, I owe thanks for his support over the years and recently as Director of UKCLE. Thanks are due to Dr Lisa Hill, University of Adelaide, for commenting upon and correcting Chapter 4; and to William Twining, University College London, for his helpful comments on Chapter 3. To Clark Cunningham, Georgia State University, tireless clinician, endless innovator, and Larry Grosberg, New York Law School, I owe a debt for many kindnesses and for fascinating discussions about standardised clients and the American scene generally. Thanks also to Nigel Duncan, Inns of Court School of Law, for permission to quote text from a *Law Teacher* article in Chapter 9, and especially for his endlessly stimulating conversations, his sharing of a lifetime dedicated to teaching, learning and its research. To all participants in the SIMPLE project I owe a debt for keeping me grounded in the realities of simulations.

Thanks to Cynthia Baker, Indiana University Law School, for helpful conversations about fictional constitutions at Lake Arrowhead; and to David Johnson of New York Law School (some day we'll get round to a virtual version of Norton Juster's book). The Zeugma Group – Karen Barton (GGSL), Sefton Bloxham (Lancaster), Patricia McKellar (UKCLE) – have been influential in more ways than they can ever know in the drafting of Part 3. Karen found time to comment in detail on Part 3, as did Fiona Westwood, and helped to clarify many theoretical issues arising from our practice.

My thanks to staff at the Butler Library, University of Columbia for their generous assistance while consulting Dean Stone's papers; to the Library staff at Edinburgh University, Special Collections, while consulting manuscripts of Adam Ferguson's lectures; and to staff at the University of Groningen Library for showing me Isidore of Seville's *Etymologia*.

Most of the chapters have been presented in one form or another at legal education seminars and conferences in the University of London (IALS), BILETA, UK Centre for Legal Education at Warwick University and elsewhere – my thanks to colleagues and participants who commented upon work there. Students, too, have been an endless source of inspiration, insight and wit – my thanks to them, and particularly to the research assistants who have worked at the GGSL over the last seven years. My research assistant Tina Boswell has been invaluable to the production of this book. Thanks also to Alison Kirk at Ashgate for her patience and foresight.

Finally, more personal debts – to Euan and Magnus, for their patience when I should have been with them; and to Nicola, without whose love and support none of this would have happened.

To Nicola

Education either functions as an instrument that is used to facilitate the integration of the younger generation into the logic of the present system and bring about conformity to it, *or* it becomes 'the practice of freedom', the means by which men and women deal critically and creatively with reality and discover how to participate in the transformation of their world.

Foreword, Freire (1999, p. 16)

Introduction

Begin, ephebe, by perceiving the idea
Of this invention, this invented world,
The inconceivable idea of the sun.

[W]e do not have to go to knowledge to obtain an exclusive hold on reality. The world
as we experience it is a real world.[1]

Approaches to Theory

Legal education is not just law learned in universities but also in further education, schools, solicitors' offices, Citizens' Advice Bureaux, clinics, offices, the Bar and the Court. Although the book deals predominantly with Higher Education (HE), those of us in HE institutions can learn profoundly from considering the research that has been carried out on learning in other institutions, in workplaces and in other disciplines, including education itself, and the fundamental questions that are addressed there.[2] What is it that we do when we say we teach or study law? How does it differ from other disciplines? What effect are ever-larger numbers of undergraduate students, dwindling resources and burgeoning masters programmes having on the learning experience? What relationship should the undergraduate degree bear to postgraduate education and professional practice? How can the relationship of education to legal education be characterised? What is the role of technology in legal education? These questions are complex and often recursive, bearing one on another.

What these and most other questions concerning legal education have in common is that they operate within a specific historical context and structure. Indeed, they would not be asked were it not for that historical structure. As Leont'ev puts it in his discussion of the concept of activity:

> If we removed human activity from the system of social relationships and social life, it would not exist and would have no structure. With all its varied forms, the human

---

1   Stevens (1978), 'Notes Toward a Supreme Fiction', lls 1–3, p. 380 and John Dewey, cited in Biesta and Burbules (2003), p. 25. Future references in this book to Dewey's work are to the standard critical edition, *The Collected Works of John Dewey*, ed. Jo Ann Boydston (1969–91), and published as *The Early Works* (*EW*), *The Middle Works* (*MW*) and *The Later Works* (*LW*). These designations are followed by volume and page numbers. Here, *LW*, 4, p. 235.

2   'We' includes not just HE staff and students in the UK but in common law jurisdictions generally.

individual's activity is a system in the system of social relations. It does not exist without these relations. (Leont'ev, 1981, p. 47)

The contextual point was made in a similar way by the philosopher and educationalist John Dewey:

> There is no such thing as an ability to see or hear or remember in general; there is only the ability to see or hear or remember something. To talk about training a power, mental or physical, in general, apart from the subject matter involved in its exercise, is nonsense. (*MW*, 9, p. 107)

Any view of legal education, from the micro-level of classroom interaction to the macro-level of state and international educational policy, is subject to this rule of context. It is inevitable, then, that a book on legal education written by an academic with no professional legal experience will deal with the university generally; but we shall discuss professional as well as academic education; and deal with larger social concerns, too – indeed, they cannot be left out of any discussion of legal education.

In all this, we shall encounter theory as well as practice. Theory, as Julian Webb, Fiona Cownie and others have reminded us, matters a lot.[3] It is much more than a set of abstract concepts that explains practice. It enables a clearer understanding of legal educational practice and experience. It may take many forms – conceptual analysis, research reviews, model building or analysis, ground-up theory, activity theory and the like. Theoretical approaches therefore have a degree of sophistication or 'thickness', to adopt Geertz's term. Some may be little more than conceptual frameworks or scaffolds, while others may be thoroughly researched positions that are embedded in practice and with a body of literature attached to them. Many theories overlap or feed off each other.[4] Theories will often rival each other; and in their alternative views of phenomena they give us the opportunity to see things differently.

But if theory matters, we need to be cautious about the place of theory in discussion of legal education for two reasons. Firstly, in education (and particularly educational psychology) there are strong positivist traditions of empirical theory and research that hold to what might loosely be termed a 'black box' view of human learning. The tradition is most closely associated with laboratory research paradigms, and adheres to a pre-test, test and post-test model of research. Such a paradigm, while powerful, requires careful reading and application. Tests or research conducted on samples of students will produce results that may be quantifiable and reproducible in experimental conditions; but the conditions of actual teaching and learning in universities provide a very different setting.

---

3   For our purposes here, I shall take as my definition of theory, 'a systematic account of relationships among phenomena' (McMillan and Schumacher 1984, p. 14).

4   See for instance the constellation of concepts surrounding constructivism – situated learning, collaborative learning and so on.

Theory based upon experimental research, therefore, while used throughout the book, is treated with caution.

Second, and related to the first point, it is often the case in education that an openness to alternatives in theory is essential. Legal education rarely tolerates theoretical absolutes.[5] This is not to say that there are no guiding principles or ethical principles involved. Far from it – legal education is full of such principles. But it is simply a reminder that the quotidian, the everyday, plays a powerful role in what we do as educators. Sfard put this well:

> When a theory is translated in an instructional prescription, exclusivity becomes the worst enemy of success. Educational practices have an overpowering propensity for extreme, one-for-all practical recipes. A trendy mixture of constructivist, social-interactionist, and situationist approaches … is often translated into a total banishment of 'teaching by telling'. What is true about educational practice also holds for theories of learning. (Sfard, 1998, pp. 10–11)

It is for these reasons that I take a broad, interdisciplinary view of education and experience. The actual experience of education will be the focus of analysis here. As ever, Dewey puts the issue in a nutshell for us: '[t]he fundamental issue is not new versus old education nor of progressive against traditional education but a question of what anything whatever must be to be worthy of the name *education*' (*LW*, 13, p. 62, Dewey's emphasis). In this sense, while there are effective ways to educate as proven by the research, in practice there are likely to be various ways to achieve such effective education, since students, institutions and communities need alternatives. In the process of exploring those alternatives, undergraduates move toward graduation, graduates move from being novices toward becoming competent practitioners and practitioners move toward becoming experts. It is a process of gradual transformation and the analysis of this process is what lies at the core of this book. The questions raised by such transformations are deeply ethnographical. On a wider social plane, for instance, how do infants adapt to social life in a kindergarten? How do little children become school pupils? How do girls and boys become partners, mothers, fathers?[6] This is one meaning of the book's title. It is about the transformation that takes place while students are in our care, the slow transformation brought about by their learning a discipline, exploring professions, entering them, the slow and essential process of growing in wisdom, of coming to know who you are and what you are capable of.

---

5   Regarding learning outcomes, Richard Lanham made the point well. 'Imagine waking up in the morning and being entirely Clear, Brief, and Sincere to everyone you met […] you'd lose your spouse the first day, your job the second, and your reason the third' (Lanham, 1993, p. 242).

6   I am not suggesting that Garfinkel's approaches are phenomenographical; but there are many analogies between an approach such as his view of ethnomethodology and the research methodologies of Marton, Säljö and other phenomenographers.

In Dewey's sense it is a search for forms of education that can be worthy of the name. Just as students transform in time, so do we ourselves as teachers. Education and legal education are profoundly practical domains, suffused with theory. It is living *phronesis*. Research on education should send us back to practice at least thoughtful, possibly intrigued, certainly with new or renewed ideas, and ought to facilitate change within practice and context. Reading is only the first stage of this participative process, though – as Dewey has it:

> Experience is the result, the sign, and the reward of that interaction of organism and environment which, when it is carried to the full, is a *transformation* of interaction into participation and communication. (*LW*, 10, p. 28, my emphasis)

Dewey's vision is enacted by others – Shulman, for instance, has called for sustained scholarship that has three fundamental qualities – it should be public, it should be a critical review and evaluation, and it should be accessible for exchange and use by others in the community (Shulman, 1998, p. 5).[7] And Bernstein, a Carnegie scholar, has described the alignment between teaching practice and student performance as a 'transactional relationship', echoing one of Dewey's key terms (Bernstein, 1998, p. 77). This book, which takes a dialogic view of research, should be judged by this standard.

Does the book, though, have no other theoretical contribution to make than well-meaning cautions as to the use of theory? It is time to say what readings it is guilty of.[8] The title speaks to the main theme, that of transformation, because it is becoming clearer to many of us involved in legal education that our current educational approach to legal education is, in the longer term, unsustainable. It is heavily front-loaded, still aimed at school-leavers predominantly at a time when the law school student population is diversifying in age as well as experience and culture (Francis and McDonald, 2006, pp. 92–108; Anderson et al., 2003). We categorise and subcategorise law to our students, creating matroshka dolls of legal concepts; we divide study into hierarchies with division of labour. We teach intensively jurisdictional law for three or four years, then deal with globalisation and globalised law in brief special courses, redolent of the way EC Law used to be taught in the 1970s. We divide off academic and professional learning to the serious detriment of both. In the UK LLB and that of some other jurisdictions we still, on the whole, relegate ethical inquiry and practice to vocational courses; and we have little impact on and almost no input to professional educational initiatives.[9] In the US, too, often the second and third

---

7   See also Stenhouse (1983, p. 185).

8   'As there is no such thing as an innocent reading, we must say what reading we are guilty of' (Althusser and Balibar, 1970, p. 14).

9   All of these points have attracted serious comment in the legal educational literatures of common law jurisdictions. The ethical point has come under sustained critique – see for example Webb (1998 and 1999) and Hutchinson's (1999) splendidly excoriating piece in the same journal issue – for him, and for many others, myself included, it is a situation 'depressing beyond words' (p. 301).

year experiences are dilutions of the first. In most common law jurisdictions there is evidence that our students are disciplined, urged to conform; they tell us in too many studies that, whatever we may think we are teaching, they experience a loss of creativity and personality when they study law.[10] The latest empirical research tells us that we force them to use institutional ICT (information and communication technology) structures at a time when personalisation and customisation of web interfaces is intuitively the norm for many students. Many of our twenty-first century law schools still inhabit an industrial system of education inherited from a twentieth century mired in nineteenth-century structures – a system that is entrenched by the massification of higher education.[11]

Underlying much of our current practice as legal educators are variants of the liberal law school.[12] The liberal position, though, is under intense pressure. It derives from a model of university design that grew out of British and German industrial societies and the historical relations between university and state in that period. Within the limits of the state-education Fordist compact of the earlier twentieth-century, this design worked adequately to serve the needs of both state and universities.[13] But increasingly the model is breaking up, economically, commercially, culturally, educationally, not merely under pressure from chronic underfunding and increased demand on resources, but under the pressure of neoliberalist policies and globalisation. As Kress puts it, '[t]he relative stabilities of the class societies of industrialized states, with their economies founded on industrial mass production, are being replaced, or at the very least overlaid, by the highly fluid arrangements of lifestyle groupings' (Kress, 2000, pp. 133–45).[14] Such groupings are highly vulnerable to the market forces that drive both the neoliberalist agenda, and globalised finance.

Under such pressure we need to inhabit a critical legal education that stands, to quote the Scots poet Hugh MacDiarmid, 'whaur extremes meet', that embraces multiliteracies and is multimodal.[15] We need curricula that take account of the blurring of the domains of academic and everyday work and leisure, authority and purpose, market and individual choice, knowledge-in-itself and knowledge-for-others. In addition there are three pressing issues we need to address. We need to:

---

10 The literature is extensive, consisting of both empirical work and autobiographical accounts. For example Elkins (1985), pp. 27–55, Goodrich (1996), Turow (1997) and Krieger (2002), pp. 112–29.

11 The results of such massification and its 'trajectory' are explored briefly by Bradney and Cownie (2000), pp. 4–5.

12 The literature is extensive. See, for instance, Birks (1994), Twining (1995), Brownsword (1996 and 1999) and Bradney (1999 and 2003).

13 Though the relationship was always an uneasy one, even in the nineteenth century. For an exploration of one mid-nineteenth-century moment of this, see Davie (1961).

14 For a powerful critique of the effects of neoliberalism and globalisation on legal education, see Thornton (2001).

15 See for instance the positional statement of the New London Group (1996).

1) *Account for knowledge generation and evolution of knowledge and hold ourselves responsible for that*

   Theories of learning that are focused on the singular mind bracket the world and set it aside. The world cannot be set aside. We are ineluctably part of the world and it of us, and our social relations affect generation of knowledge. In the past 30 years, fresh views of knowledge have formed – constructivism, situated learning and activity theory, to name a few – which have as much to say about the activities of academics and everyone involved in education as they have about student and professional learning. We owe ourselves, our students and our discipline a duty to learn about and contribute to the development of these ways of knowing, and where appropriate, to integrate them with more familiar models of learning.

2) *Take account of globalisation*

   Many aspects of HE globally will change hugely in the next 30 years. Cross-border HE statistical projections give an indication of the scale of change. Between 1999 and 2004, the number of mobile international students grew by 41 per cent to 2.5 million; by 2025 that is computed to increase to 7.2 million (Böhm et al., 2002).[16] Traditionally the cross-border higher education market has had less to do with altruism than expansion of university and departmental revenue bases. By 2025 the patterns of student enrolment will change significantly. If UK and US institutions wish to pursue the market, projections are complex but point in one direction:

   > student enrolments will expand only modestly in OECD countries by 2025, rising from 46 to 51 million, but in non-OECD countries, enrolments will rise from 69 to 255 million. (Kritz, 2006)

   There are many issues raised by such projections. One of the more foundational ones might be the problem of how classic liberal theory, at its heart a statement of enlightenment and nineteenth century views of rational activity of the mind, based upon elite values regarding the conservation and transmission of knowledge (replete with highly westernised, northern-hemisphere narratives at that), will cope with such change? There are of course international high-level frameworks being developed for dealing with financial and cultural shifts. The Lisbon Convention, for instance, builds recognition of forms of education on the basis of trust rather than scrutiny of course equivalence. But these are merely structural, tied to specific areas (for example, European education) and, although structural facilitation at this level can be helpful, unless there is significant, embedded change at local levels – jurisdictions, regions, universities,

   ---

   16 See also UNESCO Institute for Statistics (2004). In Australia, for instance, global demand for international K-12 education (offshore and by e-learning) is expected to increase nine-fold up until 2025 and is already Australia's eighth-largest export sector, according to Böhm et al. (2002).

law schools, individuals – our participation in the process of cross-border HE exchange is likely to be relatively ineffectual, regardless of our motives and the cultural capital of the common law in our courses.

3) *Account for engagement with the world*

There is, for instance, still too little engagement between higher education and the professions. This does not mean that we ought to turn our law schools into vocational schools. In fact it means we ought rigorously to reject such an approach. But this book does argue for deeper, more serious engagement with the professions in the work that they do in society and that we should look to models of education and educational research in other disciplines and professions and other jurisdictions to provide us with exemplars and models we can build upon.

I have said that the concept of the liberal law school requires re-appraisal. But liberalism is much more than a collection of theoretical positions: it is a powerful affective impulse about the nature of knowledge, society, the individual, privacy, freedom, and the like. It is reasonable to point out where it can be improved and how one may achieve that improvement and to offer alternatives, in theory and practice, to its superstructure. In this book, therefore, I shall take a critical approach to the liberal model. This approach is based upon a *transactional* approach to legal education, one that finds its roots in pragmatic education, drawn from the work of John Dewey. As a prolegomenon to what follows in subsequent chapters it will be useful to outline some of this pragmatic foundation.

Dewey, one of the great figures in twentieth-century education, was a watershed for many streams of philosophical ideas. In him gathers the idealism of the later nineteenth century, with its Hegelian bias; social Darwinism, early psychology, aesthetic theory, realism, and much else.[17] Key to his philosophy of education was Pragmatism – the movement that, beginning in the later nineteenth century with James, Pierce and others, rejected the traditional dualistic construction of knowledge and the world, focused on the experience of the subject in context and was critical of the effects of capitalism and industrialism on American society (Menand, 2001).

We can illustrate this by considering a key early article, 'The Reflex Arc Concept in Psychology'. Written in 1896 – the year that the Laboratory School opened in Chicago University – it is one of the most influential papers in the domain of late-nineteenth-century culture, and ranks in importance with Freud's contemporaneous work on the aetiology of hysteria. In it, Dewey rejects the current theory of sensori-motor coordination which posited a stimulus-response arc for experience. This theory 'no matter how it may prate of unity … still leaves us with sensation … idea … and motor response, or act, as three disconnected

---

17 As recent researchers have shown, Dewey's debt to Hegel was fairly long-standing. See Garrison (2006). For a general account of Dewey's approach to Pragmatism, see Sleeper (1986).

existences' (*EW*, 5, p. 100). In what was to become a typical strategy in his essays on law and method, Dewey criticises this theory by analysing the methodological bases of it:

> We ought to be able to see that the ordinary conception of the reflex arc theory, instead of being a case of plain science, is a survival of the metaphysical dualism, first formulated by Plato, according to which the sensation is an ambiguous dweller on the border land of soul and body, the idea (or central process) is purely psychical, and the act (or movement) purely physical. (*EW*, 5, p. 104)

Dewey adds to this criticism of implicit metaphysical dualism within the arc theory the observation that the theory's logic is flawed: '[a] state of things characterizing an outcome is regarded as a true description of the events which led up to this outcome' (*EW*, 5, p. 105). As Dewey pointed out in his conclusion to the paper,

> [t]he reflex arc theory ... gives us one disjointed part of a process as if it were the whole. It gives us literally an arc, instead of the circuit; and not giving us the circuit, of which it is an arc, does not enable us to place, to centre, the arc. (*EW*, 5, pp. 108–9)

Dewey's concept of the circularity inherent in the cognitive learning process is clearly allied to theories of the circle of hermeneutic analysis, a progenitor of the cybernetic feedback loop, and the cognitive learning cycles of Kolb and many others.[18] These family resemblances were later traced by Pragmatism's later twentieth-century relatives, those involved in the neopragmatist debates. But early in the twentieth century, Dewey's interdisciplinary concept was deeply influential. In *Education and Democracy* – published 20 years after the reflex arc article and one of the most influential educational texts of the twentieth century – we can see the same move to define culturally-accepted dualisms – mind and body, mental percept and the world, theory and practice – as merely parts of the arc, not the circuit. We shall see evidence of it in the paper 'Logical Method and Law', where Dewey denies that any one set of legal rules can be identified as providing certainty and stability in legal judgement. Instead, Dewey advocates a process of constant checking and re-checking, an awareness of the instrumentality of role-based concepts, a feedback loop oriented to the future.

---

18 With regard to hermeneutics, Dewey's concept of logical enquiry in law prefigures Gadamer's use of the phrase 'tension' (*Spannungsverhältnis*) to describe the state of the act of textual interpretation: 'In both legal and theological hermeneutics there is the essential tension between the text set down – of the law or of the proclamation – on the one hand and, on the other, the sense arrived at by its application in the particular moment of interpretation, either in judgement or preaching' (Gadamer, 1975, pp. 274–5).

These ideas were based upon a radically new understanding of European philosophy, what might be termed an *anti*-epistemology.[19] Instead of defining mind over against the world, Dewey recast the problem as one of interactions within nature, interactions which take place ceaselessly – thought, for instance, is 'the interaction between elements of human nature and the environment, natural and social'.[20] This interaction, later called *transaction* (because Dewey felt that 'interaction' still gives the sense of individual parts), is at the heart of Dewey's conception of understanding and learning – a conception that he only began to fully develop in the middle of his long life. It is a concept that powerfully conditions the idea of reality, and therefore, as several commentators have pointed out, the term 'transactional realism' probably is closest to what Dewey wanted to describe. Thought itself becomes existential, and not separated from the act of inquiry and its context. Inference thus becomes a temporal event, one justified by the context, and by the experience of the thinker. Sleeper has described the term thus:

> [k]nowing is ... regarded as a transaction that takes place between an organism and its environment, and its occurrence denotes changes in relationships as existential events, actual changes in the real world. (Sleeper, 1986, p. 92)[21]

But knowing is only one mode of experience. Experience is formed for us by our contact with culture, which includes language, rituals, social groupings, ceremonies, habits and taboos – the whole enculturated, saturated experience of society – and therefore experience also includes ethical, aesthetic, religious, practical modes and much else.[22] For Dewey, experience was formed from action in the world and the transformation of living entities, and it is for this reason that he opposed the stimulus-response theory of the reflex arc, with its sense of completed actions that are really so only in retrospect. Instead, he saw it as an iterative process: '[t]o "learn from experience" is to make a backward and forward

---

19 The word is used by Biesta and Burbules (2003), p. 10, whose impressive interpretation of Dewey's educational work I follow below in my own understanding of Dewey's value for contemporary education.

20 *MW*, 14, p. 9, Dewey's emphasis; cited Biesta and Burbules, (2003), p. 10.

21 See also Vanderstraeten (2002, p. 234), who rightly argues that 'Dewey's analyses of the transaction of organism and environment can be read as an account of the construction processes that lie beneath all human activity. Dewey's work anticipates, if it does not explicitly articulate, much of what is important and interesting about constructivist epistemology and constructivist pedagogy'. Dewey is at once a remarkably accessible and remarkably difficult educationalist. Reading him is a vertiginous experience: one has at times the feeling of the ground dropping away from under you as you discover the depth of philosophical issue he references. Misreadings still appear – see Phillips (1996) and Glassman (2001). For a reply to Glassman, see Prawat (2005) and for a forthright reply to Phillips, see Petrovic (1998).

22 For a helpful table contrasting traditional views of experience with Dewey's view of it, see Hildebrand (2003, p. 36).

connection between what we do to things and what we enjoy or suffer from things in consequence.'[23] It is an approach to experience that seeks to jettison the 'spectator' theory of knowledge attributed to Greek philosophy, to turn its gaze to different procedures, and very different problems:

> [p]hilosophy recovers itself when it ceases to be a device for dealing with the problems of philosophers and becomes a method, cultivated by philosophers, for dealing with the problems of men. (*MW*, 10, p. 46, cited in Sleeper (1986), p. 100)

What were these problems for Dewey? Look around you, he would have said: vast inequities in wealth within democracies, totalitarianism, poverty, famine, disease, genocides, wars on a world scale, marvellous technologies used for inhuman purposes. And underlying these conditions, a western worldview that gives us the hideous choice of the 'inhuman rationality of modern science or the human irrationality of common sense' (Biesta and Burbules, 2003, p. 17), where values are relegated by science to the realm of the spirit, instead of remaining immanent within the transactions of 'actual changes in the real world'.

Dewey's philosophy of knowledge led him inevitably to a philosophy of culture, and to a philosophy of education. Within that, a number of concepts are important, notably the idea of *habit*. As Biesta and Burbules point out, the concept is one angle of an important triangular explanation for Dewey of how we act in the world. Three aspects of habit are important. First, according to Dewey habits are not formed by repetition (since 'the ability to repeat can only be the *result* of the formation of a habit'); secondly, because action is always transaction, the trigger for habits does not lie only in the external environment; and thirdly, habits give meaning to our environment, in the sense that experiential learning leads to more differentiated meaning in the world.[24] The world thus moves from being – in terms redolent of James (Henry, not William) – 'a vast penumbra of vague, unfigured things' to becoming 'a figured framework of objects' (Biesta and Burbules, 2003, pp. 36–7). Such knowledge-objects (both everyday as well as highly symbolic objects such as equations or legal cases) are created from transactions which take place in society and are mediated by social forms and communication.

Balanced against habits is the second angle of the triangle – impulses, which seek to restore habits when they are thwarted in some way: '[h]abits by themselves are too organized, too insistent and determinate to need to indulge in inquiry or imagination. And impulses are too chaotic, tumultuous and confused to be able

---

23 *MW*, 9, p. 147. As Dewey put it in a later essay on Copernicus, '[the world] is not in its primary phases a world that is known, a world that is understood and is intellectually coherent and secure. Knowing consists of operations that give experienced objects a form in which the relations ... are securely experienced' (*LW*, 4, p. 235).

24 And they are, of course, essential to identity-formation – as Dewey pointed out, '[w]ere it not for the continued operation of all habits in every act, no such thing as character could exist. ... Character is the interpenetration of habits' (*MW*, 14, p. 18).

to know even if they wanted to' (*MW*, 14, p. 124). Balanced against impulse is the third angle – intelligent thought, which can reflect upon the conflict of habit and impulse, and make webs of meaning from them.

Habits in themselves can become intelligent habits when deliberate thought about the habit is applied *via* the process of inquiry (foreshadowing Schön's reflection-in-action). This happens when thought interacts with habits and impulses – as Koschmann put it, Dewey 'believed that it is possible to develop habits for productive inquiry through extensive practice, just like any other kind of skill'.[25] He defined inquiry as the 'controlled or directed transformation of an indeterminate situation into one that is so determinate in its constituent distinctions and relations as to convert the elements of the original situation into a unified whole' (*LW*, 12, p. 108). The unified whole, though, was by far the end of the matter: inquiry was a condition of constant re-appraisal for Dewey.

Learning is therefore a transaction: not the acquisition of knowledge about the world (which like the stimulus-response model separates mentality and reality damagingly), but the acquisition, coordination and practice of habits, impulses and dispositions towards action in the world. As a result of learning, the world becomes richer, more meaningful, for the learner.

But this is not the only interest we may have in Dewey's concept of transaction. Toward the end of his life, Dewey wrote an extraordinary work, until recently little regarded by educationalists, entitled *Art as Experience*. It is a book that is relevant to the practice and theory of legal education. There, he defines experience of art as transactional: it is 'active and alert commerce with the world; at its height it signifies complete interpenetration of self and the world of objects and events' (*LW*, 10, p. 25). It is always and everywhere historical: '[a]n experience is a product, one might almost say a by-product, of *continuous and cumulative* interaction of an organic self with world' (*LW*, 10, p. 224). Immersed in the moment, we cannot articulate it until raw data is identified, schematised. Thus when I look at a wooden mallet, according to Dewey, I see the expressiveness of the object, its quality as defined by use, shape, materials – a quality I can transfer to other types of mallets – copper, rubber, rawhide, and so on. For Dewey, though, expressiveness can become dulled with familiarity: 'apathy and torpor conceal this expressiveness by building a shell about objects' (*LW*, 10, pp. 109–10). In contrast, the act of dwelling upon experience was imbued with imagination, without which transfer of process between objects and between concepts was inconceivable: '[a]ll *conscious* experience has of necessity some degree of imaginative quality' (*LW*, 10, p. 276, Dewey's emphasis).[26]

---

25 Koschmann (2000, p. 157). See also Sullivan (2000).

26 For a helpful interpretation of Dewey's aesthetics, see Alexander (1987). It is interesting that Dewey's aesthetic position helped develop the early, and highly influential 'reader-response' movement, which developed specific theories about how we read texts, and literary texts in particular. See, for example, Rosenblatt (1978).

It is thus that imagination becomes a central concept in Dewey's construction of experience. It is the great function of art to enable us to see anew our experience, our schemas and our habits of thought. The quality of attention given to experience is important and separates aesthetic from other types of learning experiences. Thus, when what he calls the 'intrinsic meaning' of an object predominates over the 'extrinsic meaning' then the experience becomes focused on the aesthetic object. For Dewey imagination is a fundamental part of the way we construct our experience and schemas of complex phenomena such as music or law.

If it is integral to all mental events to a greater or lesser extent, imagination ought to be a fundamental element in legal education, and we should enlist it in the art of teaching law and legal skills so as to enable students to use it in learning the art and science of the law. The arts and other disciplines – literary objects and literary theory, medical education, musical education, educational theory, rhetoric, the cognitive sciences, the clusters of cross-disciplinary concepts emerging around new uses of ICT – these embody approaches that can be of vital use to us; but only if we explore them and use them within our legal educational practice. Legal education has always *borrowed* concepts and methods, but this metaphor does not focus us sufficiently on the sources of those concepts and methods. Examining the theories and theories-in-use in other disciplines, we can begin to appreciate how other versions of artistry might be employed in our own discipline. Such open-texture is essential, I would argue, to the continued health of legal education; for should we not remain open to other disciplines, the results will be an impoverishment of the theoretical roots of legal education and its practice.

This has been the briefest of summaries of a subject that Dewey himself spent more than five decades writing upon. As we shall see throughout the book, there are many advantages to adopting Dewey's view of knowledge. I said earlier that Dewey was a watershed: not just for previous thought but for later educational thought, too. Many others have acknowledged his influence.[27] Constructivism and situated learning, for instance, are but two approaches to learning that widely acknowledge Dewey as a source.[28]

And yet it might be thought that someone born in the same year as the publication of Darwin's *On the Origin of Species* might have little to say to us about legal education in the twenty-first century. And to anyone brought up in Scottish and English jurisprudential traditions, Dewey's approach is oddly

---

27 Take for instance the fields of ICT and medical education. In the former, Garrison et al. (2000 and 2001) have designed a valuable community of inquiry model that was constructed from Dewey's practical inquiry model, and incorporated domains: social presence, cognitive presence and teacher presence. Their concepts were helpful in the design of multimedia learning, and are cited in Chapter 9 of this book. In medical education, see the work of Koschmann (2001, 2003 and 2006).

28 See Garrison (1995). One can find his influences even in instructionist approaches to education – see, for example, Thurmond and Wambach (2004).

aslant what one might take as the mainstream of legal philosophy.[29] But Dewey's achievement as a philosopher, while systematic after a fashion, belongs more to the critical tradition – that of Kierkegaard, Nietzsche, Heidegger, Wittgenstein and Arendt – and it is in this capacity that he is valuable to a critical *educational* jurisprudence.[30] To anyone who has read educational scholarship of the last 40 years it might appear that Dewey has been overtaken by the bulk of that scholarship. But his achievement as an educationalist was to transform profoundly educational theory and practice in America and elsewhere by reversing the polarity of theory-practice such that powerful ideas arose from practice and experience, and were theorised in practice – his Chicago Laboratory School is a case in point (Tanner, 1997). Dewey's achievement also lies in his social and political criticism and in his unceasing and inspirational support of the cause of democratic freedom and social responsibility, which has particular resonance for legal education, ethical education and the role of lawyers and professionals generally in society. I would hold that that reversal of polarity and the strong bonds between Dewey's philosophy of learning and his commitment to democratic society still hold a valuable message for us in many aspects of legal education; and this book explores some of those educational streams stretching from Dewey down to us, through us and into the future.

In subsequent chapters, then, elements of Dewey's Pragmatism and transactional realism are used as critical tools to help us clarify a vision of transforming legal learning. This does not mean that readers need to accept a Pragmatist programme in legal education. By the end of the book I hope you are persuaded sufficiently at least of some of Dewey's ideas, and possibly interested enough in some of the implementations to develop them for yourself – as Dewey himself said, 'a working model is not something to be copied; it is to afford a demonstration of the feasibility of the principle, and of the methods which make it feasible' (*MW*, 1, p. 56). If not (as is likely, because the experience of teaching is often more powerfully persuasive than reading about teaching), then the book contains a structure of ideas and collection of examples that may at least contribute to the development of future theory and practice in legal education. As well as being a formal discipline, education is a subject like religion, politics or money: we all have our deeply held ideas about it and how it could be improved. Most important of all, therefore, this book is an invitation to you to share your own ideas on how legal education could be transformed.[31]

---

29 Some are frankly baffled, in part because of Dewey's radical recovery of the American Realist and Pragmatist tradition. I agree with Brian Leiter that Hart's critique of Realism in Chapter 7 of *The Concept of Law* is a misunderstanding of the Realist enterprise. See Leiter (2006, p. 8).

30 See Sleeper, 205–6. See also Stephen Toulmin's sensitive introduction to Dewey's 'The Quest for Certainty', in *LW*, 4, pp. vii–xxii.

31 The final chapter of the book will be posted on a wiki at http://www.transforming. org.uk. Comments on the chapter and discussion of alternative futures for legal education are welcomed on this site.

Preview of Chapters and Themes

The book is divided into three parts. The first part examines some of the central issues in the book's approach to legal education. The second analyses three episodes from legal educational history, while Part 3, concerned with present and future, examines some approaches to technology-enhanced learning in law.

Part 1: In(ter)disciplines

Interdisciplinarity is one of the key themes of this book – an implementation of transactional realism. It is important to our own research practices as academic staff, and holds significance for us in the ways that we can use educational theory in order to understand our own practices (Feitelson and Stefik, 1977).[32] Other disciplines have long acknowledged how theory and contingent situations impinge upon each other – in medical education, for instance, there are regular meta-debates centred on journals, on how medical and other disciplines should be used to develop theory and practice.

Thus Chapter 1 explores some of the problems in adapting this approach. What is interdisciplinary activity and how might we best perform it in our legal educational research and in our teaching? Three approaches are outlined – interdisciplinarity in subject matter, in method and as meta-awareness – and the three are discussed in three case studies, namely a taught unit within a module on Jurisprudence, the place of rhetoric in legal education and the use of PBL to enhance problem-solving in the legal curriculum. The chapter ends by describing a model of practice adapted from the work of Peter Galison that could be useful in structuring our interdisciplinary research.

Chapter 2 goes on to examine the links between research and practice. What is the relation between the two? How can we best use research in our practice? The latter question is a critical one. Systematic experimental and design research is always a necessity but it is not enough. Practices developed in research can be used to drive the re-organisation of legal education, whether small-scale and local

---

32 See the work of Feitelson and Stefik on the research practices of geneticists, who observed that researchers did not set out an entire research programme, but rather appeared to relate each emerging research observation to their overall research aims. In the process, they constantly generated and sorted hypotheses that would explain the changing situation of the research results, interrogating the pre-existing research literature and its findings as they did so. Paradoxically, this paper arose from the AI Knowledge Systems cluster of projects at Xerox PARC, the aims of which were to extract features of human expertise and embody them in machines that would then function as integrated elements of a community. This approach is largely discredited, but from it arose a number of useful projects and approaches to knowledge-building. Quoted in Suchman (1987, pp. 187–8). As Suchman put it, '[t]he experimenters' expertise lay not in completing the plan, but in the ability to generate hypotheses continually, and to exploit serendipity in the course of the experiment'.

change in classrooms, or fundamental structures in law schools and the three case studies are contributions to such thinking. First we consider a representation of the teacher-student relationship in literature and music. Next we consider a method of music education, the Kodàly Method. Finally, we consider the use of standardised clients in the teaching and assessment of client interviewing. The three case studies are linked thematically to the three case studies of Chapter 1 and these and other matters are discussed in the conclusion to Part 1.

Part 2: Laminations

The middle passage is historical: how and why it is so requires a little explanation. As Twining pointed out some time ago, a knowledge of our discipline is essential to who we are; and it is all to easy to forget our own story in this regard, versions of which are filed away under a different directory called legal history, or history of legal education (Twining, 1967, p. 396).[33] This is as much the case for the history of legal education as it is for the history of law itself. All the more reason, therefore, that we should turn our gaze to the past, to the reasons why we are here as a discipline, and how our assumptions about legal education come to be as they are. Part 2 therefore consists of three meditations on historical moments, starting with the most recent, in the 1920s, and moving further back into our foundations – eighteenth-century moral philosophy, and some of the tools of legal learning in medieval universities.

Chapter 3 focuses on the encounter between Dewey and the realist reformers in Columbia University Law School. It investigates, in part through analysis of primary materials, the implications of the encounter and the grounds for failure in the experiments there. It goes on to explore the implications of this for the current New Legal Realism movement in the US and contemporary curriculum innovations.

Chapter 4 starts with a description of rival concepts of competence as these are presented by Ronald Barnett, and goes on to locate a source of ethical dichotomy in eighteenth-century Enlightenment concepts of moral education. We take a moment in the development of that fissuring, namely the Moral Philosophy lectures of Adam Ferguson, delivered to students at Edinburgh University (including law students). The moral and ethical dimension of Ferguson's solutions to the social problems around him are analysed (including the tensions created by the expansion of commerce and capital, and the ethical dilemmas this posed); and this discussion of the ethics of educational discourse is set in the context of Gillian Rose's discussion of the broken middle in ethics and the law. The chapter ends by relating the triune discussion (Barnett, Ferguson and Rose) to contemporary methods of ethical education in the law school.

Chapter 5 moves further back in time, to medieval forms of reading and writing. I argue that the highly sophisticated form of textual conservation and

---

33 See also Twining (1997, ch. 4).

transmission known as the gloss enacts forms of communication quite alien to our own contemporary textual practices, but which are strikingly similar to communicative forms embodied by the wireless web and social software. The implications of this for contemporary legal educational culture are discussed.

All the chapters in Part 2 function as comparisons of historical events to our own contemporary situation: Chapter 3, the emergence of realist educational ideologies; Chapter 4, the development of Enlightenment virtue ethics; and Chapter 5, the deep structures underlying the technologies of reading and writing in medieval and twenty-first century learning. They are by no means comprehensive accounts of these events, but it is hoped they offer fresh perspectives on important aspects. Historical analysis is of course inescapably postmodern and fragmented, a field of contending interpretations. It could be argued, as relativists do, that we cannot find anything in the past except what our own preconceptions and analyses of it supply us with. Or we could take another view, that common, albeit evolving forms of a discipline exist through time (legislation, courts, texts, curricula), and should be the subject of sustained historical inquiry. I shall take the view here that it is possible to understand, in a limited way, aspects of the cultural production of meaning in past societies and that, in doing so, it is possible to achieve a measure of distanciation from our own practices sufficient for us to understand social, educational and technological processes that may hitherto have remained hidden to us in both the past and the present.

While the view of the past I present here is by no means nostalgic, it may be argued that this use of the past is strongly teleological; and I would not deny this. But a teleological use of the past does not presuppose a Whiggish view of history and the relentless progress of cultural development that that view espouses. Far from it: Part 2 attempts to recover from the past lost conceptual perspectives and processes which have been erased or partially forgotten, and which are resonant – are at the very least fascinating – commentaries on our contemporary dilemmas. Thus the historical convergence of Pragmatism and the realist curriculum that occurred at Columbia holds important lessons for any contemporary attempt at curriculum (re-)building. Ferguson's creation of a virtue ethics derived in part from Stoic and Aristotelian sources, and allied to a Hutchesonian view of the *sensus communis*, can help contribute to a fresh perspective on our own adaptations in contemporary ethical education. Hypertext and the wireless web recovers a sense of the text which, since the rise of Ramist propaedeutics, Renaissance hermeneutics and above all the massively dominating presence of the printed text, we have lost; and one *locus* for understanding this lost textual art is the *glossa*. In a sense, therefore, the highly sophisticated textual forms of the Glossators can in many respects be seen to be the progenitor of much of what we currently *have not yet achieved* in our web-based teaching and learning, and therefore gives us interesting models for future textual production. The past, in other words, offers us a glimpse of alternative futures – and not merely the more immediate past of the twentieth century, but beyond the reaches of what one might regard as modern society. As E.P. Thompson put it,

[w]e shall not ever return to pre-capitalist human nature, yet a reminder of its alternative needs, expectations and codes may renew our sense of our nature's range of possibilities. (Thompson, 1991, p. 184, quoted in Norrie (2005), p. 72)

This applies even more to other jurisprudential and educational traditions in other societies and other times – the cultures of learning within Jewish and Islamic legal traditions, for instance. If there is no comment here on these and other ancient and highly sophisticated traditions of learning it is only because of my ignorance of their culture and languages.

Part 3: Metaverse

Where Part 2 is primarily historical, Part 3 looks more to the immediate future of legal education by taking examples from the present, particularly the context of e-learning. Chapter 6 begins by describing aspects of contemporary games and simulations that are multi-user virtual environments (MUVEs), the principles underlying the collaborative and social activities within them, and how they can be turned to legal educational use. Chapter 7 describes simulations currently in use in a postgraduate professional course called the Diploma in Legal Practice at the Glasgow Graduate School of Law and offers examples together with adaptations of transactional learning theory underpinning the practice. Chapter 8 analyses how such simulation-play affected the curriculum, and how the curriculum, staff teaching, administration and much else in the Diploma has been re-structured by transactional learning. In particular I show how the subject of Practice Management, hitherto a relatively peripheral subject, became a lynchpin for the whole programme of study. Chapter 9 presents examples of the resources and media that can be distributed in cyberspace to support the simulations described in Chapters 7 and 8 and examines some of the results of a research project that set out to discover how such resources affected the quality of student learning.

Part 3's discussion of the present of legal education may seem to be dominated by technology. In writing about it, I am not arguing that the only interesting educational innovations today are in technology nor that transactional learning can only be implemented through use of ICT. Far from it: the extraordinary work being done in clinical education, trans-systemic curriculum design, professional learning and many other *loci* throughout all common law jurisdictions are examples of inspiring educational initiatives. But if this book is about the transformation of legal education then we need, as Bilimoria puts it, to generate and legitimise the creation of 'new and vital teaching and educational structures and practices conducive to improving student learning' (Bilimoria, 2000, p. 704). While there is a rich and sustained literature developing around legal clinic, for instance, there is still insufficient theory and practice that is developed around either the use of simulation or the use of ICT in legal education. The theory is out there: over the last 30 years there has developed a distinguished tradition of anthropologists, ethnologists and educationalists who move between educational concepts and cybernetic concerns – Gordon Pask, Gregory Bateson, Sherry Turkle, Diana Laurillard, to name a few – and that tradition is, with the development of the internet, growing into a complex and fascinating literature.[34] It is a line of research that has attracted proportionately little comment from legal educationalists, though, given the huge uptake in ICT by law schools in recent years.[35] It is becoming increasingly urgent that we engage with this and other lines of research, and develop implementations based upon its insights into the relationships between technology and education specifically, and between technology and society more generally.

In my analysis, I hope to avoid two simplistic positions. First is that of technological determinism – the idea that technology is a relentless juggernaut, careering out of control – and secondly, the concept that technology is a value-neutral toolset that can be applied to whichever ends we choose. Both positions assume a view of society and the effects of technology within it that are not borne out by serious research (Burbules and Callister, 2000). The truth is at once simpler and more complex: technology is social, and society is technological, and their effects, one on the other, are profound. If we adopt a technologically-determinist approach, we become victims not of technology but of those in the global capitalist grid who control it; and if we take a technologically-neutral approach, we are in effect guilty of irresponsibility and insensitivity, as well as accepting of a 'neo-liberal globalization paradigm' (Clegg et al., 2003, pp. 39–52).

Part 3 therefore exists as an in-depth case study of the use of technology within a single programme of study. It contains both theoretical approaches and implementations that stem in part from Dewey's transactional realism and other educational approaches, all of which are harnessed to the attempt to effect a transformation of legal education. On another level, it presents an example of an alternative curriculum, one which is much more Pragmatist in its approach, with distinctive views of learning, assessment, ethics, teaching, technology and much else.

Finally, in the Afterword, I draw together the themes of the book and try to glimpse, in a highly hubristic account, what a student's experience may be like 40 years hence, in 2047.

---

34 The internet, as Phil Agre notes (2002, pp. 171–89), is most often used as a shorthand for the notion of distributed computing – a synecdoche which is also present in terms such as 'cyberspace', 'the web', and so on. It is this sense of the word that will be used in this book.

35 There are of course shining exceptions to this – commentators such as Abdul Paliwala, Peter Martin, John Mayer have given us powerful instances of both theory and practice to draw upon; organizations such as the Centre for Computer-Assisted Legal Instruction (CALI), and the British and Irish Law Education Technology Association (BILETA) have provided platforms for the dissemination of theory and practice. But I think that most working in the field would agree that there is still a lack of sustained theory to underpin our practice in our discipline.

It will be evident from this summary that the three parts of the book have a rough symmetry – where Part 1 deals with the nature of legal education through an exploration of theory and practice, Part 2 turns to episodes in legal education's rich history. Part 3 deals with technology-enhanced learning and in doing so looks more to the future, while being soundly (and paradoxically) based in the last chapter of Part 2. There are many other parallels and contrasts within and between the chapters, for my method is unashamedly eclectic in character.[36] No-one – phenomenographer, constructivist or pragmatist – has the *ur*-theory that can wholly explain to us who we are and what we do in legal learning and teaching.[37] Most have insights worth listening to, depending on who we are, where we come from, what we want to learn. Often the richness of insight comes from an archaeology of the commonplace, a careful uncovering of what lies hidden under the topsoil of our quotidian assumptions about learning the law, and about ourselves.

---

36 And it moves constantly between theory and practice, as befits the matter of education. To those who suspect such moves are category errors, I would answer that this – in the words of Twining – merely 'combines appropriate theory ... with explicit concern for method' (Twining, 1982).

37 As Dahllof has said, '[t]oo much attention is directed towards finding ... 'the best method', even though fifty years of educational research has not been able to support such generalisations. Instead we should ask which method – or which combination of methods – is best ... for which goals, for which students, and under which conditions' (Dahllof, 1991, p. 148, cited in Entwistle, 1995, p. 32).

PART 1
In(ter)disciplines

Chapter 1

Trading Zones

We demand a rooted place and a dispersed existence all at once
Galison and Jones, 1995, pp. 99

What is written in the Law? What is your reading of it?
Luke 10:26

Legal education. In these two words we are bringing together two very different disciplines – law and education – and in this and the next chapter I'd like to explore just what is involved when we engage in interdisciplinary research and teaching. From the outset there is a key distinction to be made between cross-disciplinary or multi-disciplinarity research and interdisciplinarity, as a Royal Society report on the subject pointed out:

> Pulling together a group of experts from different disciplines to contribute to a single project does not constitute interdisciplinarity. Indeed, in most cases the resulting research is multidisciplinary in nature.
>
> Multidisciplinary research involves people from different fields co-operating: working together towards a common goal but staying within the boundaries of their own fields. They may reach a point where, because of the restrictions and limitations of their disciplines, they cannot make further progress. They may then be forced to work at the fringes of their fields, and forge new ones. At this point the research becomes interdisciplinary. (Royal Society, 1996, p. 15)

And there are defensive mechanisms operating at the boundaries of disciplines, as Becher has pointed out:

> Tribes of academe ... define their own identities and defend their own patches of intellectual ground by employing a variety of devices geared to the exclusion of illegal immigrants. (Becher, 1989, p. 24)

In spite of this, disciplines have for some time now had more of an open architecture than before: trespassing appears to be a common activity, not only between what might be regarded as cognate disciplines such as law, literature, history, theology and philosophy, but between the sciences and social sciences (Klein, 1995). The effect of Darwinian science on Victorian literature, for example, has been charted by Gillian Beer and others (Beer, 1983; 1995; Levine, 1988; Stafford, 1994; Jordanova, 1986). More particularly, the biological hypothesis of organic memory has been analysed by Laura Otis who, in her study, excavates the history of this way of thinking about the body throughout the nineteenth century, and takes case studies of European literature as examples of how the theory was propagated and represented to society. She reveals how the science becomes analogous to other things in literature; and how in turn these things mirror the science to society: '[a]s in image reconstruction, the image [of the organic memory hypothesis] became clear only when viewed from many perspectives simultaneously' (Otis, 1994, p. xii).[1] In jurisprudence, Roberto Unger developed his notion of 'expanded discourse' in defence of a version of interdisciplinarity (1983, p. 561); while the concept of autopoesis arose from biological autopoesis, and its application by Piero Sraffa, Nikolas Luhmann, Günther Teubner and others to social sciences, then law in particular.[2]

Other commentators have observed the topographical metaphor and their language points up the difficulty of the activity. To gain control over knowledge, Foucault has commented, we allocate to it a spatial position, a 'fix', between existing bodies of knowledge. Thus contained, we can begin to build a concept of the discipline, create a central core of practices and ideas, guard the penumbral borders between it and other disciplines. But – and again quoting from Foucault – within any present discipline there are fissures, 'kinds of virtual fracture which open up the space of freedom understood as a space of concrete freedom, i.e. of possible transformation' (Foucault, 1988, p. 36). These fractures present us with the opportunity of exchange between disciplines as they are presently conceived: exchange conceived as 'transmissions, transferences, interferences' (Foucault, 1988, p. 37). Within a discipline, similar fractures occur. Often a discipline will want to deny its origins or distance itself from its rivals and often there will be a number of interpretations of the historical process within the discipline, or rivalry between subdomains within a discipline. Stephen Bann has described this process well with reference to art history:

> art history, in defining itself as a discipline over against connoisseurship, understandably took over the positivist paradigm of nineteenth century archival research. But in doing so it also inevitably (though no doubt unconsciously) took over the prejudice which

---

1   On p. 8 she discusses what Gould termed the 'analogistic tradition' in his book on Haeckel (1977, p. 40).

2   Maturana defined autopoesis as follows: 'We maintain that there are systems that are defined as unities, as networks or productions of components that 1/ recursively, through their interactions, generate and realize the network that produces them; and 2/ constitute, in the space in which they exist, the boundaries of this network as components that participate in the realization of the network' (Maturana, 1981, p. 21). As Arthur Jacobson (1989, p. 1649) points out, Sraffa's (1961) economic theories pre-date Maturana, and possibly supply a paradigm for the application of biological theories to the field of social sciences, and for Luhmann's (1982, p. 366) assertion that social systems themselves are autopoietic.

was so ingrained among archive-based historians against the serious historical value of artistic representations of history. (Bann, 1989, p. 104)

As Bann points out here, interdisciplinarity is inextricable from historical process: as disciplines mutate, they are constantly shape-shifting, particularly at the edges where they lie against other historically-adjacent disciplines. That being so, how difficult it is to cross the borders between disciplines depends on the state of the discipline. Some borders are strictly policed; others depend on a form of Schengen Agreement, where there is a complex of understandings about what constitutes good practice in comings and goings; between other disciplines the borders are historical only – the scene of great debates, long since settled or now deemed irrelevant.

However, the extent to which it is possible to 'forge' anew, as the Royal Society report put it, is questioned by some commentators. Stanley Fish, for example, has argued that interdisciplinarity, in seeking to eliminate boundaries between disciplines, has set itself an impossible task. According to him, interdisciplinarity can only redraw boundaries, not abolish them. One discipline may annex another, can borrow methodologies, models or theories from another, or a new discipline can be created which takes as its subject the study of disciplines (Fish, 1989). To Fish, then, interdisciplinarity in the form of boundary-abolition is almost a form of indiscipline.

I suspect that Fish is wrong in this view, and I shall say why at the end of this chapter. It is undeniable that boundaries are essential to a discipline, but much depends on what happens at the border crossings: what will be permitted, what will thrive once inside and what will be rejected. If we take a domain as eclectic as cognitive science (which grew from disciplines as amorphous as philosophy, psychology and several medical sciences such as neurology and anthropology) it might have been thought that this subject would have formed its own discipline. As Gardner (albeit hardly a dispassionate observer, but one with inside knowledge) put it, '[t]he hope is that some day the boundaries between these disciplines may become attenuated or perhaps disappear altogether, yielding a single unified cognitive science' (Gardner, 1985, p. 17). The last 20 years, though, have seen less the formation of a new discipline than the growth of sets of theories within the discipline of psychology, many of which have been appropriated in creative and fertile ways by other disciplines.

The situation with legal education (as opposed to law generally) is subtly different. Depending on how one defines it, it can overlap with humane arts, social sciences, economics or business process. It is also an education for a profession. Often the interdisciplinary peripheries and the core knowledge seem to be in tension with each other. But this is a false antithesis. Legal education has always developed interdisciplines for itself. Even Christopher Langdell could not resist the parallels.

We have ... constantly inculcated the idea that the library is the proper workshop of professors and students alike; that it is to us all that the laboratories of the university are to the chemists and physicists, all that the museums of natural history is to the zoologists, all that the botanical garden is to the botanists. (Langdell, 1887, pp. 123–4)

How can interdisciplinarity be carried out in legal education? The subject is notoriously difficult to categorise, but we can outline three approaches – interdisciplinarity in *subject matter*, interdisciplinarity in *method* and interdisciplinarity as *meta-awareness*. One can, for instance, deal with what is commonly regarded as legal subject matter but using another discipline's methodology. A good example of this is the work of Amina Memon on law and psychology, and particularly in the areas of eye witness memory, child witnesses and jury decision-making.[3] Memon's work is clearly of value to legal academics and practitioners, but her research methodology is thoroughly that of psychological data analysis, as are the journals she publishes within and the research groups of which she is a member. Alternatively, one can take concepts and materials from one's own home discipline and use these within others. Ian Hacking, for example, has described how he exports concepts properly belonging to analytical philosophy into domains as varied as experimental physics and multiple personality (Hacking, 2004). Finally, one can analyse the basic structure of research that is used in another discipline in order to examine how it may be adopted and adapted within legal education.

To exemplify these three approaches, I shall take three case studies. The first is an example of interdisciplinarity in subject matter, as it was embedded in an undergraduate level three jurisprudence module. The second, focusing on the emergence of rhetoric as a discipline, illustrates how interdisciplinarity can be used as a methodology within legal education. The third is an example of interdisciplinary research parallels between legal and medical education.

Case Study 1: 'Representations of Justice'

This case study formed part of a pre-existing module on jurisprudence. The module ran for a full semester (12 weeks) and, before the introduction of 'Representations of Law', consisted of two six-week units. The first was a historical analysis of the thought of key figures (Aquinas, Austin, Hart, Finnis, for instance), and the second focused on jurisprudential topics: punishment, justice, Critical Legal Studies and the like. Within this framework, the 'Representations of Law' unit was an option in the latter six weeks of the module, so that students could choose this unit instead of the existing topics. Teaching was carried out by a

---

3   See Memon and Bull (2001), Gabbert et al. (2004) and Memon et al. (2003).

combination of lectures and tutorials, and the module was assessed by essay (30 per cent weighting) and examination (70 per cent).

Tutors were selected because of their practical experience as well as their academic qualifications. They were aware of the aims of the unit, of the need to cohere with each other's work on the unit, and the thematic basis to the unit methodology. Above all, the unit had to be interdisciplinary from the students' point of view. It would have been a bar to student understanding of the unit if the separate sections had remained multi- rather than interdisciplinary. We shall see whether that in fact occurred.

If students were to view the unit as interdisciplinary, there would have to be something that bound the units together. I decided to adopt a thematic approach to the units, based on a number of subjects or *topoi*, in the rhetorical sense. These themes would be based upon the concept of the representation of law in society: more specifically, law as representation. This term was adopted for a number of reasons. First, I wanted to spotlight for students the idea that law is embodied in many ways and by various media in the world, and that we can, as an intellectual task, attempt to understand this process of embodiment. Understanding this task means understanding theories of what we might call embodiment or representation. It also means understanding how such theories are built and how they work in specific contexts in the world. In this approach, specifics were not to be the handmaids of theory: specifics were to embody theory, so that students could examine how theory could be applied to, and was influenced by, specifics. This approach, therefore, was both theoretical and concrete: it aimed to bridge the gap between jurisprudential understanding and student knowledge of the world.

In this sense, I wanted the concept of 'representation' to be as general as possible, knowing that students would encounter different aspects of this term from tutors in different sections of the unit. In my introductory lecture I outlined a number of ways in which the idea could be used in different disciplines – in film and law,[4] in literature and law,[5] graphical representation in cognitive science,[6] the computational model of mind and semiotic views of representation.

The unit was divided into four sections:

1) Discourse Analysis and the Semiotics of Law;
2) Indigenous Peoples and Land Law;
3) Law and Literature;
4) Law, Film and Television.

---

4   Wiegand (1997) and Corcos (1997)

5   I used Ian Ward's (1995) useful discussion of the distinctions between law and literature.

6   Scaife and Rodgers (1996) and Shannon (1993).

The first unit considered how a number of discourse and semiotic practices functioned within law, particularly with reference to oral and written language. The subtopics included: language, linguistics and justice, forensic linguistics in the courtroom; and the detection of deception in texts. They also included the subject of normal and abnormal communication and the underlying assumptions of these and the implications for law of semiotic analyses within a context of critical theory.[7] Class discussion and activities centred on definitions of semiotic analysis and application to aspects of language in legal discourse. The final topic was that of miscommunication, and led into the second unit, 'Indigenous Peoples and Land Law'.

In this second unit, students studied a number of key cases and statutes applying to First Nation peoples in Canada and set these in the context of their lands, history and culture.[8] The class also learned something of the reality of contemporary First Nation life and culture from their tutor, who had first-hand experience of indigenous communities, the political movements, the effect of SLAPP suits, and the legal strategies by which First Nations are attempting to reclaim rights and lands.[9] Links were also made between this second and the first unit: Peter Goodrich's essay 'Modalities of Annunciation', which begins with a moving narrative of the evidence presented by the Haida people in their struggle to prevent the logging of the Queen Charlotte Islands, was used to help students apply what they had learned about the process of semiosis to the evidential process in court (Goodrich, 1990a).

The third unit focused on representations of law in literature. These included excerpts from Dickens', *Bleak House*, Scott's, *Waverley* and *Heart of Midlothian* and James Kelman's *How Late it Was, How Late* and some of his short stories. In the first, students analysed Dickens' presentation of legal procedure by using semiotic analysis; in excerpts from Scott, they explored Scott's creation of Highland culture as an aboriginal culture, and court process (in *Heart of Midlothian*) as a collection of voices (Goodrich's text was useful here); in Kelman's novel they analysed an interview between a DSS claimant and a doctor, using some of the tools of conversational analysis they had encountered in unit one, and some of the concepts of client counselling they had used in another third level module,

---

7   Class texts included excerpts from Giddens (1991a), Lyons (1972), Coupland et al. (1991) and Banks and Baker (1991).

8   Cases included *Daishowa Forest Products Inc v. Friends of the Lubicon Cree* (1998) 39 O.R. (3d) (Daishowa is a Japanese transnational paper corporation, and an international boycott of Daishowa attempted to stop Daishowa's plans to clear-cut unceded Lubicon Lake Indian lands in northern Alberta. Plaintiff sought damages and an interlocutory injunction); and *Delgamuukw v. British Columbia* [1998] 1 C.N.L.R. (Gitksan and Wet'suwet'en hereditary chiefs' claim to aboriginal land title; relevance of oral history and native law and tradition as evidence). Relevant statutes included the Indian Act 1985, Constitution Act 1982, Royal Proclamation, 1763.

9   SLAPP stands for 'strategic lawsuit against public participation' and is a form of lawsuit designed to prevent the organisation of consumer boycott.

Clinical Legal Skills. Most of the class time, however was spent analysing Scott's short story 'The Two Drovers' and Scott Turow's novel, *Presumed Innocent*. In the first we analysed Scott's use of the clash of legal and personal values to highlight the cultural differences between communities; and in the second the use of voice to narrate a personal story within a legal context. Key concepts for this unit were those of narrative voice and genre (Swales, 1990).[10]

In the final unit, 'Law, Film and Television', students studied excerpts from the film videos of *The Verdict*, *The Client* and *Presumed Innocent*. They also compared episodes of *Murder One* and *Kavanagh QC*, using the analytical tools they had learned in the first and third units: that is to say, analysis of what is perceived to be 'normal' genres in film and TV contexts; analysis of dialogue, particularly in court-room scenes; discussion of the extent to which political and professional power and legal issues are engaged in the films and episodes; the extent to which legal issues are mediated by the form of the genre. The tutor, an independent TV producer who was also Creative Writing Fellow at Glasgow and Strathclyde universities, drew upon film theory as well as the semiotic concepts used in the first unit to analyse the tapes; and of course followed through into the visual medium the textual analysis of *Presumed Innocent*.

The unit was designed so that themes could be tracked through various classes. It was possible, for example, in 'The Two Drovers' to refer back to the literature students read in the second unit on First Nation concepts of justice and its workings within a community, and compare this to Scott's treatment of the ideas of justice and honour in the short story. Throughout the unit, it was made clear to students that in their assessed essay and in the examination they would be expected to draw analogical interdisciplinary links between different knowledge sets, and they were given examples of this type of analysis. During the law and literature unit in particular, they practised mini-arguments in class, using semiotic tools of analysis upon literary texts. In this way, some of the forms of interdisciplinary argument were modelled for them, and they had the opportunity to practise, in a relatively safe environment, constructing argument for themselves using the texts studied in the classes.[11]

---

10 For example, students were introduced to the following definition of genre as this applied to legal texts as well as literary texts:

'[Genre] is a recognizable communicative event characterized by a set of communicative purpose(s) identified and mutually understood by the members of the professional or academic community in which it regularly occurs. Most often it is highly structured and conventionalized with constraints on allowable contributions in terms of their intent, positioning, form and functional value. These constraints, however, are often exploited by the expert members of the discourse community to achieve private intentions within the framework of socially recognized purpose(s)' (Swales, 1990, p. 58).

11 The model of writing practice used here was that of 'intensive-writing'. For brief practical guidelines on this model, see http://writing.umn.edu/tww/policy/index.htm.

Of the 12 students who took the unit, all welcomed the variety of the texts and visual media. Several of them commented that it made jurisprudential analysis much more exciting for them to apply it to film and television, in particular:

> I especially liked thinking about the films, though I found it difficult because when you're watching, even if you've seen the film before, you get involved in following the story rather than analysing it. I found I had to take wee bits and just concentrate on them.

This method of 'chunking' was similar to other students' method of dealing with the difficulty in jurisprudential texts. This is borne out by what seemed to be the general agreement of the students that the first unit, on semiotic analysis, was the most difficult to understand – as one put it candidly, 'I didn't really see the point of this at all'.

Shifting disciplines was always going to cause difficulty, and it did for most students. One student, though, commented that once she had shifted from unit one to unit two, it was easier to make the move in the succeeding units – evidence, perhaps, for the student's developing 'situation-sense' in interdisciplinary research: once she was able to perceive a thematic content and make the conceptual shift from the first discipline to the second, the cognitive move was easier to make to the third and fourth units.

Two students commented that they could not understand the unit. One commented 'I couldn't understand what was going on. We jumped from one idea to the next, and I didn't really know what to do'. This comment points to one weakness of the unit, namely the briefing given to tutors. While the interdisciplinary nature of the unit was emphasised, and the need for contextual analysis on the unit, the tutors did not receive sufficient information on the classroom techniques which would be common to the unit – for example, use of analogy as a heuristic, and the use of intensive-writing sessions in every tutorial; or the use to which the semiotic theory was to be put in various sessions.

Feedback on tutor performance was very good; but feedback on the unit generally was uncertain and mirrored general student bafflement about the underlying structure of the unit. From the outset, it was important that the unit should combine disciplines. The question arose at the start as to whether it should be interdisciplinary or multidisciplinary, but this crucial question was never satisfactorily resolved. As a result (and as the Royal Society report quoted at the start of the chapter predicted), despite careful planning of *content*, the underlying *structure* of the content was incoherent and this was reflected in feedback from students. The Jurisprudence module generally tried to clear a critical space for reflection on justice and society; and the Representations unit went further in destabilising notions of western, globalised, capitalist, justice. But it was not sufficiently coherent. It attempted to integrate localities (Queen Charlotte Islands and Glasgow, for instance) within a theoretical structure that would allow for the play of critical faculties. But the result was unsatisfactory for two reasons: first because the theoretical structure was treated in the unit as a master narrative, overwriting other discourses; and secondly, the unit failed to integrate student experience with the voices speaking from other times, other places.[12] As a result, students were unable to make sense of ideas for themselves and thus learning could never become comprehensible to them – let alone transformative – no matter how liberating the content of the unit may have been (Tsui, 2004).

How might the unit have been improved? As Tanner points out in discussion of the curriculum planning of Dewey's Laboratory School at Chicago University, 'an interdisciplinary team is not a curriculum design, nor will it necessarily give birth to one' (Tanner, 1997, p. 78). There was not enough common planning time for tutors to become effective facilitators, nor did I allow for enough integration between them in my planning. In addition, the development of the syllabus was wrongly planned, and went against the grain of Dewey's developmental curriculum. In his approach, education is successful when it starts from where the learner is and develops toward increased abstraction and alienation. If semiotic theory were the ground plan for the syllabus, I should not have started with an outline of the theoretical concepts but, rather, ended with a summary of them and brought out the concepts experientially for students within the interdisciplinary plan, which should have been designed not as a series of blocks but as an ascending spiral.

Case Study 2: Rhetoric – the Protean Discipline

Rhetoric, or compositional studies, is now well-established not only as a discipline but as a set of approaches that can be used in other disciplines. This was not always the case. The subject was moribund for much of the twentieth century and while the groundbreaking work of Perelman and Olbrechts-Tyteca was inspirational in redefining what had become largely a historical subject, it was only in the early 1970s that the subject began to re-emerge in the USA as a vigorous discipline.

The engine of revival was the pattern of research techniques used to study writing practice that was derived from psychology and education. The early work of Scardamalia and Bereiter (1982) and Flower and Hayes (1981, 1989), for instance, moved away from the previous prescriptions of historical rhetoric by questioning what good and poor writers actually did when writing.[13] In their work there is close observation of writers at work, involving statistical analysis

---

12 When, of course, postmodernism tells us stories of the end of master narratives – see Lyotard (1984, pp. 27–41).

13 As Flower and Hayes (1989, p. 283) put it (sketching out lines of research), there was a realization that what was required was 'a far more integrated theoretical vision which can explain how context cues cognition, which in turn mediates and interprets the particular world that context provides. What we don't know is how cognition and context do in fact interact, in specific but significant situations. We have little precise understanding of how these "different processes" feed on one another'.

of results, but largely codification of responses to writing situations, and the analysis of 'verbal protocols' or think-aloud statements made by writers as they wrote.[14] Hand-in-hand with this went the formation of models of writing – the identification of writing processes; how writers approached the tasks they were set, the effect of different contexts and factors on writing processes, and so on. And at a more abstract level there was discussion of models, processes, research from related disciplines and so on. 'Related' disciplines, of course, gives the game away. Rhetoric was in effect becoming a discipline in its own right within departments of English Studies and it was doing so by borrowing methodologies and recasting these to provide the data that would define its identity as a research discipline.[15]

The result was a body of research that not only transformed rhetoric itself but also invigorated the study of composition and writing in other disciplines in the USA. As it did so, it defined its own relationship to contemporary academic culture – to postmodernism, for instance, to discourse and feminist theory, or the general move in the last two decades from cognitive-based research in communications research towards social and community-based forms of analysis.[16]

In the UK (where rhetoric has, admittedly, a different disciplinary trajectory) the recent work of Lea and Creme is an example in point. Their approach to writing is based on what has been termed the 'academic literacies' approach to student writing in higher education. It builds upon the more cognitivist approaches of earlier rhetoric and compositional studies research, but takes into account literacy practices as these are embedded within social situations and specific discourses. In an article on myths in student writing, for instance, they argue against a generally-accepted 'deficit' model of student achievement in writing, identifying four myths in circulation regarding student performance:

*   students lack basic skills;
*   some groups of students can't write;

---

14 See for instance Flower and Hayes (1984). A valuable resource for the history of compositional studies is the bibliography on the College Composition and Communication website at http://www.ibiblio.org/cccc/scopc.html. It is significant that the bibliography was first constructed in the late 1970s because there was no other major bibliographical listing for the subject. Up until as late as 2000, the MLA International Bibliography excluded content relating to pedagogy, under which it classified rhetorical research – see http://www. ibiblio.org/cccc/history.html. Exclusions often work to create a sense of community.

15 See Flower and Hayes (1985), rebutting criticism of protocol analysis of Cooper and Holzman (1985). These and many such similar debates regarding research methodologies helped to define status, prestige and above all directions within the discipline.

16 See for instance Wood and Cox (1993) and Kress (1997). There have of course been revisionist and more traditional approaches to rhetoric. See for example Ehninger (1968); Vickers (1989). For a rebuttal of Vickers, see Goodrich (1990b). As Goodrich put it, 'the revival of rhetoric in legal studies runs the danger of archaism and worse of a blinkered refusal to accommodate theory to changing technologies of practice' (Goodrich, 1990b, p. 563).

- there is one way of academic writing;
- academic writing is depersonalised.

They then proceed to

> unpack the relationship between so called 'poor writing' and disciplinary and subject-based knowledge. For example, students may, indeed, write in long sentences, using a preponderance of nominalizations, embedded clauses and passive tenses. This may be a response to wanting to sound academic and impersonal and to appear to have mastered the 'academic socialisation' process. (Creme and Lea 1998)

In this as in much of their work, they analyse the social practice of student writing within a particular discipline, rather than treating writing skills as a generic set of technical competences that can be transferred smoothly to and from different discourses.[17] Their awareness of the rhetorical context is in some respects a continuation of the work of Bourdieu in this regard. For him, students' imitation of academic discourse amounted at times to a form of 'creolized' language (Bourdieu et al., 1994, p. 4).[18] Note how an awareness of the power relations between students and academics is implicit in Bourdieu's analysis, as it is in the New Literacies movement. The concept of identity is bound up with these relations, particularly in the way that student writers think about their audience and the audience's expectations (Ivanic, 1998).

Much of the work of the New Literacies movement is an investigation into the relationship between discourses and individual writing practices. A study by John Hilsdon, for example, analysed student work on an Arts interdisciplinary course where student writing was perceived to be at an unacceptable standard. Using questionnaires, interviews and sample analysis of student essays, he concluded that problems associated with student writing 'seemed to result from aspects of communication and style in constructing arguments and articulation of points

---

17 See for example Bhatia (1993) and Lea and Stierer (2000).

18 The passage is worth quoting in full for its powerful critique of the discourse double-bind as a 'rhetoric of despair': 'Many university students are unable to cope with the technical and scholastic demands made on their use of language as students. They cannot define the terms which they hear in lectures or which they themselves use. They are remarkably tolerant of words lifted from the language of ideas but applied inappropriately or irrelevantly, and they accept sloppiness and incorrectness with resigned indifference. The lexis and syntax of examination scripts and essays written during the year offer a still more unchallengeable test of linguistic misunderstanding. Constrained to write in a badly understood and poorly mastered language, many students are condemned to using a rhetoric of despair whose logic lies in the reassurance that it offers. Through a kind of incantatory or sacrificial rite, they try to call up and reinstate the tropes, schemas or words which to them distinguish professorial language. Irrationally and irrelevantly, with an obstinacy that we might too easily mistake for servility, they seek to reproduce this discourse in a way which recalls the simplifications, corruptions and logical re-workings that linguists encounter in "creolized" languages.'

and ideas, *rather than from errors in surface features of English such as spelling and grammar'* (Hilsdon, 1998).[19] In more detail, Hilsdon pointed out that students required more guidance in areas such as:

- describing, defining and explaining concepts or points;
- supporting a position with reasoned argument;
- reporting, referring to and quoting the views of others;
- evaluating information, views and ideas;
- summing up points and coming to conclusions.

He explicitly makes the connection between his study and the work of linguistics theorists such as Halliday, discourse analysis and the New Literacies movement.[20] His conclusion was that 'remedial English' classes were unnecessary: what was required was support for students in the key tasks of constructing argument: 'the kind of language awareness work needed is where the language of the subject, and the forms in which discourse about it can be constructed, are discussed and held up for critical appraisal' (Hilsdon, 1998).

Such forms of language awareness are required in every discipline and are different in each. But what is generic to all is the importance of taking into account issues of identity, knowledge and power relations in helping students to understand the issues at stake.[21]

The value of rhetoric to legal education is slowly emerging from the research that is being carried out – too little research, however, and still not enough practical embodiment of that research in the UK. The situation is different in the USA. There, since at least the early 1990s, Stratman and others have researched the contexts within which students and lawyers read texts, and the strategies they adopt to do this and have mapped out at least three rhetorical approaches. Such research findings have been confirmed by Deegan, Lundeberg and others. In one study Christensen examined how 24 law students in the top and bottom 50 per cent of their class read a judicial opinion (Christensen, 2006). Students read by think-aloud protocols; she then interviewed students at the end of their readings to determine the strategies they were aware of using.

---

19 His emphasis. Within the BA Combined Arts modular scheme he analysed 50 pieces of student work and interviewed 119 out of 720 students and 20 from a total of 50 staff.

20 For example Halliday (1978) and Kress (1988).

21 Some researchers have argued that this line of rhetoric research actually underpins the more generally-accepted 'approaches to learning' literature. See Haggis (2003) where she suggests that 'whilst the model may be successful in creating a generalised description of the 'elite' goals and values of academic culture, it says surprisingly little about the majority of students in a mass system' (Haggis, 2003, p. 89). She goes on to suggest that the new 'academic literacies in specific contexts' approach might be a complementary alternative (p. 99).

Her findings were significant: the more successful law students read differently from the students who were less successful in their classes. Unsuccessful readings were more rambling, less purposeful. Unsuccessful readers started with little contextual understanding gained from their reading (for example, where the case was litigated, its procedural history and so on) and their confusion clouded their subsequent readings because they did not resolve their confusions before they moved on into further matters in the case. Successful readers were highly purposeful. They took time at the start to understand the context of case and, if they were confused, they could engage a sense of auto-monitoring in which they prioritised whether the confusion was minor or major and required analysis and clarification before they proceeded. Finally, poor readers used 'default strategies' much more and relied on them unthinkingly to reproduce meaning from the texts.[22] Indeed, as Christensen says, 'heavy reliance on default strategies seemed to prevent some students from engaging in any meaningful case analysis' (p. 34). By contrast, higher-performing students 'relied more extensively on reading strategies from the problematizing and rhetorical categories, and limited their use of default strategies' (p. 35).

Christensen's use of the terms 'problematizing and rhetorical categories' derives from Dorothy Deegan's earlier work on law students' approaches to reading. 'Problematizing' refers to those strategies that enable a reader to solve problems within a text: 'they ask themselves questions, make predictions, and hypothesize about developing meaning' (p. 6). Christensen contrasted these strategies to those of unsuccessful readers:

> [t]ypically, readers [who used default strategies] would restate or paraphrase portions of information, often underlining and/or making margin notes [... which ...] were not specifically initiated from or tied to explicit questions or hypotheses.[23]

There are teaching strategies developed in the rhetoric literature which are designed to help students with these and similar problems. Maharg (2000a, pp. 85–90) documents the attempt to tackle the genre difficulties facing students in first-year legal studies by using an 'essay conference', modelled on the guidance given by Scardamalia and Bereiter, whereby students were encouraged to 'internalise' structures of argument and where the tutor would scaffold the defining features for the student.[24] I began to realise that Scardamalia and Bereiter's model of

---

22 Default strategies are the generic learning devices taught at school and university basic induction courses to students to enable them to identify and remember meaning within texts, for example, underlining text, highlighting, circling key words, marginalia and so on.

23 Christensen quoting Deegan (1995, p. 161).

24 In the words of Scardamalia and Bereiter (1986), 'A more readily internalizable form [than dialogue] might be the "assisted monologue" ... where the talking is primarily done by the student, with the teacher inserting prompts rather than conversational turns' (quoted in Maharg, 2000a, p. 90).

the 'assisted monologue' could be adapted to be more productive. Instead of adopting a 'prompt' role, I adopted more of a collaborative role in understanding the students' construction of meaning – what Carl Rogers described as being a 'confident companion' to the student.[25] Just why this is so is quite complex, but for our purposes here we might note that the literature on Rogers and counselling was useful in determining how an approach based on rhetorical analysis of student performance might be enhanced.[26] In other words, concepts and procedures from two disciplinary fields provided a solution to a problem of giving effective feedback to students in legal writing conferences.

Another approach to reading explored by Stratman and others is that of 'rhetorical reading'. The term derives from Haas and Flower's now classic work on rhetoric and reading, and defines the situation where the reader constructed 'a rhetorical situation for the text, trying to account for the author's purpose, context and effect on the audience' (Haas and Flower, 1988, p. 176). These situational traits lie at the heart of much of Flower's *oeuvre*. Her recent work draws upon the earlier cognitive studies to outline a synthetic theoretical approach to the construction of negotiated meaning in writing, in which rival voices and social forces play a critical role (Flower et al., 2000, p. 8).

These approaches to rhetoric, negotiation and identity are explored by James Stratman in his work on law students' reading. In one study, for instance, Stratman conducted a think-aloud protocol study with 56 first-year students with the aim of discerning 'when students are having difficulties as critical readers and when they are having difficulties as contextually sensitive legal problem solvers, or when in fact they are having difficulty connecting these two processes with each other' (Stratman, 2002, p. 57). It is a subtle point, and goes to the heart of the methodology of the New Rhetoric. Do problems arise in cognitive approaches, or in the structure and content of the genre, or in the encounter between the two? Stratman chose to approach this problematic by constructing professional roles for the students, and asking them to assume one of these roles while reading the judicial opinions – an advisory role, a policy role or an advocacy role. Stratman also added a role that students would be very familiar with – that of preparing for a law class. Use of these roles, Stratman hoped, would enable him to filter out the occasions when students read more critically, and with a more problem-recognition and -solving bias.

His findings were very significant. The assignation of role affected the reading task that students were given. Sophisticated reading strategies such as problem-recognition rates were more apparent and were higher when students assumed one of the three professional legal roles than they were when students assumed the role they normally took, namely as students preparing for class. In other words

---

25   The phrase comes from Rogers (1980), p. 142.

26   Though much better known for his therapeutic *oeuvre*, Rogers was of course deeply interested in education. For application of some of his ideas to legal education, see Maharg (2000a).

when students adopted a professional purpose, it enabled them to read more effectively. Purpose is linked to identity in Stratman's studies and this is confirmed by Christensen's study on reading. There, students' reading was analysed by think-aloud protocols; but unlike the earlier studies of Oates, Deegan and Lundeberg, Christensen asked students to adopt the role of a practising attorney (Christensen, 2006, p. 15).[27] Her results led her to conclude that 'students comprehended text better when they assumed the role of an actual attorney as opposed to reading as a law student preparing for class' (2006, p. 26). More specifically, Christensen noted (and provides evidence in the protocol scripts) that such students

> read the facts of the test case more closely (to determine whether their client's case might be analogous to the facts of the opinion); they noted the respondent's punishment (to inform their client of potential consequences) and they noted the procedural posture of the case more accurately (understanding that the court was reviewing a mutual agreement). (p. 25)

It is worth reading this passage closely, because it explains much about the connection between reading with purpose and identity. It is not the case that when students adopted the professional role, they then read with purpose. Rather it is the reverse: they read more effectively because the professional purpose focuses their attention on the legally-relevant details of the case appropriate to their purpose. Their legal task enables them to read the case more successfully. Christensen draws the conclusion that as teachers we should assign our students specific purposes when they are set reading tasks (p. 27) because students comprehend more when they read with purpose.[28]

This is one interpretation of her results and of Stratman's research. But a broader reading would take into account the mediational role that professional identity plays when introduced between the dyad of student and text. It is a theme in Stratman's research, in Flower's research (particularly her work on 'rivalling' and negotiated meaning – Flower, 1994; 2003) and in the Academic Literacies research too. As we shall see, this can be used to effect in legal education, and in surprisingly profound ways.

---

27 Compare the studies of Oates (1987) and Lundeberg (1987). In the latter study Lundeberg did however compare the reading patterns of law student and expert (that is, practitioner) readers and found striking differences between the two groups.

28 One can, of course, set tasks that are too specific. One should be cautious of the 'erosion of learning' that can occur when students' attention is directed too strongly to aspects of a text – see for example Marton (1976, pp. 125–8) and Marton and Booth (1997, p. 169), commented on by Maharg and Muntjewerff (2005, pp. iv–vi).

Case Study 3: PBL and Legal Reasoning

Few now doubt that educational theory is important to teaching in higher education.[29] This is true of other disciplines too. As an approach to learning, problem-based learning (PBL) is generally taken as being a Good Thing in medical education, but this has not stopped the flow of research literature in medical education analysing why, under what conditions and to what extent it is good for the education of doctors, nurses, dentists and many others to be problem-based. This is in part a recognition that while general guidelines to PBL exist, its implementation can differ quite significantly from one medical faculty to the next; and that a number of different models exist, from pure PBL to hybrid models.[30] It is also a recognition that as a heuristic, PBL has the power to change how doctors practise and in particular, to change *what* they know (domain knowledge) and how they solve problems.

According to some of the literature, students on a PBL course show no decrease in science domain knowledge compared to their traditional course counterparts (Albanese, 1993, pp. 52–81). They are more likely to use that knowledge in problem-solving activities than students on more traditional courses and to perceive that they have developed more effective problem-solving and communication skills and a greater sense of personal responsibility than did students who received lectures (Bransford et al., 1989). These differences extend down to the detail of personal methods of study (Newble and Clarke, 1986 and Nolte et al., 1988).

Other researchers found that PBL students could be weaker on basic sciences (Vernon and Blake, 1993). Colliver reported no overall and convincing evidence that PBL could significantly improve knowledge base and clinical performance to the extent justified by the resources that were required for the task of implementing PBL (Colliver, 2000). It has to be said, though, that many other studies contradict these findings.[31] Norman and Schmidt (2000), for instance, observed that a number of studies reported positively on PBL learners' abilities to recall information, in part because remembered information helps learners to construct explanations; in part because elaborations of remembered information enables the integration of new information; and also because the contextual learning activities of PBL enabled information to be recalled more easily at a later point. In a two-year comparison study of a traditional curriculum against a PBL curriculum, Eisenstadt found that PBL students tested lower on test scores at the end of the study than traditional students, but retained much more after re-testing a year later (Eisenstaedt, 1990).

If the studies are contradictory, what the great majority of them agree upon is that PBL is a sufficiently powerful heuristic to have changed the way that medical

---

29 See for instance Cownie (2000).
30 For a general introduction to PBL, see Schmidt (1983).
31 See for example Vernon and Blake (1993) and Hmelo et al. (1997).

teachers now think about problem-identification and problem-solving. The studies carried out by Patel et al. (for instance, 2000) confirm this. In their comparison of an admittedly small sample, they discovered that PBL curriculum students tended to solve problems by reasoning from the data of the problem to explanations. This they termed 'backward reasoning', contrasting it with the 'forward reasoning' of experts, which proceeded by comparing data against previous experience of data types, to achieve a congruence between the two. Backward reasoning, they held, generated multiple explanations, some of them erroneous, while forward reasoning gave rise to fewer clinical errors. Perhaps most controversially, they identified forward reasoning in the practice of students undertaking traditional curricula and identified its source as domain knowledge, not problem-solving heuristics. In other words, according to their results, PBL appeared to be teaching students ineffective reasoning methods. In response to this type of research findings, some researchers have advocated better methods of presenting domain knowledge in place of a move to full-scale PBL (Claessen and Boshuizen, 1985).

It seems to be a persuasive point. But whether or not backward reasoning – or 'hypothetico-deductive reasoning', to give it its proper title – is ineffective is debatable. Forward reasoning may be useful for the diagnosis of relatively straightforward clinical problems, but even experts use backward reasoning when presented with uncertain or ill-structured problems, or when they move from a domain they are confident in to one in which they have less domain knowledge (Bergus et al., 1995). Moreover, accurate diagnosis relies on what some researchers have identified as an accurate and well-remembered network or semantic structure that is a form of schema (Bordage and Lemieux, 1991).[32]

What the literature proves is that experimental cognitive psychology research literature on this point of problem-solving is contradictory. Why is it, then, one might ask, that PBL has become so popular in the health sciences? One answer is that it has many other benefits that traditional approaches to health education do not offer. For instance, students enjoy problem-identification and problem-solving and engage more readily in active learning (Amos and White, 1998, Barr and Tagg, 1995 and Duffy and Cunningham, 1996). They make greater use of background reading, have more positive attitudes to the instructional milieu and they take greater personal responsibility for their work.[33]

But if we step back for a moment from the detail of the research itself, we can see what is happening as regards PBL interdisciplinary research strategies. Medical practitioners and medical educators have liaised with cognitive scientists, or learned about cognitive educational research themselves, in order to understand more

---

32 Note the resemblance between Dewey's description of experience, cited in the Introduction at p. 22–5 and the descriptions of backward and forward reasoning above.

33 See, respectively, Blumberg and Michael (1992), de Vries et al. (1989) and Lieux (1996).

about the processes of learning involved.[34] Cognitive psychologists themselves report on these processes and results. What we have, then, is a community of disciplinary practitioners in medicine cooperating with another disciplinary community in cognitive science. As a result, the standards and approaches of one community – experimental cognitive psychology – is brought to bear upon medical education, which becomes subject to forms of discourse, measurement and judgement appropriate to this disciplinary community. In turn, the medical community evolved its own special forms of educational expertise – PBL itself and statistical and psychometric approaches to assessment, such as standardization of patients (of which more in the next chapter). It has to be said, of course, that the statistical bases of cognitive science and medical science mean that *au fond* there are many overlaps between the two disciplines.[35] As one study puts it,

> systematic reviews of controlled studies that focus on outcomes resonate with a community which has seen the success of randomised, controlled trials in biomedical science. The complexities of educational interventions may indicate that this is not the most appropriate tool for research in this area and may have contributed to the difficulties that the authors had in coming to a definitive answer. (Farrow and Norman, 2003, p. 1132)

Recently, though, other discourses have entered the field, notably situated learning, constructivist learning and teamwork learning. Regarding the last, Bleakley has noted that despite the emphasis in health care upon interprofessional teamwork,

> [i]ndividualistic models of learning continue to be privileged within medical education … Where clinical skills are collaborative, such as resuscitation team activity, we need learning theories with explanatory and predictive power for such contexts. This is a health-care imperative, where the majority of medical errors are systems-based and quality of teamwork is linked with improving patient outcomes. (Bleakley, 2006, p. 152)

Bleakley compares research based on acquisition metaphors to research based on metaphors of participation where collective work is 'more than the sum of any recollections individual team members might bring to the work situation' (p. 153) and he goes on to explore aspects of theories of identity-formation, narration, the rhetorical strategies of practitioners, models of ethical awareness, the role

---

34 See for instance the interesting early history of the Standardized Patient movement, as recounted by Wallace (1997). See also Schmidt (1993), p. 432.

35 Including the use of meta-analyses of research – see for example Newman (2001).

of activity theory, distributed cognition and dynamicist learning in complex adaptive systems.[36]

These bodies of theory are not replacements for cognitive research. Rather, their explanatory and predictive power is appropriate to particular situations, particular purposes. But we must be aware that they often carry with them implicit concepts of what a good doctor actually is; and this points to one of the dangers of interdisciplinary research practice, namely that one uses techniques that have hidden consequences for results and for implementation. We can see this danger being negotiated in high-quality interdisciplinary work in legal educational research, such as Stefan Krieger's careful exploration and adaptation of Patel et al.'s medical educational cognitive research (Krieger, 2002).[37] Krieger argues that the role of doctrinal or domain knowledge is an essential pre-requisite to the learning of clinical skills and that attempting to teach both at the same time causes cognitive overload in students. He also draws upon Patel's argument regarding backward and forward reasoning to claim that we may not necessarily be teaching best practice models to our students. Both he and Patel are right of course: domain knowledge is crucial to the development of schemas and scripts.[38] But in drawing heavily upon Patel and her tradition of research, Krieger commits himself to the division of basic science knowledge learning and clinical work that PBL from the start has tried to heal. Also important is the ethical and narrative context of practitioners' scripts, their contribution to growth, identity and the effect of communities of practice upon the development of reasoning skills (Wenger, 1998). Is it possible to do what Krieger advocates in his eminently sensible guidelines for traditional curricula in his paper and integrate traditional domain learning fully with clinical or simulation work? Is it possible as he describes it, to overcome the inflexibility of scripted practice and encourage a balance between 'entirely scripted and completely open-ended lawyering'? (Krieger, 2004, p. 205). Part 3 of this book describes an attempt to carry out just such an integration.

---

36 Bleakley is also interested in the aesthetic dimensions of looking and judging – see the project involving three medical practitioners and three visual artists into processes of clinical and aesthetic judgements in the visual domain, in Bleakley et al. (2003). See also the curriculum experiment on these lines at Stanford University, http://news-service. stanford.edu/news/2003/february19/artmed.html. This aspect of legal education will be explored in the next chapter.

37 Another example is Blasi (1995).

38 As Krieger puts it, referencing Patel, '[o]ver time, the explicit "textbook" knowledge becomes tacit knowledge as the practitioner develops scripts for handling different kinds of problems' (ibid., 199). See Patel and Kaufman (2000, pp. 197–214). See also Wiley (1993, pp. 716–18).

Summary

These three case studies illustrate approaches to interdisciplinarity in method, content and meta-awareness. In the case study 'Representations of Justice', we analysed the reasons why interdisciplinary content-structure was unsuccessful. In the case of rhetoric, we discussed how aspects of the research in that discipline can be adapted in legal education as a methodological approach to reading and writing; while in the third, through a brief analysis of a set of issues in PBL, we saw how important it is to be aware of the cultural context of research underpinning approaches to learning in other disciplines, before transplanting that research to the legal domain. The examples provide intriguing comparisons. For example, the findings of Stratman and Deegan on reading capability contrast with those of Patel, in that the success of Stratman's and Deegan's strategies, arising from the adoption of professional roles at a fairly deep level, provide an alternative to the separation of domain and clinical learning advocated by Patel. In this third case study, which set of disciplinary guidelines should we follow when teaching law?

Whatever we want to do, *how* we go about interdisciplinary work is crucial. And to describe this process I shall adapt another discipline's phrase and describe the field of interdisciplinarity as a 'trading zone'. The phrase comes from Galison's groundbreaking study of the material culture of modern experimental microphysics. Galison shows how the contemporary need for coordination between large research teams of scientists, engineers, computer programmers and many others (quite different, as Galison notes, to the earlier existence of the solitary physicist) creates a dynamic 'trading zone' in which theorists, writers, experimenters, instrument designers, policy-makers, politicians and others meet, share knowledge and do collaborative research (Galison, 1997). Parties traded content and method; they imposed constraints on each other; traditions coordinated but without homogenising; they communicated in pidgins and creoles to express and absorb each other's essential concepts. The trade is never neutral – as Galison points out 'nothing in the notion of trade presupposes some universal notion of a neutral currency' (1997, p. 803): indeed, 'trading partners can hammer out a local coordination despite vast *global* differences' (1997, p. 783). It is the nature of the local cultures and exchanges that matter profoundly, as we shall see in the next chapter.

Galison's position, as he acknowledges, is common with that of Donald Davidson and Hilary Putnam, both of whom challenge the idea that, within different disciplines, 'different schemes or paradigms render mutual intelligibility impossible' (Galison, 1997, pp. 840–41). Davidson – in a move typical of Dewey's anti-epistemology – rejected the dualism of this position, arguing that even the recognition of disparity and difference between conceptual schemes presupposed a body of knowledge about those schemes.[39] The position is one answer to Fish's

---

39 Galison (1997, p. 841), citing Davidson (1982).

antifoundationalist statements regarding the impossibility of interdisciplinary work.

Above all, we ought to begin to recognise what has been for some time now the case, and which will become increasingly so in the future, namely that the problems that educators are faced with every day are quite simply not solvable in any particular discipline. They can often be patched or fixed temporarily but, for more thoughtful and serious responses, one often needs the resources of a number of disciplines. But for this to happen, teaching needs to be considered as a field worthy of extended thought and analysis. As Shulman observed,

> [t]oo often teaching is identified only as the active interactions between teacher and students in a classroom setting (or even a tutorial session). I would argue that teaching, like other forms of scholarship, is an extended process that unfolds over time. (Shulman, 1998, p. 5)[40]

The process involves, according to Shulman, vision, design, interactions, outcomes and analysis. Vision and analysis are common in research projects, but the three middle elements are critical to legal education. Design is a process rather similar to the design process in architecture, where there are multiple real-world factors that have to be managed.[41] The heart of the process is the educational interaction and the outcome of that interaction which, as Bernstein observes, involves 'a "transactional relation" between teaching practice and student performance' that is a '"benchmark of excellence in scholarly practice"' (Bernstein, 1998, p. 80).

The relation is constantly evolving, unfinished. But if it is constantly in flux and evolving, it needs close attention as to its evolution, which is an intensely personal affair. Indeed, good teachers nearly always dwell upon their teaching and create of it something from the references to other forms of teaching, other models of learning that they have in their repertoires. And there lies part of the problem with teaching as thought process, which teachers have reported almost as an unconscious process:

> [t]oo many times, my good ideas about teaching are lost because they pass through my brain as fleeting thoughts or as unwritten resolutions to 'do better.' The opposite is also true. I repeat mistakes or make do with old strategies because I have not taken the time to rethink my game plan for a lesson or activity. My sense is that the very act of capturing those fleeting thoughts, of formalizing the game plan, of facing the failures, and of underlining the successes will help me to new places with my teaching. (Langsam, 1998, pp. 60–61)

One academic used a portfolio approach to help him:

---

40 Shulman (1998), as quoted in Bass (1999).

41 One reason why the architectural salon was adopted by Schön and Argyris as a place where reflective educational design could be studied.

[w]hat most surprised me was how the portfolio increased my sense of unrealized potential in the classroom. I began to see teaching and learning in a more scholarly way – comprising a body of knowledge much in the way one's 'discipline' does ... I began to read more selectively in the research literature on teaching and learning, discovering new ideas and strategies for use in the classroom that made me more aware of the cognitive atmosphere in my classes. I saw – increasingly – many more opportunities to apply principles of good practice in my classes. (Mignon, 1998, pp. 69–70)

The 'transactional relation', then, exists not just between teaching and learning, but between teaching as an activity in the world and as an object for analysis and research. We shall return in Part 3 to this concept of the transactional relation in a different context.

Chapter 2

The Empty Quarter:
Interdisciplinary Research and Practice

As John Dewey remarked in *Democracy and Education*, society not only exists *by* transmission and *by* communication, it exists *in* transmission, *in* communication.

Stenhouse, 1983, p. 19

Introduction

I have argued in Chapter 1 for the application of Galison's metaphor of a trading zone to be applied to the interdisciplinarity of legal education. However, in applying the metaphor we need to be aware of the different contexts of use between research scientists and legal educators.[1] One of the key points of Galison's research was the extent to which the research cultures and methods of particle physics research had been profoundly affected by the material culture of the research teams. The same is true of the material culture of learning. But in legal education the community often uses the same basic structure repeatedly (a seminar, for instance), altering content, micro-structure, adapting to context of student knowledge, aims, wider context of the seminar and so forth. Practice, in other words, requires a sense of ongoing and cumulative activity *within* a discipline; continuity of practice in concept, ideology, material objects and method; and the critical task of educational dissection or archaeology. It also requires a set of standards by which the community of practice judges its performance, individually and as a community. How might Galison's research communities fit with this type of practice?

In this chapter we shall consider the relationship between research and practice. We shall then consider three brief case studies. The first is a poem, 'Johan Joachim Quantz's Five Lessons', written by the poet W.S. Graham; the second, Zoltán Kodály's particular form of choral education; while the third concerns the use (derived from medical education) of standardised clients within legal education.

---

1 Note that this is not a matter of two contrasting activities – research and teaching. As I shall argue throughout this book, legal educational research arises from the experience of teaching and learning and must feed back into it. The two activities are thus synergistic in nature.

In each we shall examine the standards at play and how legal education can draw upon those standards.

Many categorisations of research start out with something like Donald Stokes' quadrant of scientific research activity (see Figure 2.1) (Stokes, 1997, p. 73). Top left describes pure research such as Niels Bohr's work on atomic models; top-right, Pasteur's work on bacilli (fundamental research with specific practical aims) and lower-right, Edison's entirely technological work (for example, on the electric light bulb). Stokes's lower-left quadrant is not empty: it is given over to what he calls 'research that systematically explores *particular* phenomena without having in view either general explanatory objectives or any applied use to which the results will be put' but which, significantly, remains nameless (p. 74).

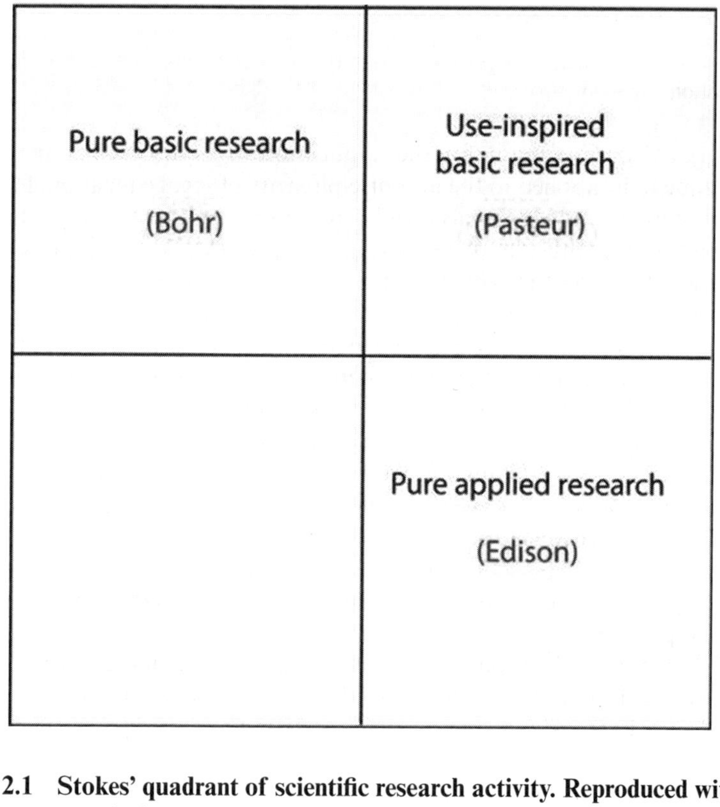

Pure basic research (Bohr)	**Use-inspired basic research** (Pasteur)
	Pure applied research (Edison)

Figure 2.1   Stokes' quadrant of scientific research activity. Reproduced with permission.

As a number of studies have since pointed out, Stokes' quadrant model does not do justice to the complexity of research, in its motivation, practice, culture or result. In education for instance, Shaffer and Squire (2006) have pointed out that Stokes' account is based upon an incomplete view of Pasteur's own practice.[2] They point out that Pasteur's quadrant of 'use-inspired' research, to which much educational research is consigned by educationalists themselves, narrows the subject of research. The quadrant forces researchers to focus on what Sabelli and Dede have called *scholarship of practice*: questions that speak to practitioners' concerns – '"curriculum, pedagogy, assessment, professional development, etc" – with an eye toward improving extant practices' (p. 4). The point of such research is to move from small-scale research innovations to larger-scale implementations. But as Latour points out vis-à-vis Pasteur's work on the anthrax bacillus, Pasteur's scientific method was much more complex and knowing than a simple move from laboratory to field trials.[3] The isolation of the anthrax bacillus and the development of a vaccine took place in his laboratory, to be sure; but Pasteur's field trials succeeded because the conditions of the trial 'were carefully negotiated so as to recreate in a farm setting the conditions of Pasteur's laboratory that were essential to the success of the vaccination'. In other words the success of the vaccine in the field was due to a 'transformation of farming practices to mimic the conditions of Pasteur's research' (p. 7). As Shaffer and Squire point out, Pasteur's

> own practice was, as Latour suggests, not merely "use-inspired basic research"; it was a series of levers by which problems and contexts were more deeply understood, tools and techniques were developed, and systems and practices were reorganized in light of the resulting process of inquiry. (p. 8)

Such levers should be developed in educational research, they urge, and should include systematic experimental and design research. In the process they point out the need to 'reconceptualize the process of "dissemination" as one of "transformation," in which practices developed in controlled settings become images that drive the reorganisation of schooling in fundamental ways'. Such transformational practices, in research, design and practice, are precisely what this book calls for. But they cannot take place unless we pay close attention, as did Pasteur when he moved from laboratory to field, to the process by which we implement changed practices. We need, in other words, to become researchers of our own practice.

Such an idea is nothing knew, but as the example of Stokes' quadrant demonstrates, it is easy to misunderstand the process by which it happens. One of the most influential origins of such process-thinking and teacher-researcher theory in general, is the work of the educationalist, Lawrence Stenhouse, who spent part of his career as director of the Humanities Curriculum Project (HCP) from 1967–72. His work in this post was in a number of senses the culmination of much of his theory and practice as an educationalist. The HCP was innovative

---

2   The authors argue convincingly against Sabelli and Dede and others (2001) and adduce recent research on Pasteur's methods, including that of Latour (1983, pp. 141–70).

3   I am indebted to Shaffer and Squire for these references to Latour: although I was aware of his work on network theory, I was unaware of his detailed research on Pasteur.

in that it was a cross-disciplinary initiative that aimed to educate school pupils via small-group work under the direction of a teacher as a 'neutral chairman'. It produced a wide variety of media for pupils and teachers to use – books, looseleaf papers, posters, slides, film strips, OHP transparencies. It employed innovative methods of discussion, project work, small-group work and evaluation (Stenhouse, 1983, p. xvii). Taken forward by Jean Ruddock's work in the late 1970s and early 1980s, it influenced methods of small-group teaching in HE (Hopkins and Ruddock, 1985). At the time, it was an innovative form of school discourse, using new forms of structured and interdisciplinary materials.[4]

Or so it seemed. But as Stenhouse himself acknowledged in the Foreword to *Authority, Education and Emancipation*, the Project's materials were influenced by the work of the Danish educationalist, Hartvig Nissen, on nineteenth-century Scottish encyclopaedic readers – reading books containing pieces on a huge variety of subjects, including world history, geography, pneumatics, astronomy, plant physiology and etymology. Stenhouse notes how Nissen idealised the connection between education and democracy in nineteenth-century Scotland (a connection still the subject of much fond mythologising).[5] Stenhouse was strongly attracted to the ambition of such an aim, as he reveals in a significant passage:

> And yet ... how to reinterpret in the contemporary school that aspiration towards a democratic intellect which might increase the powers and independence of the pupil? There was, it seemed to me, a need to increase the seriousness of the content of reading materials in schools if this content were to be seen neither as the occasion for an exercise nor as matter to be mastered, but rather as the cultural basis of interaction within the learning group. (Stenhouse, 1983, p. xiii)

Stenhouse's nostalgia for the 'lad o' pairts' tradition in Scotland does not cloud his judgement. Note the moves that he makes here: increase in powers and independence (or emancipation as he calls it later in the volume) arise not as an exercise, nor in mastery learning, both of which Stenhouse explicitly rejected. Interaction within the micro-culture of the group was the key for him and through it he hoped to embody the culture of democracy at the deepest and most influential level in schools.[6]

The HCP is still a rich mine for educational research, but as regards the subject of this chapter, there are two aspects of it that are of interest: Stenhouse's position

---

4   It is worthwhile to note that the term 'Humanities' as used by Stenhouse is close to the Scottish sense of the term, namely Latin and 'humane letters' (Stenhouse, 1983, p. xv).

5   See Hearn (2000).

6   Stenhouse was perhaps not as aware (or perhaps as interested) as social theorists such as Anthony Giddens in the extent to which social reality defined consciousness – an awareness that was at the source of Giddens' redefinition of the relationship between micro- and macro-sociological phenomena in his theory of agency and structure (Giddens, 1984). Nevertheless he would have been sympathetic to the direction of this critique.

on the objectives movement in education and his view of the teacher as researcher. Among the innovations in the Project methodology was the rejection of the then newly-fashionable aims and objectives movement. Stenhouse made a number of serious criticisms of the effectiveness of aims in education:

- being general, they gave little guidance in planning interventions;
- objectives tend to become '*ad hoc* substitutes for hypotheses' (1983, p. 81);
- they give the illusion of predicting what ought to happen;
- they imply the idea of 'teacher-proofing' the curriculum, thus losing the value of 'divergent interpretations' (1983, p. 82);
- they stop pupils having their own objectives;
- they inhibit speculation;
- they have unexpected consequences for schools as institutions as well as teacher practice.[7]

In place of aims and objectives, Stenhouse advocated 'standards', based on learning process or input, rather than learning outcomes or output. Instead of treating knowledge as a set of observable behaviours and instead of handing teachers a blueprint of what was expected as the learning outcomes of a class, the standards tried to 'produce a curricular specification which describes a range of possible learning outcomes and relates them to their causes. The style of its formulation is: "If you follow these procedures with these materials with this type of pupil, in this school setting, the effects will tend to be X"' (1983, pp. 82–3).

As Stenhouse admits, the problem with this honesty as to consequences is the complexity of the method. Nevertheless, the standards approach does take account of the complexity of the local situation and how important that is to any teaching intervention. The work of the HCP confirmed this. Even after rigorous

---

7   This is a summary of what Stenhouse says (1983, pp. 81–2). In this, Stenhouse was in complete agreement with MacIntyre's statement that '[p]ractices must not be confused with institutions. Chess, physics and medicine are practices; chess clubs, laboratories, universities and hosptials are institutions. Institutions are characteristically and necessarily concerned with what I have called external goods. They are involved in acquiring money and other material goods; they are structured in terms of power and status and they distribute money, power and status as rewards'. As a result of this tension, MacIntyre observes wryly, 'institutions and practices characteristically form a single causal order in which the ideals and the creativity of the practice are always vulnerable to the acquisitiveness of the institution, in which the co-operative care for the common goods of the practice is always vulnerable to the competitiveness of the institution' As a result, MacIntyre comments, 'without justice, courage and truthfulness, practices could not resist the corrupting power of institutions' (MacIntyre, 1985, p. 181). It is a remarkable passage and one entirely applicable to legal education and the role of the aims and objectives movement, semesterisation and many other institutional practices, both within the universities and within the legal profession, which require to be critically examined in their effects on educational practice.

testing and piloting of materials, it was found that in some schools teachers reported success, in others, failure (1983, p. 85); and the standards methodology was an attempt to explain to teachers the reasons why this was so and how local situations might be engineered – Pasteur's approach – to obtain success. In this approach, Stenhouse points out how innovations require us to re-think context in a fundamental way.

Above all, Stenhouse saw the importance of the teacher as researcher of his or her own practice. In its time, it was this aspect of the HCP that was perhaps most misunderstood and still to this day is a radical intervention. In the US, for instance, there was a parallel project to HCP in the Harvard Social Studies Project, that was quickly abandoned under the pressure for top-down, even 'teacher-proof' curricula, following the post-sputnik return to conservative and instructionist educational practices.[8] By contrast, Stenhouse wanted teachers to site their practices within three broader contexts: other disciplines, society and history. He was certain that if this did not occur, teachers themselves would be undermining their own history and place in society. He gave an example of how the first of these might be carried out and it is worth quoting in full:

> What is demanded of the teacher [within HCP] is not extensive knowledge of all the subjects touched upon, but the recognition of the need, as his teaching develops, to extend his understanding of the principles of each subject area. ... A teacher who is mounting an area of enquiry on law and order needs to be aware of the existence of a field of study, jurisprudence and legal theory, which has its own tradition. Given this awareness, his education should allow him to explore such a field judiciously. To suggest that teachers cannot cross the boundaries of their subjects, even when they are working on the basis of inquiry and discussion rather than of instruction, is to condemn each of us to live within the narrow confines of his specialist academic education. (1983, p. 92)

But it was not merely other disciplines that Stenhouse wanted practitioners to investigate and use: it was their own teaching practice, too:

> Idea and action are fused in practice. Self-improvement comes in escaping from the idea that the way to virtuosity is the imitation of others – pastiche – to the realization that it is the fusion of idea and action in one's own performance to the point where each can be 'justified' in the sense that it is fully expressive of the other. So the idea is tuned to the form of the art and the form used to express the idea. (1983, p. 159)

What Stenhouse is arguing against is the separation of research from practice. He is also arguing for specific types of research. Research generally, in addition

---

8   Like HCP, the Harvard Project emphasised interdisciplinary resourcing, teacher-as-researcher and discovery teaching strategies. For an account of the Harvard Project see Oliver and Shaver (1966). True to the Deweyan tradition, it contains a ringing declaration of the ethical commitments of modern democratic society, much of which is aligned to the underlying transformational assumptions of the HCP.

to being much the more prestigious activity, takes place in different places, using different methods, has its results presented in different public spaces and to different ends than teaching. The result is that the insights that derive from teaching practice have nowhere to be identified, nurtured, compared, analysed in detail, elaborated and returned to the world of practice. Nor do they have a place in the public arena to be debated by practitioners, where the intensely private world of the classroom and experiences drawn from that domain can be publicly described and explored.

Stenhouse's emphasis on the public arena is particularly important for legal education. He believed that this arena should be historically sited, too, so that practice is informed by archives, records, case studies, as well as general theories and practice-based theories. There are many problems inherent in this and Stenhouse was by no means blind to the difficulty of the task – the reluctance, for instance, of many educational theorists to descend (the metaphor is apt) into practice, rather than remain on the higher ground of more abstract theory, which generally attracts more status in research terms. Nevertheless, the public nature of the task was key, not just because it gave access to otherwise inaccessible parts of the curriculum, not just because it gave status to the activity of practice-based research, but because it was instrumental in both creating and sustaining the tradition of research.

It is perhaps not too much to claim that Stenhouse was aiming to draw together the view of research as an activity based in evolving historical traditions of thought (MacIntyre) and the Habermasian process of contemporary social groups struggling to achieve a workable consensus; but it is not quite an action research approach, either.[9] Stenhouse's view of the teacher-researcher is, in a sense, a portrait of the teacher as artist, remarkably close – as we shall see below – to concepts of communication and teaching that derive from other disciplines. The language he uses above is that of art and he often drew the comparison between teacher and artist. In this, Stenhouse can be compared with Schön's project to develop a *phronesis* of practice and with other attempts to define an epistemology of practice. R.S. Peters, for instance, was quoted by Stenhouse:

> ... most of the important things in education are passed on [...] by example and explanation. An attitude, a skill, is caught; sensitivity, a critical mind, respect for people and facts develop where an articulate and intelligent exponent is on the job. Yet the model of means to ends is not remotely applicable to the transaction that is taking place. Values, of course, are involved in the transaction; if they were not it would not be called 'education'. Yet they are not end-products or terminating points of the process. They reside both in the skills and cultural traditions that are passed on and in the procedure for passing them on. (1983, p. 48, quoting Peters, 1959, p. 92)

---

9 Though it is close to it in many aspects. For research resources on action research, see http://www.bath.ac.uk/~edsajw/.

The language Peters uses in the late 1950s is strikingly similar to that used by constructivists in the late 1990s. Situated learning, authenticity of task related to student experience, the development of substantive discipline knowledge within a strongly ethical structure – all this is implied by both Peters and Stenhouse and the above passage, as with so much that they wrote on the subject, opens up the central importance of the teacher's articulacy and artistry. Indeed, Stenhouse and Peters both direct us to ask the question: if we consider using constructivist approaches to legal education with our students, why should we not approach the learning of staff using the same approaches?

In doing so, Stenhouse was not blind to the realities of practice or the difficulty of the task of creating a research-practice culture. He acknowledged it would take at least a generation. Experience since then has indicated it may take a lot longer, not least because the subject is highly political. Soon after the end of the HCP, the Conservative government introduced a national curriculum under the banner of 'back to basics', with an agenda that stalled or set back many of the changes that Stenhouse was trying to introduce into the comprehensive system of schooling.[10]

Much has changed since the HCP. There are conferences based on action research; the British and Scottish Education Research Associations (BERA and SERA) both focus on publicly-funded research into classroom practice and on practice-based research. In legal education, we have the Higher Education Academy and other conferences on the scholarship of teaching and learning; and the UK Centre for Legal Education, the LILAC conference, legal education streams at SLS conference, in the States there is the AALS conference, specialist organisations such as CALI and much else. But much remains to be done to raise the status of inquiry-based practice. In the UK, how does QAA support this endeavour? Could it do any better? Has benchmarking developed teaching skill, inhibited it, had any effect at all? What effect do our systems of accreditation and objectives have on student learning? Has the RAE encouraged or inhibited legal educational research? Has it encouraged *active* and practice-oriented research? Is there sufficient training for legal educators in empirical and theoretical research methods? Do the regulatory bodies in professional education listen to legal educators and their experiences? Do we present them with sufficient evidence in the form of 'resistant readings' (Kress, 1988, p. 7) to inform their strategies? The lessons Stenhouse has for legal educationalists are clear. Unless we focus on what is valuable in our practice of teaching and bring that into the light of public debate, we will remain in the hands of external agencies and authorities including government who know little of what goes on in legal education and whose aims are not ours. Our activity will thus become more and more trivially technical, as Stenhouse recognised and Dewey before him:

---

10 A process that New Labour has enthusiastically continued. See for instance MacLure and Pettigrew (1997); see also MacLure and Stronach (1993) and Kress (1988).

In the name of scientific administration and close supervision, the initiative and freedom of the actual teacher are more and more curtailed. By means of achievement and mental tests carried on from the central office, of a steadily issuing stream of dictated typewritten communications, of minute and explicit syllabi of instruction, the teacher is reduced to a living phonograph. In the name of centralization of responsibility and of efficiency and even science, everything possible is done to make the teacher into a servile rubber stamp. (*LW*, 2, 122–3)[11]

As a result we shall be led by whatever fashionable policy happens to be in place, rather than guided by theory derived by us from our own practices and supported by our sister disciplines.

But which sister disciplines? Which practices? The following three cases studies are a part-answer to these complex questions.

Case Study 1: The Precision of Ordinary Language: 'Johan Joachim Quantz's Five Lessons'

W.S. Graham was born in Greenock in 1918 and died in 1986. In 1938, after completing his apprenticeship in engineering, he studied philosophy and literature at Newbattle Abbey and thereafter dedicated his life to writing poetry. He lived most of his working life as a poet in Cornwall, close to the community of painters and sculptors living around St Ives.

Language and the difficulty of communication were central to Graham's work. He expresses this in a letter, discussing his long poem, 'The Nightfishing':

> Because although I wanted to write about the sea it was not the sea only as an objective adventure (if there is such a thing) but as experience surrounding a deeper problem which everybody is concerned with.
>
> I mean the essential isolation of man and the difficulty of communication. (Snow, 1999, p. 144)

Graham could express it teasingly, too, as in this letter to Ruth Hilton:

> I'm seeing you now. You're seeing me now and this is us meeting and we at least know that. Though I wish some other person were looking to see us both seeing each other across the old nuisance of language which gets a bit dark or hazy or is it steaming up because we're breathing too close for comfort. I've tried to wipe my side clean how's yours. (Snow, 1999, p. 210)

As this extract reveals, it was the performative, dynamic aspects of language that attracted and puzzled Graham. As he observed (with a nod to Heraclitus) in his early statement of poetic intent, 'Notes on a Poetry of Release',

---

11 Quoted in Maharg (2006).

The most difficult thing for me to remember is that a poem is made of words and not of the expanding heart, the overflowing soul, or the sensitive observer. A poem is made of words. [...] All the poet's knowledge and experience [...] is contained in the language which is obstacle and vehicle at the same time. The shape of all of us is in this language. [...] Each word is touched by and filled with the activity of every speaker. Each word changes every time it is brought to life. Each single word uttered twice becomes a new word each time. You cannot twice bring the same word into sound. (Snow, 1999, pp. 379–80)

It appears again and again in his poetry. His readings in Schopenhauer and Heidegger reinforced his convictions regarding the essential problems of communication not just in the more abstract poems, but in the deeply personal ones too. Take for example these lines from 'The Thermal Stair', a powerful elegy on Graham's friend, the painter Peter Lanyon, killed in a gliding accident in 1964:

You said once in the Engine
House below Morvah
That words make their world
In the same way as the painter's
Mark surprises him
Into seeing new.

* * * *

You said "Here is the sea
Made by alfred wallis
Or any poet or painter's
Eye it encountered.
Or is it better made
By all those vesselled men
Sometime it maintained?
We all make it again."

Give me your hand, Peter,
To steady me on the word. (Graham, 1979, pp. 155—6)

The concept of language making things anew for us is a common modernist trope. Graham extends it here by re-enacting the voice of the dead in formal register describing the aesthetics of art and juxtaposes it with the deeply personal – 'Give me your hand, Peter ...'. Graham never underestimated the power of plain and spoken language: its force is apparent in the syntax of his best work.

We can see this in 'Johan Joachim Quantz's Five Lessons'. The poem takes five instances in the musical education of Karl and juxtaposes them in five stanzas. Starting in winter and ending with spring, the five lessons span Karl's progress from beginner to professional in one artwork. Such time-play is a typical modernist ploy that Graham was well aware of. One could compare it to the work of Nicholson in the St Ives community where Graham was a fairly central figure, or Hepworth and their contemporaries. The work of another modernist, Eduardo Paolozzi's *Untitled Fragmented Head* (1984) is a good example, where the head is composed of disparate parts. Paolozzi was inspired by a Surrealist game where each artist drew a body part, folded the paper over and circulated the paper to the next player. The paper was eventually unfolded to reveal a sort of monster or *cadavre exquis* made up of strange juxtaposed elements.[12]

J.J. Quantz, a eighteenth century flautist, author of a book on flute technique, minor composer and flute tutor of Frederick the Great of Prussia, is at first glance an unlikely subject for Graham. The poet never taught, but he had respect for those who were good teachers – as he says in an early letter, 'Unless you're first and never-wanting-to-do-anything-else a teacher, you're better out of it all and all the energy into the right thing' (Snow, 1999, p. 30,). Neither was Graham a trained musician. Nevertheless he found Quantz's book fascinating for a number of reasons. One of these was the difficulty of musical communication, which he often noted and which for him was a problematic akin to that of language and meaning. As he says in a letter to Ruth Hilton, who first brought Quantz's text to his notice,

> … why am I not aware more the intended shape of the musical object? It takes an effort of memory to 'observe' the musical object as one object. (Snow, 1999, p. 200)

In another letter, explaining the genesis of the poem, he tells of how he is attracted by the musical aesthetics of Quantz's text and its practical emphasis on flute playing (Snow, 1999, p. 330). The conjunction of abstract and highly practical clearly paralleled Graham's own approach to language and the communication of meaning in his poetry. Graham read deeply, if erratically, in philosophy (pre-Socratics, existentialists, Sartre, Heidegger); but when he sought to investigate the problems he would seek a resolution of the abstract through the concrete, leaving the reader to reconstruct the abstract. Nor was this the result of a poetic focus upon the concrete detail only. Many poets are much more abstract than Graham. But it is the very fusion of abstract and practical that attracts Graham.

The poem, spoken in Quantz's dry, severe tone (not unlike the tone of much of his book), deals with the evolving relationship between Quantz and one of his pupils, an anonymous Karl. The poem, though, can hardly be said to be student-centred. Karl figures as a cypher: it is the relationship of Quantz to music, the place of the tutor, the contrast between abstract and practical and other concerns that are the focus of the poem. In the second lesson, for instance, when Karl is 'now nearly able to play the flute', Quantz tells him:

> Now we must try higher, aware of the terrible
> Shapes of silence sitting outside your ear

---

12 See http://fr.wikipedia.org/wiki/Cadavre_exquis.

Anxious to define you and really love you.
Remember silence is curious about its opposite
Element which you shall learn to represent

Enough of that. Now stand in the correct position
So that the wood of the floor will come up through you.
Stand, but not too stiff. Keep your elbows down.
Now take a simple breath and make me a shape
Of clear unchained started and finished tones.

The tone is one of command, perfunctory at times. We may think of its plainness and apparent simplicity as more appropriate to the technical language of instrument playing; but Graham uses this syntax for both the practical and the abstract discussion within the poem. The result is a remarkable embedding of the philosophical and abstract within the quotidian and the technical aspects of music-making – a form of aesthetics derived from form and practice, not philosophy. The language develops this: a breath that is 'simple', tones that are not merely 'finished' but 'started' as well. This is elaborated in the final lesson: 'Remember Karl. Begin with good / Nerve and decision', with this last line exemplifying the practice Quantz wants Karl to follow. Quantz teaches Karl to be the locus of evaluation in his playing and to listen closely to his own performance:

Go on now but remember it must be always
Easy and flowing. Light and shadow must
Be varied but be varied in your mind
Before you hear the eventual return sound.

The third lesson emphasises the place of music derived from folk forms in Karl's education and the immediacy of the form within its context:

Play me the dance you made for the barge-master.
Stop stop Karl. Play it as you first thought
Of it in the hot boat-kitchen.

Later, in the fourth lesson, Karl becomes inducted into art music:

                    Karl,
I know you find great joy in the great
Composers. But now you can put your lips to
The messages and blow them into sound
And enter and be there as well. You must
Be faithful to who you are speaking from
And yet it is all right. You will be there.

It is a passage that stands for the difficulty of interpretation of art, that entirely avoids the question of literal interpretation and focuses instead on the necessary role of the musician as interpreter, 'a little creator / After the big creator. And it can be argued / You are as necessary'. Quantz can now see in this penultimate lesson Karl's increasing sophistication in the complex act of interpretation. No longer is the tone commanding, admonitory. There is more of fellowship about the act of tuition:

> Take your coat off. Sit down. A Glass of Bols
> Will help us both. I think you are good enough
> To not need me anymore. I think you know
> You are not only an interpreter.
> What you will do is always something else
> And they will hear you simultaneously with
> The Art you have been given to read.

Quantz is clearly speaking of Graham's concerns: the difficulty of communication, the performance of art in the creation of meaning. Graham offers insight into the abstract nature of the problem, but his solutions are always practical. In the fifth and final lesson the final stanza of the poem deals with this and other matters:

> One last thing, Karl, remember when you enter
> The joy of those quick high archipelagoes,
> To make to keep your finger-stops as light
> As feathers but definite. What can I say more?
> Do not be sentimental or in your Art.
> I will miss you. Do not expect applause.

The combination of practical and abstract also includes the moral and ethical. Quantz warns against this and against the vanity of performance.

How might such an art-work be useful in the context of legal education? Can one legitimately 'research' the application of this poem to legal education? I think we can. In the first instance, I think it important that 'application' is precisely the wrong word; as is the implicit idea that the poem belongs in a separate category, which might be termed 'law and literature' or some such. Recent scholarship of this and related *topoi* can be accommodated if we think of the direct links between the text and legal education. The power and deceptive clarity of Graham's poetry points up the invidious distinction made between literature and ordinary language, where literature is defined as in some way or other value-added. Such a distinction trivialises the complexity of ordinary language and impoverishes the options open to both literary criticism and legal education. But rather than take the position that there is no such thing as literary discourse or legal education which can be identified as such and therefore separated out once and for all from other forms of utterance and community discourse, it would be more accurate to state that there is no such thing as ordinary language or ordinary educational encounters. As Stanley Fish pointed out some time ago (adducing Chomsky and Austin's speech-act theories), ordinary language is 'extraordinary because at its heart is precisely that realm of values, intentions and purposes which is often assumed to be the exclusive property of literature' (Fish, 1981, p. 108). It is a point that is made not only by the Academic Literacies movement, but by the New London Group as well (New London Group, 1996 and Gee, 1996, pp. 44–66). The same is true of every educational intervention that involves dialogue: at its heart lies a social encounter. With this in mind we could note the following approaches to research:

1) The poem stands in its own right as an aesthetic object and has value for that.
2) It is useful to understand how another discipline deals with these issues. What are the standards that Graham applies to his work? How do we interpret those standards? What are the community standards by which interpretation of Graham's art is judged?
3) The poem embodies a number of the performative issues that students need to deal with – in negotiation, interviewing, advocacy, for instance. How do we presently deal with those issues in legal education?
4) The poem comments on the teacher-student relationship and as such it could be useful to foreground the relationship in legal education and create of it an object for discussion.
5) It treats of epistemological and communication issues relevant to the education of law students and relevant to every legal educational encounter.
6) The aesthetic is important precisely because of the imaginative qualities it foregrounds in the educational process. How do we use and value imagination in legal education?

Case Study 2: The Kodály Method: Practice, Theory and Performance in Music and Legal Education

The choirmaster enters the room. The choir of 60 or so children continue to chatter among themselves, though they keep an eye on the figure who has moved over to some sheets of music lying on the piano and is sorting them. He has a quick word with two assistants, then turns to the choir. He claps his hands and begins to sing to them, 'Hello everyone', using only a major third interval, ascending. The choir chants back, 'Hello' in the same interval, descending. The choirmaster sings back, using the same interval but with different words; and the choir responds. The lesson has begun. It continues with vocal exercises. The choirmaster no longer sings but, after a chord from the accompanist on the piano, signs to the choir with his hand – the so-called Curwen hand signs. The choir sings the notes signified by the sign. The choir is then divided into two and practise pentatonic sequences, signed by the choirmaster and an assistant. They divide into three and play a game called 'Avoiding do', in which the aim is to keep the pentatonic sequences sustained for as long as possible without returning to the tonic.

Meanwhile several assistants are taking the junior choir, ages 5–8, in another room. They divide the children into small groups. Each small group has a leader who is one of the children or an assistant. The leader gives out a rhythm to the small group – ta te-te [rest] te-te. The children think for a moment, then organise themselves into groups that mimic the shape of the crotchets, quavers or rests: a single child, two children facing each other with their arms around their shoulders, one sitting on the floor and two in the same position as the other two. The leader tells them if they got the shape of the rhythm correct. If not, he or she simply repeats and points to the group of notes/children that are wrong. There is a moment as the rhythm is rehearsed mentally, silently, by the children; the group re-forms and invariably the correct pattern is established.

All of these activities and many more like them take place on Monday evenings in the Henry Wood Hall in Glasgow. The choirs are the junior and probationary choruses of the Royal Scottish National Orchestra, led by Christopher Bell. They are learning to sing via a system of musical education that has become known as the Kodály System, after the Hungarian composer and educationalist, Zoltán Kodály who is associated with the method.[13] Kodály was not the only begetter of this system, however. It evolved in Hungarian schools, under his guidance and under principles initially derived by him; but it has been developed by others since 1950, when the first music primary school was set up in Kesckemét, Kodály's home town. There are now Kodály Societies and Institutes across most of the western world developing Kodály's system of musical education.

The system consists of a number of deceptively simple activities and concepts:

•   rhythm symbols and syllables are used to denote rhythm;
•   hand signals are used to represent tonal relationships;
•   music first learned is often the music most to hand, particularly folk music.

Like another early twentieth-century composer and educator, Hindemith, Kodály gave much emphasis to the construction of rhythm; but he goes well beyond this to a tactile, concrete sense of not only rhythm but notes on the page. As far as possible, every activity in the practice room is subsumed to music: it is a form of music immersion. But as well as this, the concept is rigorously child developmental in its learning sequences. Thus, in terms of sol-fa, the youngest classes learn sol-mi and sol-mi-la patterns, particularly the ascending intervals, which are the harder to memorise and sing. They go on to learn accented and unaccented beats, thence the barline, in duple metre, 3/4, 4/4 and 6/8. More advanced choirs

13   See Lambton (2006) and the website of the British Kodály Academy. For further musicological sources, see Ránki (1987), Choksy (1999) and Houlahan and Tacka (1998).

sing music with *ostinati*, both melodic and rhythmic and work on inner hearing and melodic dictation.

The result of this is that, from the start of their musical education, children begin to learn the basic building-blocks of musical literacy and analysis; and they do so in a method that has three important properties. First, the method is strikingly child-centred, not subject-developmental. Second, the gradations between levels of achievement are based on a matrix of skills and knowledge that is derived from a model of child development. Third, all human faculties are enlisted, not just the aural. Children use visual memory perception as well as aural memory. They learn to distinguish the notes they are to sing from others in part-singing almost from the first day and to focus on melodic line and rhythm. Above all, they enjoy themselves.

What has this to do with legal education, you might ask? Surely this is specialised music, not legal, education; children, not young adults are being taught; and the end product is musical performance. But there are, I would hold, many fascinating parallels and contrasts to be drawn between aspects of legal education and the grammar of the Kodaly method, that are of interest to legal educators, are worthy of research and I list some of them below:

1) The method is developmental. It is based upon a steady increment of sophistication and complexity in musical understanding.
2) Children learn incrementally, building upon skills and knowledge, constantly reviewing and previewing what they are learning or about to learn.
3) Performance is the goal, but children are also encouraged to improvise, compose and use their known musical vocabulary at each level.
4) The performative skills are not treated in isolation. They are linked in a fundamental way to the musical theory that the children learn.[14]
5) Theory is not learned in theory classes, but is learned via practice. Practice and theory thus are intertwined.
6) As many of the senses as possible are involved in the production of music.
7) Games, activities, warm-ups, are used to focus attention on specific aspects of musical performance.
8) Time spent in rehearsal is aimed at performance to the highest standards; and a complex performative network consisting of tutors, administrators and volunteers as well as professionals supports both rehearsal and performance.

None of this is particularly the province of musical education. We can see some of it in problem-based learning (for example, the complex matrix of skills, knowledge and attitudes used by PBL designers); much of it can be seen in the texts of Pestalozzi, Montessori, even Rousseau – the founding documents of the

---

14 Compare this, for instance, to the positions of Patel and Krieger as regards PBL outlined in Chapter 1.

child-centred movement in education.[15] Balkin and Levinson have pointed out in a number of articles how, among the 'humane arts', as they term them, the performative arts are quite close to law's practice and function. Scores and scripts are similar to constitutions and statutes; the 'triangle of creators, interpreters and audiences' shapes the success of performances; and in both law and music performance is sustained by complex networks within conservatories and law schools – involving administrators as well as academic staff – and also within performance areas: law chambers and courts, concert halls and performance programmes such as Proms concerts (Balkin and Levinson, 2006, pp. 155–87, Levinson and Balkin, 1991 and Balkin and Levinson, 1999).

And yet, much of it has yet to filter through to legal education. Games, simulations, role-plays – these are increasingly the province of the professional end of legal education; but there is no reason why we should not start them from the first day of legal education in our law schools and continue this right through undergraduate education.[16] This applies as much to the skills of academic argument as it does to the more professional skills. For example, what do our students understand of the rhetorics of the student essay? How do we teach the building blocks of legal literacy in undergraduate life? How do we manage the gradations and standards of work between early years in the LLB or (in the USA) JD qualifications and the Honours programme in the LLB or JD final year?

As an example of this, let me quote from a research project I carried out with undergraduate first-level law students. The project aimed to explore the relationship between their prior writing strategies and their writing on the law course – what had changed, why and how the new discipline was altering their writing strategies – by conducting a number of interviews over the course of which students drafted and redrafted their work.[17] A number of students in the first interview observed of their work that they were 'stuck' – unclear about what to write, how and unclear about standards. As a result, the students were uncertain about what they should produce, how they were to go about the task, what criteria will be used to judge performance. They attempted to reproduce methods and models of achievement that appeared to serve them in the past, but which, in their legal writing, condemned them to what Bourdieu (quoted in Chapter 1) characterised memorably as a form of 'creolized discourse'. Uncertainty as to language, purpose and process contributed to uncertainty of argument structure and poorer quality of written work.

---

15 A parallel that has already been made – see for example Christensen (2007) and Curtis (2006).

16 For examples in professional education see UK Legal Education and Training Group at http://www.letg.org.uk. See also Gunsalus and Beckett (2006).

17 Students were required to write two 500-word essays. The author interviewed students (5–10 mins max.) pre- and post-essay, using techniques originally developed in-depth by Carl Bereiter and Marlene Scardamalia. For the methodology used in these intervention protocols, see DiPardo (1994), Swanson-Owens and Newell (1994), Hartley and Chesworth (1998) and Lillis and Grainger (1998).

Is it possible to move students from this stuck position to one where they can begin to feel in command of their writing, at least to some degree? It is and the remarkable point about many of the techniques advocated by compositional and rhetoric theorists cited in Chapter 1 is that they involve variants of the Kodály method. Here is a mature student discussing her frustration in expressing herself within the constraints of disciplinary argument:

Sarah	So I knew myself it was just absolutely, totally, it's not what I wanted it to say, it's not exactly what I wanted it to say, I mean, Friday afternoon at half past three I was still typing it out and I thought 'This is ridiculous, I've usually got everything done by now'. I just couldn't for the life of me get what I wanted down on paper and I thought there is no point in changing it now it's too late – it's to be in for four o'clock. Just a fail. I just knew it right away. I was like that, 'There's no way that's gonna pass'.
PM:	It's a bad feeling, isn't it?
Sarah:	Oh no, I knew myself I even said, I says, the essay is a lot of crap, I says, it's total and utter rubbish that's in it (Maharg, 2000, pp. 92–3).[18]

Following my advice, Sarah made three alterations to her writing methods. First, she kept the text in as unfinished a state for as long as possible. Second, she used diagrams and sketch maps of the essay structure, linked to to-do lists. Third, she used tape recordings to help her manage the complex sets of lecture notes, reading notes and essay fragments out of which she assembled her argument. She had already used a variant of this 16 years earlier in secondary school. Here is Sarah again after submitting her second essay draft:

Sarah:	[...] I actually taped it first [...]. I sat and I had all my notes down. I just relayed off what I wanted to say and then just took it bit by bit [...] So I took your advice on Wednesday night and I was up to four o'clock on Thursday morning doing that essay right enough. I did! [...]
PM:	But did the taping of it work?
Sarah:	Yeah. I find it a lot easier, a lot easier, because my brain works faster than my writing so if I've said it all right – I've added that bit and that bit – so that's fine I'll just write it out, what I've said and then I can add the bits in here and there. And I thought well that's it – perfect, got it.

---

18 Quoted in Maharg (2000). Student quotes are reproduced with student permission. Student name has been changed to preserve anonymity. As a result of this and other interviews a number of new modules were developed that integrated writing skills development with substantive law and that developed cumulatively at levels one, three and four (Honours dissertations) within a four-year BA law degree at Glasgow Caledonian University. The methodology of the interview technique is discussed in detail in Maharg (2000). Particularly useful in thinking about student–staff talk was Mercer (2000). Models of talk – disputational, cumulative, exploratory – are, as Mercer, admits, simplifications of a complex reality, but it is a necessary process to explore that reality with students.

Sarah here was really engaged in a task as cognitively and as performatively complex in its own way as part-singing in a choir. She had to cope with the demands of disciplinary argument, use terms of art with precision, be aware of the demands of the essay question, organise structures of legal argument, use her past experience and many other demands on her cognitive awareness. The higher grade she achieved in the second essay was perceived by her to be the result of the discovery that the way she worked 16 years before could be adapted as a valuable heuristic at university. That method was highly oral and graphic-based. She was discovering, to quote Flower, how the 'negotiation of inner voices shape[s] the *hidden logic* of the text' (Flower, 1994, p. 55). In recovering that multimedia method (close in form to the Kodály method), it is not too much to say that Sarah was recovering part of herself and her creativity that she had forgotten; and she was recovering, too, a sense of self-worth and dignity by finding personal ways in which to learn how to attain the standards expected of her in the complex discourse of the law as taught within a university. It is not too fanciful to picture her negotiating those voices at her ear, anxious to define her, in Graham's terms. For like Graham himself – who is both Quantz and Karl in the poem – Sarah was a first-generation tertiary education student, negotiating the social ground as much as the intellectual.

Kodály's approach has been confirmed by research within the social cognitive tradition, with its acknowledgement of the importance of the social context of learning. In his article on memory for instance, Tulving (1985) hypothesised that episodic and semantic memory may be associated with distinct forms of awareness, that is, remembering and knowing. His proposition was taken up by Conway et al. (1997) who refined the concept by focusing on the relationships between episodic memory and remembering and semantic memory and knowing. They suggested that remembering existed within the personal structure of episodes and that this remembering gradually becomes a form of knowing by a process of schematisation – what they called the 'remember-to-know' shift. To prove their hypotheses, Conway et al. analysed how students actually learn, taking as their subjects students who were studying first-year Psychology modules. The students were assessed by multiple-choice examinations after their research methods module. What Conway found was revealing. The remember-to-know shift seemed to occur because of the nature of the module and its placing in the curriculum. It was a practical module and aspects of it were encountered by students throughout the rest of the Psychology curriculum, in different situations. Students could thus put their research module learning into practice under different conditions and in association with different parts of the curriculum. Conway et al. suggested that this form of learning facilitated the remember-to-know shift. It is a form of Kodály's intense focus on practical embodiment of abstract knowledge, encountered within different contexts.

Case Study 3: The Gestalt and the Ethics of the Client: Standardised Client Initiative

This is a study in assessment derived from medical education that can also be used for teaching and learning. Barrows (1987, p. 17) defined the concept thus:

> The Simulated/Standardized Patient (SP) is a person who has been carefully coached to simulate an actual patient so accurately that the simulation cannot be detected by a skilled clinician. In performing the simulation, the SP presents the gestalt of the patient being simulated; not just the history, but the body language, the physical findings, and the emotional and personality characteristics as well.

Barrows rightly emphasises the totality of the experience of being a patient. If this is represented well in the consultation, the student's experience will be much more profound – as if he or she is dealing with a real patient. Originally used in undergraduate medical education, SPs are now used in postgraduate and continuing professional development in medicine, where they are used not only to role-play patients, but to assess aspects of performance (Smith et al., 2002, pp. 83–7).[19] Ker et al. point to their range of use:

> Simulated patients have been found to be valuable in areas of health behaviour change (Poirer et al., 2004) and lifestyle problems such as alcohol abuse (Eagles et al., 2001) and sensitive areas such as sexual heath (Fitzgerald et al., 2003). They have also helped in giving formative feedback on performance following simulated ward exercises (Ker et al. 2003, p. 9).[20]

SPs are most commonly used in problem-based learning curricula, but their use can be adapted to a variety of situations.[21] In the Glasgow Graduate School of Law (GGSL) we were interested in adapting the technique as a form of assessment of interviewing skills.[22] Prior to the introduction of SCs, we assessed interviewing skills by videotaping interviews of students role-playing solicitor and client. There were however many problems with this – validity (was the student client a

---

19 For an excellent history of the development and use of SPs, see Wallace (1997). As Wallace says, the key principle of the method as developed by Barrows is that 'as much as possible ... the students should be given an opportunity to learn in the same manner as the students is going to practice' (p. 9).

20 This article is a helpful introduction to bridging practices between standardised patients and standardised clients.

21 For a general introduction to the resources on PBL and legal education see the work of the UKCLE PBL working group at http://www.ukcle.ac.uk/resources/pbl/group.html.

22 The literature on client counselling is of course considerable. See for instance Felstiner and Sarat (1992), Sherr (1986), Moorehead et al. (2003); see also Smith (1995); Cunningham (1999 and 1992) and Smith (1998). As far as we are aware there is little written about the use of SCs in legal education.

believable client?), reliability (were all student client characters equally equable or awkward?) and fair (some student clients fed 'lines' to their solicitors; others did not). There were also problems with assessment of performance by tutors, who marked to a detailed 20-point assessment schedule, but whose assessments were not wholly reliable across their assessment cohort, nor could we prove that there was consistent inter-rater reliability. If assessment of interviewing skills were to be high-stakes, it required significantly improved standards of validity, reliability and fairness.

Above all, and after four years of using this procedure, it was clear that students were learning little about communications at a deep level. Basic student-to-student role-play was useful on a Foundation Course; but at a higher level of sophistication the role-play was simply not helping them to understand the critical issues of client-centred practice. Students themselves acknowledged this: we offered them the opportunity of videotaped voluntary practice with each other before the assessment, with feedback to be given on the tape by a tutor; and approximately 2 per cent of the student body took up this offer.

As a result, we developed a standardised client initiative (SCI) to train our SCs not only to role-play clients but to assess our students.[23] Lay persons would be trained to simulate legal clients (standardised clients – SCs) and would be interviewed by students adopting the role of legal trainee. To do this we had to set up procedures to deal with recruitment, induction, training, re-training and many other issues. A project of this nature could not be undertaken alone and GSSL is one of a number of international partners in the SCI, all of whom have contributed to the Initiative.

The project began when, during a legal education conference at Georgia State University's College of Law, Clark Cunningham organised a visit to an SP centre close by in Atlanta for a number of participants.[24] The project at the GGSL began with a training seminar held by Dr Jean Ker and her colleagues in Dundee Medical Faculty. They have much experience of training SCs which was very useful to us. Ker's assistance was invaluable also at a later conference where a number of us held a small impromptu seminar at which we analysed many of the problematic issues that arose regarding assessment criteria and procedures.[25] It was at this seminar, for instance, that the assessment schedule

---

23 For more information on this, see Barton et al. (2006) See also, for general information and papers, the SCI blog.

24 Those visiting included Professor Larry Grosberg of New York Law School (whose own work in the field of SCs has been invaluable to us) and Nigel Duncan, of Inns of Court School of Law, City University, London. In addition to this conference and visit, Cunningham's Effective Lawyer-Client Communication (ELCC) Project has been of great value in forming the project. The Initiative has been funded over the past three years by the Burge Endowment Fund, the College of Law in England and Wales, GGSL and the Clark Foundation for Legal Education.

25 Sixth International Clinical Conference, UCLA, Lake Arrowhead Conference Centre, October 2005.

underwent significant alteration from the form of both the original GGSL 20-point assessment schedule and the ELCC assessment form. Later, it became clear that the form had imported a number of assumptions about lawyers' behaviour in legal practice and there were a number of important debates that focused along lines of is/ought, as we sought to determine what our assessment of interviewing skills was trying to achieve. We also drafted feedback criteria for the SCs to use during training sessions. Towards the end of this period of development we began to train SCs in a series of seminars using video, peer-feedback and practitioner feedback on both the delivery of information to the student-lawyers and then on standards of assessment we expected on each of the assessment items in the schedule.

As a result of this project development, the GGSL interviewing assessment now consists of three stages, where the student:

1) is given general information about the client;
2) interviews the SC;
3) writes up a note to file on the interview.

The SC assessment schedule contains two parts. Part A assesses on eight items (on a five-point Likert scale), all of which are based on their experience of the interview. Part B is a case-specific checklist, consisting of statements answered by yes or no. The SC fills out both once the student has left the interview room. Elements two and three of the assessment count for less in the weighting of the total mark for assessment. Following small-scale pilots we organised a larger-scale pilot in the GGSL where both tutors and SCs assessed the entire student cohort (over 250 students) according to the new assessment schedule. Our aim was to discover if assessment by SCs could be as valid and reliable as assessment by tutors. After extensive statistical analysis it was clear that the results were highly significant and strongly indicated that assessment by SCs was sufficiently valid and reliable to be used for a high-stakes assessment in legal education (Barton et al., 2006).

It should be noted that what we were assessing here was not standardisation of student performance, but of assessment. Students require to learn disciplinary activities but there is a balance to be struck: in our highly organised programmes of study we must take care that the process of standardisation does not repress individuality or creativity. Dewey (like Stenhouse on the subject of learning outcomes) recognised the wider context of this, believing as he did that an education which highly constrained individuals was dangerous to a democratic polity:

> A progressive society counts individual variations as precious since it finds in them the means of its own growth. Hence a democratic society must, in consistency with

its ideal, allow for intellectual freedom and the play of diverse gifts and interests in its educational measures.[26]

How has this changed our teaching? The change is so significant and radical that we are still in the process of adapting and we shall be for some time. As things stand within the Diploma, the alignment of sophistication from Foundation Course student-on-student role-plays to SC role-plays is much more effective. SCs now give feedback to students as if in assessment and students can reflect on that assessment and undertake extra training sessions prior to their formal assessment. Student uptake on this has been remarkable: where previously around 2 per cent of the student body took up the offer of voluntary role-play with each other, this year (2006/7) over 90 per cent of students volunteered to interview an SC and receive feedback. In the near future we shall videotape this practice interview with the SC, give students the tools to comment on the video and build this into our development of e-portfolio procedures and evidence.

It is clear, though, that we are moving to a model where, after initial workshops, there will be minimum tutor input. Instead, students will enter a process of action and reflection with the SCs, a process that we shall support by hosting videos of master classes (based on the music education model) where a SC will comment upon student performance; and this will be supplemented by comment from the student involved in the interview and possibly a lawyer (but with the focus firmly on the client experience). In this way, a student will obtain information from three sources not just about the client experience, but about the standards applicable to the course. In this way we hope to focus students not merely on the standards expected of them in interviewing but that those standards are based on the client experience and the ethics of the client encounter. In the future we shall be working to develop more sophisticated SC scenarios for trainees and to develop scenarios for continuing professional development – for example, specialty accreditation processes. Note the critical point though: we are adapting our practice around the communicative and learning power of the SC encounter, which is client-based, not student-based or curriculum-based. The SC project, stemming from another discipline and deeply embedded in the research paradigms of that discipline, is thus having a transformative effect on our teaching practice.

---

26 Quoted in Aleman (2006, pp. 25–31). There is of course a wider context to standardisation than is discussed here. The entire standardisation movement in the health sciences is a huge, complex and as one might expect, not uncontroversial subject, given that it deals with matters such as professional power, objectivity and standards of clinical care and procedures. See Timmermans and Berg (2003) for an introduction to the history of the movement and a balanced investigation of the clinical and medico-sociological issues. It is a context we are aware of in the SCI and our approach is that the trade-off for education weighs more than the potential dangers. There is of course a similar potential for other forms of educational activity, such as collaborative learning, to be used for the wrong purposes (discussed below in Chapter 8).

Summary

What do these three educational moments tell us about interdisciplinary practice and research? They reveal different epistemologies, different approaches to the process of learning. All have relevance for us as descriptions of the human condition. The problem of communication that Graham wrestled with is the same problem for a student facing a SC – the incremental development of activities in the Kodály method is precisely what is needed in implementations of PBL such as use of a SC in legal education. Moreover, where Stenhouse advocated that the unpredictability of discussion in the HCP meant that student understanding could only be assessed against internal standards, not external criteria (learning objectives, for instance), Barrows advocated that the locus of evaluation in a consultation or interview was not the domain of the subject expert, but of the patient or client, who was part of the relationship at that time, in that room. It is also clear to us that such projects are probably best carried out by interdisciplinary and inter-jurisdictional teams. As we say in our article on the SC Initiative:

> In a sense, one of the benefits for the participant institutions has been the inter-jurisdictional and interdisciplinary collaboration on the project. There is so much that we have learned from each other over the length of the project to date that could not have been learned in any other way than working with each other; and this has resulted in fairly radical change, in the GGSL at least, to our working practices. (Barton et al., 2006, pp. 53–4)

What we learned from the SC Initiative was already there in Latour's account of Pasteur. There is never a simple transfer from research laboratory to field. As Shaffer and Squire point out, 'the point of the *lever model* is that the role of such experiments is not to adapt to existing practices but rather to provide guidelines for the transformation of practice' (Shaffer and Squire, 2006, p. 14). In order for the implementation of the SC simulation to succeed, we needed to base our work on the gestalt of an actual client as closely as possible; we then needed to simulate its key elements within a laboratory setting (the SC training sessions); and then we needed to develop interventions with the students through our experimental research. In doing so we also needed to adopt the relationship between theory and praxis advocated by Stenhouse (which is close in many respects to the lever model), and the intense focus on the nature of communication and the developmental scale of the project exemplified respectively by Graham's poem and Kodály's method.

In a sense all three case studies in this chapter constitute examples of Galison's trading zone, with the last one an instantiation of that practice. All are capable of significantly changing aspects of legal education. If radical change is to come about, it is only by working as Stenhouse's teacher-researchers, as Galison's traders and with other practitioners close-up, on joint projects in communities of practice that we can, in Graham's words, be aware of the shapes beyond our usual practice, anxious to define us and really love us. For this reason, following an irresistible adamic impulse, I name the empty quarter in Stokes' diagram for Transformational Research.

Part 1 Conclusion: Elasticity and Obstacle

In a keynote address the educationalist Joseph Schwab (1970, p. 4) warned against what he called 'inveterate, unexamined, and mistaken reliance on theory'. He dismissed the search for a single theory of education that would be a foundation for all, and instead advocated a 'polyfocal conspectus', a drawing together of theories and experience. The six case studies in the last two chapters have been chosen in order to shed light on each other, but principally to illustrate the necessity for interdisciplinary research and practice within legal education. In a perceptive footnote Galison compares his own practice in *Image and Logic* to that of Callon-Latour as observers of scientific research process, noting how others had seen resemblances between their methods:

> [Callon-Latour's work] emphasizes the effectiveness and elasticity of the leveraged power that comes of creating alliances and enlisting other groups toward a predetermined end. My work tends to focus on the material (and nonmaterial) obstacles that shape and delimit action in the sphere of science over time. (Galison, 1997, p. 15, n.21)[1]

There in a couple of sentences we have the problems of research and practice that we have to work with in legal education: the balance of elasticity and obstacle, of leveraged power against delimited action. The case studies in these two chapters are indicative of alliances and contexts, material and methods, failures and successes. They reveal that we can find useful experiments, descriptions, texts and progenitors in the most surprising of contexts; that our research work requires grounding in research methodologies that are not merely our own, and that we need to give careful thought to the meta-translation of that research to our own practice.

Is it true to say that more substantial achievements happen because interdisciplinary people work together over a period of time on joint projects, of the type that Galison describes in meticulous detail in his history of micro-physics? Of course not. There are many remarkable and luminous works which are not necessarily of this description. But increasingly if we are to engage in work close to practice, we need to create the space, and plan the funding to engage in such projects. What sorts of initiatives might be useful?

The best interdisciplinary initiatives are ground-up; and if they are to thrive and survive as permanent contributions to knowledge and practice then

---

[1]   He is of course writing within a horizon of other researchers into the nature of scientific disciplines and of material production in the sciences – for example Knorr-Cetina 1999, Galison 1987, Latour 1987 and Lenoir 1997).

(inter)disciplinary institutions, cultures and structures are essential.[2] They might include the following:

- institutions working together on materials or methods projects, possibly forming joint centres in order to facilitate this;
- more interdisciplinary initiatives under the aegis of the UK HEA subject centres, particularly in multi-site and international projects;
- a redefinition of the relationships between foundations that fund educational research and implementation, and their grantees;[3]
- lobby for change to the RAE process in the UK.

The last issue is, in the short- to medium-term, a problematic one for interdisciplinarians. The question of interdisciplinarity has of course exercised designers of the Research Assessment Exercise. The RAE panels have had difficulty in the past in categorising interdisciplinary research. Recently there has been no lack of research discussing how such research might be assessed. As the result of a two-year exploratory study of research and teaching practices at what they termed 'exemplary interdisciplinary institutes and programs', for instance, Gardner and Mansilla (2003), suggested that interdisciplinary research ought to be judged by the 'core epistemic' criteria of consistency, balance, effectiveness.[4] 'Epistemic' is precisely the right word to use of this type of judgement, for the decision is a situation-judgment as to the fit and the fitness of the research. In more detail, they summarise their findings of what interdisciplinary researchers judged as good work as the following:

1   in the disciplines involved (*consistency with multiple separate disciplinary antecedents*);
2   the way in which the work stands together as a generative and coherent whole (*balance in weaving together perspectives*);
3   the way in which the integration advances the goals that researchers set for their pursuits and the methods they use (*effectiveness in advancing understanding*). (Gardner and Mansilla, 2003, p. 5)

---

[2]   Despite Stenhouse's best efforts, the HCP was always going to be a structured programme alien to a local culture, and because of that, have a limited effect in its main aims (though it had many other and unforeseen positive effects).

[3]   A valuable study on this in the US has recently been carried out by the Carnegie Foundation – see Bacchetti and Ehrlich, 2006.

[4]   They defined interdisciplinary work quite simply as 'work that integrates knowledge and modes of thinking from two or more disciplines'. For a summary of the findings, see http://www.carnegiefoundation.org/files/elibrary/Foundations_and_Education_summary. pdf. See also resources at the Interdisciplines website, and the Harvard Interdisciplinary Studies Project generally.

To deal with the assessment of interdisciplinary work, the recent Roberts review of the RAE advocated 'a small number of 'thematic' panels which would provide a focus for interdisciplinary communities which have become established within the sector':

> We also propose that sub-panels should be supported by colleges of assessors with experience of working in designated multidisciplinary 'thematic' areas. This would ensure that the accepted definitions of excellence in a discipline do not prevent contributions to excellent multidisciplinary projects from being properly recognised. The areas of research covered by this facility would be identified through a bibliometric analysis of data on research collaborations. This would provide a mechanism for ensuring the value added through interdisciplinary and multidisciplinary work is properly recognised. (Roberts, 2003, p. 28, para 192)

The Roberts review is satisfied that the RAE structure of individual panels, leavened with thematic sub-panels ought to be sufficient to analyse interdisciplinary work.[5] But this does not take into account much of the cutting-edge of truly interdisciplinary work which, by definition, cannot be assessed by mono-disciplinary standards. Mansilla and Gardner (2003) put this well in the summary of their work:

> As [the researchers in their study] portray it, quality interdisciplinary understanding does not rest on an accumulated set of established disciplinary rules. Instead, each piece of interdisciplinary work revealed an idiosyncratic coordination of disciplinary insights geared to accomplish researchers' cognitive and practical goals.

One wonders whether such creativity will be given due recognition, or whether it will end up in the wrong quadrant of Stokes' matrix. As Shaffer and Squire (2006, p. 4) point out, a renewed focus on Pasteur's quadrant places

> undue emphasis on tinkering around the edges of existing educational systems without seriously reconsidering the fundamental values or organizing structures behind schooling. In short, it has led to a privileging of research programs that work within the current constraints of schooling rather than those that have the potential to change it.

As it stands, and if such an outcome holds for the 2008 and subsequent RAE exercises in the UK, transformative interdisciplinary work may well continue to be disadvantaged.

---

[5]   According 'RAE 2008 Panel criteria and working methods', section 2, paras 52–5, there will be provision for cross-referral and specialist advice – not quite the Roberts model.

PART 2
Laminations

Chapter 3

The Road not Taken:
Realists and the Curriculum

One cannot understand the history of education in the United States in the twentieth century unless one realizes that Edward L. Thorndike won and John Dewey lost.
(Lagemann, 1989, p. 185)

[Dewey's] method of dealing with problems is still and always will be the great and needed method: Take a fresh look, look to see what is there, and what it is about, and re-pose your issues in those terms.
Llewellyn (1959), quoted in Twining (1985, p. 367 at n.126) and reprinted in Twining (2002, p. 131).

Dewey and the Realists

It is one of the interesting features of the realist movements in the first half of the twentieth century in US law schools that there is no single manifesto that can be said to stand for the practice of all and no version that is a general statement of the purpose and method of all. A number of scholars have attempted this (Summers, 1983, for instance) but to date, the best jurisprudential work has been either biographical (Twining, 1973) or analyses of specific aspects of their work (Schlegel, 1995). This chapter focuses not on the jurisprudential aspect of the realist initiatives, but on some of the educational aspects, and in particular the early evolution of the reforms in the 1920s at Columbia.

As often happens with curriculum reform, the realist interventions there and later at Yale came about as accidents of time and circumstance as well as planned campaigns. The reforms were influenced by at least three pre-existing conditions. First, the Law School was financially straitened during World War I, as were many other law schools, when staff were difficult to recruit and students even harder. Afterwards, numbers of students expanded, and the correspondence of Dean Harlan Fiske Stone with staff applying for posts expands considerably, too.[1]

---

1 Stone was Dean of Faculty 1910–23. His office files (Stone (1911–24), 69 boxes) are preserved in Special Collections, Butler Library of Columbia University, and include an extensive collection of Faculty correspondence and papers, correspondence with the NY Bar Association and AALS and personal papers and memorabilia. These files are a valuable source of information on the Columbia reforms. Stone's contribution to the

With the expansion in staff and students came the opportunity to expand the curriculum. In addition, staff began to offer relatively unusual courses – Spanish Jurisprudence, for instance.[2] Second, there was considerable re-organisation of the curriculum at Columbia in order to create a set of internally-coherent subjects, and much discussion as to the order and detail of the various subjects.[3] Third, there was dissatisfaction with the skills, knowledge and attitudes of students arriving in the JD programme from undergraduate programmes of study and this was the catalyst for experimentation with new processes in assessment.[4]

Such innovations are an indication not merely of President Nicholas Murray Butler's ambitions for his Law School, but of the interdisciplinary dynamism that existed within the law faculty and which was in part developed by Dean Stone's appointments.[5] It is clear from the correspondence between Herman

Columbia reforms is described below. For more information on him generally, see Stone and Mason (1953) and Konefsky (1946). Papers relating to his period as Chief Justice, 1925–46 are preserved in the Library of Congress.

2   In a fairly typical exchange J.H. Moore, author of *Moore and Houston's Problems in Business Law*, offered his services to Stone 'as my interest has become more concretely centered in the law than in any other phase of economics'. See letter to Stone, 20 April 1920 (Employment-Teaching, 1919–20, Misc. Corresp. Box 41).

3   Stone's correspondence with Y.B. Smith reveals this during 1920–21. As Stone says in his Annual Report for 1922: 'The curriculum of the American law school is in some respects a makeshift, the resultant of forces many of which bear little logical relation to each other. The exigencies of the personnel of the teaching staff, the form and scope of particular text or case books, the constant tendency manifest in most educational enterprises to multiply courses, the undue overlapping of courses and the failure of any school in recent years to make a systematic revision of its curriculum are some of the elements contributing to the failure of law school curricula to realize to the fullest extent the needs and tendencies of present day legal education' (Columbia University Bulletin of Information, Annual Report of the Dean of the School of Law, 1922, Misc. Corresp. Box 62).

4   Stone put it thus in his Report: 'When the college degree was made the basis of admission to the law school it was assumed that a first degree in liberal arts or science of the better American Colleges was a certificate of fitness to do successfully the work of the law school, but experience has demonstrated that this assumption was a false one' (ibid., p. 31).

The Law School was only one of a number of disciplines undergoing fundamental curriculum alteration. In September 1919 the Social Sciences at Columbia instituted an interdisciplinary course in 'Contemporary Civilization' (a course that has lasted right up to the present) while the Humanities planned a two-year General Honors Course based upon canonical texts that was the basis of the 'Columbia Sequence' in the 1930s. See Carnochan (1993), chs 6 and 7; and [author unknown] (1946). Though beyond the scope of this chapter, it is fascinating to compare the curriculum reforms in other faculties with that of the law faculty.

5   Stone himself was prepared to consider fairly radical solutions to the three-year envelope of the JD programme. As he argued, 'Must the curriculum leading to the first degree in law be narrowly technical or may there be a judicious admixture of those courses

Oliphant and Stone that they were both keen to attract staff to Columbia who could establish the School's leadership in the new curriculum – Oliphant sought to attract figures such as Magill, McMurray and Karl Llewellyn to Columbia, for instance.[6] That Columbia gradually came to see itself as a national leader in this regard is implicit in much of their correspondence.[7]

As Dean, Stone appeared to play a cautious role – open to the reformist position, but not one of their camp, as he made clear in an article published in 1923 in the *Columbia Law Review*. But he did have his own ideas about what needed reforming, and why. In the article he states his own position, citing a number of fundamental problems that he considered contemporary legal theory required to address: 'the multiplication of its authoritative literature; the vague and shifting content of its terminology; the uncertainty and confusion and lack of symmetry which is gradually permeating our law through the accumulation of precedents which are out of harmony with its system and its social objective' (Stone, 1923, p. 337). For him,

> the problem of simplifying our law in its statement and in its mechanism is due not alone or principally to the volume and character of its literature. It is one which is inherent in the nature of the common law and the method of its creation. The common law doctrine of precedent, whereby the judicial decision not only determines the rights of litigants who invoke it, but becomes the authoritative source of legal precepts to govern future cases, is at once the secret of its strength and the source of some of its weaknesses.

---

which tend to give to the lawyer a wider outlook and more balanced judgment of the nature and function of law? It will have to be confessed that until such time as the professional students of law in this country are in a position to pursue a unified course of six years or more in which both technical and liberal training are interwoven and pursued with the same thoroughness with which they now carry on the work of the professional school, there can be no ideal solution of this problem' (Annual Report, 1922, p. 33).

6   In an undated extended memo to Stone (who comments favourably upon the draft) he advises: 'The faculty probably did not know that Llewellyn and I talked pretty frankly before we got through and that it was not until I suggested the possibility of three such men, himself, Magill and myself tackling the job at one place that he sat up and became interested. He wants in on that set-up. The thing which has put him to thinking is the thing to follow up. I know beyond doubt that salary, rank etc will not shake him. We can get him, in my judgment, only if we move out vigorously toward making the set-up at Columbia which will convince him that leadership in this thing we have been talking about will be established in our school' (Memo from Oliphant to Stone, undated, Stone–Oliphant correspondence, 1922–24, Misc. Corresp. Box 50).

7   See for example the advertisement for a replacement for Stone as Dean of School – '[...] Columbia Law School is itself embarking upon a period of inquiry and a series of experiments which, if properly led, will mean a contribution of legal education, to which only that made by Harvard in the latter part of the last century will be comparable' (Memo from Oliphant to Stone, 14 March 1923, Stone–Oliphant correspondence, 1922–24, Misc. Corresp. Box 50).

According to Stone

> [i]ts development is not systematic, its precedents which collectively are its substance, because of the very method of their creation, lack a foundation of scientific and philosophical generalization on which all systems of law must ultimately rest if they are to endure and do their appointed work. (1923, p. 320)

Clarity, as well as systematisation, was a problem for lawyers – what he termed lack of a realistic understanding and of an accurate definition of many of its most fundamental concepts:

> The terms right, power, duty, privilege, title, possession, ownership, constantly fall from our lips, but always with varying and elusive significance and application. (1923, p. 327)

Here and elsewhere, Stone made suggestions as to how the common law tradition needed to alter not only to cope with increasing volume of precedent and legislation, but to 'adjust the conflicting demands of the doctrine of *stare decisis* to the demands of logical system or of social need and convenience or both' (1923, p. 321). He pointed to the 'method of sociology' as being one way in which the law could be restated. He was however sceptical about whether such interdisciplinary work might be useful in the long term:

> The result of these investigations has been to place great emphasis on the 'method of sociology' or 'sociological jurisprudence' and to establish in our legal thinking that trinity of juridical theory-logic, history and the 'method of sociology' – as the source of all true legal doctrine. We are told that the application of logic and history must be tempered by the 'method of sociology,' and that we must enlarge our scheme of jurisprudence so as to embrace within it the operations of a program of 'social engineering.' (1923, pp. 327–8)

Instead, he advocated a reconstruction and re-statement of the law based on careful historical study –

> We must look rather to the creation of some agency which can be made a part of the common law system to perform the function of examining and stating our legal doctrines in systematic fashion. (1923, p. 328)

– and he saw this agency as the function of the developing modern law school.

The article is interesting for a number of reasons. First, it is more committed to deep disciplinary change than one might expect from a cautious Dean; and is thus indicative of the fairly deep thought that was being given, even at this early stage, to the redesign of the curriculum. Second, Stone is clearly looking for help to define what the agency he desires might be, if it is not to be sociological. The timing of the article is interesting, too, for soon after his arrival at Columbia from Chicago

University, John Dewey became involved in collaboration with a number of different departments. In the summer of 1922 (less than a year after the publication of Stone's article) he was invited by Stone to give a 'Special Conference' on Logical and Ethical Problems of Law.[8] The seminars were organised from 1925 onwards by Edwin Wilhite Patterson who developed a genuine affection for Dewey and his ideas, and between 1925–30 they conducted the seminar jointly.[9] From the seminar sprang an essay published in the *Philosophical Review* (later published in the *Cornell Law Quarterly* and in a book, *Philosophy and Civilization*) entitled 'Logical Method and Law'.[10] In this essay Dewey is concerned to define the form of logical enquiry used by law. In doing so, he notes the 'apparent disparity which exists between actual legal development and the strict requirements of logical theory' (*MW*, 15, p. 68) and quotes one of Holmes' apothegms – 'The actual life of the law has not been logic: it has been experience' (*MW*, 15, p. 69). Dewey agrees with Holmes, but only in so far as one defines logic as strict syllogism. As he points out, 'No lawyer ever thought out the case of a client in terms of the syllogism. He begins with a conclusion which he intends to reach, favourable to his client of course, and then analyzes the facts of the situation to find material out of which to construct a favourable statement of facts, to *form* a minor premiss' (*MW*, 15, p. 72). Dewey emphasises in this form of logic 'principles of interpretation' over against rigid rules, and the role of general rules as working hypotheses, needing to be constantly tested by the way in which they work out in application to concrete situations (*MW*, 15, pp. 75–6).

He also questioned the term 'legal logic', noting that there are a number of different types of logic: '[w]hat Justice Holmes terms logic is formal consistency,

---

8   Summer, 1922, and part of the series Special Conferences in Jurisprudence held at Columbia Law School. Other invited speakers included Dean Roscoe Pound on Sociological Jurisprudence and W.W. Cook on Some Problems in Legal Analysis. See Isaacs (1923). According to Nathan Isaacs who attended the course, there was a parallel between Dewey's course and the text that Dewey published in 1910 entitled *How We Think*, in that the subject of the course was how lawyers thought, and how legal thinking could be differentiated from ordinary thinking.

9   See Jones (1957). Jones cites a passage from Patterson's *Jurisprudence: Men and Ideas of the Law* (1953), pp. 480–81, where Patterson makes a telling point about the optimism of Dewey's whole cast of thought: 'Dewey, through his primary interest in education, stresses the adaptability and latent capacity of mankind rather than its limitations. ... Once I asked Professor Dewey 'Why do you talk only of the influence of the social environment on the individual and not about his inborn traits, which limit and determine his destiny in life far more than his education or other environmental influences?' After a pause, he replied 'I suppose it's because we can't do anything about them' (Jones, p. 613).

10   *MW*, 15, pp. 65–77. I agree with the suggestion of Ann Sharpe, textual editor of the Carbondale edition of Dewey's works, that the course and article were related (*MW*, 15, p. 438). For comment on the textual history of Dewey's article, see *MW*, 15, pp. 437–9. A history of Dewey's extensive emendations to two later versions of the article is listed at *MW*, 15, pp. 450–55.

consistency of concepts with one another', which concepts 'once developed have a kind of intrinsic inertia on their own account; once developed, the law of habit applies to them' (*MW*, 15, p. 69). We have already seen in the Introduction (pp. 24–6) how essential habit was to a pragmatist theory of experience and learning. Here it is applied to a theory of legal logic where, Dewey notes, if it is encouraged it leads to a 'mechanical jurisprudence' (quoting Dean Pound).

In place of this he advocated a logic that was '*relative to consequences rather than to antecedents*' (*MW*, 15, p. 75, his italics). For Dewey, this 'infiltration into law of a more experimental and flexible logic [was] a social as well as an intellectual need' (*MW*, 15, p. 77). While acknowledging that rules of law should be as definite as possible, Dewey points out that the regularity of decision springs not only from the rules themselves but from uniform and relatively static social conditions. However, where 'new devices in business and communication bring about new forms of human relationship' (*MW*, 15, 74), then the power of 'antecedent assurance' (*MW*, 15, p. 74) is diminished.

Dewey was in no doubt about the potentially revolutionary shift that he was describing in this essay. Though highly abstract when read on its own, the essay actually dovetailed neatly with other legal realists' concerns about the nature of *stare decisis* and the narrowly technical account of the doctrine that had been developed at Harvard.[11] His account of legal rules as 'working hypotheses needing to be constantly tested by the way in which they work out in application to concrete situations' (*MW*, 15, pp. 75–6) is a remarkable opening-up of the doctrine, a profoundly democratic view of law in society, and an interpretation of law as a discipline contributing to the social good. The basic move – to create a logic 'relative to consequences rather than to antecedents' – is one he uses constantly in education. Look at the context and the results, he might have said, to determine whether an approach works, and be prepared to modify even the most apparently entrenched principle.

In this brief essay we have a pre-eminent example of the effect that sociologists and philosophers had upon the American legal realists.[12] Dewey's language is pragmatist – the emphasis upon new forms of enquiry, the language of progressive, evolutionary reform, the social ameliorism and underlying optimism; an insistence upon the uncertainty of legal rules and their artificiality; the dwelling upon experimentalism and instrumentalism.[13] In a sense realist views of legal process

---

11 Llewellyn's concerns found voice much later in *The Common Law Tradition – Deciding Appeals* (1960) which, as Twining points out, was over 30 years in the making and began with investigations into judicial decision-making. See Twining (1973) p. 204.

12 On this subject see, Twining (1973), Hunt (1978), Duxbury (1995) and Schlegel (1995).

13 As Jerome Frank put it, 'law may vary with the personality of the judge who happens to pass upon any given case'. Quoted in Morton White (1978), *Patterns of American Legal Thought*, p. 123.

accorded with pragmatist views on educational theory.[14] In his general defence of pragmatism Dewey put this well:

> [p]ragmatism ... does not insist upon antecedent phenomena but upon consequent phenomena; not upon precedents but upon the possibilities of action. And this change in point of view is almost revolutionary in its consequences. An empiricism which is content with repeating facts already past has no place for possibility and for liberty (*LW*, 2, p. 33).

In it we can see many aspects of the anti-formalism of the legal realists, not least a version of what Llewellyn was to call 'situation sense'.[15] As Dewey put it in a later essay, 'law is through and through a social phenomenon; social in origin, in purpose or end', and he later defined law as an 'inter-activity ... [which] can be discussed only in terms of the social conditions in which it arises and of what it concretely does there' (*LW*, 14, pp. 117; 118).[16]

It is significant that in this essay and elsewhere in his legal writings Dewey, ignores the pre-existing literature on legal problem-solving and legal education generally. Interested in the process of pedagogy as he was, and quoting from Holmes' *The Common Law*, he could hardly fail to be aware of the educational developments in the legal domain, particularly those of the latter half of the nineteenth century. The dominant heuristic, the influential Langdellian case method, analysed appellate decisions within a heuristic framework of logic that was heavily prescriptive and text-derived, and which did not at all examine the rhetorical bases of the texts themselves.[17] As Langdell put it, adducing scientific analogies for his own practice – '[l]aw, considered as a science, consists of certain principles or doctrines. To have such a mastery of these as to be able to apply them with constant facility and certainty to the ever-tangled skein of human affairs, is what constitutes a true lawyer' (Langdell, 1879, p. vi).[18] The analogies

---

14 See Chapter 8 of *Reconstruction in Philosophy* (*MW*, 12, pp. 187–201), where he attacks the generalist tendencies of individualistic socialist and organic social philosophies.

15 Llewellyn (1960). See Twining (1973, pp. 216–19).

16 Many realists of course supported interdisciplinary thinking. As Llewellyn put it, '[t]he social sciences are not staked out like real estate. Even in law the sanctions for harmless trespass are not heavy' (1930, p. 465).

17 Implementation of the case method differed from law school to law school, and from class to class. In addition Langdell's development of it altered from his early to his later career – see Kimball's impressive study of Langdell (1999).

18 Recall also his celebrated analogy of law with sciences, cited in Chapter 1 (p. 40). President Charles Eliot made this point more acutely when he declared that the 'law library and not the court or law office, is the real analogue of the hospital', quoted in Chase (1979, pp. 341–2) The point was repeated again and again in instructional texts. In one 1924 instructional manual, for instance, case analysis is described as '"laboratory work" of solving specific problems' – see Daly (1924).

of library to laboratory seems to align legal science and legal education to the methodologies of taxonomic sciences.[19]

Dewey resisted this idea vigorously in his essay. Where Langdell derived doctrinal principles from texts of decisions and applied these to 'human affairs', and sought to separate law from these affairs so as to clarify the legal decision-making process, Dewey plunged into those 'affairs' with his practice-oriented logic of what practitioners do in practice.[20] In his essay, in fact, Dewey goes to the root of a confusion between legal enquiry as a science – which it patently is not, in the sense that, say, enquiry into subparticle physics is a scientific activity – and legal enquiry as a rational activity. In this sense his essay is a meta-critique of legal logic, one that has, as the last sentence of the essay points out, profound consequences for legal education.

In addition to the Special Conference at Columbia, it would appear that Dewey and Patterson also taught a course to students entitled Logical and Ethical Problems of the Law. The course readings survive amongst Stone's papers in the Butler Library in Columbia and consist of two parts: a collection of 'Theories of Concepts' (pp. 1–24c) and 'Formation and Application of Legal Concepts' (pp. 25–64).[21] The first section has a sub-heading 'Conception – General Introduction' with a single reading, namely an extract from Dewey's educational text, *How We*

---

19 And in particular with the study of Agassiz and his students at Harvard in the Lawrence School. Schweber makes the telling point about the descriptive, rather than the analytical, aim of such an endeavour. And in another passage, Schweber observes that Langdell's method banished extra-legal principles: 'law was referential only to itself. Like the natural theologians of an earlier era, Langdell's students would reason by inference to already-determined principles ....' As Schweber shrewdly observes, even on its barest terms such an analogy pointed up the methodological impoverishment of the Langdellian approach: '[l]egal education was no surveying expedition [...] the science classes were intended to teach a method that could later be used to make new discoveries, while Langdell's students were introduced to a landscape with known and well-surveyed boundaries. The law case was fundamentally an object of contemplation, not analysis'. Schweber (1998, pp. 631–2).

20 See Weaver (1991, p. 165): 'Langdell believed that law could be simplified into "a comparatively few absolute rules". These rules, once "found", could be categorised into doctrinal frameworks from which lawyers and judges could deduce the outcomes of cases.' For a criticism of Langdell's and Harvard's decision to 'remain in their bare cell of "technical" appellate doctrine, while all around them leading lawyers were busily transforming law practice and legal institutions', see Gordon (1995, p. 1259)

21 Located at Stone, 1923–24, Miscellaneous Papers, Box 66. The title sheet is headed 'Readings in Legal Philosophy by John Dewey and Edwin W. Patterson (Prepared for the exclusive use of students in the course in Col. U. known as Logical and Ethical Problems of the Law: An Introduction to Legal Philosophy. Philosophy 130)'. The collection is dated '1925 (NOT PUBLISHED)', though of course this is no indication of when the course started. Some page numbers are extended by letters – for example, 24a, 24b – to save retyping the series, which would suggest that this may not be the first version of the readings.

Think (*MW*, 6, pp. 177–356). The second section is divided into three, with the first section missing – '(B) "Trespass"' and '(C) Legal Personality'. These sections are striking examples of the realists' functionalist approach to case law. 'Trespass', for instance, begins with extracts on the history of the concepts from Maitland, Maine, Street and others (leavened with an *aperçu* from Cardozo).[22] This is followed by a subsection on modern applications of the law, via case law.

In his writings on law we can, not unsurprisingly, see the same patterns of enquiry as are present in the domains of education, philosophy and psychology in Dewey's *oeuvre*. In 'My Philosophy of Law' for example (*LW*, 14, pp. 155–67), he defines the relations between custom and law as being identical to those between fact and theory; and therefore legal theory ought to be dealt with in the same instrumental and experimental mode that we deal with theory. Such instrumentalism involves iteration – a constant process of checking and re-checking, but always within a circle beyond which, Dewey emphasises, we cannot reasonably go. If we postulate or seek for sources of law beyond this circle of experience – whether of the natural law or positivist varieties – then we risk reaching legal ends which have little effect on or contact with the actual effects of law in society.

Just what these consequences were we shall see in a moment when we come to consider Columbia Law School's innovations in legal curricular reform. Before we discuss this, however, we ought to consider the extent of the influence Dewey had on the Law School and the central concepts in Dewey's pedagogical discourse which would have been available to them. The studies conducted to date show no direct link between Dewey and the Law School, in the sense that Dewey was a member of the faculty revision committees or a prime mover in the early reforms. Texts such as Twining's *Karl Llewellyn*, Morton White's *Social Thought in America* or Morton Horwitz's, *The Transformation of American Law* cite neither precise links nor group networks and influences.[23] Nevertheless, the family resemblances between Dewey's radical concept of legal logic and his pedagogy are irresistible, and undeniably there. As these texts and others point out, Dewey's signal contribution to the realists' reform cause was his philosophical analyses stemming from his previous work in philosophy, psychology and education. Alan Hunt points out, for example, a 'crucial link between the Realists and pragmatic philosophy' was played by Oliver Wendell Holmes, and in Hunt's as in most accounts, Dewey has a walk-on part as pragmatist spear-bearer to the realist

---

22   From Cardozo (1921, p. 51): '[t]he tendency of a principle to expand itself to the limit of its logic may be counteracted by the tendency to conine itself within the limits of its history'.

23   Twining (1973); White (1947); Horwitz (1992, pp. 169–73). The same is true of the more detailed studies of the Columbia Law School in the 1920s. Schlegel's study is probably the most detailed treatment; but Schlegel is less interested in legal education per se and more in empirical scientific methodology.

heroes (Hunt, 1978, p. 42).[24] I would like to argue, however, that while Dewey's version of legal education and legal enquiry may have been a source of inspiration for reform of a conventional legal curriculum, it also became a source of implicit criticism of that reform, and an explanation as to why it was not developed further, either at Columbia or elsewhere.[25]

At the end of WW1, then, the curriculum at Columbia was the conventional admixture of Langdellian and more traditional methods. In 1922–23, however, it was the research plan for functional law courses which with their 'challenge to the accepted taxonomy of the law and their disturbing impact on the unity and the proportions of the curriculum' that stimulated the later, more extensive innovations (Currie, 1951, pp. 331–83 and 1955, pp. 1–78).[26] To an extent one must agree with this origin. But as Kuhn has taught us, innovations are only accepted if in some way or other they are seen as being extensions of paradigms already acceptable. Dewey's work at Michigan and Chicago, his writings on law, his earlier presence in the Faculty, all this would have given support to reformers such as William Underhill Moore, Oliphant and others, and would have helped to have made the radical possible in terms of realist shifts in the curriculum.

The Columbia experiment really took effect in the years 1926–28. In the period prior to this, the Faculty re-engineered its law courses along what it termed 'functional' lines, including in the courses substantial materials derived chiefly from the social sciences. Herman Oliphant pointed this out in a memo to Stone, commenting on the work of the American Law Institute on subjects for study and restatement of the curriculum. He correctly identified the Institute's choice of approach as being crucial, 'the choice being whether the rules of law shall be studied in their business setting as functional devices for accomplishing ends in the work of the world, or studied with the purpose of constructing a logically symetrical [*sic*] body of law'. The ground for this choice was significant: 'in a very true sense, there is in the abstract no law of contracts i.e., apart from contracts such as used in particular fields of business or other human activity, such as in the organisation of business, the securing of credit, the marketing of goods, etc.'[27]

---

24 Alan Ryan (1995, p. 167) is the most recent to characterise Dewey's influence in this way: 'In the argument between 'legal realists' and their critics in the twenties and thirties, the leading legal philosophers of the day, Roscoe Pound and Karl Llewellyn, assumed an implicit alliance among Beard, Veblen, Holmes, and Dewey, with no attempt to give chapter and verse for agreement on particular points, but clearly expecting to carry conviction as a gesture toward a shared world view, shared political allegiances, and a common methodology.'

25 For example, Yale, to where several key Columbia faculty transferred after the deanship crisis.

26 Currie's account of the Columbia reforms provides us with the classic account of the curriculum, synopsising as he does the mass of original documentation, and I rely heavily on his account. However as will be clear below, I do not agree with all his conclusions regarding the reforms.

27 See memo to Stone, 26 February 1923 (Misc. Corresp. Box 50).

The process began, then, with the piecemeal development of courses so as to include economic and sociological studies amongst the study materials (Currie, 1955, pp. 5–7). This was nothing unusual – it was happening at Harvard amongst other law schools. But at some point early in the reform period, the decision was taken not merely to add new materials to what was seen as an already crowded curriculum, but to reorganise the *entire course of study* along functional lines (Currie, 1955, p. 8). Currie's analysis of the reformers' reasoning is perceptive: the reformers argued that duplication of curricular structures and materials could be avoided if the 'doctrinal classifications' which were the traditional bases of instruction were replaced by 'functional classifications' (1955, p. 8).

As Currie charts it, the main work of the curriculum reformers was carried out, under the direction of Herman Oliphant, by a number of committees, each charged with responsibilities for creating syllabus and course materials.[28] The results of this massive reorganisation are described in Stone's *Summary of Studies*; and Currie with justification calls the new definition of legal studies that this document represents 'an epoch-making event in American legal education' (1955, p. 13). However, it became clear to at least some of the committees as they attempted to integrate legal with non-legal teaching and learning materials, that while it was easy and desirable to set up a research institute along functionalist lines, it was much more difficult to overthrow what were seen by some as the shackles of doctrinal classifications, and to replace these with a functionalist curriculum (1955, p. 34).

And it was also difficult to throw off the training of a lifetime and truly inhabit other disciplines. As Schlegel points out, the problem was partly that of interdisciplines and socialisation within disciplines. Walter Wheeler Cook, for instance, greatly admired Dewey, but his interpretation of Dewey's method took place squarely within the boundaries of his own legal training and identity.[29] Underhill Moore's meticulous statistical studies of parking (undertaken later when he was at Yale) created datasets that overwhelmed his methodology, when perhaps a more ethnographic approach to research methodology might have been more appropriate.

The problems are evident in Oliphant's perceptive paper addressed to Faculty entitled 'The Revision of the Law School Curriculum'.[30] There, he outlines the problems and the solutions to curricular reform, grouping them as 'whom shall we teach, how shall we teach, and what shall we teach?' (p. 1). 'Whom' resolved itself into questions of preparation for the law course, with solutions adopted that will be described below. The 'how' issue involved moving away from the casebooks – [n]either in [the case method] nor in the making of case-books will a

---

28 See Currie (1955, pp. 23–64), for a detailed account of the work of the committees.

29 See Patterson (1950, p. 619).

30 Stone (1923–24, Miscellaneous Manuscripts and Typescripts, Box 66). The report is dated 29 October 1923, with an undated addendum.

substantial contribution to legal education be made by continuing or attempting merely 'to outharvard Harvard' (p. 4). Oliphant was right of course about this; and he makes a point that describes the *raison d'être* of the realist approach to curriculum reform: '[n]o development of major importance will occur in the field of method during the coming two decades unless necessitated by a shift in the content of courses' (p. 3). But as we saw in Dewey's paper on legal logic cited above, 'method' (that is, how legal logic was operationalised) was critical to content, and not necessarily dependent upon content. This point was not well understood by realists, who reached for new content first, and sought to derive a methodology from that new content. But the realists did not need to wait for new content before they examined and altered method, any more than did the medical schools after the Flexner Report, or indeed Dewey himself, when founding the Laboratory School.[31]

Thus, Oliphant's discussion of 'what' dominates the rest of the paper, and is for him the way forward. He summarises the practical issues:

> The multiplication of courses in present day law curricula approaches if it is not already, a positive evil. It cannot continue indefinitely. And yet the feeling grows that students are going out only partly trained for numerous specialized bodies of law are developing and we have not caught up by our tantalus-like addition of new courses. This suggests that in some of our so-called basic courses we have not got hold of some of those things which are really basic in the functioning of law with the result that this now hidden matter is constantly cropping out here and there as specialized and apparently unrelated problems. (p. 6)

The solution, in his eyes, was to re-organise curricular content:

> It is believed that, if we are really to get at the fundamentals, the organization of the curriculum must be more in terms of the human relations dealt with and less, as largely now, in terms of the logical concepts of the conventionally trained legal mind. (p. 6)

But – and it is a crucial point – Oliphant ignores *how* these new courses will be taught. He considers this earlier, again in terms of content, only to reject it:

> A somewhat radical change in the model effected by including other materials than decided cases and by using problems or skeleton, [*sic*] cases, promises sufficient results to warrant careful study by the Law Faculty. It might well consider modifying the use of the case method in some of the advanced courses. But these changes if made would not constitute an outstanding development. Moreover, this mechanical problem cannot be the center of interest in a study of the curriculum. (p. 3)

---

31 Flexner was concerned with both curriculum content and methodological structure. As he pointed out in a later study (Flexner, 1925, cited in Cooke et al., 2006, p. 1341): '[s]cientific medicine in America – young, vigorous and positivistic – is today sadly deficient in cultural and philosophic background'.

Remarkably enough, what he almost proposes here is an early form of PBL, but he mistakes the radical nature of the proposal by categorising it as a 'mechanical problem'. Reading his paper now with half a century of research into learning and teaching research and innovation, it is easy to see how wrong he was to dismiss such concerns as 'mechanical' problems. In his attempt to take a creative swerve round the dominance of Langdellian methodology it must have seemed that to emphasise content was the only way to outflank the Harvard method with an 'outstanding development'. Yet it was such mechanical problems that were the core of Dewey's pragmatist reform in the Laboratory School, and were considered in detail in the highly-influential Flexner Report's recommendations on medical schools earlier in the century. But nowhere do we find at Columbia a detailed discussion of educational method. Langdell's case method worked as an educational method, because it was grounded in texts (case books), in methodology (Socratic questioning), in procedures (repetition, the grid of seats, etc).[32] The realists neglected to learn the educational lessons from this, and as a result, their implementations were weaker and could not be as easily reproduced by colleagues within the law school or disseminated to other law schools. Grant Gilmore, commenting on his experience of legal education at Yale in the 1940s, made the striking point about the traditional form of the curriculum, in spite of its realist background:

> [w]ithout exception, the courses they taught were entirely standard exercises in case law (or, occasionally, statutory) analysis, which would not have been out of place at Harvard. (Duxbury, 1995, p. 146)[33]

In the event, the faculty's main aim of thorough-going curriculum reform was not achieved. Some reformed courses were taught as fully functionalist entities with extra-legal materials, while others were not delivered as planned for a number of reasons – Currie lists these as being lack of finance (1955, p. 66), the difficulty of overcoming disciplinary barriers (1955, p. 68); the intractable nature of some areas of law when approached from a functionalist angle (1955, p. 73); the resignation of key Law School reformers, who took up positions at Yale and Johns Hopkins, and experimented there with smaller versions of the Columbia reforms.[34] But as Currie points out, there are two other reasons why the experiment in realist legal education at Columbia failed. First, business was

---

32 As we shall see in Chapter 5, the importance of readable, usable texts in spreading ideas should never be underestimated. As Corns (2000, p. 103) put it, discussing the Reformation Geneva Bible – [it] is a splendid self-study package; indeed, the ultimate CAL package – Calvin-assisted learning'.

33 Duxbury also cites Cavers (1943) who noted that by the 1940s, although the problem method was gaining ground, a number of realists still clung to the Langdellian case-method more evidence that the realists needed to give much more thought than they did to heuristic methods. Cited at Duxbury (1995, p.253).

34 Twining (1973) gives the details of these in Chapters 3 and 4.

a 'dominant concern and justification of law' at Columbia (1955, p. 74). Five of the seven curriculum 'chapters' fall within business law categories. Currie attributes this to the leadership of Marshall and Oliphant, oriented as they were to the Chicago School of Business.[35] Second, he observed that the 'greatest of the manifold difficulties associated with the assimilation of nonlegal materials seems ... to have been the lack of any sharp conception of the purpose to be served by such materials' (1955, p. 72). These two points are perceptive, but it could be argued that there is a third reason, one perhaps more fundamental than these two points. The emphasis on business law within the overall aim of embedding nonlegal materials within the legal curriculum had the effect of shifting the attention of faculty reformers from functionalist and pragmatic methodology (*how* they were going to achieve their goal) and led to a concern with empiricism (*what* they would teach to achieve their goal).

One can see this emerge from Stone's correspondence with the reformers. For Stone, the major problem was that there had been no effective revision of the curriculum for 30 years or more.[36] The solution was not just tinkering with the mechanics of the current curriculum. The curriculum had become already too complicated and over-taught. He proposed what Underhill Moore and others had argued for, namely

> a simplification of the educational methods by reaching a clearer and more accurate understanding of the relation of law to this same function which it endeavors to control and by studying its rules and doctrines as tools or devices created and placed in the hands of the lawyer as a means of effecting that control. (1923 draft Report, p. 11)

However Stone is vague in this document, as in others, about the ways his School will achieve these ends. Here he is describing the problem and the solution:

> [the problem] naturally divides itself into two subsidiary problems. The first one is the problem of so re-arranging and organizing the subjects of law school study as to make more apparent this relationship and to bring together the various branches of technical law study in law schools into their proper relationship with the particular social function with which they are concerned so as to present them in their true

---

35 Leon C. Marshall, economist and noted figure in business education had been invited from Chicago University (where Oliphant knew him) as a visiting professor to facilitate the reformers' task as chairman. See Twining (1973, p. 47).

36 Stone commented drily on the accumulating curriculum, '[s]tarting with the fundamental courses in Contracts, torts, Property and Equity, we have added courses in Insurance Law, Public Service Companies, Unfair Competition, Restrictions on Trade, Industrial Relations, Creditors Rights, Statutes, Damages, to number only a few of the many new courses [...] until at last we are beginning to realise that the logical outcome of this process must be that students who come to us to be trained as lawyers must remain with us for the rest of their natural lives in order to be trained properly to begin the practice of their profession'. Draft Report to the President of the University on the School of Law, 30 June 1923, p. 9 (Misc. Materials folder, Misc. Corresp., Box 63).

proportion and relationship to the social enterprise and the same time save the dissipation of energy and effort which goes on when that relationship is not perceived. (1923 draft Report, p. 11)

The problem here is that Stone's solution is a rationalisation of subjects, for example, creditors' remedies that appear in a range of different courses with no cross-curricular thinking between the subjects. He does not propose, as did Dewey, that radical alteration to the curriculum essentially involved rethinking the relations of law and society such that the fundamental aim of law in society was challenged.[37]

The second subsidiary problem was that students arrived in law school having experienced no systematic approach to the social sciences. His solution was the creation of an 'undergraduate course of study in economics and social science [...] which would be of value to the student planning to take graduate courses in law or business'.[38]

The point becomes clearer when we consider that jurisprudence (a subject which, if anywhere, could provide the clearing where staff could analyse, with students and for themselves, the functionalist methodology of the curriculum), together with legal history and comparative law, were dismissed by the reformers as being 'important only in so far as they contributed to the teleological criticism of law – largely in terms, it must be presumed, of commercial and economic ends' (Currie, 1955, p. 74; see also pp. 63–4). Though understandable in the

---

37 The faculty revision took effect with an initial 'analysis and survey of all the courses offered in the law school', wherein every instructor 'prepared a complete descriptive memorandum of his course, giving in detail the subjects discussed and the method of treatment' (1923, Draft Report, p. 15).

38 Stone corresponded with Professor James C. Egbert, Director of the School of Business, Columbia University, on the matter. He outlined the matter thus: 'I have come to realize that a large part of my difficulties as a law student arose out of my ignorance of business transactions. Many lawyers have expressed the same thought to me and said that they found with me, that the difficulties arising from the same cause continue into practice and present constant obstacles that are overcome only slowly and painfully.'
Stone suggested in his letter an ambitious two-year outline of work:

Year 1	Weeks
The Structure of Business	5
Banking	
Accounting	10
Year 2	
Investment Finance	6
Insurance	6
Marketing	
Transportation	6
The Relation of Business to the state	6
(Taxation, Franchises, Regulation)	

context of business law, the low profile given to jurisprudence is remarkable, given the radical ambitions of the reforming faculty. It indicates a fundamental flaw in the reformers' methodology and thinking about legal education which was highlighted early on in the process by an anxious Dean Stone. In an article in the *Columbia Law Review* Stone declared himself sceptical of the ability of 'sociological jurisprudence' to deliver principles of sufficient scope and rigour to organise the curriculum:

> Many years ago, Mr Justice Holmes in classic phrase reminded us that 'the life of the law is not logic but experience'. ... But can we in any proper sense speak of the application of this principle as a 'method'? Has sociological jurisprudence any methodology, any formulae or principles which can be taught or expounded so as to make it a guide either to the student of law or to the judge? ... If not, then sociological jurisprudence will not tend to reduce the accumulation of anomalous doctrines; it may even add to it. (Stone, 1923, pp. 327–8)[39]

In many respects Stone's article can be read as a questioning, if not a rebuttal, of the approach taken by Dewey in his course and article on logical method and law. Stone even uses the same apothegm from Holmes' *The Common Law*, and gives it his own sceptical interpretation. Simplification of the curriculum for Stone meant searching, as for the dominant theme in a *roman à clef*, for the principle theme, here that of 'social utility', which would give meaning to the burgeoning detail of the legal curriculum. He questioned whether such a principle could be found; and the failure of the Columbia project would seem to have proven him right. But I would suggest that both the curriculum reformers and Stone's early article exhibit a misunderstanding of both the meta-critique of legal method which Dewey offered on pragmatic principles and his educational pragmatism. For Dewey, there could never be a simplifying principle, no science of 'sociological engineering' which would simplify the complexity of legal learning and its logics.[40] From Dewey's perspective, therefore, Stone was mistaken in his scepticism, and the reformers were misguided in their attempt to convert the entire curriculum on the basis of this essentialist empiricism. If the realists generally were to be as successful in their implementations as the educational approach of the Langdellian case method they would need to give much more thought to classroom practice, and to the definition and implementation of realist educational principles.

It was a lesson that was not learned from the Columbia experience. After the deanship crisis of 1928 the faculty split, with Yntema, Marshall and Oliphant joining Walter Wheeler Cook at the research-based Johns Hopkins Institute of Law, and Douglas and Underhill Moore going to Yale. Their later careers were based firmly in social science research and the law. Those who were left took forward some aspects of the previous efforts at curriculum redesign. Casebooks became

---

39 23 *Columbia Law Review* (1923), pp. 327–8.

40 Ibid. Note the superficial analogy that Stone makes here between legal method and scientific methodology.

more contextual, setting the law within social data and descriptive passages.[41] Their approach to professional training was one of 'enlightened vocationalism', but few of the radical ideas of the early reformers were implemented.[42]

Those ideas can hardly be said to form a coherent programme of reform, any more than they did jurisprudentially. As we have seen, there was much debate, many fascinating ideas, but underlying educational philosophy played little part in the debates. The subsequent trajectories of both the 'Prudents' and the 'Scientists' at Columbia and Yale and Johns Hopkins respectively proved this to be the case. Two decades later, for instance, Underhill Moore and Charles Callahan published a book entitled *Law and Learning Theory: A Study in Legal Control*.[43] The first half of the book summarises the results of Moore's detailed parking studies in New Haven – part of a general theory of behaviour. However, it became clear that a general theory could not be derived from the data and therefore in the second half of their book Moore and Callahan applied to learning theory for principles to explain aspects of their results. The theory they turned to was strongly behaviourist, derived from 'the work of Pavlov, Thorndike, Watson, Hull and others', where, in an experimentalist and reductionist account, 'behavior is determined by the relation between four factors – drive, cue, response, and reward'.[44] That alternative methodologies were available to them, one need only look to the Chicago or Ecological School approach, based in the sociology department of the University of Chicago, where since the 1920s urban sociology and urban ethnographical studies had been carried out – methodologies perhaps more sympathetic to realist aims.[45]

Dewey and Thorndike

There is one more interesting aspect to Dewey's involvement with the Law School at Columbia. Earlier we saw that Oliphant had outlined a concern to Stone regarding the increasing numbers and the quality of intrants. Stone himself was

---

41 As Twining observes, some were more innovative than others in this approach, citing Llewellyn's *Cases and Materials on the Law of Sales* as an example of this – Twining (1973, ch. 7).

42 Twining's phrase, private email on file with the author and cited with permission. There were of course no general statements made by the Columbia reformers themselves, apart from specialised statements on law's function, etc. Llewellyn was later to tackle the subject in an article on the subject; but as Twining observes, while the article is perceptive about aspects of the reforms, and – wisely – avoids generalisation on such an amorphous subject, it is not useful as a 'coherent introduction to realism' (Twining, 1973, p. 71).

43 Moore and Callahan (1943). The book was one of a number of studies published by the Institute of Human Relations at Yale.

44 Moore and Callahan (1943, p. 61).

45 See for example Bulmer (1984).

concerned.[46] As a result, the law school turned to a member of Teachers College in Columbia, namely Edward Lee Thorndike, who had just published what was to become one of the most influential texts in American educational history, *Principles of Learning* (1921). The book outlines Thorndike's work in the field of educational psychology, and his revolutionary approach to the science of human behaviour. Thorndike is now regarded as a pioneer of instructional design – both the behaviourist B.F. Skinner and the cognitivist Robert Gagné acknowledged their debt to him – and in particular his work on experimental design, combined with statistical analysis and the management of teaching, has been the foundation of approaches to standardisation of outcomes in schools (Tomlinson, 1997).

Thorndike was hired by the law school to conduct a series of 'psychological examinations' on first year law students.[47] The details of the initiative, in Stone's correspondence, reveal the scale of the enterprise.[48] Later termed 'General Placement Examinations', these early tests were trialled in the three sessions 1925–27, and Thorndike observed that the Educational Psychology division

---

46 Stone put it thus in his Report: 'When the college degree was made the basis of admission to the law school it was assumed that a first degree in liberal arts or science of the better American Colleges was a certificate of fitness to do successfully the work of the law school, but experience has demonstrated that this assumption was a false one' (p. 31).

47 The entry test was described thus by Stone in his Report: 'It was therefore deemed advisable to invite the assistance of the psychologists of the University under the leadership of Professor E.L. Thorndike in preparing such a test for the members of the entering class for three successive years, the results of the test to form the basis of study and comparison with the law school records of the students examined, both by the examiners and the law faculty. It will thus be possible to gather a body of data of great importance in perfecting a method of selecting the members of the law school student body, and in verifying and and comparing the value and trustworthiness of the method adopted' (p. 35).

48 See Stone, 1923–24 (Faculty Correspondence, Box 50). Thorndike's work included early stimulus-response theory, and scales and ratings for a variety of domains, including hand-writing, art, and psychological scaling for the US Army during World War I. See Jonçich (1968). From the correspondence between Moore, Stone and Thorndike it is clear that Thorndike, who was then director of Columbia University's Teachers College Institute of Educational Research, had been consulted on forms of assessment. Stone commented: 'He thinks the study worth making and that as a result we might be able to shorten our labor on examinations somewhat, altho he does not encourage the belief that the psychologist could give any adequate substitute for our present method of testing the student's analytical ability.'

The financial accounts for the experiment are also preserved. In May 1922, for instance, Thorndike presented the law school with a detailed account, amounting to the substantial sum of $767.95 for the design work, setting, scoring and correlation of the results against marks obtained by first year law students (clearly an attempt to discover if the entry test results could be predictive of Law School performance). For further information on Thorndike and the law school, see Grant (1929); for use of multiple-choice assessment, see Wood (1925).

would by the spring of 1932, provide 'annual tests, different in content, but equivalent in significance and difficulty, for use, under suitable restrictions, by any institution desirous of exact information concerning the calibre of its student body' (Thorndike, 1931, p. 99). In that last phrase one can foresee much of the subsequent history of the LSAT in American law schools – debates over the influence of law school rankings, weighting of LSAT scores, alongside grade point or other averages, 'whole-person' approaches, the real predictive value of the test, the effect on the entry of students of colour, the role of the LSAT in affirmative action programmes, and over-reliance on the LSAT.[49] Some elements of these debates were raised by the pioneers in the Law School; but it is fair to say that many of them were left unresolved.[50]

It would perhaps be too easy to contrast Dewey and Thorndike directly, as the chapter's epigraph does. There were actually many points of similarity between them, as Koschmann points out – both were colleagues at Columbia, both were on the progressive wing of educational change, both believed in the capacity of science to contribute to educational theory and improve practice (Koschmann, 2000, p. 314). There were also significant differences – Thorndike, the brilliant and painstaking experimentalist, was no philosopher; Dewey was relatively uninterested in experimental design. This is perhaps the key lesson for Dewey's influence upon faculty at Columbia Law School, for as Koschmann points out, 'Dewey developed a more profound and better-elaborated model of human problem-solving, but he was at best an armchair psychologist, leaving it to others to actually undertake the program of study' (2000, p. 316). As Tanner has pointed out with regard to Dewey's Laboratory School in Chicago, Dewey's approach allowed others to flourish by giving them the space to flesh out the Deweyan structure; but it was a weakness for a general strategy of legal education – which is what the realist endeavour desperately needed.

But in spite of his eminence in educational matters, Dewey was not brought into the plans regarding the curriculum structure of the reforms. In place of the analysis and critique that he could have brought to bear on the pattern of the reforms, there were relatively shallow, though enormously vigorous, changes made to the curriculum. Thorndike was consulted on issues of assessment, as

---

49 According to LSAC, the LSAT is 'designed to measure skills considered essential for success in law school' – Law School Admission Council (2005) LSAT AND LSDAS Information Book. The literature on the LSAT is of course extensive, and for those law schools in the UK adopting the LSAT, is essential reading. See for instance Weinstein (2001), Henderson (2004);, Thomas (2003), Kidder (2001), Delgado (2001) and Edwards (2006).

50 It would be unfair to characterise Law School concerns as simply focused on numbers. In an article published in the ABA Journal responding to the Carnegie Foundation Report on legal education, for instance, Stone discussed the principles that, in his view, should lie behind law school entry criteria – principles which are conservative even by the standards of pre-New Deal America, and at a considerable distance from the social and political views of Dewey, Jane Addams and their circle. See Stone (1921).

we have seen, but these were on a fairly detailed level. He was not consulted on curriculum-wide issues, either, which were decided on content-based criteria, and on a sociolegal basis. Educational research was thus defined either as intensely local, detailed and scientific interventions (Thorndike) or else as new functionalist content. Dewey's key educational principles were relatively ignored, and pragmatist educational approaches as a consequence were nowhere in sight.

Llewellyn, though, was never in doubt as to the significance that Dewey could have had for the early reformers at Columbia. According to Twining, Llewellyn blamed Patterson for this, 'in that he had treated Dewey first and foremost as a logician' and had diverted him from analysing legal processes.[51] This may well be the case, though as we have seen Dewey's paper was a response to concerns about method that were being raised by the reformers. It is certainly the case, though, that Dewey could have played a much greater role in the re-design of the curriculum. Reading Llewellyn on the subject, one has the impression of lost opportunities.

Afterword: New Legal Realists

Realism as a lure for theory and practice has never really gone away: it has been there in the substratum of American legal scholarship, as Duxbury has pointed out (1995, p. 158). Recently, however, there has been a revival of realist theory and practice in legal scholarship. According to one definition, New Legal Realist scholars (NLR) 'bring together legal theory and empirical research to build a stronger foundation for understanding law and formulating legal policy' (Erlanger et al., 2005, p. 339, especially n.7).[52] The intervening decades of research and commentary have made the field of law and society much more sophisticated, and for some there is a debate about whether we need to return to the original realists.[53]

The key phrase for legal education in this definition is 'understanding law'. How is the NLR understanding enacted in educational initiatives? The website does describe one aspect of the developing NLR model as being 'Bringing

---

51 Twining (1973, p. 423, n.130). As Twining puts it, 'Llewellyn's private ambition ... was to perform the role of a Dewey in jurisprudence, trying to do for law what the great man had done for other subjects. The most pleasing compliment that could be paid to Llewellyn was to compare him to John Dewey' (ibid.).

52 See also New Legal Realism website at http://www.newlegalrealism.org. As might be expected, there is some controversy attending the name itself.

53 See for instance Bill Henderson on the Empirical Legal Studies blog, answering Brian Leiter's posting, and asserting the need for NLR, observing that for him, 'NLR is really about developing a theoretical framework (or a workable consensus) on how and when to utilise relatively new research tools and perspectives' – http://www.elsblog.org/the_empirical_legal_studi/2006/06/leiter_on_new_L.html.

Empirical Research to Legal Education'.[54] The movement has set itself the task to 'develop a new set of approaches to interdisciplinary research on law' (Erlanger et al., 2005, p. 339). This includes an analysis of the forms of translation that occurs between social sciences and law. Within legal education the founders note that this involves

> bringing new legal realist translation into the core law school curriculum ... to ... create a beneficial erosion of traditional boundaries between 'stand-up' and clinical teaching, between doctrinal and social science approaches, and between students as recipients of already-acquired information and researchers of the source of social science data. (2005, p. 361)

The aim is laudable, the detail lacking, but it may be that this will be fleshed out later.[55] The conference on NLR at Wisconsin recently included a panel on legal education, where Louise Trubek defined the emerging NLR framework as 'based on an empirical understanding of both the changing socioeconomic world and the changing practices of lawyers'; and observed that '[l]egal education is an integral part of constructing legal practice, and is now confronted with the challenge of changing its pedagogy to reflect the new practice of law' (Trubek, 2005, p. 456).[56] As she points out, 'the narrowness of contemporary legal education' is problematic (ibid.). She identifies two boundaries that have to be overcome: first, that between public interest law and mainstream practice, and second, the boundary between 'clinical programmes and traditional teaching methods'; and she points to the need to consider 'pedagogy, substance, and status' (2005, p. 472). But as long as there are calls for legal education merely to *reflect* legal practice it will be difficult for legal education to be radical enough to transform the curriculum – which, after all, was the aim of the realist pioneers at Columbia and elsewhere.

As we have seen in Chapter 1, there already exists transformative work – Stefan Krieger's sensitive and acute interdisciplinary work is only one example amongst many legal educators in the US. But as Trubek points out, there needs to be a more substantial and practical shift before the JD curriculum shifts significantly. The point about law and society is true also of legal educational theory and practice: in the last 50 years or so our thinking about legal education has generally become more sophisticated, because we are willing to listen more to Dewey, as well as to Thorndike. It may be that the NLR movement is an opportunity to engage new theory and engender new practice within the JD curriculum which in its essential shape has not altered much since the realists (Rubin et al., 2006, p. 466). But there is one significant difference in comparing law and society research and law and education research. If the realists were indeed perplexed about social science

---

54 www.newlegalrealism.org/D_model.php.

55 For a description of an Empirical Methods class outline linked to the aims of this group, see Law and Econ Prof Blog at http://lawprofessors.typepad.com/law_econ/2006/09/empirical_metho.html.

56 See also Hayes (2004).

methodology through lack of training amongst other reasons, they did not need to be so in education: the pragmatic practice and theory of Dewey was already there for them, had they wished to develop it. It is there, too, for NLR scholars, and much burnished by later scholarship. Will they develop it?[57]

Others, too, have been at work in developing new forms of curriculum innovation. Harvard Law School has embarked on a major review of its first year curriculum – the first such in over a century – which will, inter alia, give students the opportunities to address 'complex, fact-intensive problems as they arise in the world (rather than digested into legal doctrines in appellate opinions), and which will lock into the already reviewed second and third years'.[58] At Stanford there is considerable alteration of the second and third years of the JD programme, in order to 'combine the study of other disciplines with team-oriented, problem-solving techniques and expanded clinical training that enables students to represent clients and litigate cases – before they graduate'.[59] Perhaps one of the most radical innovations is McGill Law School's trans-systemic approach to common and civil law jurisdictions. It is a polyjural experiment which, at a deep level, dislocates many assumptions about jurisdiction-based legal analysis, and has the potential not merely to reflect but to change aspects of the practice of law.[60] The key to their innovation is a profound re-alignment of curriculum structure and methodology, from the most theoretical aspects to the most practical – an approach that Dewey would have thoroughly approved of.

---

57 There are a number of interesting suggestions emerging from the movement. Elizabeth Mertz, for instance, points out how recent work on linguistics and rhetoric could be used in NLR classes – see the Empirical Legal Studies blog, Elizabeth Mertz posting, 'Building interdisciplinary communities', at http://www.elsblog.org/the_empirical_legal_ studi/2006/06/building_interd.html .

58 See Harvard Law School, News and Events, October 6, 2006, http://www.law. harvard.edu/news/2006/10/06_curriculum.php.

59 See Stanford Law School News Centre, November 28, 2006, http://tinyurl.com/ y4ujld.

60 Strauss (2006); Morissette (2002).

Chapter 4

'By the End of This Module ...':
The Intimate Dimensions of
Ethical Education

Lawyering theory literature makes it clear that morality matters. It matters to the law, it matters to clients, and it matters to lawyers as well.

(Kruse, 2005, p. 458)

To reduce human action to a constellation of terms such as 'performance', 'competence', 'doing' and 'skills' is not just to resort to a hopelessly crude language with which to describe serious human endeavours. In the end, it is to obliterate the humanness in human action. It is to deprive human being of *human* being.

(Barnett, 1994, p. 178, his emphasis)

What is the city over the mountains
Cracks and reforms and bursts in the violet air
Falling towers
Jerusalem Athens Alexandria
Vienna London
Unreal

(Eliot, 1963, p. 76)

Ronald Barnett: The Lost Vocabulary

The descriptors of competence, quality, learning outcomes and curriculum design have a language and set of metaphors that drive our thinking regarding the nature of legal education in our law schools. Like all educational terms, they have a socioeconomic, cultural and ethical history behind their implementation. This chapter analyses some aspects of our educational language, and argues that there might be other ways we can conceptualise of, and name, the ethical in legal education.

One of the reasons why the issue is problematic, I would argue, lies in the restricted nature of concept and language that we use to describe the task of ethicising the curriculum, and the identities that this language gives us. Such identities are, to use a term from cultural psychology, embedded within a particular field of cultural practice, which ensures that we see ourselves and our tasks in a particular frame of reference (Cole, 1996).[1] Activities are saturated in cultural significances. Our activities as teachers are closely bound to how we view our identities as teachers, and what helps us to become ourselves are the systems of resources, the symbolic systems we use, the representations of our discipline, the technologies we use, and above all the concepts and language that we deploy to understand what we do when we communicate with students. The problem for us is that if we are to change at a deep level our activities of teaching and learning, we need to re-conceptualise our tasks, and for that we require to engage with the language that we use to conceptualise our tasks.

The necessity to do this has been pointed up by Ronald Barnett in much of his critical work on higher education, and particularly (for our purposes here) in his book, *The Limits of Competence* (Barnett, 1994). There, he adduces two versions of competence: academic competence, linked to knowledge of a discipline, its contents and methods of analysis, and vocational competence, with its operational definition of competence set within the world of work outside the academy. This has been described many times before and since Barnett, and needs no rehearsal here. As Barnett points out, though, these versions are actually *rival* versions of competence, and their rivalry can at times be debilitating both for students and disciplines. In place of both sets of competences, Barnett puts forward an ambitious third way, a programme of 'life-world becoming', in which he attempts to transcend both academic and operational competence. In so doing, he identifies the common ambition of both definitions of competence:

> [d]isciplines, objective knowledge, occupational standards, skills and the whole ragbag have to be seen for what they are: ideologies exerting power and constraint, requiring a certain form of human development. In this sense, both the academics and the operationalists are in league in framing *their* conception of ideal human being and in requiring the student to conform to it. If we see higher education as a form of becoming in which students become *themselves*, an altogether different notion of becoming is required. (1994, p. 191)

Barnett's critique here and in later books deserves serious consideration, particularly its implications for the relation between ethics and curriculum design. It is not merely that the concept of competence is teacher-centred, or dominated by the discourses of state and employment. The two versions are at a much deeper level oppressive of the personal growth that students undergo in higher education. Barnett aligns the two sets of competences with Goffman's 'total institution' in which 'the identities of the inmates were entirely formed and sustained by the institution' (ibid.). Barnett is careful not to adopt the language of libertarian education, in facile opposition to this: he sees disciplines as necessary formulations of thought for students to work through and with which they need

---

1   See, for example, the work of Lave and Wenger (1991) and Wenger (1998) on this, which applies as much to educators and their enculturation as it does to apprenticeship learners.

to become familiar. Instead, and though he does not mention it explicitly, Barnett here employs the language of phenomenological commentary on being to explain how we might construct a curriculum at once liberating and disciplined.

But as many phenomenologists have pointed out, such transcendence is not possible without historical knowledge of the condition we are in. For both students and teachers, it would require self-awareness of the conceptual changes required in their perception of their respective identities to achieve what Barnett advocates. It is undoubtedly a tall order for both students and staff, as Barnett himself acknowledges:

> This self-construction is anathema both to the academics and to the operationalists since it stands independently of the worlds both of academe and of work. And the severity of its demands are not self-evidently attractive to students-as-customers. It is a process of becoming, therefore that is unlikely to find many takers. (1994, p. 192)

In his book Barnett offers a broader description of what he means by taking a constellation of terms and exploring them in more depth. What he calls the 'lost vocabulary' is set against the new vocabularies of capability, enterprise, transferable skills, work-based learning and the like. He explores, carefully and elegantly, new meanings in the terms 'understanding', 'critique', interdisciplinarity' and – most audacious and perhaps least successful – 'wisdom'.

The point has been made a number of times by commentators on legal education. Stuart Toddington for example has observed vis-à-vis competence frameworks that

> […] a laudable but insufficiently theorised consensus on the need for curricular 'relevance' has resulted in a narrowly 'professional' understanding of legal skills. This […] is inhibiting the development of an imaginative and critical conception of not only the essential nature and wide importance of legal skills, but of the very idea of legal education. (1996, p. 69)

There are, though, two elements that are underplayed in Barnett's critique. The first element is the absence of a collection of practical examples of the four qualities he dwells upon. The absence of these examples weaken his argument, for if the qualities that he espouses as alternatives to traditional academicism and new operationalism are to be developed, then this must arise from grounded action within a curriculum, not just from theoretical descriptions of the possibilities of such alternatives. The second is the practical effect that the historical awareness of disciplines has upon teaching. Barnett mentions this several times, but partly because his text aims to be a generic critique of higher education, he downplays the effect that lack of *critical* awareness of historical context can have within a discipline. Such lack of awareness is one of the greatest barriers to change, precisely because it legitimises orthodoxy and contributes to silent enculturation in educational practice.

Adam Ferguson: Enlightenment Ethics and the Stoic Tradition

The debates around competence are not new. In one form or another they are evidence of a profound debate about the nature of ethics and the place of moral philosophy within society's higher educational structures stretching back through the nineteenth century, through Enlightenment and Renaissance discourse to the Aristotelian distinction between *sophia* and *phronesis*. In their modern shapes the arguments crystallised in Enlightenment educational discourse, particularly within the civic humanist tradition that was, as Pocock and others have observed, an essential ethical discourse for European moral thought. As such, the arguments underpin many of our assumptions underlying the teaching of legal ethics.

I shall illustrate this by analysing a short passage from a lecture given by the Professor of Moral Philosophy at Edinburgh University, Adam Ferguson, in the academic session 1775–76. But before that, some background information is required about Ferguson and his intellectual milieu.[2] Ferguson (1723–1816) was one of the central figures in the Scottish Enlightenment. He was born in Perthshire, which was then a county straddling the two principal and very different cultures of Scotland, Lowland and Highland, on what was then the boundary of the Highland Line. He came from a distinctively Highland family who were firm adherents to the Hanoverian cause, and this affected much of his view of historical development in Scotland.[3] After university he joined the military early in his career as chaplain to the 42nd Regiment (Black Watch).[4] Thereafter, and with the assistance of Hume and other friends, he was appointed to the Chair of Moral Philosophy and Pneumatics at Edinburgh University, and in this capacity he lectured, in his class of Moral Philosophy, to many of those who would go on to become lawyers and advocates in Scotland. His *Essay on the History of Civil Society* (first published in 1767) was a bold and novel attempt to reclaim the tradition of active citizenship and apply it to the modern state. He followed this

---

2   The view of Ferguson's work below is, as will be clear, influenced by Lisa Hill's interpretation of his work. Her book represents the start of something approaching a renaissance in studies in Adam Ferguson. Two major collections of edited essays, drawing on historians, philosophers, sociologists and political scientists, are planned in the next two years: Heath and Merolle (2007) and Heath and Merolle (2008).

3   For a brief, balanced biographical essay see Chapter 3 of Kettler's (2005) monograph on Ferguson.

4   He was suited to the commission, being both a fluent Gaelic speaker and a government supporter. Evidence of Ferguson's military experience comes from a letter written to Alexander Carlyle: 'and I pray you remember that when a shell falls near you: You are not to run away but ly flat down till it burst & then take to your heels as fast as you can, lest any more should come' (Letter to Alexander Carlyle, Bath, 26 May 1781, Ferguson MSS). Ferguson spent nine years as a chaplain before resigning his commission, and saw active service at Fontenoy and elsewhere. He was serving with his regiment in Flanders during the defeat of the Jacobite army in 1746 and the subsequent destruction of Highland society.

with an *Institutes of Moral Philosophy* (1769) and later, two volumes of *Principles of Moral and Political Science* (1792).

Ferguson's place in the Scottish Enlightenment is an interesting one. A civic humanist by inclination, he attempted to bring together a number of concerns that stemmed not merely from his intellectual background, but from the social and political problems he perceived around him.[5] Many Scottish Enlightenment figures were similarly motivated – Adam Smith, Lord Kames, David Hume, William Robertson. But Ferguson's *weltanschaung*, distinctive in his own lifetime, differed in a number of important respects from that of other figures. He offers a complex model of historical continuity which challenges both Hume's and Adam Smith's philosophy of history, and the primitivism of Rousseau. Ferguson combines a subtle analysis of the emergence of modern commercial society with a critique of what appeared to him to be its abandonment of civic and communal virtues. Where Smith and Hume generally approved of the economic and material changes wrought in society within recent times (legitimising the rise of the commercial, for example, for its effect of liberating social orders from feudal superstructures), Ferguson was much more critical of the new structures and their effects on society. Where Rousseau and others pointed to the contractarian basis of society, he also drew attention to conflict as an engine of change, and investigated the effects of moral and emotional motives to action. It was on account of this *social* trajectory that Pocock described Ferguson's account of social becoming as 'perhaps the most Machiavellian of the Scottish disquisitions of this theme' (Pocock, 1975, quoted in Hill, 2006, p. 39).

The key concerns of the civic humanist tradition lay in citizenship and virtue. For Ferguson, following Seneca, Cicero and the Stoic tradition, it was inconceivable that society could exist at all without the binding qualities innate in civic virtue and benevolence. One of Ferguson's major influences in this regard was the teaching of Adam Smith's predecessor at Glasgow, Francis Hutcheson, and in particular Hutcheson's concept of what he called the 'moral sense' – that is, the means by which we make distinctions between concepts and moral categories. Hutcheson's exposition of the moral sense is complex and sometimes obscure, particularly in its cognitive aspects, and it is not my intention to venture too far into his arguments; but it is necessary to grasp his concept in outline, for it was important to late enlightenment jurisprudential and educational thought.

Hutcheson's concept of the moral sense departed from a central tradition in seventeenth century natural law. Stair, for example, could declare authoritatively from a natural law position that 'Law is the dictate of reason, determining every rational being to that which is congruous and convenient for the nature and condition thereof' (Dalrymple, 1981, I,1,1). Hutcheson disagreed with this view of the moral basis for action. For him, the process of deciding how to act was not so much a matter of comparing notes with Reason as apprehending, at a

---

5   Ferguson's reputation has only recently been revived. Hill (2006, p. 5, nn.22–7), provides a useful list of references.

much deeper cognitive level, what was right or wrong in any situation – hence his concept of a moral sense based on the '*natural Affections* and *kind Passions*'. As he protested in a public letter, '[T]he old Notions of *natural Affections*, and kind *Instincts; the Sensus communis*, the *Decorum,* and *Honestum*, are almost banished out of our Books of Morals; we must never hear of them in any of our Lectures for fear of *Innate Ideas*; all must be Interest and some selfish View' (Hutcheson, 1969–70, VII, p. 475).[6] As the last lines indicate, Hutcheson was directly opposed to the view held by Locke in his *Essay* regarding the origins of virtue. He believed, *contra* Hobbes and Mandeville, that the moral motivated us by providing us with self-interested reasons for acting in a moral way.[7]

The concept sounds emotivist, but it is much more complex and subtle than that, especially in the form that Hutcheson presents it in *An Inquiry into the Original of our Ideas of Beauty and Virtue* (1725). In this text Hutcheson's construct of our apprehension of virtue and right conduct is a 'beatific' moral theory, advocating that the happiness of society can be achieved by the beneficence and moral virtue of its agents.[8] Furthermore, because our moral sense is the foundation of natural law, so rights in law derive from this sense too – even the rights which accrue to those for whom there are no corresponding obligations, such as animals and unborn children, for instance.[9]

Ferguson was influenced by Hutcheson's interpretation of the moral sense, but went beyond it, for he disagreed that a purely beatific moral theory could account for and influence the fast-developing character of later eighteenth-century Scotland. In that period, Scotland was a place of remarkable contrasts – the perfect example of the three-stage development of civil society drawn up by Ferguson in his *Essay* (Ferguson, 1996). Bjorn Eriksson has summed it up succinctly:

> [T]he highland clans could ... be characterised as belonging to the shepherd stage. The stage of agriculture was still vivid in mind even if farming was in a process of transformation into a capitalistic, market-oriented production; and the stage of commerce was rapidly gaining in the second half of the eighteenth century when the

---

6   Hutcheson (1969–90, VII, pp. vii–ix) quoted by Moore (1990, p. 48) and Mautner (1993, p. 54).

7   See for instance Hutcheson (1969–90, II, pp. vii–ix); see also Moore (1990, p. 49) and Campbell (1982, p. 170).

8   Haakonssen (1990, p. 78). Haakonssen stresses that Hutcheson's theory was not mere moralising: '[For Hutcheson] morality was a matter of qualities in persons, but empirically ascertainable ones' (p. 72). I follow Haakonssen in taking Hutcheson as the start of a line of Scottish moral philosophical investigation stretching to Dugald Stewart, James Mill and beyond – ibid., p. 62. See Hutcheson (1969–90, I, pp. 249–76) for a discussion of the concepts of 'Obligation and Right, Perfect, Imperfect, and External, Alienable and Unalienable' at section vii, vol. I, pp. 249–76.

9   Haakonssen (1990, p. 80), quoting and analysing Hutcheson (1969–90, V, pp. 309–16).

Scottish lowlands were the economic wonder region of Europe. (Eriksson, 1993, p. 272, quoted by Hill, 2006, p. 191)

But the costs of such astonishing change to the wonder region were heavy, and Ferguson commented on these in the *Essay* and in his *Institutes*. The radical disjunctures within society, and the growing disparities in wealth and poverty, together with the growing division of labour and breakdown of traditional societal bonds seriously concerned Ferguson. Throughout his work, he tried to balance the burgeoning capitalism of Scottish commerce and industrialism with community, and find ways to accommodate both wealth and virtue in society. For this reason, as Hill points out, we find in Ferguson a watershed of different and ancient discourses: the discourse of civic humanism, and the discourse of rights (Hill, 2006, p. 21). Ferguson is an attractive thinker precisely because he attempts such a balance. As Hill points out,

> most of Ferguson's thinking seems to hover in the middle ground between Smith's progressivism, modernism, liberalism and laissez-faire-ism and Rousseau's romantic, egalitarian and *dirigiste* tendencies. (2006, p. 40)

He refuses to site himself in any particular tradition. He is a mesocosmic figure, peculiarly modern in his refusal to exist comfortably within a tradition, and instead inhabits the peripheries of those traditions, making of them a new and cohesive tradition from his own acute analyses of civil society. On the one hand, for example (and foreshadowing Freud and Marx) he emphasised how important was conflict in society, in bringing about social change and improvement at every level. He pointed out how love of challenge and difficulty was an integral part of society. On the other, he mounted a remarkably powerful defence of the concept of benevolence as a regulator of social order, and a goal of social activity.[10] Throughout, he is insistent that human activity cannot be understood in isolation, but only in a social context. In this he disagreed with Rousseau's treatment of a state of nature, and always pointed out the social nature of historical and contemporary society. As always, he was prepared to deal with a complex reality, rather than reduce it to an over-riding passion or drive. Thus he disagreed with Mandeville about innate self-interest – society, he believed, was much more complex in its action and motivation than the mere reduction to self-interest. He also disagreed with Smith and Hume about the moral order best suited to a fast-developing nation such as Scotland then was. Beneficence (in quite similar terms to that expressed by Hutcheson) was a powerful motive for human action, precisely because of our social nature and context: a person is 'by nature, the member of a community: and when considered in this capacity, the individual appears to be no longer made for himself' (Ferguson, 1996, p. 59,

---

10 Compare for instance, the claims of the French Materialists, for whom society and its parts were described in mechanical terms – see for example Julien de La Mettrie, *L'homme Machine* (1748), quoted by Hill, p. 76.

quoted in Hill, 2006, p. 89). Ferguson advocated that our happiness lay in the service of others; that beneficence, not wealth, should be the aim of society.[11] In this context, Hobbesian moral individualism is dismissed by Ferguson: people act from many motives, not merely rationalist ones, and therefore what appears to be in retrospect an orderly progress of civilisation, defined by concepts such as social or original contracts, is actually, according to Ferguson, at the human level merely random.[12]

Ferguson's appeal lies not only in his refusal to let philosophical systems blind him to the stark realities of capitalist shifts in later-eighteenth-century Scotland, but also in his refusal to admit that a complex and sophisticated philosophical tradition two millennia in the making had little of worth to say to him or his society. Rejecting utilitarianism, he creates an ethics based upon self-interest and benevolence, upon competition and stoic communitarianism (Hill, 2006, p. 85).

Put thus, Ferguson sounds like a moralist; as if he should be aligned with the more puritanical texts that appeared in the later eighteenth century deploring the wealth and luxury of commercial and ruling classes. This would be to misinterpret his position, however. Ferguson was above all a practical philosopher, deeply concerned with the moral, economic and cultural state of Scotland in particular and Britain generally. To this end, as Hill points out, he followed no neat ideological programme, but instead positioned himself between intellectual cultures represented by the ancient civic humanism of Cicero and Seneca and the proto-liberalism of his own era, a version of 'liberal-stoicism' (Hill, 2006, p. 26). What was striking about Ferguson's position was its refusal to dismiss the Stoic position and adopt wholesale a utilitarian displacement; and his scepticism of the very concept of society's progress, particularly in a capitalist society. He conceived the use of moral philosophy to lie in the problematic areas of 'choice, practice and conduct' (*Institutes*, 6; Hill, 2006, p. 207). As these are infinite in the variety presented to us in social interactions so our learning in ethics never ceases. Ferguson thus perceived moral learning as 'a teleology without an attainable *telos*', in the neat formulation of Hill. She quotes a range of Ferguson's metaphors: ethics is 'a "baffled project", an infinite "curve", and a perplexing "labyrinth" rather than a precise goal' (Hill, 2006, p. 207).

The tension that Ferguson holds in balance is typical of his approach to society and ethics. It is evident in his most famous book, *An Essay on Civil Society*, which, as Hill observes, bridges 'Machiavellian humanism with the nineteenth century focus on the theme of alienation' (p. 162). In this work there is a concern to keep society balanced so that (to use the terms quite close to the sense that Hannah Arendt uses them) public and private realms of conduct are balanced, and a sense of community is possible through recognition of 'common affairs' (Ferguson,

---

11 And in his descriptions of this he rarely applies to Christian precepts or writings, preferring instead secular, often ancient, authors.

12 As Hill points out, such a view of human activity is remarkably close to autopoietic accounts of social activity and organisation (Hill, p. 103).

1996, p. 208). Such common affairs, not far from Hutcheson's *'sensus communis'*, are a crucial aim for Ferguson, but the journey is never completed. In common with the Rousseau of the *Social Contract*, Ferguson deplored the dominance of private interest over the public commonweal.[13] Society – multivarious, protean – is constantly re-negotiating common affairs, between the essential poles of peace and benevolence on the one hand (he believed in innate goodness), and conflict and competition on the other.

He also held that habit was of central importance in moral development. This is an ancient theme, first mentioned by Aristotle as the mean between deficiency and excess, and acting in particular ways according to the principles of practical intelligence or *phronesis* (Aristotle, 2002, II, p. 6). Ferguson developed the practical application of habit, noting that it acted as a memory of moral progress, and regarding it as a faculty of human nature that was sensitive to social approval or disapproval (Ferguson, 1792, p. 234). It enabled individuals to act ethically in a manner that was self-regulated; and what was true of the individual was true of society as a whole.

Ferguson's emphasis on habit or 'manners' was part of a larger concern in later eighteenth century Scotland with the education of youth, and in particular the mechanisms by which ethical behaviour could be encouraged. John Dwyer has sketched out how widespread this ethical concern was in Scottish society. As he pointed out, if Rousseau lays claim to the first serious treatment of youth in modern educational literature (in *Emile*), it was Scottish civil society which demonstrated how ethical education could 'support the traditional moral community of a stratified nation' (Dwyer, 1987, p. 90). But where much of this discourse consists of redactions of civic humanist sources to normative values by moderate clergy and others, Ferguson's conception is much more complex. He recognises not only how habit can be pressed into the service of ethical behaviour, but also its profound psychological base.[14] What Ferguson describes in certain passages approaches Dewey's concepts of the world's vague penumbra that becomes clarified as a 'figured framework of objects' (Ferguson, 1996, p. 11). In other words habit forms ethical action precisely because it is not mere repetition but consists of transactions with the world that are freighted with meaning.

Turning now to the draft lectures on Moral Philosophy that he delivered, the subject-matter and tenor of his lectures is a remarkable contrast to what we might regard as a twenty-first century view of education. In 1775–76 he lectured on seven subjects – rudiments of the natural history of man, theory of mind, knowledge of God, moral laws, jurisprudence, casuistry and politics – then spent the final

---

13 It should be pointed out that Ferguson rejected many of the basic tenets of Rousseau's position on education, denying that a state of nature could ever exist and emphasising the study of social forms as the ground of educational development (1996, p. 9).

14 Hill, for instance, notes Ferguson's prescient descriptions of emotional transference, conditional responses and childhood responses: see 2006, pp. 146–7.

lecture emphasising the practical value of these studies for the business of life. The language of his discourse reveals the true ambition of the enlightenment educational project in Scotland: Ferguson took as his subject in the lectures 'Human Nature, the present condition and future prospects of mankind'. His subjects generally were the 'first and most general Principles of Pneumaticks and moral Philosophy' (Ferguson, 1775, p. 1, *recto*). He defined 'Pneumaticks' for his audience as 'the knowledge of mind or Spirit', and moral philosophy as 'the discernment of right and wrong in the Characters and Manners of Men' (1775, p. 1, *recto*). Ferguson was aware of the wide interests of his audience, speaking as he did to the student body of the Arts Faculty:

> I am to speak of Human affairs to you who are yourselves men and deeply interested in what relates to mankind. You are at once the Subjects, the Evidence and the Judges of what is to be advanced. (1775, p. 4 and *verso*)

The focus is firmly on the social, and on human society. As he says in the 'Prefix' to lecture 49:

> Our principal Object in this place is to discuss the first and most important of all questions – What is best for Mankind? In order to solve it the nature of man and the subjects presented to his Choice should be known. I have considered what the scene of human Life presents upon a general view of the species. (1775, p. 541)

Like every good lecturer, Ferguson went on to preview his subject. He also spoke of the manner of delivery:

> I think it is a hard and unprofitable task to attempt writing the Lectures. They are delivered to be understood not to be written.
>   It may be useful nevertheless to take some short notes in aid of the memory and afterwards compose for yourselves what you conceive on the subject of each days Lecture.[15]

---

15 Ibid., p. 16. It is interesting to note that Ferguson expected students to read fairly widely in the texts mentioned on his course, and he also expected coursework to be carried out by students: 'It is of great use to the Student to take Notes of what occurs in the Course of his Studies and to build upon thos Notes at his Leisure more full & compleat Informations on the Subjects that Interest him. / This Attempt may give in certain Professions a Facility in a Practice which is of great use. / It will serve to exercise the Talent for Composition & to imprint the subjects of Knowledge on the Memory. And I shall expect at Different Periods to receive Speciments of this sort which may prove a Useful Exercise to you and give me some Satisfaction with respect to the Proficiency you are making' (1775, p. 20).

The lectures set out the structure of Ferguson's inquiry, and are at times dauntingly abstract.[16] They are arranged in summary in his *Institutes of Moral Philosophy* (1769). The book (subtitled 'For the use of Students in the College of Edinburgh') was written as a text for Ferguson's course in Moral Philosophy in the University of Edinburgh, and summarises the structure of the lectures. There are eight parts: the natural history of man, theory of mind, knowledge of God, moral laws and their general applications, fundamental law of morality, jurisprudence, casuistry, and politics. The drafts of the lectures themselves, which exist in manuscript form, elaborate upon the argument structure of the *Institutes*, and discuss many more examples. The following passage is fairly typical:

> Now is your time to begin Practices and lay the Foundation of habits that may be of use to you in every Condition and in every Profession at least that is founded on a literary or a Liberal Education. *Sapere and Fari quae sentiat* are the great Objects of Literary Education and of Study. … mere knowledge however important is far from being the only or most important Attainment of Study.
>
> The Habits of Justice, Candour, Benevolence, and a Courageous Spirit are the first Objects of Philosophy the Constituents of happiness and of personal honour, and the first Qualifications for human Society and for Active life.[17]

The passage repays close reading. It is important to realise that the general, philosophy-based course of instruction that Ferguson taught was known to him and others as a humanist course of study, and described as 'liberal' in that sense ('literary' was another adjective for the same *cursus*). The first line begins with mention of habits – which, as we might expect, Ferguson foregrounds as a key mode of experiential learning. What sort of things are to be learned – the gaining of wisdom and the ability to express oneself – is signalled by the quotation from Horace, Epistles, I, iv, which is addressed to the poet Albius Tibullus – a poem written in the *carpe diem* tradition.[18] It does not express the desperate urgency

---

16 Some students may have complained, for Ferguson writes an addendum to an early lecture: 'Gentlemen may think it an error to have placed first what is most abstruse. But we must learn to prefer what is useful, to make the Surmounting of difficulties our pleasure' (1775, p. 56).

17 Also quoted in Sher (1990, pp. 117–18), quoting Ferguson's Lectures,1775–76, fols 540–41.

18 The relevant section of the 16-line epistle reads:

> Non tu corpus eras sine pectore; di tibi formam,
> di tibi diuitias dederunt artemque fruendi.
> Quid uoueat dulci nutricula maius alumno,
> qui sapere et fari possit quae sentiat, et cui
> gratia, fama, ualetudo contingat abunde,
> et mundus uictus non deficiente crumina?
> Inter spem curamque, timores inter et iras
> omnem crede diem tibi diluxisse supremum;
> grata superueniet quae non sperabitur hora.

of seizing immediate pleasure, however.[19] Rather it speaks of a way of life, based on typical Horatian values of moderation, sophistication, irony.[20]

The 'Objects' of this course thus go beyond 'mere knowledge', and include the qualities listed by Ferguson in the next paragraph. It is a list that goes *behind* our own typical triad of skills, knowledge, values. Ferguson has no hesitation in listing these qualities because they are perceived by him to be the virtues that underpin his civilisation. Indeed, as many commentators have pointed out since Pocock's ground-breaking history of the development of Stoic *virtus* in western political, economic and moral thought, the Senecan forms of thought underlying these terms are a powerful magnet for ideas that would have already been part of the undergraduates' moral universe.

The qualities he adduces – and again, introduced as 'Habits', so important is this concept– are carefully chosen. Justice is a critical faculty, because Ferguson refers to justice in general, not merely the action of laws.[21] 'Benevolence' is matched by 'a Courageous Spirit', and all are essential elements of philosophy, happiness, honour, and society. It is an extraordinarily wide claim, but the merging of philosophy with the other three would not have seemed inappropriate to either Ferguson or his audience. 'Personal honour' is an interesting quality. As I said, Ferguson would have been well aware of the high importance associated

---

You are not merely a body without any feelings.
You have been given beauty, wealth and the means to appreciate things.
What more would a nurse wish for her sweet little one
Than wisdom, the power to express what he feels,
Much kindness, health and fame,
An elegant way of life, and enough money?
Amid the hope and worry, fear and anger,
take every day that dawns as your last –
the unlooked-for hour will be a welcome surprise.

19   As does Andrew Marvell in 'To His Coy Mistress', for instance :
Let us roll all our strength, and all
Our sweetness, up into one ball;
And tear our pleasures with rough strife
Thorough the iron gates of life.

20   Surfeit and its corrosive effects in society was a typical theme in the lectures, sometimes expressed as value or quality in human activity. See for instance the following passage on wealth: '1st What is Wealth / 2nd What is its comparative Importance: & the Value of the Arts that Procure it. / They derive a value from their End. / They derive a value also from their Effect in cultivating human Nature' (1775, p. 245).

21   He makes this clear later when he discusses briefly the Rousseau-esque concept of the social contract. He asks: 'Qu. 1 In this account of the origin and progress of Government; what place have we left for the Social Compact, etc' and gives the answer: 'I have already observed that the Social Compact is a mere fiction of natural Law. And that the Obligations supposed to be thus established are better founded in humanity & Justice. / So that men instead of recurring to the Social Compact may recurr to the principles of Justice and humanity, etc.'

in Highland cultures with personal honour. His knowledge of Highland and Lowland cultures and their way of relating one to another probably contributed to his insight into the qualities that determined behaviour within a culture.

With the final two words of the passage Ferguson points to the future lives of his students. At first glance 'Active life' may seem like a contemporary version of operational competence – the preparation of students for the life of citizenship, or the world of employment or the professions. But the term means much more than that for Ferguson. He, and his students, would have been aware that the concept was one part of the ancient diptych of *vita activa* and *vita contemplativa*.[22] Ferguson was thus pointing up a key element of his moral philosophy – the need for a vigorous activism among all levels of society in the nation.[23] Taken as a whole, the discourse represented by this passage was profoundly influential in the rhetoric of higher education in Scotland, at least until the Royal Commission into Scottish Universities of the mid-nineteenth century.[24]

The passage holds much significance for us. Imagine, if you can, this passage being spoken as part of the introductory lecture to a programme of study in your institution. Is there any part of it that would *not* puzzle students and staff? Perhaps more importantly, in our post-industrial, postmodern world, can we ever be as confident as Ferguson about the values that ought to underpin our society and our profession? What would we say today if we were to try to make similar statements to our students? Would our educational values be our moral values, and would the two be integrated with each other? Curiously enough, Barnett has what looks at first glance a similar passage in his book:

> Wisdom is not the only virtue that is having a poor time of it in the modern university. Patience, humility, generosity, perseverance, thoroughness, carefulness, quietness: these might once have been felt to be signs of a strength of character. No longer. In

---

22 Analysed in depth by, among many others, Arendt (1958).

23 The following passage from the lecture drafts illustrates Ferguson's advocacy of the 'Active Principles', as he called them, in human affairs. He outlines what such principles consist of; and note the subtle intertwining of the qualities set out above: 'The Active Principles of human Nature may be referred to three Objects. Self Preservation Advancement & Society. / The Principle in every instance is good but the proper [use] or the abuse of it depends on the supreme directing Power of Wisdom. / Attempts have been made to found Systems upon some one of these principles partially or separately. / All the Phenomena of human life are but diversifyed appearances of the Law of Self preservation or Interest. / As Ambition is one of its forms Benevolence is another. The mind in both instances only urges to its own gratifications. / … / Others imagine that the distinction of right and Wrong is to be taken from the Principle alone. That nothing can be right which is selfish [and] nothing can be wrong which is Social. / But this also is probably an Error. The Principle in every instance is wisely constituted. The proper use of it is right the abuse is wrong. / Such is the maxim of reason also relating to Ambition or the principle of Advancement it is wisely constituted, the proper use of it leads to perfection & happiness. The Abuse of it leads to many foolish and vain pursuits' (1775, p. 575).

24 See, for example, Dwyer (1987).

an age of self-promotion, self-presentation, visibility, efficiency, work-rate, personal performance indicators and sheer competitiveness, character traits such as these come to be seen as signs of personal weakness. (pp. 151–2)

But where Ferguson is confident and forward-looking, Barnett's words are a mourning, for lost values, lost vocabularies. Where Barnett struggles in his book to articulate a position between rival versions of competence and a third position, Ferguson taps into an ancient tradition of moral and civic thinking, and transforms it for his students, his society. His students would have recognised that his Senecan discourse stemmed from humanist and scholastic roots that go back several centuries in Scottish intellectual culture. He is unquestionably of the opinion that the discourse is vital to his culture in eighteenth-century Scotland. In his words, moral philosophy, history and intellectual culture become practical models for contemporary life in Scotland.

The comparison of Ferguson and Barnett is, of course, unfair. Where Ferguson writes within a rich philosophical tradition, no such immersive discourse is available to Barnett, writing after Darwin, Nietzsche, Freud, the global disasters of two world wars, the Holocaust. And where a prescient Ferguson warns of the corrosive effects of materialism, the division of labour and *anomie*, and the rise of the bureaucratic state, Barnett must deal with the full effects of these massive social changes. Barnett is right to dismiss the competence answer:

[a] higher education designed around skills is no higher education. It is the substitution of technique for insight; of strategic reason for communicative reason; and of behaviour for wisdom. (1994, p. 61)

A strongly competence-based education cannot provide an adequate conceptual structure for legal students or trainees. At best it provides second-order description of conduct and knowledge, as Stenhouse recognised more than 20 years ago, and Dewey before him. Alone, and acting as performance criteria or learning outcomes, such statements can become impositions on students, setting up a dialogue of learned helplessness. If these are the criteria of assessment, students argue reasonably, show us examples of acceptable performance that we may copy. For students, the focus thus moves from organic development of self to the copying of forms of behaviour and the rote resumption of knowledge. Performance criteria thus become ever more detailed, and student performance ever more baroquely imitative in order to comply with assessment criteria. In this environment the space for the growth and development of ethical awareness is diminished. What is required is the first-order ethical structure that arises not from the ethical intuitions of students or staff, nor from the impositions of a set of ethical guidelines, but from the moral dialectic of self, profession and society.

But how are we to express this dialectic relationship in our legal educational curricula today? Are we bound to Barnett's rival versions, or his unpalatable alternative? This chapter is not an elegy for lost vocabularies, lost certainties

– which were in any case hard-won even for Ferguson. But unless we have a historical awareness of the values shift, and the possibilities open to us in theory and practice, we will remain thirled those of others. Linden West expressed this well when, talking of adult students in the Medway towns, he remarked:

> [f]or adults as well as children, affirmation, holding and inclusion, especially for those on the margins, provides a basis for existential legitimacy, core cohesion and authentic engagement in the world. The problem has been that education and educators have lacked a compelling language to interpret and theorize the intimate dimensions of learning and self-development within a connected and historical frame of reference: or, to state it differently, to interpret what it takes, emotionally, socially as well as intellectually, to keep on keeping on even in the most oppressive and fragmented of times. (West, 1996, p. 208)

Such 'intimate dimensions' are critical to the ethical project, for they are the ground by which ethical thought becomes part of identity. West again:

> [...] reclaiming a past – emotionally, biographically, intellectually and culturally – is essential to claiming a future, built more on one's own terms than upon those of others. (1996, p. 211)

The reclamation space to develop such moral understandings is critical, and it can only happen in a community of justice in the law school. By 'space' I do not mean the creation of yet another module. I mean it as architects use the word – a place defined by its context, as much as identity is defined by circumstance. We can visit the neo-classical structures of Ferguson's *oeuvre*, but we cannot live there.[25] We need other spaces around which are the ethical structures built by us for our own times. Not *new* structures, for how could we inhabit a totally new architecture, an architecture that denies the past; but a space that is created by teaching methods, learning opportunities, curriculum design; by the exploration of classical ethical structures as well as the counter-culture of postmodernism; by the description of real legal practice and professional culture, the archaeology of its hidden foundations and re-appraisal of its motives, methods, consequences; and the practice of justice within the law school.

Gillian Rose: The Broken Middle

The political scientist Gillian Rose has, among others, made the point that ethical structure depends upon us recognising sources of power and analysing their vectors, victims, wielders, effects. Postmodern ethics, in their concern to overcome the coils of western metaphysics, divest themselves of philosophy, and remain dualistic: 'between

---

25 Their lineaments are unreal to us, Eliot's falling towers. I agree with Norrie (2005, p. 28) that there is no return to the classical tradition.

inner morality and outer legality, individual autonomy and general heteronomy, active cognition and imposed norm' (Rose, 1992, p. xii). Such dualism, according to her, results in the diremption of law and ethics, where philosophy is 'over-unified', is 'turned into social theory', where '"truth" is revealed to be a value among values; "rationality", "justice" and "freedom" to be types of domination'.[26] The middle between such dualisms is broken, is always broken, and we seek anxiously to mend it, soothe away the break, the diremption of law and ethics, make it whole again by an array of inauthentic ethical devices. Her analysis of the relationship of law and ethics, *The Broken Middle*, is an uncompromising, dramatic analysis of how deep the broken middle fissures our postmodern society, and how much we strive to overcome it. Rose castigates – it is not too strong a term – not just post-structuralist attempts to overcome the diremption of the middle, but the adoption of Levinasian ethics as a deconstruction of the brokenness into holiness, which for her is yet one more repetition in a long series of philosophical and ethical repetitions:

> Levinas cannot suspend the ethical. Instead he dirempts it – separating love and law: eros redefined as the peace of paternity, as law and commandment, 'law' redefined as freedom, being, the state. (1992, p. 258)

The Broken Middle is a dark and sombre text: at the end we are urged to return to philosophy, avoid *accedia*, and 'resume reflexively what we always do: to know, to misknow and yet to grow' (1992, p. 310) It is left to Rose's final book to give us clearer indications of what she means by this. The opening lines of *Mourning Becomes the Law* contain a list whose tone is redolent of Barnett's words:

> One by one all of the classical preoccupations of philosophy have been discredited and discarded: eternity, reason, truth, representation, justice, freedom, beauty and the Good. (Rose, 1996, p. 1)

But her words are a call to action based upon a clear-eyed view of the alternatives. In an interpretation of Poussin's painting of Phocion's wife retrieving the ashes of her husband who was executed unjustly by Athenians, she claims the action is 'a protest against arbitrary power, it is not a protest against power and law as such' (1996, p. 26). It is a placing of the ethical squarely within the city, within experience:

> [e]thics and domination, the good and violence, the community and the law, do not belong to two worlds, to two cities, to two different methodologies. (1996, p. 36)

Against neo-liberal politics and the fantasies of communitarianism, Rose argues that the

---

26 Note that Rose does not deny the achievement of social theory (Weber and Durkheim form key elements of her analysis), but she argues that its theoretical basis is more complex that it appears.

impure paradoxes of the disposition of power renew virtue in life and in death. To know the violence at the heart of the human spirit gives death back its determination and its eternity. (1996, p. 141)

She imagines the abandonment of Athens, 'city of rational politics', for Jerusalem, where the community would dedicate itself 'to difference, to otherness, to love – to a new ethics' (1996, p. 21). The enormity of the task, though, is described in her next words, chilling in their consequences:

> What if the pilgrims, unbeknownst to themselves, carry along in their souls *the third city* – the city of capitalist private property and modern legal status? The city that separates each individual into a private, autonomous, competitive person, a bounded ego, and a phantasy life of community, a life of unbounded mutuality, a life without separation and its inevitable anxieties? A phantasy life which effectively destroys the remnant of political life? (1996, pp. 21–2).[27]

Many of her anxieties were also those of Ferguson, and for some of the same reasons, caught between the Athens of political rationality and the Rome of stoic virtue, and Edinburgh of the new commerce, and knowing that the effects of the third city are profound but hidden, in the soul of the individual, and in the unregarded social processes of society. Ferguson's sophisticated equivocation was one answer. Barnett is similarly caught between rival versions of competence, and his middle, his dialectic response, is that of 'life-world becoming'. In terms of legal ethics and legal education, we are caught between the rational, normative structures of professional ethical codes, and radical critique of one sort or another, the journey to Jerusalem.

If there is indeed a first-order of ethical qualities, what are these qualities, and how can we approach them with our students? I would argue that there is no need to create a new ethics or abandon Athens: we need to re-think the city, re-imagine what an ethics based upon a philosophy of the broken middle might actually mean for us. We have models: as Rose points out 'the three great thinkers of *power before ethics,* Machiavelli, Nietzsche and Weber, each renew the classical tradition in ethics for the modern world' (1996, p. 140). But in moving from high- and middle-order theory, how can we develop this body of thinking about ethics for legal education?

Intimate Dimensions of Ethical Practice

Perhaps the first point to recognise is that, as legal educationalists, we cannot avoid our own implication in theory or practice, West's 'intimate dimensions' quoted above (p. 127). To read and create theory is to be subject to methodological

---

27 Rose's theoretical stance summarised here is elaborated in Rose (1984). For an application of Rose's concept of the broken middle to education, see Tubbs (1997).

reflexivity, to be faced with the question of one's own practice. Nowhere should one become a spectator, a neutral voice, so involved in the technical language of 'operationalist terminology' (Rose, 1996, p. 245) that one becomes blinded to the ethical. Second, is the key point for Rose – the embedding of the ethical within the city, the act of returning Phocion's ashes within the city. The act is essential if mourning is to be completed, the circle accomplished, and justice restored, not to Phocion, but to the city, by which action the mourner 'returns the soul to the city, renewed and reinvigorated for participation' (Rose, 1996, p. 36). Such a return cannot be attempted as a list (or 'constellation of terms' as Barnett has it in one of the epigraphs to this chapter) of competent, professional, or even ethical qualities. It is, after all, not in the statement of qualities *per se* that ethical behaviour is tested, but in the clash and dissonance of one quality against another. In the case of Phocion's wife, it was obedience to the law of the city set against love and piety, all qualities that the city equally praised. In other words, it is not in the discussion of or reflection upon qualities, but in *action* that ethical education is enacted.

Clearly clinical experience, properly organised, is seminal to this approach. So too are simulations. Both methods enable students to develop and reflect upon intuitive, experiential knowledge, ways of coping, discerning, sensings of professional development, the 'social spaces' of training, the awareness of changing identities. It also helps them to learn about what is involved in the legal 'custom complex' (Schweder et al., 1998 pp. 865–937), the distinctive networks, hierarchies, heterarchies, agents, boundaries, bodies of expertise and connecting relationships within the legal profession. For young lawyers, learning is as much about learning the networks, relationships, reputations and contacts within the field as it is about knowing drafting conventions in a joint venture agreement, or the regulated ethics of client care, rebellious lawyering or any other form of legal practice. Real world practice problems, not hypotheticals, are the best context. In all of these activities ethical practice is represented and conveyed not only by grand gestures, but also and perhaps as meaningfully by the merest of signs – tone of voice, carefulness in communication, thoughtfulness in thinking of others, generosity in interpreting motives, in allowing others social space to speak and contribute. These signs define the tenor of the middle, the relationship between self and other; and they begin in educational relationships – those of the early years, right up to tertiary education. Such relationships are not a preparation for civil life – they *are* life, wholly continuous with other communities of civil society. And we are not speaking merely of the relationship between teacher and student, supervisor and trainee, but more importantly between student and student, between trainees, and between newly-qualified lawyers, between lawyers and others in society. Indeed, for Piaget, the peer-to-peer relationship was more important for the development of moral reasoning than the relationship of teacher/student. The peer-to-peer relation is also, in its intimate dimensions, more open to the development of empathy.

But as Dewey and Ferguson pointed out, empathy does not grow out of the occasional action. As we have seen, Ferguson believed habit to be an essential facility for the development of moral behaviour; and we saw in the Introduction how habit was an essential element in Dewey's transactional realism: '[i]mmediate, seemingly instinctive, feeling of the direction and end of various lines of behaviour is in reality the feeling of habits working below direct consciousness' (*MW*, 14, p. 26). To develop such habits in peer-to-peer communities there need to be opportunities for dialogue between peers to *matter* in the educational framework of values.[28] In addition, situational factors heavily influence behaviour.[29] There needs to be a curriculum based not merely on democratic forms of governance, but on democratic habits of cooperation, public spirit, where the law school integrates into the wider community around it, experimentally, inventively, ethically.[30] The literature on this has been well developed. From Piaget to Kohlberg, to Rest and many others one can discern the lineaments of a critical social cognitive tradition that is being taken forward by specific professions in specific ways.[31]

On the whole, it is probably true to say that, so far, we have learned these lessons intellectually; not experientially. Our competence statements seldom approach the sophistication and subtlety of recent research across a range of disciplines on how ethical education can be enacted.[32] How many of our law schools integrate clinical or experiential learning deeply and widely in the curriculum? How many can be

---

28   Chapter 8 gives some examples of this in practice. For an exploration of law student personal and institutional values, see Evans and Palermo (2003).

29   The social psychology literature on character and situation is extensive. For a discussion of some aspects of it, see Wendel (2005) and Doris (2002). Legal context has been extensively analysed – see for example Boon (2005).

30   See for instance Breger et al. (2004) and Christensen (2006). See also Bergman (2003).

31   Piaget (1932). With regard to Kohlberg's work, see Power et al. (1989); see also Kohlberg (1969), Kohlberg et al. (1983), Kohlberg (1981), Rest and Deemer (1986, pp. 28–58) and Rest et al. (1999).

For illustrative literature in accountancy, see Dellaportas et al. (2006). The literature in medical education is very considerable. See in particular the work of David Stern, and literature on professionalism – for example, Ginsburg et al. (2000), SS6–11 and Prislin et al. (2001), SS90–92.

32   A similar point is made by Boon (2005), who argues for ethical education not just at the postgraduate, but at the undergraduate stage as well – as do others, such as Chapman (2005). Boon points out both the cautious version of integration (using a module in English Legal System or some); but also puts the more radical and transformative version: '[t]he increasingly consistent criticism of a common legal education is that it is a compromise in preparing students for widely divergent and specialized fields of practice. Specialization has undermined the rationale of the common core of doctrinal study. Why is there a need for such a large common core when most graduates will use relatively little of the material they learn?' (2005, p. 65).

said to use the methods of Kohlberg's just communities?[33] Have we investigated how we might use technology to support democratic and ethical learning in law?[34] For democracy and ethics cannot be far from each other when we consider ethical and moral learning in the law. Isobel Armstrong noted as much, in her book *The Radical Aesthetic*, where she compared Dewey's account of experience and art with Rose's broken middle. The comparison is startling at first, but entirely justified, for Dewey's 'commitment to ideas of community' (Armstrong, 2000, p. 19) is based upon personal experience of commitment, ideas and community; and is close to Rose's insistence that the work of ethics will be a mourning for a lost ethics, incomplete, undone, until 'the mourner returns to negotiate and challenge the changing inner and outer boundaries of the soul and of the city; she returns to their perennial anxiety' (1996, p. 36).

---

33 There are of course inspirational examples – the work of many individuals in projects and institutions such as that of Philip Plowden and colleagues at Northumbria, Chandler and Rowbotham (2005), Minnesota Justice Foundation (http://www.mnjustice. org/); and the work of organisations such as the Clinical Legal Education Organisation, and the Global Alliance for Justice Education (GAJE – www.gaje.org). But as is generally recognised, such work still needs to be embedded in law schools widely and deeply.

34 See for example the valuable discussions and examples contained in Shane (2004).

Chapter 5

Codex to Codecs:
The Medieval Web *Redivivus*

What is everywhere passes unnoticed. Nothing is more commonplace than the experience of reading, and nothing is less well known. Reading is taken for granted to such an extent that at first glance it seems nothing need be said about it
(Todorov, 1978, p. 39).

So we beat on, boats against the current, borne back ceaselessly into the past.
(Fitzgerald, 2000, p. 172)

Introduction

That technology has a profound effect upon society cannot be doubted (Winston, 1998, Nardi, 1996, Slevin, 2000 and Einon, 1995). That it is socially constituted, and mediated by culturally embedded practices is also widely accepted.[1] That computerised information technologies in particular are having a profound effect upon the practice and theory of law, one need only look to the changed practices of the legal profession and the administration of justice. In legal education, while the use of ICT generally has a higher profile through the ubiquitous use of learning management systems, the use of ICT is still variable. We have yet to attain what Ernst Cassirer called 'mature constructivism', namely the self-reflexive view of the development of technology within the history and culture of the domain (1946). In part this may be because of our focus upon learning, at the expense of other contextual factors such as learning ecologies, social economies, motivation and prior knowledge. It may also be because we do not investigate sufficiently the introduction and development of technology within legal education. It is the purpose of this chapter to uncover some aspects of that forgotten story, which are valuable not in a historical sense only but also because they help us understand some of the changes we are undergoing in our own technological revolution in the early twenty-first century. First, we shall consider the context of medieval reading and writing; then the construction of glosses as a device to accommodate the

---

1   See for example Suchman (1987), MacKenzie (1990), McGrew (1992), Lemonnier (1993), Bijker (1995 and 2001), Bijker and Wiebe (2002), Latour and Woolgar (1979) and Rammert (1997).

information explosion around key texts such as Justinian's Digest; and finally we shall consider the parallels with web-based forms of data presentation, networked learning and social software.

Medieval Text and the Glossed Manuscript

Problems of Interpretation

A number of commentators have compared the shift from manuscripts to printed texts, and from printed texts to hypertexts. The comparison, frequently invoking the magic of Gutenburg (*pace* McLuhan) is a dangerous one, but it is illuminating for what we are about to discuss, mainly because it illustrates first the difficulties in comparing past and present, and second because it illustrates the dangers of making assumptions about forms of communication, whether past or present.

A good example of this is the relationship between manuscripts and books. It is axiomatic that the earliest books, that is, incunables, imitated the form of manuscripts. Printers copied the overall shape, letterforms (rubrics, incipits – that is, the first few words – large initials and illustrations), bindings and parchment sizes so that their books were sometimes mistaken for manuscripts. For this reason it was until recently assumed that printers simply imitated manuscripts either because they wanted to preserve the uniqueness of the manuscript (and its high price), or else they imitated manuscripts simply because it was the only literate form available. But as Margaret Smith and others have pointed out, the concept of imitation does not do justice to the complexity of the relationship between late medieval manuscripts and incunables. By examining the ways in which printed texts appropriated the form and texture of manuscripts she came to the conclusion that printed books did not so much imitate as emulate manuscripts, and principally for economic reasons (Smith, 1994, p. 25).

The distinction between emulation and imitation is narrow, but it is important to the way in which printers perceived the legacy of the manuscript, and how they used this in order to articulate the concepts of information linkage and hierarchy within the text. Thus, rubrication was left to scribes to add by hand to printed texts not merely because it was difficult to print red text and the cost-effectiveness of the process did not justify the attempt; but because red text was an integral part of the reading schema in late medieval texts. It was used in decoration and for functions such as the initial strokes in capitals 'headings, text-, chapter- and subdivision beginnings, lemmata and references to authorities'.[2] If a genre which had hitherto appeared with rubrication as an integral part of its

---

2   Smith, 1994, p. 37. As Carruthers points out, scribes were sometimes described as the 'painters' of manuscripts, and she notes the etymology of the Latin verb *distinguere*: '"divide up," "mark", "punctuate", and "decorate", all activities pertaining to the fundamental task of divisio' (1990, p. 225).

meaning structures suddenly appeared without red letters, it would have seemed highly odd to its readers. Printers thus were not so much following rubrication *per se* as the conventions by which meaning was created and ordered within the text. It took some time for printed books to develop a quite different set of conventions appropriate to its form which would be recognised by a book's readers: the evolution of the incipit into the title-page (almost entirely unknown in manuscripts) is a good instance of this.[3]

In a similar way, I would argue, generalisation regarding the relationship of one form of textual meaning to another (here, that of manuscript text to printed text) is fraught with danger. For this reason, rather than describe comparisons between print and hypertext interfaces, later in this chapter I shall attempt to consider how internet-based hypertext transforms or skirts the underlying conventions which, almost unconsciously, we apply when we read texts. In effect hypertext revives technologies that lie *behind* the print revolution of the fifteenth century and which have been generally eclipsed by that event – in particular the technology of the glossed manuscript.

If comparison of hypertext to text is difficult, then comparison of hypertext with medieval *glossa* would appear to be little short of presumptuous. Before we discuss this textual form in its context (a context which may help us to begin to appreciate the remarkable properties of this scholarly tool), there is a debate surrounding interpretation and reading that should at least be referenced here.

Commentators on communication have taken a variety of complex positions with regard to the effect that communicative media have had on historical cultures; and the debate has continued for the past 40 years or so. On the one hand there are those who claim that the move from orality to literacy brought about profound changes not only in the general culture of a society, but also in modes of cognition.[4] Amongst their claims, they argue that written forms separated text from context, made the concept of grammar possible, and (perhaps most interestingly for legal scholars) made possible the concept of context-free logic (Hcim, 1987).[5]

Against the positions advocated by this more radical group are those of what might be regarded as less technologically-determinant commentators.[6] They argued that it was impossible usefully to distinguish the effects of literacy from those cultural forms mediated by educational processes; and that the evidence for wholesale cognitive transformation was weak if present at all in societies that had undergone transmission changes. This position has been confirmed in the

---

3   Smith, 1994, pp. 35–6. See, for example, the first page of Alciati's *De Verborum Significatione*, reproduced at figs 4 and 6, pp. 44 and 46 in Maclean (1992) and discussed there at 1.4.3, pp. 37–8.

4   See for example Goody and Watt (1963), Havelock (1963 and 1976), Ong (1976 and 1982) and Olson (1994).

5   Michael Heim aptly called this the 'transformation theory'.

6   Cole et al. (1971), Scribner and Cole (1981) and Greenfield (1983).

work of Elizabeth Eisenstein, Michael Clanchy and Mary Carruthers; and it is the approach that is adopted, with some modification, in this chapter. It should be noted that none of the above commentators deny the profound changes wrought in society by technology, whether by script or by book. They analyse in detail the introduction of technology, its use and effects, on particular societies. What is useful about Carruthers' research, for example, is that she shows how contemporary cognitive research can be applied to the activities and procedures involved in medieval reading, writing and memory. Her comparisons of the mnemonic techniques of Cicero and Quintilian, as these were embodied in the texts and practices of Hugh of St Victor and others, for instance, and the comparisons she draws between this and cognitive research into memory and writing serves to demonstrate the complexity of medieval textual practices.

Manuscript Reading and Writing

If the more radical approach to literacy and cognition is not adopted in this chapter, there are still many strands of the arguments that are valuable to our understanding of medieval manuscript culture. Ong, for example, points out the visual quality of much medieval textuality (Ong, 1986, p. 226). This 'visualist drive' is 'marked by an increased sensitivity to space which is apparent', says Ong, in medieval art and in the rules and procedures used by scribes to arrange words on pages – lines of research taken up by Carruthers and others.

It is of course impossible to be completely sure how medieval readers understood their texts, but what we do know about their textual practices reveals that their understanding of text, and their understanding of what they were doing when they read, wrote, remembered and used texts was radically different from our own. We can appreciate this if we consider aspects of the writing systems developed in the early medieval period. Medieval writers were closer than modern writers to the final product which their readers would use, because they were closer to the methods of production, and could make decisions regarding their physical materials. One of the first decisions, apart from which instrument to use for writing, was which material to write upon. After 1307, there were three available to writers.[7] Wax tablets inscribed with a stylus were used for brief writings, summaries, quick thoughts. The wax was re-usable, since the wax could be smoothed over and used again. Paper was relatively scarce before the advent of printed books, and was used for informal writings (perhaps one reason why so little of it has survived). Parchment or

---

7   That is, if we discount tally-sticks, a common medieval administrative tool. The introduction of paper made from rags was a late medieval and probably a local phenomenon. According to Clanchy (1993, p. 120), paper was scarcely known in England before 1307, when it is first mentioned in a register from King's Lynn. Other materials, of course, were pressed into service. The earliest recorded polyphonic music in Scotland (c.1450) was found in the main drain of the Cluniac monastery of Paisley, inscribed on a slate (Paisley Museum). Thanks to Nicola Maharg for drawing this to my attention.

membrana was the commonest writing material. Parchment was commonly the skin of cattle, sheep or goat which was scraped, stretched and prepared for writing. It was used for a variety of writing purposes: for pocket-sized books, for administrative 'pipe rolls', records of fines and plea rolls, notatarial instruments, ecclesiastical documents such as Gratian's *Decretum,* or considerable literary productions such as Books of Hours or the Winchester Bible. It was a highly durable material, and writers were aware of this when they committed their words to the *membrana.* As a result they wrote with a different sense of the status of the text than a modern writer would have, writing on paper. In the first place, they would be aware that the text they were composing, by dictation (*ars dictaminis*), or by writing, was unique: no other would be identical. Secondly, this text was not transient or fragile like paper or wax, but long-lived: later medieval writers had proof of this because of the survival of previous manuscripts from much earlier periods.

If relationships to materials were different, the act of penning words onto the page also involved radically different procedures, conventions and cognitive processes to our own writing practices today. In late antiquity, from around 200CE onwards, for instance, the main form of writing was *scriptio continua,* that is, continuous writing without spaces between words or sentences. As Parkes has pointed out, word separation was first used in the West by Irish scribes, whose first language would not have been a Romance language, and to whose readership Latin was an alien language:

> its speakers tended to regard Latin primarily as a written or 'visible' language used for transmitting texts: they apprehended it as much by the eye as by the ear. (Parkes, 1991, p. 2)

As a result, Irish scribes developed new graphic conventions which, as Parkes points out, relied on the ancient grammarians Donatus and Priscus, who gave them a sense of the word as 'an isolable linguistic phenomenon' (Parkes, 1991, p. 3). The scribes arrayed these isolated parts of speech on the page by separating them with spaces.[8]

This new relationship to representation of language on the page extended also to new forms of punctuation. These also followed grammatical units: the *punctus* or period, the system of marks placed at different heights in the line to indicate the importance of the pause (1992, p. 8), and the small '7'-shaped mark which indicated the end of sections. Also employed was the *diple* or arrowhead, an early form of quotation mark, used whenever scripture was quoted. In Anglo-Saxon manuscripts, this is used in two forms: a large *diple* to indicate the start of a quotation, and a smaller one to indicate its continuation in subsequent lines. The beginning of the quotation was marked by a *hedera* or ivy leaf, a device

---

8   In contrast to their practice when transcribing their own spoken language, which they did according to syllable. For further information, see Parkes (1992) and Saenger (1991).

common throughout Europe, and one of the oldest punctuation marks.[9] As Parkes points out, Bede introduced a 'system of letters placed in the margins to indicate the patristic sources for his commentaries', for example, AM for Ambrose, HR for Jerome, with the first letter sited at the start of the quotation, and the second indicating the end (1991, p. 15). Parkes suggests that this 'may well be the ancestor of the modern footnote' (ibid.); it may also be one of the roots of the twelfth-century gloss. What is interesting to a modern reader is that the paratactic material appears not at the bottom of the page, or the end of a section or the end of the manuscript, but in the margin beside the text. As paratactical material grows to commentary, the margins of texts grow to accommodate it. The siting of the material in the margins has an interesting effect on the status of the commentary. It becomes much more a dialogue of (near) equals, or a debate between text and commentary. In our modern books we have no exact parallel. The footnote is clearly *parataxis*, not *taxis*, and even when the footnote is placed beside the margin, it is still subordinate to the main text on the page.

These methods of arranging text itself so as to give the reader a sense of the organisation of meaning on the page came to be further developed throughout the twelfth and thirteenth centuries. Sometimes these devices were employed in order to aid memorisation of textual meaning. Mary Carruthers has highlighted the extent to which the layout of the page was powerfully governed by mnemonic concerns and devices (Carruthers, 1998, chs 1 and 2). Sometimes, the devices were alphabetic, and were designed as finding tools. The collection of canonical texts assembled by Cardinal Deusdedit in four books with a list of subjects dealt with by each book, is an early example of this.[10] As scholarship within the schools grew, there also grew the necessity to find material within a text. Some texts, such as Gratian's *Decretum*, were in effect finding tools themselves, consisting as they do of textual quotation for the most part. Other texts required special marks or layout design to facilitate searching. Rouse and Rouse, in their study of these techniques have summarised them: '[i]nnovations in layout of the manuscript page are surely the most highly visible of all the twelfth-century aids to study – such techniques as running headlines, the size of initials, paragraph marks, cross-references, and citation of authors quoted'.[11] Rouse and Rouse cite Bosham's edition of Peter of Lombard on Psalms as an example of the highly elaborated forms of these tools (1991, p. 199). Their conclusion gives a sense of how important these devices are, not only for medieval readers, or even modern readers, but for modern readers of medieval texts:

> The utility of the devices of layout worked out in the twelfth century is evident: we still use virtually all of them today, save that we have moved the marginalia to the foot of

---

9   Parkes (1991, pp. 108–10) cites an example of a text: Bodleian Library, MS Bodley 819, fol. 16.

10   See von Glanvell (1991).

11   Ibid., p. 198

the page. And whenever one has occasion to turn directly from use of a well-laid-out twelfth- or thirteenth-century manuscript to look for something in the exceptional modern printed text that does *not* have, for example, running headlines or clear paragraph divisions, one has an annoying sense of lost ground. (1991, pp. 200–201)

The introduction of alphabetisation, as Rouse and Rouse point out, is similarly symptomatic of a 'manifestation of a different way of thinking' about both text and its meaning (1991, p.204). From early on, alphabetisation had been employed for simple lists; but its use within large and authoritative texts signalled a change in the way in which such texts were being read. It reveals on the part of the writer 'a tacit recognition of the fact that each user of a work will bring to it his own preconceived rational order, which may differ from those of other users and from that of the writer himself' (1991, p. 204). This is particularly evident in the *distinctio* collections of the twelfth and thirteenth centuries: Peter of Cornwall's *Pantheologus*, or the *Alphabetum* of Peter of Capua, for example (1991, pp. 211–14).

The Thirteenth-Century Scholarly Text

It is the thirteenth-century scholarly manuscript which demonstrates the sophisticated use of such textual devices. At this time, there was an increase in the numbers of lay people who could read and write.[12] The variety and numbers of manuscript books, and legal and administrative documents increased substantially, as did their dissemination, giving rise to further literacy.[13] The growing universities stimulated demand for more copies of books (giving rise to the *pecia* system of book copying and dissemination), while the model of the university college library was quite different to that of the ecclesiastical library. The new Aristotelian learning and the requirements of the mendicant orders for texts which would support their work gave rise to new forms of scholarship and more complex forms of learning. The comparison between the attitude towards reading taken by the early Benedictine Rule, for example, in comparison to that of the Dominican, could not be more marked. As Petrucci remarks, the 'earliest Benedictine monasticism was not a monasticism of *scriptoria* and books': monks were not allowed to own writing materials, and 'the *lectio* of the earliest Benedictine monasteries was limited to the *Regula*, liturgical books, the Bible, and a few other religious texts'.[14] Reading went hand in hand with prayer and *meditatio* (Leclercq, 1961, pp. 88–91). By contrast, thirteenth-century scholarly

---

12 In a famous passage Bonaventura (1882, pp. 14–15) defined four ways in which books could be written: by a scribe who 'scribit aliena, nihil addendo, vel mutando', by a compiler who 'scribit aliena, addendo, sed non de suo', by the commentator who 'scribit et aliena et sua', and by the author who 'scribit et sua et aliena, sed sua tamquam principalia' To this should be added the fact that many authors did not write their texts, but dictated them to scribes. See Carruthers (1990, pp. 170–74; 211–14).

13 This is one of the themes in the sophisticated argument of Clanchy (1993, p. 21).

14 Petrucci (1995, p. 34).

reading involved textual comparison, searching and collation, and the application of textual scholarship and logic to the text by the reader. New reading purposes required new forms of text. Thus Dominican preachers were equipped with texts which they carried around with them as aids to preaching in the mission fields of town and country.[15] As Rouse and Rouse comment,

> [e]arly thirteenth-century Bibles not infrequently contain, as well, brief indexes, in rational or alphabetical order, of biblical 'themes' for preachers – for example, the index of texts useful for preaching against the Manichees (that is, the Cathars) that is found in early Dominican pocket Bibles. (1991, p. 215)

These indices were achieved by using alphabetisation, arabic numeration, division into chapters and *distinctiones*. Passages were further divided into sevenths using the first seven letters of the alphabet A–G, which then served as 'the smallest and most specific unit of reference'. This could then be used in conjunction with chapter-reference; or 'as the Bruges Cistercians did, with reference to a folio and column, to delimit the portion of the column intended' (Rouse and Rouse, 1991, p. 244). Other devices used included consideration of the best order of a work and communicating this to the reader (*ordinatio*); use of *rubricae, litterae notabiliores*, majuscules, paraph marks, running titles.

These devices were invaluable as guides to the more sophisticated forms of writing being developed by scholars in the thirteenth century. The *compilatio* was one of these – a compilation of extracts of works of authority or *auctoritates*, chosen by the compiler and re-arranged, often without commentary, so that its effectiveness as a genre lay in its juxtapositional strategies.[16] Parkes' comments on the interaction of *ordinatio* upon *compilationes* (indeed the necessity for a clear and precise *ordinatio* in order to guide readers through the bewildering mélange of extracts) are a valuable reminder of the instrumentality of reading within medieval culture, when so much authority attached to ancient and ecclesiastical *auctores*. In this respect the *compilatio* could be used on its own or as a bibliographical aid to another text.

The *compilatio* spawned a scholastic industry: 'the big compilers like Vincent of Beauvais and Hugh of St. Cher had smaller compilers to help them', while scribes learned the new forms of abbreviation and conventions, and applied them, in the manner of a journal's house style, to an author's text (Rouse and Rouse, 1991, p. 69). These changes in reading and writing affected the legal world as much as Church scholarship, and are evidenced not only by the forms of books produced but by the sheer numbers of them owned by private readers. As Petrucci (1995, p. 210) points out,

---

15 Although as Rouse and Rouse point out (1991, p. 247), the 'need for preaching tools was not limited to, nor did it originate with, the mendicant orders'.

16 See Parkes (1991, pp. 35–70; 62–4).

While in 1273 the library of the late Accursius (or what remained of it) counted only 73 volumes, all in law except for a lonely Vegetius, in about 1350 the library of Giovanni Calderini, another jurist and professor at Bologna, comprised 294 books. These were ordered by subject in twelve sections, showing that alongside the crushing presence of juristic texts (more than 50 works) and of works of philosophy and theology (81) there was also a broad representation of classics (27) and biblical and patristic literature (more than 50 works).

Parkes usefully summarises the effect of all this:

The late medieval book differs more from its early medieval predecessors than it does from the printed books of our own day. The scholarly apparatus which we take for granted – analytical table of contents, text disposed into books, chapters, and paragraphs, and accompanied by footnotes and index – originated in the applications of the notions of *ordinatio* and *compilatio* by writers, scribes, and the rubricators of the thirteenth, fourteenth, and fifteenth centuries. (1991, p. 66)

This is a key point, as we shall see when we consider hypertext. Medieval writers developed and used these research tools not as a result of the new technology of printing, but in response to the increasing demands of quantity and sophistication in the cognitive *materia* that they required to deal with.[17] They altered their own technology to deal with this.[18] But principally, there was a need in readers to order and search the greater quantities of complex materials with speed and precision; and writers responded to this.

Law, Reading and Writing

In the legal field, Clanchy gives evidence that the conventions of the form of medieval text were similar to that of other forms. He makes the point that Carruthers makes about the use to which medieval writers put signs in documents as ways to index and track the information in the document:

The use of a sign, like [a] hand with outstretched index finger, to mark a particular item in a document was a simple way of facilitating the retrieval of information. Such signs are not essentially different from the rubrics, capital letters, running titles, introductory paragraph flourishes, and other aids to the reader which are usual in medieval manuscripts. (1993, p. 172)

---

17 Contrary to the argument of Walter Ong, for whom the advent of printed books gave rise to indices and alphabetisation of arrangement. See Rouse and Rouse (1991, pp. 254–5).

18 For example, parchment was scraped thinner so as to allow for more pages within the same size of book; pens were used with a central point instead of an oblique, allowing for a more cursive, flowing hand and smaller letters – very useful when compiling a gloss to a main text (Petrucci, 1995, p. 196).

Clanchy effectively corroborates what Carruthers says about the importance of order on the page, and applies this generally to administrative and legal documents. He goes on to quote Hugh of St Victor, using Carruthers' translation and general approach:

> To fix something in the memory, it is of great value when we are reading to take pains to imprint (*imprimere*) on the memory through the imagination not only the number and order of the verses or sections in the books, but also at the same time the colour, shape, position and placement of the letters: where we saw this written down and where that; in what part (of the book) and in which place (on the page) we saw it positioned – whether at the top, in the middle, or near the bottom; in what colour we discerned the shape of a particular letter or the ornament on the surface of the parchment. I think there is nothing so effective for exciting the memory as meticulously paying attention to the surroundings of things (*circumstantias rerum*), to those features which can occur accidentally and externally. (1993, p. 172–3)

Hugh of St Victor is here giving reasons as to why books should be ornamented. As Clanchy points out, '[e]ven the most business-like manuscripts required some embellishment, in the form of rubrics and enlarged initials, to enable the user to find his place in the book' (1993, p. 280). He cites the Domesday Book as an example, with its 'vermilion paint for three distinct types of rubrication – capital letters for the names of shires and other headings; shading for the initial letter of each paragraph and certain abbreviations; underlining for the names of places and tenants' (1993, p. 280). He also cites more prosaic legal texts, namely parliamentary statutes in the Harvard Law Library collection, dating from 1290–1310. They contain a variety of devices, from illuminated initials, rubrics and figures which index contents (Clanchy cites 'a boar and a deer in a wood and a man shooting a deer with a longbow [which] accompany the text of the charter of the Forest' – 1993, p. 281).

As Clanchy and many other commentators on medieval reading and writing point out, these devices had mnemonic purposes:

> Learning by heart according to Hugh's method did not mean the oral repetition of phrases until their sounds became a recording, but the visual scanning of a page until its images were imprinted in the mind's eye like a photograph. The medieval schoolmen 'printed' books, before the invention of the mechanical process of printing, by scanning texts and accessing 'through the imagination' the pages imprinted on their minds. (1993, p. 173)

Clanchy cites an example of this – the system of Robert Grosseteste, chancellor of Oxford university and bishop of Lincoln. He devised a code of around 400 symbols, placed in margins, to identify and summarise topics: upturned V, crescent moons, dissecting lines and figures. As Clanchy puts it, 'Grosseteste located them on the pages he read in order to map his path through the thicket of scholastic texts' (1993, p.179). These marginal annotations are similar in their indexing effects to the plea roll clerks' 'practice of making annotations in the margins and cross-referencing entries' (1993, p.180).

Glossa

Unlike the *summa* which aimed to synopsise scholarship on various subjects, the *glossa* consisted of a main text written in a large hand (*textualis formata*) around which accreted comments or glosses, both marginal and interlinear. The method developed from the study of the Bible, and was used with texts which were designed to be authoritative, particularly within the context of university teaching.[19] In the thirteenth century in particular, this form of writing was one of the principal methods by which intellectual tradition and scholarship was altered *via* commentary and criticism. It is significant that the practice of the gloss dies with manuscript culture after the introduction of printed texts. It survives thereafter only in print form as a fossilised version: printed books were seldom laid out to be glossed.

The scholarly manuscript book in the thirteenth century and after was often laid out in a form which encouraged glossing: the main text was set in the middle of the page in a narrow column in large letters, with plenty of marginal space. The most sophisticated examples are glosses on the Bible, and on Canon and Roman law. Gratian's *Decretum* is fairly typical, and it is worthwhile to spend some time examining the form of the *Decretum* (c.1140) as an example of *glossa*.

Unlike the *Corpus Iuris Civilis*, whose sources are fairly uniform, canon law was the product of a variety of different source texts: sermons, patristic writings, letters, papal decretals, reported speeches, the Bible and many other writing forms. Many of these, particularly the older texts, were already embedded in other texts, often in variant readings. It would appear that Gratian worked from a comparatively small number of sources, many of them recent collections of canon law.[20] While the possibility of linking and cross-referencing these is almost infinite, the potential for textual corruption, variation and contradiction was everpresent. If Gratian's text were to live up to its name as the *Concordia Discordantium Canonum* it would have to harmonise the discordant texts. Gratian did so by providing a commentary upon his authorities called a *dicta* whenever there was contradiction, or whenever he required to link the sources together. The commentary reveals how coherent meaning can be derived from the authorities and, where there is contradiction, how the contradiction can be solved.

---

19 The existence of a gloss gave a text much more authority. As an instance of this, Carruthers cites the example of Boccaccio's romance epic *Teseid* which Boccaccio wrote in *textualis formata*, then added a commentary in a smaller hand to his own text. As Carruthers remarks, 'Boccaccio is both the originator of his text, and its reader; his own commentary invites commentary from others' (1990, p.218). By this, Boccaccio was claiming for his text 'the immediate institutional status of an "auctor"' (ibid.).

20 Gratian, 1993, p. xiii. In the following paragraphs I follow Thompson and Gordley's translation.

His text is divided into 3,800 texts or *capitula*, which are further gathered around *topoi* or *distinctiones*. Sometimes these *capitula* form sets of narrative, as with the 'fictional cases or *causae*' (Gratian, 1993, p. xiv). As described by Katharine Christensen in the Introduction to Gratian's text, they are

> designed to pose an interlocking set of questions about a given legal situation. Some are elaborate to the point of striking the modern reader as far-fetched, a sort of ultimate story problem, but every twist and turn proves significant as each question is dealt with in a series of capitula.

The logic and layout of Gratian's own text can be illustrated by taking an example – Part 2 of Distinction Eight (Gratian, 1993, pp. 24–8). It begins with a passage of *dicta* which, as well as introducing the particular subject of Part 2, also acts as a bridge between the first and second parts:

> Now natural law similarly prevails by dignity over custom and enactments. So whatever has been either received in usages or set down in writing is to be held null and void if it is contrary to natural law
> So, Augustine says in *Confessions*, III, viii:
> [quotation ...]
> Also, Pope Nicholas wrote to Hincmar, archbishop of Rheims:
> [quotation]
> Also, Augustine, in *On One Baptism* [...]
> [quotation]
> Also, Gregory wrote to Guitmund, bishop of Aversa:
> [quotation]
> Also, Augustine in *On Baptism I* [...]
> [quotation]
> Also in *On Baptism* [...]
> [quotation]
> Also, Cyprian to Pompey in the letter against Stephen:
> [quotation]
> Also, to Caecilian, in *Letters*, II,iii:
> [quotation]
> Thus it is obvious that custom is subordinate to natural law.

Set out like this, we can see the structure of this particular Distinction. In essence what we have is a dialogue set up by Gratian between his *topoi* and his sources. The resultant text is dialogic in a Bakhtinian sense, in that the authorities Gratian quotes are embedded within his argument. The quotations are rarely restatements of Gratian's *topos*, and thus there is a tension between the two forms of writing: we must look in the passage from Augustine or Gregory or Cyprian for the parallel that Gratian wants us to see.

Gratian's own text, however, attracted other commentators, who added their gloss to his text. This collection of comments, known as the 'Standard Gloss' (*Glossa Ordinaria*), stabilised about three-quarters of a century after Gratian wrote the original text, and was incorporated into future versions of the text. The comments, some anonymous, some signed with initials, were added around Gratian's text which came to occupy the centre of the page. The glosses themselves underwent small-scale revisions, supplementing each other, sometimes one gloss replacing another. The initial compilation of these glosses was carried out by the jurist Johannes Teutonicus, canon of Halberstadt, around 1215, and this was further revised around the mid-century by Bartholomaeus of Brescia. Other additions were made in the fourteenth century.[21]

All the glosses are referenced to the main text using *signa* so that the texts can be directly applied. The glosses form a variety of comment upon Gratian's dialogic text, turning it from a dialogue between Gratian and his sources into a multi-vocal conversation. The glossators corrected Gratian, commented upon his sources, added other sources which agreed or disagreed with his own, and they even argued with earlier commentators (Gratian, 1993, pp. xvii–xviii). We can see this in practice if we turn again to Distinction Eight. There, even in one Distinction, the glosses take a bewildering variety of forms. There are simple clarifications[22]; advance organisers[23]; contradictions[24]; elaborations of argument[25], and many more such devices. The glosses are distinguished from the main text not only by place on the page, but also by letterforms. The main text, written in large *textualis*

---

21   Gratian (1993, p. xvii). See also Duggan (1963, pp. 18–19).

22   For example, gloss to 'those' in the first *dicta* of Part 1: 'that is, the Apostles'.

23   That is to say, statements which synopsise what Gratian is about to expound in detail. The gloss on Part 2, for instance states 'He states that natural law differs from others in dignity, for an enactment or custom contrary to it is void. He proves this in the following *capitula*'.

24   For example, gloss on *capitulum* 2: 'It says in this capitulum that offences against human conventions are to be avoided so that the agreement of the people and the customs of the society be observed and no violated by anyone but enjoy perpetual validity. If, however, God commands something contrary to agreement or custom, then he should be obeyed. For if a king is to be obeyed in his kingdom or city, much more is the king of all creatures to be obeyed.'

25   For example, the gloss on 'law' from Augustine, 'For according to divine law 'The earth is the Lord's and the fullness thereof [Ps.23:1]': 'So it appears that something is possessed not by divine law but by human law alone. To the contrary is C.23 q.7c.1, where it says that something is possessed by divine law. But this is not contrary because it says there that all heresy may be raised against a claim for restitution. Note that it is not licit for a heretic to possess anything. C.23 q 5 c.35; C.23 q.7 c.1; C.23 q.7 c.2. Also, it may be argued from this text that when there is a claim for restitution, we must ask by what law the claim is made: by an interdict or by the authority of the court. Also, a claimant is obliged to explain the basis of his claim and what action is brought under canon law. X 2.1.15; X 2.3.3, notwithstanding X 2.1.6. The solution, I believe, is that the basis and the kind of action must be given so that the judge can make a decision according to the kind of action. X 5 3.31. Nevertheless, one is not compelled to specify an action, for according to [civil] ordinance the basis alone is sufficient. Cod. 6.33.3. Bar.' (Gratian, 1993, p. 24). The abbreviation 'Bar.' stands for 'Bartholomaeus Brixiensis'.

formata, is surrounded by commentary in a smaller hand. This had considerable mnemonic potential, much more so than a printed page without rubrics or any other form of functional lemmata. As Carruthers puts it,

> the glossed format seems deliberately designed to present memorable variations of letters ... and colours, for each page is unique. These different hands became conventionally used for these different kinds of text; the large hand developed into fully-formed Gothic script; the small squatter hand was used for commentary, even in books that did not reproduce a source text. Clearly, they were used to form a visual cue to the sort of text with which one was dealing.[26]

It has been said that glosses are really a form of footnotes. Christensen, for instance, describes the *Glossa Ordinaria* as 'more like a series of footnotes than a continuous text' (Gratian, 1993, p. xvii). The likeness is clearly there, but only in a limited sense. Modern footnotes are clearly *parataxis*. They support the main text in a variety of ways, but they seldom seek to replace or argue with *taxis*. Our expectations of footnotes and their functions are based upon this subordinate role; and their place on the page (in the great majority of texts at the bottom of the page or relegated to a section at the end of a chapter or the end of the book) reflects this. The *glossae* which surround Gratian's text, however, are quite different. They use the first person at times, and they use many different forms, some of which we have seen. We can never be sure what attitude the next *glossa* will take towards Gratian's text. The result is not a footnote: more a collection of critical commentaries. But here again we must beware unhistorical readings of medieval attitudes towards scholarship. Gratian's glossators were highly respectful of his achievement. More often than not, they elaborate his original *dicta* or his authorities. This is one of the reasons why they surround his text on the page, and are written, as Carruthers observed generally of *glossae*, in a smaller hand. Christensen is right to say that the *Glossa Ordinaria* 'makes very little sense if read in isolation' from Gratian's text (Gratian, 1993, p. xx): once again, we can see in medieval reading and writing the extent to which the text was authoritative in that it generated ongoing commentary.[27] In this sense the *glossa* had no close parallel in forms of information presentation until the video age. Perhaps the closest comparison might be the voice-over video technique, which achieves for us a seamlessness with regard to the visual material that the gloss achieves with its accompanying *textura*.[28]

---

26 Carruthers, (1990, pp. 215–16, referring to de Hamel, 1986, pp. 36–7).

27 As in the example of Boccaccio in footnote 19 above.

28 One must of course be aware of the extent to which glossators prescribed their own production of gloss comment. Gloss production was not limitless. There grew up conventions and rules regarding what could be glossed, which depended on rules contained within an authoritative text itself – see for example *Corpus Iuris Civilis*, D50.16–17. As Maclean points out, it is clear that 'conservative forces were at work to preserve technical vocabulary and the terms of debate from change; and that the realm of law and

The gloss, of course, was not a perfect tool of analysis and comment. The effort to squeeze more and more information onto the page could lead commentators or scribes to reduce the gloss to a series of obscure abbreviated comments. Furthermore, glossators were well aware of the form's limitations as a text of full authority. By the end of the twelfth century, in fact, scholars were beginning to appreciate the importance of the text in its context and the greater authoritativeness this gave the glossed extracts.[29] As Carruthers and others point out, glossed texts were frequently institutional in nature, and used by students at university. Carruthers, following de Hamel, points out the extent to which glossed texts were used as teaching texts: consequently those which were glossed tended to be institutional, highly authoritative texts, to which not only a *glossa ordinaria* would be attached, but which would have ruled margins in which readers could append their own marginalia and *notulae*.[30]

Quite apart from the difficulty of deciphering complex abbreviated Latin abbreviations so typical of glosses, the visual effect is, for modern readers, bewildering at first, then enriching. It is so because there is a multiplicity of voices all speaking on the same page. This multivocality is typical of the experience of reading a gloss, and the adjacency of gloss to text actually increases this experience. Usually a modern text will only include different voices in a critical edition of a work. There, the critical apparatus will be restricted to the bottom of the page or the end of the chapter or even a separate volume. The physical separation emphasises the critical distance, which is enforced by copyright law and culture. To have the glossators' comments cheek-by-jowl with Gratian's words emphasises, to a modern reader at least, the closeness of the community of scholarship and its engagement with Gratian's text.

As a convention of reading, juxtaposition was a common device. Petrucci points to it when he traced from late antique Mediterranean culture the form of the early medieval 'miscellany in which several texts of different authors are more or less coherently juxtaposed in a single container' (1995, p. 1) Carruthers highlights another aspect of the miscellany, the *florilegium*, which she defined as a 'compilation of extracts and maxims derived from the great writers of the past

---

legal interpretation operated as a coherent and recognizable practice' (Maclean, 1992, pp. 139–40). Maclean argues for continuity between interpretive rules in medieval and Renaissance texts, between glossatorial and Ramist systems: see 1992, pp. 85; 103–4; 107; 112; 122–3.

29 As Rouse and Rouse exemplify: 'Geoffre of Auxerre describes how Gilbert of Poitiers, in his defence at the consistory of Reims in 1148, arrived armed with the *codices integri*, to the consternation of Bernard and his other accusers who had brought with them only a sheet of extracts as their documentation; and the accusers returned, the next day, equipped with their own whole texts' (Rouse and Rouse, 1992, p. 216).

30 Carruthers, 1990, pp. 214–18, following de Hamel, 1984; 1986.

... [which was] basically the contents of someone's memory, set forth as a kind of study-guide for the formation of others' memories' (1990, p. 174).[31]

These concepts of adjacency and dialogue and of close contiguity in scholarship between text and reader are oddly aslant our own textual culture. Brian Stock, for example, demonstrates how, in Eadmer's description of Anselm's compositional practices, the central activity was that of dialogue between Anselm and his brethren, then between Anselm and his readers. Carruthers dwells upon this important point to illustrate the differences between medieval and modern reading habits. She quotes Eadmer at length, and it is worthwhile considering this passage for the view that it gives us of the medieval concept of the text:

> This work [the *Proslogion*] came into the hands of someone [Gaunilo] who found fault with one of the arguments in it, judging it to be unsound. In an attempt to refute it he wrote a treatise against it and attached this to the end of Anselm's work. A friend sent this to Anselm who read it with pleasure, expressed his thanks to his critic and wrote his reply to the criticism. He had this reply attached to the treatise which had been sent to him, and returned it to the friend from whom it had come, desiring him and others who might deign to have his little book to write out at the end of it the criticism of his argument and his own reply to the criticism.[32]

The idea of one copyrighted, integral work which cannot be copied or added to, the intellectual property of the text as a legal entity which can be purchased and sold and litigated upon – all this is very far from Anselm's view of his text and his readers. The appended critical work is treated by Anselm henceforth as an integral part of his own text. It is so for two reasons: it is seen by Anselm as a rigorous examination of his argument and therefore worthy to be included (and I think we can take his pleasure in this as unfeigned). Secondly, as Carruthers succinctly puts it, for a medieval writer, 'a text achieves full authority not by closing debate but by accumulating it' (1990, p. 213). In so doing, it achieves originality in the eyes of its readers. The concept is highly reader-centred and strikingly different from a modern view of criticism and commentary. Had Anselm and Gaunilo been modern writers, Gaunilo would have written a separate article or book, to which Anselm would have replied and incorporated into the second edition of his own text, in a preface, in footnotes or in textual revisions. In the medieval manuscript, however, Gaunilo becomes Anselm's 'co-equal reader' (1990, p. 213) because what matters is not the writer, but the reader-centred text and its place in the community of readers.

In his account of the art of teaching and learning the law, the lawyer Franciscus de Zabarellis (1360–1417 – Zabarella for short) gives us insights

---

31 She gives the example of *De universo of Rhabanus Maurus*, which she describes as 'a web of *interpretationes* of the various matters relevant to Scripture, arranged by keywords that are themselves organized not alphabetically but "logically" (starting with God and the angels)' (1990, p. 175).

32 Carruthers (1990, p. 212), quoting Southern (1963, p. 31).

into how one community, a university class, used glosses.[33] He advised teachers that they should start with the statement of the law, then introduce glosses and commentaries later in a lecture series, rather than overwhelm students with too much detail at the start of any lecture series; and to recapitulate and illustrate points so that students had the opportunity to annotate their texts at points of difficulty (Morrissey, 1989, pp. 27–33).[34] To students, he recommended studying directly from sources, rather than using secondary textual materials; finding more experienced students who could act as mentors (and becoming mentors themselves); developing good memory for text, but not being obsessed with memorising everything; knowing principles that could apply to complex and subtle problems; living a life of moderation (like Ferguson, he quotes Horace – *Epistles*, II); having a knowledge of moral philosophy, and being men of faith and prayer (Morrissey, 1989, pp. 33–7).

It is clear that the gloss technique allowed the writers to define themselves as a community of writers whose tradition and communicational technique and method was defined by the gloss. Students learned the gloss technique by actually doing it for themselves, constructing their own mini-glosses. Zabarella's text is fifteenth century, but it surely recapitulates principles of teaching and learning with glossed texts that good teachers and students would have followed for generations.

Hypertext and the Wireless Web

Hypertext: Definition and Experience

As Dillon has pointed out, ICT has emerged so swiftly from its cluster of related disciplines that it has not had time to develop 'a robust intellectual tradition' (2004, p. 138). Nevertheless, if there is a common theme to the many texts on computers and writing it is that the space in which writing is performed is important to its meaning. This is as true of medieval writings as it is of computerised text. Furthermore, medieval writers were as aware of the concept of writing space and

---

33 See Morrissey (1989, pp. 27–74). This consists of an Introduction by the editor, Morrissey, together with a text of the tract and critical apparatus. Zabarella spent 25 years teaching at Florence and Padua until called as a cardinal (Morrissey, 1989, p. 27). Morrissey's Introduction is a graphic account of medieval teachers and learners. From it we learn that Zabarella, as well as being a highly-regarded legal counsellor and spokesman, was popular with students – 'when in early 1408 Venice planned to send him as part of an embassy to the Duke of Savoy, the students proclaimed that they wanted him to stay home to teach them and protested so violently that his appointment was cancelled' (Morrissey, 1989, p. 28).

34 Morrissey cites Odofredus, a thirteenth-century commentator on Roman law, to illustrate that what Zabarella advocated was standard practice. See also Haskins (1923, pp. 42–6).

the arrangement of text within that space as word-processor users are nowadays. As Carruthers puts it

> from earliest times medieval educators had as visual and spatial an idea of *locus* as any Ramist had, which they inherited continuously from antiquity, and indeed that concern for the lay-out of memory governed much in medieval education designed to aid the mind in forming and maintaining heuristic formats that are both spatial and visualizable. (1990, p. 32)

Concern for order and layout have occupied commentators on the web, too – not just those concerned with web layout and design, but at a deeper level those who are concerned with what the experience of hypertext actually does to our concepts and practices of reading and writing. There are of course many obvious differences between *glossa* and hypertexts. Volume of materials stored, speed and method of retrieval, presentation on-screen are three of the major changes to manuscript culture that change the context utterly. Nevertheless, hypertext takes over some of the functions of the glossatorial method, principally adjacency and interaction *via* annotation in the text; and in this section of the chapter we shall explore the concept of hypertext and explore its use in social software.[35]

Hypertext has been defined many times and the chief components of most definitions are the presence of nodes and links. The literary critic and early theorist of hypertext applications, George Landow defined it elegantly as 'an information technology consisting of individual blocks of text, or lexias, and the electronic links that join them' (Landow, 1994, p. 1). This duality of stasis and kinesis can be identified in most of the evolutionary literature of hypertext, even from the earliest texts.[36] It is a duality which is at the heart of all hypertextual activity. But if it seems rather elementary to us now, more than a decade after the early browsers opened up the web for us, we still need to bear in mind Margaret Smith's comments above regarding the relationship of incunabula to manuscript culture. In many ways, the web's relationship with earlier forms of media is uneasy: as a new form of information presentation, it requires to develop *out of* the rhetorical structures and expectations set up by almost half a millennium of text production and usage by readerships.

---

35 The term 'social software' is generally attributed to Clay Shirky, who defined it as follows: 'Social software, software that supports group communications, includes everything from the simple CC: line in email to vast 3D game worlds like *EverQuest*, and it can be as undirected as a chat room, or as task-oriented as a wiki (a collaborative workspace). Because there are so many patterns of group interaction, social software is a much larger category than things like groupware or online communities – though it includes those things, not all group communication is business-focused or communal. One of the few commonalities in this big category is that social software is unique to the internet in a way that software for broadcast or personal communications are not' (Shirky, 2003).

36 See Bush (1945, pp. 101–8), Nelson (1965) and Engelbart (1988).

Early research on applications analysed the extent to which hypertext actually enabled learning and understanding of complex intellectual materials. Landow, for instance, made the claim that hypertext enables active learning (Landow, 1992, p. 121).[37] Others, however, questioned whether hypertext can do this, and if it can, under what conditions it might do so. Jonathan Smith, for instance, observed that in using Landow's teaching and research tool, *The Dickens Web*, his students 'often struggled just to process the material at the two ends of a link, and hence they tended to see the abyss rather than the bridge' (Smith, 1996, p. 125).[38] Smith did report that students' learning improved, but from his own experience in the use of *The Dickens Web* he argues that 'students must be taught how to read hypertextually' (1996, p. 128) and, if they are expected to *write* in hypertext, this needs to be learned as well (1996, p. 126, my emphasis). His point about writing is of course borne out by the culture of glossed manuscripts. The culture of this particular textual form had to be learned by writers: like all genres, there was nothing in it natural or innately comprehensible. Its symbols and structures were powerful learning tools; but they needed to be mastered before they could be used effectively.

Others have supported this point of view. In a trenchant article, McKendree et al. point out that to draw analogies between the experience of hypertext connectedness and structures of the brain or the mind is to fall into a version of the homeopathic fallacy. As they point out, hypertext is an effective learning tool when it 'makes explicit the connections between chunks of information in the domain'. However, they make it clear that comprehension of these connections is 'contingent upon the learner processing the links in a meaningful way. ... merely moving from one screen to another is unlikely to give the learner any insight as to the implied connection between the two screens' (McKendree et al., 1995, pp. 74–82).

Underlying these criticisms of hypertext is the awareness that reading and writing in hypertext is different from reading and writing books and requires us to learn quite different skills from those we have developed in order to understand the products of our print culture. But those skills, as many volumes of research into teaching and learning with technology point out, can be the basis for much

---

37 Landow's work has been seminal in the development not only of hypertextual pedagogical applications, but in literary theory as well. For examples of his work, both theory and practice, see his collection of websites.

38 A similar but more detailed description of the use to which one class put the Perseus Project can be found in Martin (1995). Martin's conclusions are similar to Smith's: 'the greatest challenge for me as teacher remains, it seems, to model for them the behavior in doing research as discovery and as expression of that discovery that I take for granted in my own life .... My conclusion ... is that Perseus gave them a chance to learn how to learn as researchers in texts. They still need lots more practice at it, to be sure. ... In reality, however, Perseus gave them the boost they needed to learn to learn by discovering and then making sense of what they discovered.'

learning from e-learning and multimedia applications. Collaborative learning, for instance, finds considerable support in the research literature.[39]

Hypertext does not only link up pages of text. Hyperlinks can of course be used to link graphics and pictures, sound and video. In the realm of hypermedia, particularly on the web, it is rare for one author to be responsible for all aspects of the production and mounting of materials. Teams of authors and web programmers frequently work together to produce the final product: 'the electronic environment is a rich context in which doing work and sharing work become virtually indistinguishable' (Bikson and Eveland, 1990, p. 286). These team productions frequently raise problems of authorship, as this is defined in the traditional, book-centred sense of the word. Landow describes this well when he narrates the process by which he and at least ten others created the graphic overviews of *The Dickens Web* (Landow, 1992, pp. 99–100). As he concludes:

> Hypertext has no authors in the conventional sense. Just as hypertext as an educational medium transforms the teacher from a leader into a kind of coach or companion, hypertext as a writing medium metamorphoses the author into an editor or developer. Hypermedia, like cinema and video or opera, is a team production. (1992, p. 100)

Or, we might add, like a thirteenth-century *glossa ordinaria*, with its multiple authors, its implicit indebtedness which makes the concept of quotation and the device of quotation marks almost irrelevant. The tools of the *glossa ordinaria*, whatever the subject-matter, compare well with the advice of our own contemporary cognitive science – they embody many of the guidelines to good reading practice and page layout, including the classic three or four column format so often used on web pages. What is interesting, though, is how much these tools are needed in the situation of the computer and the internet. In word-processed documents viewed on-screen, for example, there is little or no sense of page, only a perpetually scrolling document. Page breaks are marked weakly, but do not contribute to the sense of a page in the traditional sense. The same could be said of a page on the web, where pages exist without the contraints of books or book bindings and their parataxis such as title page, etc. In these situations, it is all the more important to use the type of mnemotechnic and placing devices to which medieval readers and writers were accustomed and which, as we shall see, we are beginning to recover through the revolution known as social software.

Hypertext, Social Software and Communities

If hypertext can seem to exemplify many aspects of the glossed literature of the thirteenth century, the analogy between medieval page and wireless web must surely be a tenuous one. And yet I am not sure that this is the case. There are striking parallels in the ways we use media in order to achieve the same ends of

---

39 See for example Crook (1994) and Laurillard (1992 and 2002).

community-readership, community-interpretation and the creation of professional knowledge tools; and in particular, those applications we know as 'social software' or 'social bookmarking' tools.[40] These include applications based on file-sharing and peer-to-peer networks wherein users can share audio files (Napster, Kazaa, podcasts), pictures (Picasa, Flikr), textual information (blogs and wikis) and hypertext links themselves (del.icio.us, Furl).[41] A useful constellation of the phrase's meanings (about the closest we can get to a definition) is provided by Tom Coates in a discussion on his blog.[42] Social software:

1   remov[es] the real-world limitations placed on social and / or collaborative behaviour by factors such as language, geography, background, financial status and so on [...];

2   compensat[es] for human inadequacies in processing, maintaining or developing social and / or collaborative mechanisms[...];

3   creat[es] environments or distributed tool-sets that pull useful end results out of human social and / or collaborative behaviour. (Coates, 2003)

Social software of course was not the first type of application to enable communication between users within a computer environment. But what is significant about this genre of software is that the interchange between individual and social networks implicit in this definition takes place within a space of production which, to quote Lefebvre, is critical to the success of the application. Social software appropriates connectivity: the space of connection becomes a *detournement*, in Lefebvre's terms, a re-use of the concept of connection, and in so doing a cultural re-definition of possible connections and their social outcomes (Lefebvre, 1991).[43] This networking phenomenon is not based on file applications, but on the concept of linkage and communication itself: ease of linkage according to one's communicational needs and the needs of one's audience are critical markers of success. In the next chapter we shall investigate another *detournement*, namely how such a space can be adapted to simulations. For now, though, it is sufficient for social software to observe the close relationship between code and personal communications. The success of Friends Reunited and Genes Reunited is based on this. Friendster, an early version of friendship networks, has recently

---

40   There are numerous discussions of this on the web. See for example www. onewisdom.pbwiki.com/SocialSoftware.

41   http://www.napster.co.uk/; http://www.kazaa.com/us/index.htm; http; http://audio. weblogs.com/; http://picasa.google.com/; http://www.flickr.com/; http://del.icio.us/; http:// www.furl.net/.

42   The term 'blog' derives from weblog, and is attributed to an early blogger, Jorn Barger.

43   First published 1974, Lefebvre's concept of detournement was derived from earlier Situationist definitions – see the first issue of their journal, *Internationale Situationniste*, 1958. It also derives from Lefebvre's reading of Marx and of course Georg Lukacs' seminal *History and Class Consciousness*.

been eclipsed by MySpace, which allows more personalised communication than Friendster. As a commentator in *Business Week* noted, quoting an early investor in MySpace, 'we just realized that to allow people more personalization and control would give people more attachment to their web pages'.[44]

As expressed thus, the concept is very different from *glossa* at first glance. While a user's MySpace home page may have mnemonic functions for any particular user, its primary aim is self-expression and sharing of personal data. And yet, at a deep level MySpace succeeds because it forms a space filled with intuitive tools for content-sharing and communications between user and audience.

Perhaps the most profound implication of the social software revolution in recent years is the implicit acknowledgement in these tools that the web is an immeasurably complex ecology, one composed of people, practices, values and technologies (Nardi and O'Day, 1999). A number of qualities mark it out from previous use of hypertext systems such as the early *Dickens Web*. First, the system is not merely based upon code, but also upon inter-relationships and dependencies of those taking part. For this reason locality, not in a topographical sense alone, but more in Bourdieu's sense of *habitus*, is crucial.[45] Secondly, applications typical of this ecology depend on users creating and sharing content. Users can, for instance, construct a 'lens' which can filter or aggregate content from other sources; they can measure content crudely by a 'tag cloud', in which links with more data attached to them appear as larger-sized text – they become in effect a form of *textura*. Throughout the functionality of this tool, as with blogs, there is a concern to compress information and to present it in as manageable a form as possible. Size of text is one device for doing so. In blogs, 'post continuation' is another, where extended posts can appear on the blog as their first couple of lines only, and if the user wishes to read on, he or she clicks a 'More' button.

Some social software applications support a pictorial view of knowledge – see for example CmapTools which offers shareable concept maps – one might compare the thumbnail illustrations within initial letters and other uses of colour and diagrammatic techniques in medieval manuscripts.[46] Illustrations within glossed manuscripts and other medieval manuscripts of course related tightly to

---

44 http://www.friendsreunited.co.uk/?li=f; http://www.genesreunited.co.uk/genesreunited.asp?wci=yourhome; http://www.friendster.com/; http://www.myspace.com/. The quotation derives from http://www.businessweek.com/ap/financialnews/D8FNN7JG0.htm?campaign_id=apn_home_down&chan=db.

45 The term is an important element of his theory of social and cultural reproduction, referring to socially acquired and embodied systems of dispositions (Bourdieu and Passeron, 1977).

46 See http://cmap.ihmc.us/. Event visualisation is another form of graphical information tool. See Chung et al. (2005). The article includes a table of event visualisation tools and techniques. For two examples of event visualisation in courts, see the Bloody Sunday Inquiry at http://www.bloody-sunday-inquiry.org.uk, and the DVD compiled by the Prosecution for jurors in the Soham murder trial, described at http://www.guardian.co.uk/soham/story/0,14010,1108312,00.html.

textual content, often with a mnemonic function. Illustrations used in concept maps have similar functions.

But it is the wiki and the blog which offer perhaps the closest parallels to *glossa* communities and forms of thought and action. As Butterfield (2005) points out, blogs and wikis express a number of fundamental qualities that distinguish them from other forms of communication on the web, namely direct forms of personal/ professional identity; a high awareness of the presence of others for whom writers write; relationships that can develop between writers; and the coalescing of groups that emerge from these relationships. Wiki production, often carried out by a widespread team of authors working within a community context, in a number of important ways returns us to the knowledge community of the gloss, where text production is collaborative, shared across the web of meaning and aimed at the creation of an explanatory text.[47]

Blogs, like glosses, are dynamic, in that they link and comment but, of course, the speed of blog information travel is exponentially faster than the webs of glosses. Communicative devices between writers and audiences includes comments, trackbacks, RSS, permalinks, blog indices and such like. These link discussions all over the web and its 'blogosphere'.[48] The links can be syndicated and aggregated, using special software that allows users to track concepts and discussions without moving in and out of bookmarking software or different applications. The blog page shares many of the basic qualities of a gloss – going to another text, embedded links, text as adjacent commentary, compression of textual meaning, the proliferation of commentary, and both the dispersal and reconfiguration of meaning. This of course is in the nature of hypertext: it both divides and separates meanings, and brings them together again in new contexts. Landow's use of the term 'lexia' points to how this can be so. Landow derives it from Roland Barthes's *S/Z*, from a passage in which Barthes describes a new way of reading text, one that breaks up hitherto accepted rhetorical structures within

---

For examples of initial letter foliation and interlinear illustration, see the Fitzwilliam Museum, http://www.fitzmuseum.cam.ac.uk/gallery/CambridgeIlluminations/images/ works/LRG/FM_ms251_fol54v_LRG.htm. The image is zoomable – glossators would have loved this tool, but they may also have had reservations about its capacity to distort the mnemonic value of the page.

47 Wikipedia is of course the classic example – http://en.wikipedia.org/wiki/Main_ Page. Wikis are the subject of vast commentary on the web. See for example http://www. willatworklearning.com/2005/12/are_wikis_inher.html.

48 And there are of course tools that index topics and themes – see http://www. bloglines.com/, a personal news aggregator, or Technorati, http://www.technorati.com/, which is a real-time search engine that tracks blogs in the blogosphere, can monitor the community and inform bloggers. According to a Pew Internet study carried out in spring 2003, already by then about 11 per cent of internet users were regular blog readers (http:// www.pewinternet.org/PPF/r/113/report_display.asp). The figure now is much greater – according to Technorati data, there are, at time of writing (25 February 2007) around 1.6 million posts daily – see http://www.technorati.com/about/.

texts, and which therefore disturbs reading conventions: '[the text] will be cut up into a series of brief, contiguous fragments, which we shall call *lexias*, since they are units of reading'.[49] Landow's use of lexia is different from Barthes's, of course, and probably less radical; but he uses Barthes's concept to emphasise a similar transformation in terms of the dispersal and fragmentation that text undergoes when it becomes both gloss and blog text.

Rip, Mix and Burn: The Hermeneutic Hypertext

The study of law bears significant parallels to literary hermeneutics as these are practiced in literary criticism and biblical studies. In all three, the habit of cross-referencing texts is deeply embedded in the conceptual meta-skills of the discipline. In their own domain, lawyers collate statutes chronologically; they compare cases, contrast and debate judgements. Textual comparison is a key skill in all of this. Hypertext supports this type of cross-referencing. What one early researcher, David Johnson, said about hypertext in the practice of law applies even more so to academic law –

> Lawyers think naturally in hypertext. Their fondness for footnotes and cross references indicates their healthy awareness of the potential complexity of any real legal issue … Hypertext systems will provide the tools with which – or rather in which – lawyers will embody their expertise so as to make it much more suitable for easy distribution to and use by others.[50]

But if lawyers think 'naturally' in hypertext, and while hypertext has been used to build extensive commercial databases such as Westlaw and LexisNexis, little has been done to allow users to annotate web text with the intuitive fluency with which glossators could add to a gloss. High-quality interpretive tools are needed if the hermeneutic potential of the web is to be realised. We need to create for our students the ability to create their own web gloss, add their own notes, share notes, and link to others' glosses. In the thirteenth century this created, as we have seen, a sense of authority, community, discussion and debate around texts such as Gratian's *Decretals* which stimulated further discussion and learning. The comment on a text which one launches out into a public electronic arena is very different from paper-based publication of commentary, and also from the private comments sent to an individual; and for these reasons, spaces for virtual comment rarely of themselves encourage comment, and rely upon social and communicational context to stimulate response. Vellum, by contrast, is a much more intimate medium for communication: there is privacy, individual contribution and, when the text is circulated, community discussion. The very slowness of communication can help to build a community of practice – an

---

49 Barthes (1970, p. 13, cited Landow, 1992, pp. 52–3).
50 Staudt (1991, p. 183).

'interpretive community' in which the constant movement of discipline shifts and boundaries within the community helps to create and – in a Foucauldian sense – discipline the texts which are produced.[51]

There are also a number of valuable insights we can derive for the form of teaching resources and learning contexts. Glossed literature, as we have seen, sprang from a recognition of an emerging community of texts and of authors who wished to comment upon the texts. Balanced between the stasis of the *textura* and the kinetic energy of the *glossa*, the manuscripts were powerful learning and teaching tools. But contemporary universities are only now coming to terms with the social software revolution and its consequences for learning theory and practice. As a number of researchers have noted, social software promotes connectivist models of learning and teaching, which are in direct opposition to transmissive modes of teaching.[52] It also promotes a learner-centred view of a curriculum, rather than a teacher- or administrator-centred view. Many of our current learning management systems (LMSs) in use in universities, for instance are built around an institutional view of learning: web sites are organised in a drill-down structure into course or programme pages organised centrally, by faculty or department, which in turn subdivide into class or module pages, with resources posted by academics who lead the module, with forums managed by the institution/academics; and where students have minimal ability to alter or interact with the online resources. To be sure, the ability to read and download such resources at a distance from campus contributes to flexibility of learning; but the structure of the LMS is still highly institutional. A learner-centred view of resources, knowledge, tasks and assessments would involve much more interaction and the ability of students to design their own learning environments, in much the same way as they can design MySpace, or Google's personalised home page, or their own blogs and wikis.

Central to the process of engaging with complex legal texts in such an environment would be the ability to gloss a text online with both interlinear and marginal notes; for those notes to be shareable with staff and other students, and to be set out in a number of different levels as well as different views.[53] The creation of such software is still in its infancy – Internet Explorer's current annotation functionality is hardly a promising start. When using this and similar tools, it is hard not to avoid the conclusion that, in this function at least, the internet has a lot to learn from the sophistication and streamlined simplicity of the *glossa ordinaria*.

---

51 See also Stock (1983) and his concept of 'textual communities', which maintain collective memory and empower certain people within them and can, on occasion, help people to challenge authority.

52 See for example the Connectionist community – Siemens' blog at http://www. elearnspace.org/ is a good example of the approach.

53 This point is further explored in Chapter 9.

That conclusion is drawn not just from the study of how graphics, layout and textual solutions were converged and adopted by glossators within the constraints of their technologies, culture and economy, but is also driven by the potential of the contemporary web to converge data. The problem for us now is that so much needs to integrate in order to give us the seamless functionality we wish for. The social software revolution will take us so far; but we need to go further. If I have a phone conversation with a colleague about virtual towns on the web I may want to integrate that conversation with a blog or a research paper, or extract concepts and search for further scholarly information on the topic on the web. Any of these activities would currently involve different hardware, different file formats, and the transfer of data across separate applications. The web is hardly seamless. The concept of rip, mix and burn, so influential in the contemporary music industry, and long since applied to the film industry (particularly in DVD formats) must be applied to legal education as well, and across data formats. Academic text publishers have only recently learned that it can make economic sense to allow consumers to read the portion of the book that they need, rather than compel them to buy a conceptual structure that arose in Renaissance economies and served it and Ramist pedagogies well, but now is a stop against change and innovation.

But 'read' is precisely the wrong term here: reading is merely the start of what one might want to do with data. If learners are interested in information they almost inevitably will want to *do* something with it, pull it into their own webs and structures so that that information can become useful knowledge. How might students create social webs of meaning? How might they share data, be part of a learning community online, enable seamless flow between scholarly study resources and other webs such as e-portfolios? The concepts of 'mashups' and filters expresses this well: a remix of data formats, and a dynamic re-interpretation, for both personal and community purposes, of information and knowledge, which also uses filtering technologies to strain out irrelevant data and capture the key information required by a user – these are critical creative and data-handling tools that web users require to survive and thrive in the data-rich streams of the internet.[54]

Summary

The ability to reflect on changes in the technology of reading and writing is not limited to our own times. In his study of orality and literacy in early German texts Green points out that in 1471 Guillaume Fichet, reflecting on the technologies of reading and writing, divided them into three periods: that of the *calamus* or reed pen (classical antiquity), that of the *penna* or quill pen (medieval literacy) and that

---

54 For interesting examples at time of writing, see Google Apps and particularly Yahoo! Pipes, described at Cubrilovic (2007).

of the *aereae litterae*, the recently-developed 'movable type'. Green observes that Fichet's divisions parallel the divisions of Walter J. Ong's argument, developed more than half a millennia later, regarding the nature of communications shifts, and points out that both Fichet and Ong develop their arguments precisely because they write close to a nodal point in the communications shift (Green, 1994, p. 1).

To many of us now it might appear as if we are undergoing a revolution in communications as we move from analogue to digital cultures, as computing becomes ever more intelligent, ambient and pervasive within our culture, and as more sophisticated versions of the web emerge as practical realities.[55] But as I hope I have shown in this chapter, much of what we do today in web-based communications has its analogue in earlier technologies used throughout the last millennium.

Glossed manuscripts developed over a long period of time, out of the need for a form that would facilitate information comprehension, collation, interpretation and dissemination given a huge corpus of primary and secondary materials. Medieval scholars faced their own equivalent of Barnett's 'supercomplexity' (Barnett, 1999). Supercomplexity still eclipses the rudimentary tools we have available to us to navigate and use the web effectively.[56] Social software is beginning to develop the user interfaces we need, together with the underlying code such as RSS and codec. The latter (COder-DECoder) is a software application that permits a computer to display or to create a compressed media file. It does so by removing what it decides are unnecessary audio and visual data from the media

---

55 See for example Ferscha and Mattern (2004). The semantic web is one solution to the massive size of information on the web and the accessing and storage of that information (the term 'semantic web' was first coined by Berners-Lee et al., 2001). Currently, search engines syntactically match a user's query to web pages or services. Many of these, however, are semantically incorrect or irrelevant to the user's purposes. The semantic web adds semantic data to web content, such that software agents can recognise web resources with greater clarity. Applications will also be able to manipulate potentially huge quantities of data much faster. See for instance Glaser et al., 2004.

56 The research being undertaken into such tools and their HCIs is substantial. For examples, see Cockburn and McKenzie (2004), where results showed that the addition of a third-dimension to computer displays did not aid users' spatial memory; Padovani and Lansdale (2003), where the authors argue that 'navigation tools are mediating structures for activities, such as bookmarking and learning the structure of the site, which represent cognitive investment for future retrieval. In this view, user performance is optimized by the balance of two potentially antagonistic conditions. First, the usability of tools and metaphor must free cognitive resources for planning; but also, the difficulty of the task and the need for planning must remain visible to the user'. See also Watters et al. (2003). See also Pearson and van Schaik (2003), which contains a helpful review of the research on web interactive design and where the authors reported that evidence was found amongst users 'to support the conjecture that experienced Internet users might have formed automatic attention responses to specific web page designs'.

file, and so reducing the size of the streamed file. One might compare this with the medieval glossed page, similarly a technological feat of compression.

Between the different writing and reading technologies of *volumen*, manuscript codex, printed book and electronic screen, it is axiomatic that we find it difficult to anticipate and cope with the problems and advantages of the new technology. One of the reasons for this could be that it is so difficult to understand the cognitive ground of our own technology. If the present is difficult to understand, with all the information about communication we have at our disposal, our understanding of the mentality of past readers and writers from the evidence of the technology available to us is even more difficult. Often, as a result of this difficulty, we treat past reading and writing technologies less as technology and more as museum curiosities: cuneiform, hieroglyphs, *scriptio continuo*, illuminated and glossed manuscripts. But as we have seen, each stage of reading and writing in the past represents attempts to come to grips with similar cognitive problems of conceptualisation of thought and communication, similar cultural and economic problems of coping with communicational volume and collaborative networks. The study of glosses, as with other forms of information capture, storage and retrieval, still holds valuable models for us in our own times.

It is essential that we engage in this study of past and present, the to-fro movement of which is exemplified so well by the epigraph quoted from Fitzgerald's novel. This book is being written, still, within the print-digital shift, but we have much less time to come to terms with the new environment. The changeover period in the fifteenth century from manuscript to print, in which print established itself as a major communications channel, extended across two generations. If we date the rise of electronic communications *via* hypertext not from Vannevar Bush's prophetic 1945 article, but from the rise of the Internet in the early nineties, we can get some idea of the speed of change, and the consequent need for determination, energy and foresight to retain control over the educational and communicational power of the internet The words of Lisa Jardine regarding the spread of book publication are a warning to us to enter the contested domain of information technology:

> What scandalized the serious scholar Erasmus (as it fascinated Dürer) was the fact that, not much more than half a century after the first appearance of the printed book, demand had turned it into a product beyond the control of the scholars and specialists. The book had taken over as the transmitter of European written culture, before scholars and educators had had time to come to terms with its power and influence. (Jardine, 1996, p. 228)

Part 2 Conclusion: Adjacencies

This section of the book investigates three historical moments that exemplify many of the themes and approaches of Part 1. In Chapter 3 we have the early twentieth-century experiments in realist curriculum design and the later twentieth century reformulations of this discourse. Chapter 4 discusses a historical example of ethics teaching that, by comparison with contemporary approaches to competence and ethics and concept of the broken middle can provides us with insight into our own ethical dilemmas. Chapter 5, analysing the differences and similarities between medieval manuscript culture and our electronic environments, reveals surprising parallels and contrasts between ways of creating and negotiating information environments. Throughout we see legal education altering its shape and form in many ways as it comes under pressure from other thought systems or from internal pressures (information analysis and retrieval, for instance). It is possible to see within each historical moment the process of lamination, of layers of dissonance and resolution. As Galison has reminded us, even within a discipline there are cross-ply: grains that are laid athwart each other, and which give strength to the structure as a result (Galison, 1997, ch. 9.5).

It would be easy to characterise the chapters as accounts of failures – the realist reforms at Columbia, where Dewey never really joined the trading zone, the ethical structures of stoic virtue that were already breaking down under the pressure of a highly capitalised economy and culture, the informational structures of glossed literature, which existed for a time but were replaced by other forms of text. But these historical moments were significant enough to have affected the direction of the intellectual and material culture of legal education. That the realist movement in legal education in the United States had an effect on the history of the discipline is beyond dispute, though the nature of the legacy is disputed. The movement, with all its variegations, is still controversial and stimulating enough for a version of it to be recently revived, as we have seen. As a form, glossed literature facilitated the reception of Roman law into European legal systems, and enabled the teaching and learning of highly sophisticated structures of legal argument and commentary.

Juxtaposed, these chapters also reveal a number of fascinating themes and parallels across legal educational history. Four examples will suffice. First, all three chapters exhibit interesting examples of interdisciplinarities, and the conditions under which there was failure or success. We have investigated this in detail at Columbia; it is there in the culture of eighteenth-century Edinburgh University's Moral Philosophy course (and therefore it is all the more ironical that the extent to which contemporary ethical education in law schools can be interdisciplinary is still a subject for debate). Glossed texts were not found in juristic texts only – they were common in theological texts too, as we have seen. Secondly, the material culture of legal education matters more than we commonly suppose; and asynchronous comparisons are often quite fruitful to advance our own thinking about new ways to teach the law. For example, Llewellyn's *Cases and Materials on the Law of Sales,* with its novel structure, multiple indices and densely interwoven text, is an example of a book that was innovative both as a restatement of the law and as a teaching tool; but which was difficult for students to use as a casebook.[1] Set beside descriptions of glossed texts, one can see an alternative form for the book – it would have made an excellent wiki-text (we shall investigate such alternatives in more depth in Chapter 9).

Thirdly, within a discipline there is a continuity of concerns that stretches across decades, centuries, even millennia. For instance universities have always been aware of the relationship between information and culture: it is close to the historically-constituted mission of the institution. The migration of manuscripts; the development of the technology of print – these are two means by which universities in medieval and Renaissance times sought to disseminate knowledge. The web and distance learning takes that forward another stage; but in discussion we should never lose sight of the sociocultural process that underlies such technologies. Manuscripts and books contributed to this transformation, but the learning/teaching relationship was central, also, and remains so.[2] In the same way, Ferguson was a much-respected professor; the pragmatist reforms resulted in courses that were well-liked by students; accounts of glosses by Zabarella gives us an insight into how well they were used by students.

Yet another way to think about these historical moments is to compare them to what else was happening in other jurisdictions, or in other disciplines. For instance we could compare the realist reforms at Columbia to the reforms in the school curriculum then taking place in America. In 1918 W.H. Kilpatrick, an educator at Teachers College following the position Dewey had advocated for at least the past 15 years, published a paper entitled 'The Project Method' that was to become the major alternative to the then prevalent concept of the scientific curriculum, with its highly atomistic, top-down, drill-based approach to teaching and learning.[3]

---

1   I am grateful to William Twining for drawing my attention to this text.

2   Zabarella's text, cited in Chapter 5, is a good example of this. Jardine (1996, pp. 214–15) gives another example – a narrative in a book's prefatory letter, in which the Louvain printer, Thierry Martens, describes how he published the tutorial notes of Professor Nicholas Heems on Justinian's *Institutes* (1513). The notes derived from tutorial groups that Heems took in his home, and which Martens perceived would be a commercial success if distributed widely in book form. And as we saw in the second case-study of Chapter 1, identity and reading are intimately bound up with each other – this was probably as true for medieval readers as it is for modern.

3   The scientific approach to curriculum development had been advocated by W.W. Charters and J.F. Bobbit among others and followed Taylorist principles of the elimination of wasted effort, and the management of efficient teaching.

In place of a curriculum analysed down to tiny elements and then reconstituted, Kilpatrick based the concept of project work on purposeful acts. As he declared (in typically ringing prose), 'We of America have for years increasingly desired that education be considered as life itself and not as a mere preparation for later living' (Kilpatrick, 1918, p. 323). The idea became a movement, centred around the *Journal of Educational Method*, and was highly influential throughout the 1920s and 1930s, and contributed to the social reconstruction movement that Dewey, Jane Addams and others were part of, and which in education flourished as the Progressive Education Association. The second honorary president was Dewey, who in his inaugural speech in 1928 emphasised social learning and the quality of learning above measurement of intelligence and other metrics: 'the attempt to determine objectives and select subject-matter' would only succeed 'if we are satisfied upon the whole with the aims and processes of existing society'.[4] Education was not a study in efficiency for Dewey, nor was it there to reflect society merely, or be a preparation for it. Education needed to take its place as a practical critique of society. With these words, Dewey could have been addressing the realists and their attempts to reform the legal curriculum; and his words are as much a challenge to the contemporary NLR movement as they would have been to his colleagues in Columbia in the 1920s, and as they are to all of us in legal education today.

One can also attempt to put these three moments into a wider context as regards contemporary research. In Chapter 1 we saw how useful the new compositional and rhetoric movement could be to the research and analysis of student writing practices. This, together with the New Literacies movement, has transformed research into writing practices in recent decades by taking a social cognitive and situated approach to compositional research. In a similar way, researchers such as Carruthers, Clancy and Stock treat manuscripts as cultural objects, and their careful analyses and reconstructions teach us much about the context, practices and attitudes of medieval teachers and learners.[5]

Is there anything we can learn from this for our own practices? Certainly nothing as crude as 'learning from history': this is to presuppose a *gemütlich* interpretation of educational history where progress is inevitable along a path paved with the happy lessons of history and proofs of our own superiority in separating myth from history. Are we any wiser or more virtuous than Ferguson? Any more ambitious or insightful than the realists at Columbia? With all the panoply of the information revolution in our hands are we better organised about doctrinal analysis and presentation of that analysis to our students than were thirteenth-century glossators, with vastly fewer resources at their disposal? This is not a nostalgic lament for what we have lost – on the contrary, it is a plea for

---

4   Quoted in Kliebard (2004, p. 163).

5   This approach also takes a more controversial form as the New Philology movement. For a definition of the movement's aims, see Cerquiglini (1999); and the issue of *Speculum,* 1990, 65(1) and in particular Fleishman (1990). See also Carlquist (2004).

us to explore what we have yet to find out about ourselves – and a statement of how much we stand to lose if we forget about our past. We are uniquely placed to explore and attempt to understand the richness of our traditions. Digital media may not have the preservative toughness of vellum, but we can retain and compare media in a way unparalleled before in history. In doing so we may come to a new understanding of subjects the analysis of which is problematic because it is so implicated and embedded in our culture – curriculum, goodness, reading. Twining's stylish dichotomy applies as much to legal educators as it does to lawyers: not all of us can be specialist legal historians, legal educational historians, jurists, though some of us are. But we all need a Periclean understanding of our laminated culture, and that includes a sympathetic and profound understanding of how we have come to be as we are, even as we engage in the business of helping to shape our students' futures. And we also need to be able to take a blow-torch to a curriculum pipe-join – which technological comment leads us to the final part of the book.

PART 3
Metaverse

Chapter 6

Simulations and the Metaverse[1]

George Parker:	What happened? One minute, everything's fine ... What went wrong?
David:	Nothing went wrong. People change.
George Parker:	People change?
David:	Yeah
George Parker:	Can they change back?
David: [grins]	I don't know. I think it's harder.

Pleasantville (1998)

As multiplayer game platforms become increasingly powerful and lifelike, they will inevitably be used for more than storytelling and entertainment. In the future, virtual worlds platforms will be adopted for commerce, for education, for professional, military, and vocational training, for medical consultation and psychotherapy, and even for social and economic experimentation to test how social norms develop. Although most virtual worlds today are currently an outgrowth of the gaming industry, they will become much more than that in time.

(Balkin, 2005)

Simulation Learning

As we saw in Chapter 2 in the case study of standardised clients, one of the most effective ways of skills-based learning is simulation – the creation of scenarios within which learners play roles, interact with people, create documents and make choices based on their legal knowledge, and all available data. The richness of data is critical to the authenticity of the simulation, not only to create the alternative pathways that students can choose, but also to create the sense of the sheer randomness within the simulation world. In this chapter we will investigate briefly some contemporary forms of simulation on the web within environments that have been variously called massively multi-player online role-playing games

---

1   The term metaverse comes from Neal Stephenson's 1992 novel *Snow Crash*, and is now widely used to describe the vision behind current work on fully immersive 3D virtual spaces. As Wikipedia defines the term, these are 'environments where humans interact (as avatars) with each other (socially and economically) and with software agents in a cyber space, that uses the metaphor of the real world, but without its physical limitations' – http://en.wikipedia.org/wiki/Metaverse.

(MMORPGs), or multi-user virtual environments (MUVEs – I shall use the latter term, which more satisfactorily includes simulations as well as games) and explore some of their potential for legal education.

Let's start by considering a simple tutorial hypothetical problem:

> John McDonald is a metalworker. In the workshop, he catches his thumb in a grinder and is injured. *Quid iuris?*

In those three sentences we have a story, like one of Brecht's celebrated short stories, that is almost entirely without the detail that gives it the simulacrum of reality.[2] It is constructed so as to raise relevant issues for students in tutorials as to strict liability, contributory negligence and the like. The issues would be dealt with in an unsituated, abstract way. McDonald is scarcely a real person; the details of the workshop are irrelevant. It exists solely as the ghostly backdrop that frames a conceptual discussion of Health and Safety and the law of Delictual/ Tortious liability.

We could recast it as a more complete narrative:

> John McDonald was a 59-year-old metalworker working for Melville Welding, a small (15 employees) metal construction firm. While working on part of the hood for a ventilation system, McDonald wanted to smooth off the ragged edge or 'rags' of a mild steel bar. He switched on the grinder as he had done thousands of times in the past, and presented the bar to the spinning coarse-grit wheel by laying it on the rest. The angle wasn't right, he thought, too steep; but before he had time to retract the bar, the wheel had caught it and in an instant dragged it and his thumb into the gap between the rest and the wheel where it was trapped. After several minor but painful operations he is left with a stump. He wonders if he has a claim for compensation for his injury against his employer.
> *Quid iuris?*

Clearly there is more to discuss because there is richer detail – should one use a grinder for this purpose; should McDonald have done what he did without checking the angle of the rest, and such like. But the narrative is, from the point of view of a student, also a cage. Students know that details are placed there on the page because they are legally relevant, and interpret everything in that light as part of the solution. They treat the problem as a *roman á clef*, to be solved by identifying the clues. The richer the narrative detail, the more they need to sift for the legally-relevant detail that will solve the case. They do not think beyond the cage, because the unspoken rules of the game state that the detail will be there; or if the detail is not on the page, its absence can be alluded to, but students should not construct it. They cannot seek further information because, of course, the narrative is bounded by the four corners of the page.

---

2   Some of Brecht's stories are only a few lines long – see Brecht, 1998.

Developed in this way the narrative emerges as a more expressive form of reality. As a reader, you are drawn into the narrative as you begin to explore the complexity of the situation, which you experience at least partially from the viewpoint of the injured worker. You are still, however, a passive reader. No matter how complex the details, you will still be sitting in a seminar discussing the problem. You will not be an agent within the problem. The focus will be primarily on what the law says, not how the injured claimant feels or wants, nor about the relationship between John Rutherford, the MD of the company and John McDonald, or the general attitude to health and safety in the workshop, or the effect of pills that John had been given for his depression a couple of days before the accident.

Contrast this with the situation where you represent John, and where he can contact you as a client. You move from being an observer of the situation, neutrally analysing it from the outside, to being a participant, either within a simulation or (as in legal clinics) with an actual John McDonald. The monologic anonymous third-person voice, ever-reliable, omniscient, is replaced with a variety of voices, each telling their partial truths, whose fragmented narratives must be pieced together with care. No longer are you audience: you are a player on the stage and what you do affects other players and outcomes.

The move from spectator to participant is crucial. It involves not just a closer proximity to action for the actors, but paradoxically the need to remove oneself from action and to reflect on it, both in advance of action and after it. The parallel with drama is instructive. Brecht, for example, introduced alienation effects to bring his audience much closer to the narratives and moral dilemmas of the play (Brecht, 1957).[3] Augusto Boal adapted a number of Brecht's concepts to what he called generally the 'theatre of the oppressed' (Boal, 1998). In one genre, for instance, called Forum Theatre, actors act out only part of a script that represents an oppressive situation. People in the audience could stop the play at any point and come onto the stage to continue the play as a character and suggest their own next steps in the action. The technique has obvious application to more traditional political theatre of ideas, but for Boal such theatre was also a way of enacting possible alternative civic policies in local and national government. In other words, its function was not to present solutions but to stimulate debate and practical action.

---

3   The word '*entfremdung*' or 'alienation' has also been translated as 'defamiliarisation' – see Brecht (1999). The comparison between videogames, Brecht and Boal was made by Frasca (2001) in his dissertation and I am indebted to him for permission to use the analogy here.

Virtual Simulations: Games and Research

One way in which we might achieve the move from spectator to participant in legal education is through computerised simulation applications. They are not a new phenomenon in learning. Previously used for purposes such as flight simulation, other disciplines in universities have developed them in depth for both research and teaching purposes.[4] In medicine, for instance, there are numerous examples of clinical procedures that are modelled within programs.[5] In the physical sciences there are many applications.[6] These simulations are usually based on procedures that it is necessary to carry out within a highly particular context, using tools, knowledge and skills. Often the procedure is limited in scope and is repeatable, with variations.

However, one form of simulation that is less used in universities is that of a virtual world. The concept of a virtual world is an extraordinarily rich one, particularly if one considers it within the ancient context of what might be termed conceptual urban communities. One might point to the example of Plato's *Republic*, Augustine's *urbs beata*, City of God, or Christine de Pizan's *City of Women*, where communities, frequently but not always in an urban setting, are envisaged as models of ways of living. Later we have the rise of the Renaissance concept of the ideal princely or republican city-state and later still, in utopian literature, the concept of a wholly imaginary landscape of political, economic and cultural ideals, which act as a commentary upon pre-existing forms of society. The genre underwent many changes. In the nineteenth century it turned dystopian, with grim views of the city as presented in Dickens' *Hard Times*, or broader visions of society in Samuel Butler's *Erewhon*.[7] In the twentieth century the genre changed, becoming much darker – Ray Bradbury's *Fahrenheit 450*, Fritz Lang's *Metropolis* (set in 2026), Spielberg's *Minority Report* (Los Angeles, 2053)

4　For an example of a flight simulator, see http://www.microsoft.com/games/ flightsimulator/.

5　See for example the 'Virtual Hospital: a digital library of health information' at the University of Iowa available at http://www.vh.org/welcome/tour/patientsimulations.html. Simulation is also an essential element in larger learning environments –for examples see IVIMEDS, http://www.ivimeds.org/. For work on international standards in interoperability in the medical disciplines, see http://xml.coverpages.org/ni2001-05-22-c.html.

6　See Gould and Tobochnik (1996). For examples, see Maciej Matyka's website, 'Computer Simulations in Physics' available at http://panoramix.ift.uni.wroc.pl/~maq/ eng/, and 'The Hubble Volume Simulations' at http://www.physics.lsa.umich.edu/hubble-volume/, which simulates nothing less than the universe.

7　For general collections of such conceptual urban communities see two quite different but related texts – Carey (1999) and Graham (2004). There are many interesting ideas contained in these modern renderings of utopia that are taken up in videogames – the concept of observing from a particular viewpoint, for instance: the view of the *flâneur*. As Benjamin pointed out in his heroic work on nineteenth-century Paris, this is an essential element of the modern urban experience (Benjamin, 1999, pp. 416–55).

or Ridley Scott's *Bladerunner* (Los Angeles, 2019) give us compelling, nightmare visions of our cities, as does *The Matrix*, where the world itself is revealed as nothing more than a vast computer program.[8]

The genre also supports satire of itself. In *Pleasantville*, for instance, a brother and sister – representatives of abrasive late twentieth-century living – are transported into the idyllic world of a 1950s sitcom, where the books in the library are filled with blank pages and where there is no conflict, no passion, no politics or any other engine of change in the pleasant community.[9] Their presence irrevocably alters this black-and-white world, so that the characters gradually become human, splashed with colour and, as the epigraph above shows, they experience love, curiosity and unhappiness.[10]

Within the last 10 years new forms of online games and simulations have gained huge popularity[11] These are games played out in real-time in 3D virtual worlds composed of graphics and code. On-screen, people log on, assume their 3D online character or 'avatar' and experience the world through the eyes and ears of that character. The worlds vary in size and culture. They can be futuristic or Tolkienesque or set in an historical period; some are violent places – Sony's *EverQuest*, *World of Warcraft* and the like. Others are much more representations

---

8   Videogames also have another influential progenitor. Cinema has often been a fertile space for radical architectural designs. Lang's work (said to be inspired by his first glimpses of the New York skyline, but also drawing on German Expressionist and Bauhaus architecture) is truly cinematic in its breathtaking scope and detail. Lang's work, together with that of Ridley Scott, reveal an interest not just in using cityscapes as a backdrop, but in using their detail as part of the interest of the plot. The same cinematic quality invests the work of Daniel Libeskind's Jewish Museum in Berlin or the intricate, complex model of his urban project, City Edge, Berlin (1987). These and other radical architectural visions were on display in the Barbican Art Gallery exhibition, Future City: Experiment and Utopia in Architecture, 1956–2006 (15 June–7 September 2006).

9   There is of course a real town with that name. Its website is available at http://www.pleasantville.americantowns.com/servlets/WebPage. A virtual world called *Second Life* (more of this below) has its satirical version: http://www.getafirstlife.com/.

10   There are many such constructions of urban space that attempt to re-build our concept of urban space. More recent projects include computer imagery of a twenty-first-century plug-in building by Lavaux and Riche (2001). See also the models of the prize-winning project Yokohama International Port Terminal (1995–2002) by Foreign Office Architects. Much of utopian literature involves the creation of a community or space which is the arena for experimentation and idealisation. It is, in effect, fiction for a purpose, and in reading one is often aware of the tension between reality and the idealised land, between experimental and control groups.

11   For a history, see Mulligan and Patrovsky (2003). Two key texts are Salen and Zimmerman (2004 and 2006). For a timeline of games development over the past 30 or so years, see Koster (2004). Koster's lineage could of course begin much earlier. Given the many mythical settings for games, he could have started with Wagner, or nineteenth-century translations of Norse myths, or even medieval manuscript versions of Norse and Germanic oral poems.

of reality we know in the early twenty-first century – *The Sims Online*, for instance, *There*, or *Second Life*. The games often involve quests, gaining different levels of experience, gaining goods or services, strategic planning, fighting, healing. Whatever the world, they share a number of common features:

- they contain large numbers of players, hence their name of massively multi-player online role-playing games (MMORPGs, also known as MMOs or MUVEs). *World of Warcraft* for instance has at time of writing over seven million active subscribers registered globally in the game;[12]
- the games are created and maintained by large teams of developers with their own lifecycles and are dependent on commercial success to survive;
- the games are innately social, involving players in groups or providing the backdrop for social activities;
- the activities are long term and there is no end to them other than surviving and thriving in the virtual world.[13]

In the MUVEs, the early versions of text-based multi-user dungeons or MUDs have been transformed not only by vastly improved graphical interfaces but also by innovative use of huge network capabilities, where virtual worlds can accommodate the virtual selves of many thousands of players. What has attracted the interest of commentators such as sociologists, economists and others is the extent to which the relationships between players' virtual and physical selves develop in the adventure games that they play; how the characters interact socially with each other, how they survive in the economy set for them by the developers of the game and how their presence and actions change that economy.[14]

Avatars are a key component of the game. The avatars can be chosen by players from a limited range of species and characters – elves, dwarves, men or women, wizards, etc. Players can choose a different gender if they wish. Once

---

12 For up-to-date statistics on MMORPGs, see http://www.mmorpgchart.com/.

13 Definition is notoriously difficult. Ren Reynolds, in his posting at http://terranova.blogs.com/terra_nova/2005/08/the_four_worlds.html, makes the distinction between ludic worlds (or games worlds), social worlds and civic worlds. Van Eck (2007, p. 274) has set out a useful tabular matrix of game and learning taxonomies. Book (2004) has identified the following six features of social virtual worlds such as *Habbo Hotel* and *Second Life*. They consist of space shared with many other users; they have a graphical user interface (GUI) either 2D or 3D; users interact in the world, for example, building objects; immediacy of action; persistence (that is, the world's existence is separate from individuals' presence); and socialisation in the communities.

14 Castronova (2001) describes the game as a virtual world where players are drawn to 'play parts in what becomes an evolving and unending collective drama'. For an extensive bibliography of these worlds and their development, see Designing Virtual Worlds: The Web Site, Bibliography, http://www.mud.co.uk/dvw/bibliography.html, which is an 'informal resource' for the text Bartle (2003). For slightly more dated but much wider set of resources, see The Voice of the Shuttle, http://vos.ucsb.edu/browse.asp?id=2710.

you have an avatar, you see the world through the eyes of that *persona*. You can move, communicate, collect goods, kill, damage, injure, make friends and make love, be injured, healed, die. To do most of this requires skills, social interactivity and learning within the game.[15] As Castronova observed of *EverQuest*'s world, Norrath, it is designed around an economy constructed on scarcity where avatars need to compete for resources, but where there is more equality of opportunity:

> VWs offer the essential human story of challenge, maturity, and success, but played out on a more level playing field. They offer life with an escape clause, because if things go wrong and you cannot walk or talk and everyone hates you, you can just start over. And they give you a freedom that no one has on Earth: the freedom to be whomever you want to be. (2000, p. 17)[16]

Some worlds are implicitly more violent than others; but even potentially violent games have lesser or greater levels of violence[17] Some are regulated and governed more than others.[18] These are densely immersive environments, with significantly growing economies (Castronova, 2003a and 2003b) and cultures (Dibbell, 2003).[19] Whatever they are designed to be, the games are designed by large corporations, and are one of the few areas of e-commerce to make substantial profit from pure internet activity.[20] The games themselves attract ecologies and economies.

---

15 Increasingly the advanced skill levels of some players are being acknowledged in the real world – see Brown and Thomas (2006).

16 As we shall see, Castronova's description does need to be tempered somewhat.

17 Norrath is obviously a much more dangerous world than that of *The Sims Online*; but within worlds a gamer can choose which levels of violence to play at. *World of Warcraft*, for instance, has been designed around three types of player activity: adventuring, where players fight against AI-designed creatures and aspects of the environment in the company of other players, entertainment activities, where objects can be made, bought, sold etc; and player versus player gameplay where players fight each other. See http://www.worldofwarcraft.com/pvp/pvp-article.html.

18 See for example the fairly complex law-making procedures adopted for *A Tale in the Desert*, at http://www.atitd.com/man-lawmaking.html, or the complex governance issues involved in coding an environment that presented untrammelled peer-against-peer violence in the game *Ultima Online* – see the interview with Raph Koster, Creative Lead and Lead Designer in *Ultima Online*, at http://www.escapistmagazine.com/issue/55/9.

19 For the latest figures on the MMORPG market, see http://www.mmogchart.com.

20 Castronova estimated that Sony's 'monthly revenues from *Everquest* [were] about $3.6 million' on a subscriber base of over 400,000 in late summer 2001. These numbers of players represented 'a growth of over 10 percent in two quarters' (2001, p. 9). The players themselves play for on average 20 hours per week – around four hours a day would be spent in Norrath, the virtual world of the game. As Castronova puts it with pardonable exaggeration, for many players a 'competition has arisen between Earth and the virtual worlds, and for many, Earth is the lesser option' (2001, p. 10).

In Sony's game *EverQuest*, for example, the virtual characters or 'avatars' have been bought and sold for slightly less than $500.00.[21] The virtual worlds are enormously complex phenomena – or perhaps the term 'phenomenaria' would be a more accurate term (Skaalid, 2003).

As Castronova points out, the economy of Norrath is designed so that it is possible for an avatar to survive in the game. The currency of the virtual world, though separate from that of the real world, is matched against real currency.[22] Most games have a real economy where players can use credit cards to buy goods for their avatars and where the avatars can sell 'loot' taken or traded from other avatars.[23] As Castronova points out, the real world economy of Nike and Amazon and multinational corporations such as Walmart can thus enter the virtual world. In addition, the global economics of the real world are beginning to affect the virtual world. Lineage II, for instance, exists on Korean, Chinese, Japanese and English servers. Players on Asian-language servers have, according to Castronova, 'invested much time to discover money and loot bugs ... and are now moving into the newly-opened English servers [where there is considerable purchasing power] because the returns to exploiting the bugs are higher there' (2004).

Castronova's research proves that web-based games and simulations are attracting the attention of HE researchers. Indeed, there is now a burgeoning literature on the economics of simulated games (Castronova, 2001), their definition (Bartle, 2003; Reynolds, 2005; Koster, 2004; Salen and Zimmerman, 2006), their ethnography (Delwiche, 2006; Yee, 2001), the effect they have on identity (Turkle, 1995; Stone, 1995) and social relations (Steinkuehler and Williams, 2006), cognition and literacy (Steinkuehler, 2005), education (Gee, 2004) and much else, some of which we shall explore below.

---

21 See Ondrejka (2006a, p. 174).

22 The journalist Julian Dibbell set himself the challenge to earn more from a year's trading within the online game *Ultima Online* than he could in a year of writing ($47,000). He almost made it – see his blog entitled Play Money: Diary of a Dubious Proposition, at http://www.juliandibbell.com/playmoney/.

23 https://project-entropia.com/Index.ajp. Dibbell's article, 'Serfing the web: Black Snow Interactive and the world's first virtual sweat shop' described one unscrupulous company's scam: 'They rented office space in Tijuana, equipped it with eight PCs and a T1 line, and hired three shifts of unskilled Mexican laborers to do what most employers would have fired them for: playing online computer games from punch-in to quitting time. The games they were required to play were *Ultima Online* and *Dark Age of Camelot*, two of the most popular massively multiplayer role-playing games online. As the workers sat mouse-clicking virtual trolls to death, their characters acquired skills and gold at a brisk, assembly-line pace. For this, Black Snow paid the Mexicans piecework wages – then turned around and sold the high-level characters and make-believe money on eBay, where a grandmaster dragon-tamer account from *Ultima* can fetch $200 and a Dark Age gold piece trades for roughly what the Russian ruble does' (http://www.juliandibbell.com/texts/blacksnow.html).

Other commentators have conducted extensive ethnographic research into online play. Yee (2001), for instance, has researched many aspects of players, including the power that the games have to be addictive. Many players attested to the power of the simulations, while others were more in control of what they were doing:

> It's true that I would feel a lot of pain if I had to quit *EverQuest* ... but I think that far from being the 'menace' that I've seen EQ addiction made into, it's actually a lot more healthy than (for example) people who come home in the evening and spend 4 or 5 hours watching television. In *EverQuest*, I interact with people, do creative things, think and strategize, and generally enjoy myself. I think it's not much different than other forms of recreation with friends and others. So no, I've never tried quitting. Why would I want to? I enjoy spending time playing *EverQuest*, and I don't see it as fundamentally unhealthy behavior. [f, 23]

When players were asked in the research if they had changed or grown in any way from playing the game, most replied that they did not:

> No, it hasn't really had any kind of impact on me. It's just a game. [m, 23]

> This is just a video game to me. I don't analyze it to that extreme, only use it as an escape from the stresses of RL for awhile. [m, 27]

Some others, though, thought that the experience of playing the game had had an effect on them:

> It didnt change my thinking, it did however change to a minor extent my acting in real life. I have found it easier to share and confront other people with my thoughts ... whether this is due to EQ or just me growing emotionally I am not quite sure off though. A very positive change indeed [m, 30]

> I believe I have matured in my interaction with other people. When I first began playing I was rather hot-headed and impatient. I've been playing over a year and I think I've become more understanding of other people and their points of view. [m, 19]

When asked if there was anything in the virtual world that pertained to the real world, players argued that there was:

> The game is fake of course. Were only looking at our computer screens and pixels. But the people playing it are real. With real feelings, emotions, and desires. The actions I do and things I say make a difference as people remember and form opinions about myself. Once a high level character cast a bunch of super buff spells on me and said 'soandso said you were a really nice person'. and I had never met her before. I thanked her and felt good. [m, 30]

I think that whenever you have the opportunity to interact with other people, you have the opportunity to learn something. Everyone has something to teach you, be it online or in person. After all, you learn from what someone writes in a book, and you don't meet with the person in the flesh. Why would online be any different? With as many people you interact with in EQ, how can you not at least learn something? That I think is the reason I have played EQ, the people that I meet. [f, 21][24]

These comments and many more such experiences are examples of the kind of learning that can take place in such simulated worlds. They raise interesting issues about the relationship not only between selves online but also between the virtual and the real. What, for instance, is the relation between avatar and physical self? Surely it is the case that in a game such as *EverQuest* our physical self has a number of digital identities that we can take up and use as extensions of our selves? And is this not similar to aspects of identity-formation and use within the real world? In this sense, social psychology theories of identity within the real world such as symbolic interactionism (Goffman, 1959 and 1967) are highly pertinent to the analysis of avatars as identity-constructs, and as such, of interest to educationalists.

MUVEs and Education

How could such environments be used in formal learning in institutions? There is a fast-developing body of educational research which is exploring this domain. James Gee, for instance, has researched the extent to which videogames can be used in schools and colleges. For him, the whole educational process of meaning-making 'is not about definition, it is about simulations of experience' (Gee, 2004, p. 8). Coming to the educational study of videogames from the discipline of linguistics, he uses the research base into literacy and language acquisition, some of which we encountered in Chapters 1 and 2, to argue that games can simulate contexts in which we learn as naturally as we learn language in context. For Gee, the decoding of meaning and learning rules and their consequences can be learned most effectively in contexts of practice and situated action. For example, he compares the language of instruction in a game's instruction booklet to the game itself, in this instance *Deus Ex*. 'You can access ... data at any time during play by hitting F1 to get to the Inventory screen or F2 to get to the Goals/Notes screen' (2004, p. 43). As Gee points out,

the trouble is this: in the actual game, you can click on F2 and meditate on the screen you see at your leisure. Nothing bad will happen to you. However, you very often have to click on F1 and do something quickly in the midst of a heated battle. There's no 'at your leisure' here. The two commands really don't function the same way in the game

---

24 Yee (2001). Quotations available at http://www.nickyee.com/eqt/growth.html.

– they actually mean different things in terms of embodied and situated action – and they never really *just* mean 'click F1, get screen'. (2004, p. 44).

Gee is clearly arguing against the notion that videogames or indeed disciplines can be practised straight from instructional booklets or textbooks. But he does not accept the opposite concept: that one should learn videogames only by playing these highly sophisticated games. On the contrary: a whole chapter in his book is devoted to an analysis of the complex tutorials that are constructed by games designers to help users play the games. The problems facing games designers at this point are very similar to those facing educationalists in every discipline: learners are different persons with different levels of prior knowledge and skills, different values and different learning preferences. Often learners themselves do not know their knowledge levels, or may find difficulty in recalling them. Gee explores the games' solutions in detail through an analysis of one game, namely *Rise of Nations*. Learners are presented with a menu ranging from Quick Start through to Beginning Player, to Experienced Real-Time Strategy Player to Advanced Topics. As Gee notes, this is pitched at a novice player's range of play: 'each tutorial places its basic skills in a scenario that is just a simplified form of the real game' (2004, p. 64). He calls the Quick Start element a 'fish tank', where players can play stripped-down versions of the game. There are no teachers: the *design itself* leads learners on into the tutorials. The later layers, more complex and experimental, he calls 'supervised sandboxes', where scenarios are set up, and where players have the opportunity to alter the speed of their learning (2004, p. 68).

The aim of these initial sessions is to prepare the player for the game proper. They achieve it by using the game environment itself, not by having users consult textbooks about it. The process of learning the game is fun in itself and Gee notes the feeling of 'pleasurable frustration, one of the great joys of both deep learning and good gaming' (2004, p. 71). What happens, though, if a player joins the game proper and finds it frustratingly difficult, so that it is no longer pleasurable? Players will drop out in such circumstances, so designers are careful to give them alternatives. The players can take skills tests, for example:

Tactics
Defeat the enemy troops to take control of a valuable resource without losing more than half your army in this test of generalship. (2004, p. 72)

Note how specific and positive in tone the description is – one might compare this to the usual legal educational module learning outcome, which is often neutral and decontextualised. Note also that the skills are not labelled as remedial: it is implicit in the statement that the skills are necessary and achievable. The activities are merely more specific replays of skills that were part of the sandbox activities, but which needed more practice. Players thus take control of their learning.

If players are still uncertain, then as Gee points out, every game has a substantial online social presence in the form of website chat rooms, blogs, guides, etc. There are even recordings that can be made of specific game encounters that can be posted onto the web and commented upon by peers, and which are valuable learning resources.[25] Some MUVEs, like *Second Life*, have their own online newspapers. In using these resources players become part of the social network of the game. They come to identify with the game, its values and its community of users. Their identity as players is subtly altered as they identify with other players, very often in the exchange of information about the game.[26] As Gee describes it, '[d]istributed and dispersed knowledge that is available "just in time" and "on demand" is yet another learning principle built into a game like *Rise of Nations*' (2004, p. 73).

The same principle of dispersal applies to the communications structures in MUVEs. In *World of Warcraft* for instance players communicate via a text box that operates like chat boxes, in the lower left of the screen. The channels of communication, though, are highly structured. There is a private chat which is person-to-person communication, heard only by those two which, in a social situation, can operate rather like the </whisper> command described by Shirky (2002).There are also one-to-many channels, that is, to specific groups and guilds (and to specific people within the guild, such as Officer chat). There is also a spatial channel, by which one can chat to all players within a certain radius. Finally there is zone chat which is a wider extension of radius chat, and which includes all players within a zone. This last channel is subdivided into four categories: General, Trade, LookingForGroup and LocalDefence.[27]

Chat is not just the communication of information: it also allows players to display emotions and to gesture. Players can whisper and yell. Under the 'Emote' menu they can perform routines such as applaud, beg, bow, cry, dance, eat, kiss, laugh, point and wave. All communications are captured in a Chat Log. A Combat Log similarly displays the combat actions of your avatar and those of other players nearby, as well as your combat experience, your purchases, item creation and your experience awards.

Socialisation, Identity and Governance

The roles that players take online are of course heavily circumscribed by the availability of species of avatars. Whatever the choice, there has been research conducted on *how* players act online. Bartle, for instance, drew up a matrix in

---

25 Recent research by Nick Yee suggests that 'on average, the majority of players [in his study] spent about an additional 50% of their game-playing time outside of the game performing games-related activities'. As Yee points out, 'a significant part ... of what it means to play an MMO happens outside of the game itself' (Yee, 2006c).

26 Constance Steinkuehler's research illustrates this well – see for example Chapter 4 in her doctoral thesis, where she analyses transcripts of apprenticeships, in which other avatars in the game help her to learn how to play (Steinkuehler, 2005).

27 See http://www.worldofwarcraft.com/info/basics/chat-overview.html.

which he identified four types of players (Bartle, 1999). Bartle went on to define the relations between the different types and compared them to each other in the effects they have on the game. According to him, a game is stable when the four player types are in equilibrium; and players tend to play predominantly in one of the four quadrants. Bartle's typology is based largely on his extensive experience of online games and the comments of other players. Other commentators have begun to analyse this matrix in more detail, basing their results on much larger empirical datasets. Using a factor analytic approach, for instance, Yee has drawn up a 10-component matrix that describes a more complex pattern of motives for, and styles of, gameplay (Yee, 2006b). His results are evidence that 'play motivations in MMORPGs do not suppress each other as Bartle suggested. Just because a player scores high on the Achievement component doesn't mean they can't also score high on the Social component' (2006b, pp. 4–5). In relation to gender roles, the data shows that 'male players socialize just as much as female players but are looking for very different things in those relationships' (2006b, p. 5). And he confirms that, in relation to 'griefing' or malicious gameplay, 'pre-existing depression or mood disorders are common among users who develop problematic usage with online games' (2006b, p. 6).

Games commentators have of course long recognised that the game code determines to a considerable extent the nature of social relations within a game. Nevertheless, there is much interaction between characters in a game that powerfully affects behaviour, even between strangers. In a blog posting McCracken describes the world of simulated flight controllers, who control flights arriving online at specific airports. These virtual air traffic simulators (VATSIMs) are another form of online game, where human purpose and experience, as well as the artificial intelligence of the game, control the activities of the game. This is not unusual in games – even in games with a high degree of scripted AI in them (*World of Warcraft* for instance). However, as McCracken points out, the fact that strangers are interacting with each other on an activity crucial to the nature of the actions performed, and that their relations seldom involve more than that, is part of the attraction of this game for gamers.[28] The relationship relies on a

---

28 McCracken describes this well: 'in the VATSIM case, interaction take place between perfect strangers. My game can be changed by behaviors you "throw off" in your game without really thinking about what they might mean to me. Flying into Albuquerque, I may "crash" because it just so happens that you, the controller, are inexperienced, tired, distracted, or wrestling with your sister for control of the family computer' (McCracken, 2006). For McCracken, this gives the game an interest and a depth it would otherwise not have. He compares it to Jonathan Miller's theory of dramatic character, where, according to Miller as summarised by McCracken, '[i]t is only when noise and contradiction are built into the character that the character comes to life. This is, it seems to me, pretty close to what happens when by game play is constructed not out of the programmer's anticipation of what I will find engaging, or someone's deliberate efforts to engage me, but by the far more random effects of happenstance' (ibid.).

For more information on the VATSIM community, see http://vatsim.net/.

tension – between the strangers that encounter each other, and their duty to each other to behave in a civil and professional manner within the game.

Where social relations are more complex and long-term than simple one-off transactions, the problems for game designers become exponential and the social, political, legal and cultural arguments extraordinarily profound. How should one govern an environment such as a MUVE? To what extent do property rights in the real world apply to cyberspace? Can one analyse cyberspace using the same tools of analysis as are applied in the real world? How useful is it, for instance, to apply Durkheimian categories of mechanical and organic solidarity to explore relations? Is the End-User Licence Agreement (EULA) sufficient to deter 'griefing' or malicious behaviour by in-world residents?[29]

The extent to which such legal problems also entail social and governance issues has already been the subject of fairly extensive comment.[30] Hunter's review (2002) of Sunstein's book REPUBLIC.COM shows the cultural depth of the debates, extending into politics, US culture wars, and many disciplines other than law. Other researchers have investigated the highly complex nature of the design decisions that attend the structure of a MUVE. In their analysis of the social dynamics of large-scale gaming communities, for instance, Ducheneaut et al. (2006), point out that the average play-time to climb the levels of expertise rises slowly and regularly in the best games such as *World of Warcraft*: difficulty increases gradually with the possibility of progress always within reach – a reward cycle that made previous MUVEs addictive. They point out the striking resemblance between this curve and Skinner's concept of operant conditioning – an uncomfortable comparison to which we shall return later in Chapter 8.

The principles of what Gee outlines as standard games learning design in a strategy game such as *Rise of Nations* is even more applicable to one such as *Second Life (SL)*.[31] This 3D game consists of nothing but avatars living within a society almost entirely created by them. It is an astonishingly simple concept for a game, all the more so because the game does not consist of the construction of highly complex 'blood pledge systems' as in *Lineage*, or the guilds of hunters in *EverQuest*, or the ongoing war between Alliance and the Horde in *World of Warcraft*, but consists simply of the immersion in lived experience in this environment. In so much as *SL* is a *game*, it is created by users themselves. *SL*

---

29 In a powerful blog posting and commentary on Terra Nova, for instance, Prokofy Neva pointed out how social relations between avatars in the game *Second Life* were adversely affected by what he saw as a lack of governance by the designers, who took a libertarian approach to rights within the game that were, in his opinion, unjustified. He cited the instance of the 'Bush Guy' – a player who put up hundreds of spinning 'IMPEACH BUSH' notices all over the mainland of *Second Life*, the removal of which cost other players money. See Prokofy Neva's comment at http://terranova.blogs.com/terra_nova/2006/05/strangers_dont_.html.

30 On property rights see, for instance, Johnson and Post (1996), Lastowka and Hunter (2004) and Fairfield (2005).

31 Gee summarises these design points at 2004, pp. 74–5.

encourages this, with an advanced system of avatar appearance. People in the game go on to create objects such as houses, clothes, artwork, vehicles and the like, which they can control with code, and sell for Linden dollars (named after Linden Lab, the company that created *SL*).

It is interesting that one of the key shifts quite early on in the game's development – the move to allow players to own what they created in the game – was the result of a roundtable discussion between the *SL* design team and academics who persuaded *SL* to take what was for them a bold commercial move.[32] As Ondrejka (2006), pointed out, 'such academic research and input will continue to alter both *Second Life* and Linden Lab'. Ondrejka's article is a timely call for the convergence of research and implementation of digital worlds: 'today's games require knowledge in fields as diverse of economics, law, governance, communications theory, psychology, education and cognitive science' (2006b, p. 112). Nor is this a matter of single development cycles. As Ondrejka points out, quoting Bartle (2005), despite the 'contradictory presumptions of harm and trivia' (2006, p. 111) games intermingle 'the visceral and the social' while forcing players to 'hypothesize, experiment and learn' (2006b, p. 112).[33]

That a digital world such as *SL* can be used for educational courses rather than for informal learning cannot be in doubt: one need only consider the uses made by educationalists of the environment to date. At Harvard Law School, for instance, an entire course is taught on Berkman Island within *SL*. 'CyberOne: Law in the Court of Public Opinion' analyses how the characteristics of new media such as podcasts, blogs, wikis and the like affect the arguments that are made using them. The course uses immersion in the e-domain as one of its methods of enabling students to understand the media. In addition to taking the course on a face-to-face basis, Harvard Extension students adopt avatars, attend lectures within the reconstructed buildings on Berkman Island, view video lectures within *SL* and attend tutorials there. While the presence of 'lectures' within such an innovative environment may be questionable, the design of activities in the syllabus is remarkably creative, with students asked to develop online games, collaborate in the creation of wikis on the development of argument and analyse issues of governance, identity, textuality, disputes and their resolution and the economics of MUVEs. The key theme of the course is that '"First World" and corporate domination of entertainment, media, laws and news can be balanced by the voices of individuals, groups and universities who use new media intelligently' (Nesson, 2006). While in some respects the use made of *SL* by Harvard as a learning domain may seem, in its reproduction of actual world spaces and forms of communication (for example, the lecture space) to be traditional, in its use of

---

32 Lessig (2003), 'Creators in *Second Life*', retrieved from http://www.lessig.org/blog/archives/001577.shtml, quoted in Ondrejka, 2006.

33 Ondrejka, ibid., quoting Bartle (2005). See also Bartle (2003); Ondrejka also acknowledges Johnson (2005).

SL as a platform for critical debate and learning about media and the law in the world for at least part of the student body it is highly innovative.[34]

The use of *SL* as an arena for debate about voices and within society, how we hear or suppress them, which is a key theme in the Harvard Law School course, is also central to the use made of *SL* by New York Law School. Their space in *SL*, called Democracy Island, consists of 16×16 acres of property terraformed on a hub-and-spoke design to facilitate communications between parts of the site. Its function is to act as a 3D area that can be used for civic engagement, giving voices to local groups, allowing government agencies to liaise with groups, and the like. The stated aim of the experiment is to 'reproduce the experience and strengths of America Speaks 21st Century Town Meeting'.[35] As one of the project founders Beth Noveck stated, the purpose of the space in *SL* was to enable people to exploit 'new social and visual technology to make decisions and wield power' (2005). This purpose is based upon the wider claim that we need to 'explore ways to structure the law so as to circumscribe malevolent groups while deferring political and legal decision-making to decentralised group-based decision-making. Noveck's use of *SL* is based on a sophisticated analysis of online group identity and behaviour, public deliberation and collaborative endeavour. According to her the rise of networks and their protocols, together with the emergence of 'more visual and social software' has promoted the extraordinary rise of collective action and reaction on the web. For Noveck, the sense of space that is crucial to political action in the real world ('[w]hat is a protest without a sidewalk or square?') can be supplied by *SL*. By analogy the self-representation than an avatar can create – the 'thrownness' of its being in the simulated world, to adapt a Heideggerian term – can be harnessed for political and democratic ends. To see through the eyes of an avatar is a powerfully mediated experience – gender, colour and age can be simulated to produce forms of empathic relations.[36]

Noveck's vision of e-spaces such as *SL* becoming civic and cultural arenas where social and democratic change can be enacted is, as she readily acknowledges, one more version of transformative change, not just of technological visionaries such as Doug Engelbart, but of commentators such as Santos and Teubner. For Santos, his six main forms of 'power, law and commonsense knowledge' are 'sites of production and reproduction of unequal exchange in capitalist societies', but they can be converted 'through transformative agency, into heterotopias, core sites of emancipatory relations' (Santos, 1995, p. 410). For Teubner, it is essential that we analyse 'the interaction and the systems which are to be controlled and

---

34 'CyberOne: Law in the Court of Public Opinion', Course Description, http://blogs. law.harvard.edu/cyberone/administration/course-description. The course ran for the first time in 2006/7, and there is little information about its reception at time of writing.

35 http://www.americaspeaks.org/lab/blog/, Lars Hasseblad Torres posting, 13 April 2006.

36 Note that in such an environment there is space for both action and reflection, as practised in Boal's Forum Theatre described earlier in this chapter. For a powerful account of peer vs peer fighting and racism online, see always_black (2006).

developed in such a way that they can more or less regulate themselves and control each other'.[37] Self-regulation is of course the key. Experiments such as Democracy Island's projects demonstrate that such environments, properly regulated, can indeed support profoundly democratic modes of social participation.[38]

Summary

This chapter has given the briefest of introductions to a fast-developing application of the web, namely simulation and gaming. In such applications, viewpoint shifts from that of spectator to participant. Around this shift has grown a culture of playing and simulating which educationalists are exploring as a fertile ground for learning, and an embodiment of one form of situated learning. Nor are simulations simply idle entertainment: they involve us in thinking seriously about issues such as socialisation, identity and governance.

Just as people play MUVEs for a variety of reasons so an educational simulation can have different meanings and consequences for different students. For educationalists involved in implementing such forms of learning, though, there is significant change involved, in both educational theory and practice. The epigraph from *Pleasantville* sums up the bewilderment of one character in the face of change. We can't go back: and yet as Part 2 has proven, we need to go back, to learn anew what our past was, and what our future might be like. Dewey, of course, would have recognised *SL* for what it can be (regardless of whatever else it may be) – one more example of an experimental Laboratory School in human relations.

Many disciplines are beginning to experiment with forms of role-play and simulation using technology – education (Bell, 2001; Diamantes and Williams, 1999), environmental studies (Cutler and Hay, 2000), medical education (Benbassat and Baumal, 2002), social work (Moss, 2000, 2002), business (Cox, 1999), history (Luff, 2000), psychotherapy (Riva, 2005). The latest research at time of writing suggests a considerable upsurge in interest (de Freitas, 2006). Many institutions as well as corporations are buying islands in *SL* to discover how they might use them for a variety of purposes, including training and education. But can online simulation environments support and enhance deep learning in law, and across a programme of study? The next chapter attempts to answer that question.

---

37 Noveck (2005), n. 214.

38 And they can of course be used for many legal educational purposes. See, for example, the use of utopian coursework (Dator, 1999) and the use of buildings as representations of legal order and culture (Baker, 2005).

Chapter 7

Transactional Learning in Action

> ... learning consists of building up a set of materials and tools that one can handle and manipulate ... in the most fundamental sense, we as learners are all bricoleurs.
>
> (Papert, 1980, p. 173)

Simulation-based training has been shown to be highly effective in professional disciplines.[1] In one study, nurses were taught to recognise and treat critically ill patients on a general ward by a combination of mini-lectures, workshops and simulator-based patients. The subject-matter included assessment of respiratory, cardiovascular and renal systems, and pain management. Participants completed pre- and post-course tests, which showed statistically significant improvement ($p<0.001$); and in the follow-ups at two months and six months later, participants reported long-term confidence in caring for acutely ill patients (Stedeford et al., 2003).[2]

Why might one want to use a virtual world in legal education? What are the advantages of a virtual legal world over the real one? In the last chapter we explored the educational potential of online games and simulations; and on the basis of this there are at least five reasons for using online simulations:

- Students can practise legal transactions, discuss them with other tutors, students, and use a variety of instruments or tools, online or textual, to help them understand the nature and consequences of their actions.
- The virtual world enables students to practise within an environment that is close to the world of practice, but safe from the realities of malpractice and negligent representation.
- Online simulations enable a wide variety of assessment, from high-stakes assignments with automatic fail points, to coursework that can double as a learning zone and an assessment assignment.

---

1 The medical educational literature is more extensive than most other disciplines. See, for instance, Forrest et al. (2002) and Blackburn et al. (2003). Some of the literature explores the learning environment within which simulations and simulators are used. In another study by Forrest et al. (2003), for instance, novice anaesthetists were given simulator practice, and then debriefed. The results were compared to a previous study where simulation was used without debriefing. Using a previously-validated scoring system to track technical performance, it was reported that the group which had undergone the debriefing showed no significant improvement in technical performance over a 12-week period.

2 See also Rall et al. (2000).

- Online simulations encourage collaborative learning. The guilds and groups of hunters in *EverQuest*'s world of Norrath, for instance, can be replicated for very different purposes in legal education.
- Students begin to see the potential for the C in ICT; and that technology is not merely a matter of word processed essays, LMSs and WestLaw, but can facilitate a form of learning that changes quite fundamentally what and how they learn.

Within the GGSL, it became clear, though, that if we were to begin to embed student learning within a virtual world we would need to consider why we might construct the virtual spaces. Simulations always need powerful purposes; and in a university setting they are largely specific to the needs of a discipline. It was therefore necessary to design purposes and tasks for the virtual environment. In the course of a number of internal working papers and conference papers, the concept of transactional learning began to form. This form of learning, as we saw in the Introduction, derives from Dewey's pragmatic educational discourse. In effect, students within the virtual environment would not produce meaning, activity, text as if they were acting within an academic setting. Instead (and following the rhetoric research results obtained by Stratman and Christensen, discussed in Chapter 1), we would ask them to act as if they were trainee practitioners carrying out transactions on behalf of their clients. This was not merely surface simulation of professional learning. The Deweyan transaction is much more complex than this, and involves analysis of and judgement on the world. For our purposes, on the grey zone between academia and practice, we needed to define what precisely that meant, both for our own practice and for students' understanding of the processes of learning they would be undertaking. However, before I define what we mean by 'transactional learning' and describe in detail its implementation, it would be helpful to sketch out the curricular context in which it was implemented.

Context: Professional Legal Education in Scotland

In Scotland there are a number of routes to qualification as a solicitor or advocate. It is possible to sit examinations held by the Law Society of Scotland in what are known as the 'qualifying subjects', a pass in which qualifies the candidate to proceed to a postgraduate course in professional subjects, called the Diploma in Legal Practice; but only a handful of candidates take this route. The commonest route to the legal profession is via university study. In their undergraduate years, most students study for their LLB degree in one of a variety of routes stretching from 2–4 years (six, if studied part-time), depending on their previous experience and pattern of study. This is followed by the postgraduate Diploma, which lasts for around seven months – effectively a full academic year – and which is currently offered at five centres throughout Scotland.[3] Students must then obtain and complete a traineeship of two years in a legal office, during which the Law Society of Scotland requires them to undertake a Professional Competence Course and, during their traineeship, to undertake the Assessment of Professional Competence (work-based assessment of competence).

The Diploma consists of eight subjects, including an optional subject – in the GGSL we have added another, namely the first in the following list:

1) Foundation Course in Professional Legal Skills;
2) Civil Court Practice;
3) Criminal Court Practice;
4) Financial Services and Accountancy;
5) Private Client;
6) Professional Ethics;
7) Conveyancing;
8) Practice Management;
9) *Either* Company and Commercial *or* Public Administration.

In the later 1990s the Diploma curriculum underwent revision by the Law Society, with more emphasis placed on skills-based learning, in areas such as interviewing, negotiation, advocacy, legal writing, drafting and professional research.

In the GGSL there are three full-time academic members of staff associated with the programme, and a number of visiting professors. Nearly all classes are taught by around 150 part-time tutor-practitioners (normal practice in Scottish Diploma centres) supported by an administrator, secretaries and a number of administrative support staff. The greatest area of staff expansion is probably in the area of ICT (Information and Communications Technology). Here, we have increased our staff from a single network maintenance officer to a Learning Technologies Development Unit (LTDU), the development wing of which presently consists of a learning technologies development officer, two multimedia and web designers and two applications developers. The reasons for this considerable increase in staffing will be explored below, as well as the effect that LTDU has had upon the programme of study.

Transactional Learning

The idea of learning as a form of transaction is of course not a new one. As we saw in the Introduction (pp. 21–7) it can be traced back to Dewey's fundamental argument that education arises from the interaction of a person's internal life and

---

3   The Diploma centres are based in the law schools of Aberdeen University, Robert Gordon University, Dundee University, Edinburgh University and the Glasgow Graduate School of Law (GGSL).

external conditions. Experience, he held, consists of an 'interaction', a transaction between individual and environment (*LW*, 13, p. 25). Indeed it would not be saying too much to describe it as *the* educative process.[4]

Others have taken up this transactional relationship and developed it in different directions. Chen, for instance, has applied it to the concept of distance in use of the web for distance-learning (Chen and Willitts, 1998) and Garrison and Anderson (2003, p. 19) note that in the construction of distance-learning theory recently there has been a shift of focus from 'organisational and structural constraints' (such as those of geographical distance) to 'transactional issues and assumptions' of teaching and learning. For Garrison, the shift is nothing less than a movement from industrial era conceptions of learning at a distance to post-industrial learning where peer collaboration and dialogue lie at the heart of the educational experience (Garrison and Archer, 2000).[5]

Transactional learning as an educational term is different from 'transactional lawyering' as described by Gilson and others (for instance Gilson, 1984 and Gardner, 2003).[6] It is more inclusive of the type of transactions (including, for instance, court actions), and more ambitious in its educative aims. In this respect it should be said at the outset that our use of transactional learning (TL) in the GGSL is based upon the view of learning as a process of negotiation between self and environment and as a rhetorical space. The transaction is thus not merely a legal transaction, but a dialogue between self and context. As Dewey puts it,

> [a]n experience is always what it is because of a transaction taking place between an individual and ... his environment ... The environment ... is whatever conditions interact with personal needs...to create the experience. (*LW*, 13, p. 25)

If the theory is an implementation of a Deweyan pragmatist curriculum, it also takes into account the massive body of research in legal theory and education that has been constructed since Dewey. Some of this theory acknowledges Dewey directly. The theory differs from the conversational theories of Laurillard and Pask. It bears some resemblance to the theory of transactional distance (TD) suggested by Michael G. Moore. His concept, articulated first within the field of distance education, was based upon the idea that dialogue and curriculum or syllabus structure affected learner autonomy. As dialogue increased between

---

4   As he states in an albeit early article, 'I believe finally, that education must be conceived as a continuing reconstruction of experience; that the process and the goal of education are one and the same thing' (*EW*, 5, 91).

5   See also Garrison and Archer (2000), and Vrasidas and Glass (2002).

6   Gilson and Mnookin (1995) go as far as to advocate the addition of subjects such as transaction costs economics and the economics of information to the JD programme of study. Schwarcz (2006) has recently redefined the value of transactional lawyering based on empirical work; but the conclusions he draws for legal education are uninspiring – more case work, and agreeing with Kronman on the 'importance of traditional case analysis over theory and social sciences'.

tutor and learner, so transactional distance decreased and structure became less important. Where there was less dialogue, then there was more TD, and structure became more important (Moore, 1993 and Moore and Kearsley, 1996). What is interesting about Moore's theory is that it has in recent years been applied not just to distance learning, but to other educational interventions (Bischoff et al., 1996).[7]

We also distinguish our version of transactional learning from that of Philip Jackson, for whom TL was a method by which teachers would negotiate with learners what was to be learned and how (Jackson, 1968). Jackson contrasted this method of learning exchange with the more positive heuristics of 'transformational learning' where students learned at a more profound level.

While we took into account Moore's account of the theory, we needed a body of propositions that would act as a set of guidelines for our own practice as we were developing it within the virtual world, and which would guide the implementation of the world itself. Its key features are as follows (Maharg, 2004):

1) *Transactional learning is active learning*
   Transactional learning goes beyond learning *about* legal actions to learning *from* legal actions (Gredler, 1996, pp. 571–6). There is, of course, a place for learning about legal actions. Indeed, (following the discussion of PBL in Chapter 1) transactional learning is rarely possible unless students first have a conceptual understanding of what the legal process actually entails.

2) *Learning to do legal transactions*
   We aim to give students experience of legal transactions. This learning extends not only to knowledge of parts of the transaction, but of the whole transaction, including the relational and ethical dimensions of a transaction.

3) *Transaction + reflection*
   Transactional learning involves thinking about transaction – indeed (to go back to the root of the word) thinking *across* transactions. It includes the ability to rise above detail, and 'helicopter' above a transaction; or the ability to disengage oneself from potentially damaging views of a group process, and reconstruct that view.

4) *Collaborative learning*
   Transaction as collaboration, indicating the root of the word: literally 'acting across'. We mean collaboration in two senses. First, students collaborate with staff, in the sense that tutors act as mentors or guides rather than teachers. Simulations can be discovery environments, but they often work best when student learning is 'scaffolded' by the presence of examples of good work or

---

7   Their factor analysis revealing that email dialogue decreased TD suggested to them that this form of dialogue could be used in all such teaching interventions. The universality of the proposition is a doubtful one (there are many factors involved in this type of intervention), but it at least demonstrates the potential application of Moore's proposition to areas of teaching and learning other than distance-learning.

helpful procedures, and by the availability of tutors as guides, either to answer basic information questions directly, or to suggest ways of action to students who are stuck in the process for one reason or another (Hmelo and Day, 1999).[8]

Second, students are valuable resources for each other. Collaborative learning breaks down the isolation and alienation of what might be regarded as isolated or cellular learning. There is of course a place for individual learning, silent study, literature review and so on. But students can help each other enormously to understand legal concepts and procedures by discussing issues, reviewing actions in a group, giving peer feedback on work undertaken in the group, and so on.

5) *Ethical and professional learning*

Transactional learning of necessity draws upon ethical learning and professional standards. In both undergraduate and postgraduate seminars and lectures and in their reading of texts, students engage with ideas, and form understandings of ethical and professional concepts. Within transactions they practise and link up emerging understandings with prior knowledge, and with anticipation of future knowledge within the dynamic of the transaction. The more they become familiar with the transactional method, the more efficient this process of learning ethics and professionalism becomes (Veenman et al., 2002 and Swaak and de Jong, 2001). In addition, we saw in Chapter 4 (p. 130) that profound learning about ethics can arise within the peer-to-peer relationship.

Ardcalloch: Development and Implementation

For anyone bringing together simulation and transactional learning, the immediate problem is how to simulate the complexity of practice. Simulation could be a highly hubristic concept, for even if one accepts that one can never replicate reality, the problems of simulation are huge. They involved us in designing:

- the sheer sensory and informational detail of a real world situation;
- the potentially accidental and random qualities of reality;
- communities of practice – the office, the profession, the town, the interest groups.

It became clear that ICT could play a part in the partial simulacrum of society, by helping us to represent a community to its members: in effect by representing a town. Within this town students would play the role of solicitors, and would be able to contact other professionals, institutions, public bodies, and so on, to obtain information and play the part of being a solicitor in practice. Other roles would be played by online tutors or facilitators who would masquerade as characters over the web in order to communicate in role with the students. Note that our

---

8   See also examples from Barton and Maharg (2006, pp. 131–4).

aim was not to replicate reality – impossible and not necessarily a productive educational heuristic – but to simulate aspects of it.[9] Our world would necessarily be instrumental and a place for experimentation. It would be a world where the norms of professional legal practice could be played out, where students could begin to learn what it was to be a professional lawyer, and where they could begin to create their identities as novice professionals. As the literature on skills learning has pointed out, students often need help in constructing a view of their skills.[10] The event that gives them feedback or the opportunity for reflection, however, can be separated from the skills event, thus turning learning from a mode of participation to one of spectating.

Of course, the power of the interaction that is present in Ardcalloch is very much restricted when compare to that of online games. Real students, playing the part of trainees in their virtual firms, can slip in and out of character quite easily, and the environment is rarely as wholly immersive as the 3D MUVEs described in Chapter 6. However, as we shall see, students were able to learn from the activity of 'trying on' or fitting their real selves into their online self as a legal professional. This, after all, is what many of them are going to do for real at the end of the Diploma, and we make it clear to them that the Diploma is the time for them to practise roles, values, ethics and transactions which will be very real in the coming few years.

Our fictional city, therefore, had a number of aims, namely to provide students with:

- the backdrop for legal transactions – what might be termed the 'realia' of professional legal work. The term derives from archival work, and includes a vast array of objects in that domain, such as scrapbooks, newspaper clippings, advertisements, photographs, wills, bank books, account books, etc. We have created many such objects in the virtual town;
- characters, institutions, professional networks with which they can communicate;

---

9   The virtual environment has involved many personnel. When we started to develop it, there were only two of us involved in the project – Scott Walker and myself. Scott, now our Learning Technologies Development Officer, has a background in ICT and AV; and he is responsible for the technical design of our environments. For the first few years, we employed student programmers to help us construct web pages. Gradually, we brought together a technical team which could construct learning applications using an 'agile methodologies' approach to the production of learning applications. We give special consideration to:
1) *adaptivity*. Agile methods work via processes that adapt and thrive on change. This applies as much to our working method itself as to the product of the method.
2) *the situation of users*. We think about who will be using the software and in what environments and to what purpose. We also consider our own role in the production, testing and use of the software (Beck and Beddle, 2001).
10   See Drew (1998); Bennet et al. (2000); Lucas et al. (2004).

- virtual offices within which they can work as they might work within a law firm;
- IT communicational systems embedded within the virtual community;
- as close as possible a simulation of actual legal transactions;
- a discipline-neutral environment for legal transactions that could welcome other disciplines and possibly law students working in other jurisdictions.

The last point may require a little unpacking. If, as outlined in Chapter 1, we are to take the lessons of interdisciplinary study seriously, then it would make the enterprise a lot easier to manage if there were a transactional environment that could be used by a number of disciplines – a point we shall discuss below.

There is a synergy between environment and student transactions. Clearly the environment must support the transactions; but it also ought to go beyond it. The first transaction around which the environment was constructed was the Personal Injury Negotiation transaction (Maharg, 2001b and Maharg, 2002), which was first implemented in 1999. This had been created three years earlier at another university as a simple email negotiation between teams of students. There were no realia, no virtual community tools, and there was no web-based functionality. In 1999 the first sense of an online space given to students was a webpage consisting of photo-montage, later developed as a rather crude schematic map with no interactive features. That year we also created 50 document sets, based around the same basic scenario, but differing in key details such as type of injury, wages details, names and addresses, and so on. These document details were labelled as variables and databased within a document server, thus creating out of the same basic scenario any number of different transactions.

The next year, 2000–2001, we brought a second subject into the environment, namely Private Client. A third transaction, namely Conveyancing, in which students buy and sell domestic property over the web, was added to the environment, and later others such as the Civil Court Action and Practice Management. More – such as Public Administration (liquor licence application), Company and Commercial (setting up and winding down a 'shelf' company) – are in the process of being created.

As the transactions increased in number and complexity we assembled a sense of place built around the original, very simple schematic town map described above. The following year (2000–2001) the map was redrawn so that it was graphically more sophisticated, and included website links built into it (Figure 7.1). These resources were gradually increased, and in 2001–2002 a directory was added as the number of characters, businesses and institutions grew in size (Figure 7.2).

Currently the map exists as a web page developed using Flash with many small photographs attached to streets to give a sense of an actual place. The virtual law office has similarly been developed incrementally. In the first year of operation (1999–2000), it was little more than an email address. The next year we used MS Outlook and MS Exchange server to develop a more sophisticated environment

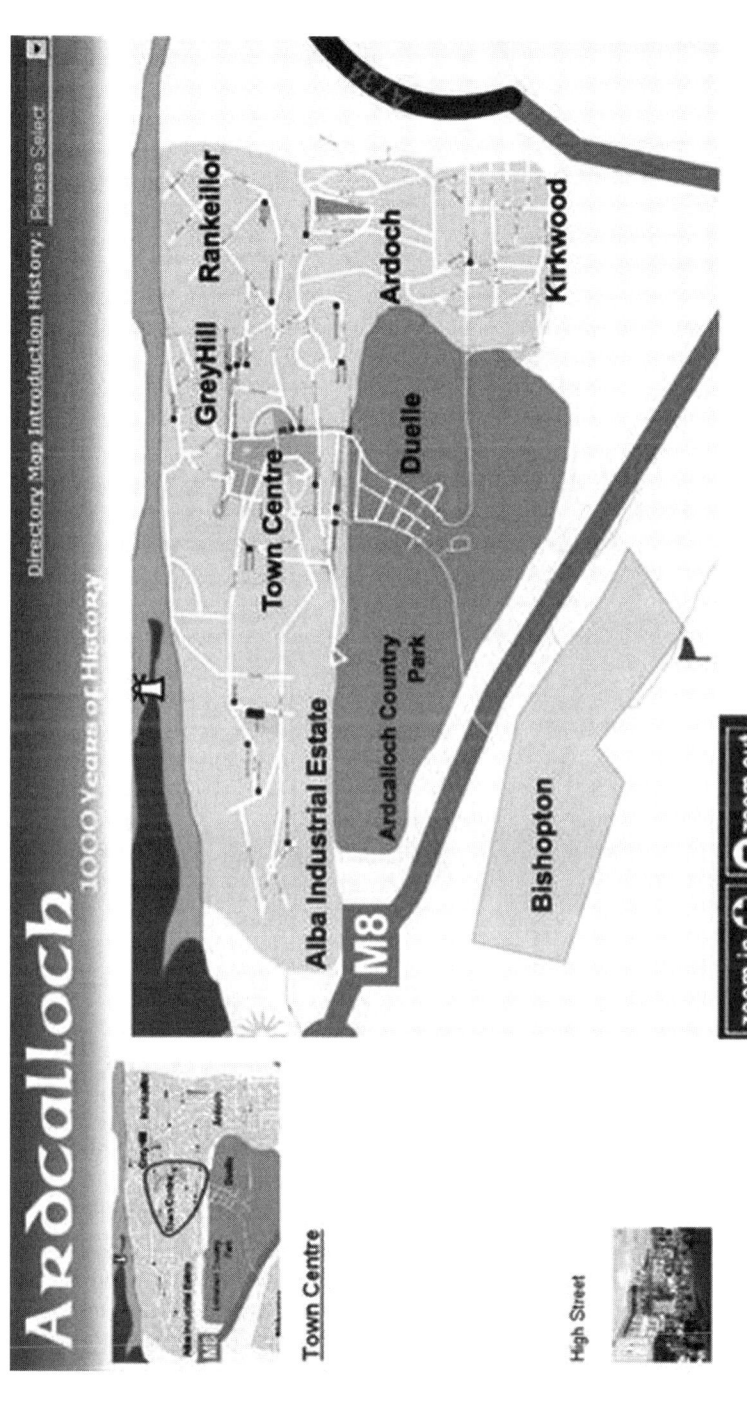

Figure 7.1 Map of Ardcalloch

Note: On the left is a thumbnail view (top left) and photographs (lower left) associated with topographical details in the town.

Figure 7.2   Ardcalloch directory

(the application was used at that time by a number of larger Scottish law firms as the interface to their office systems) and later still we built a truly web-based MS .NET application. This year the office environment has been designed around Windows SharePoint Team Services amongst other applications, with a greater range of collaborative learning tools – task organiser, calendar, firm minutes, confidential logs, discussion forums and alerting services (see Figures 7.3 and 7.4).

With transactions increasing in number and complexity, the directory became more important as a way of navigating information within the town. The first directory was relatively crude in design, but the following year we devoted considerable efforts to creating a substantial directory subdivided into categories – institutions, businesses, law firms, citizens.[11]

---

11 'Law firms' was an anomalous category because it was so specific, but it was necessary to create it because students would want to check this list most frequently, and because of the number of law firms within the town. The sheer number of law firms within the town was the subject of comment in the *Ardcalloch News*, an online newspaper (written by students), who noted in a weekly column that there were more lawyers than nurses in Ardcalloch, and wondered whether this development was good for society.

Figure 7.3   Student law firm generic front page

Note: Each of the links contains further information about the firm.

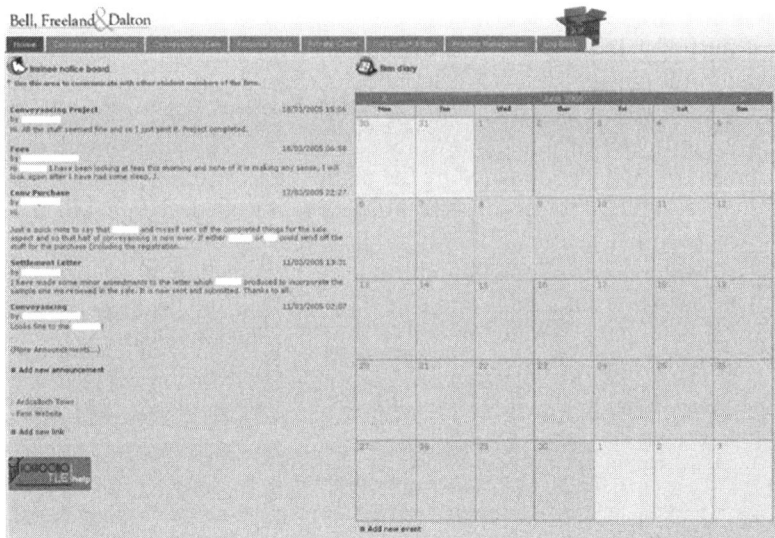

Figure 7.4   Law firm intranet page

Note: Note the transaction tabs in the strapline below the firm title.

Working within an online simulation environment affects attitudes not only towards IT but also towards how it can be used within a legal office practice. One of the issues we were concerned about was that of security – not the security of our own systems, which was an altogether different matter, involving university and departmental systems – but that affecting legal practice. Communications security and secure encryption over the internet remains a serious issue for lawyers and we needed to alert students to this in our online environment. We did so with the introduction of a fiction, namely 'AdeX' – Ardcalloch Digital Exchange. We informed the firms that under a Scottish Enterprise scheme to develop local broadband culture and communications, Ardcalloch had won a grant to install and use a wide-area broadband which also included secure digital communications systems. Lawyers could thus communicate with each other and with everyone else within Ardcalloch the need for third-party applications or delivery methods. The fiction raised the issue of internet security to students without actually inhibiting communications in the transactions.

A sense of locale is present in the history of the town (Figure 7.5). We wrote a brief historical essay on the town, available on the website by historical period, which describes the town's place in Scottish history and particularly in Scottish legal history. The history is also linked to the websites in the town that students can access. For instance, there is a Faculty of Procurators (a professional grouping of lawyers within a locality in Scotland) whose website describes its development within Ardcalloch, relations with its sister Faculty in Glasgow and its place within local legal culture in Ardcalloch and the west of Scotland. The town's development is described in detail. The centre, for example, is the old medieval heart of the town. To the northeast lies Greyhill, with its jetties and modest docks developed in the nineteenth century, and the slum housing associated with this area (currently being redeveloped as a 'Silicon Dock'). Further east is Rankeillor, with its lines of modest tenemental housing. South of this lies the unique architectural development of Ardoch, designed by the planner and visionary Patrick Geddes as a response to the problems of slum housing that were developing in Greyhill in the early twentieth century.[12] However, the actual cultural development of any place also displays discontinuities and ruptures. The creation of a fiction enables us to focus on aspects of society and culture in decline, and the local response to that, and to deploy these as an integral part of transactional learning.

On one level, what we have created is a learning management system (LMS), one that is specifically developed for students who are at the professional stage

---

12 Geddes, like some other Scottish figures of the time such as J.B.S. Haldane, was a remarkable polymath – biologist, town planner, sociologist and educationalist. In the later nineteenth and early twentieth centuries he produced a number of City Design reports that were highly influential – for example Geddes (1904) where he declared his aim to be civic renaissance, and 'the larger possibilities of civic life' (p. 215). After reading such a declaration there was only one thing to do: I co-opted Geddes to redesign urban spaces in Ardcalloch, and his unique solution of gardens and tenements can be seen in the Ardoch neighbourhood in Ardcalloch. Thus can art transform reality.

Origins

The name of the town is Celtic in origin. 'Cailleach' means 'old women' or cowled women', possibly referring to nuns. There is a legend that the priory of St Cerulus was built on the site of an earlier Celtic foundation attributed to St Kentigerna, the daughter of Ceilach, Prince of Leinster (early eighth century, d. 733). The island of Inchcailleach in Loch Lomond, where she died, is apparently derived from the same root. According to Nennius, a chapel, dedicated to her, and containing some of her bones, was erected some time in the eighth century. No trace of this has been found, though it is probable that the Premonstratensian foundation of St Michael in the fourteenth century was built upon the site of this early chapel. Nennius' account is corroborated by the *Orkneyinga Saga* which relates that Earl Rognvald, great-nephew of Saint Magnus and builder of the foundations of St Magnus cathedral, on his crusade to the Holy Land, visited her shrine around 1132 to pray for his safe deliverance. St Kentigerna must have listened to the Earl, for he returned to Orkney two years later, after a remarkable series of adventures.

There is also evidence that Ardcalloch was originally a settlement which grew up around the Clyde crossing at this point in the river, which is the lowest crossing point for the major settlement on Dunbarton Rock, on the other side of the river. It would appear that in early medieval times it was possible to walk across the river at this point at low tide. There were local stories that marker poles were driven into the mud for this purpose; and indeed there are records made by James Watt that bear this out. During the work he carried out in preparation for his report on the river in the later eighteenth century, he recorded that 'there are the remains of wooden stakes driven deep into the mud of the river, from one side to the other as if put there for the purpose of guiding travellers across the river, else for the siting of fishing nets'.

Watt's deduction was given corroboration in 1885 when workmen excavating a railway spur to the docks came upon a roadway of neatly laid stones, indicating a causeway that led down to the old ford. Local historians surmised that it was the Roman road to Dumbarton, and later archaeology has confirmed that this was indeed the direction of the road.

During the 1750s workmen repairing the roadway at the crossing point unearthed a hull composed of planks pegged to a wooden frame and set in a keel. From contemporary accounts it would appear that the vessel was constructed using viking techniques. The vessel was preserved in a house turned into a museum of the Clyde, which was later demolished by a bomb in World War II.

Figure 7.5   History of Ardcalloch, early medieval period

of legal education. On another, though, what we have is a sophisticated problem-based learning environment, one that is focused on legal transactions and that builds an online community of educational interests. These transactions and the theory behind them are explored in more detail below. Before we go on to consider this, though, we should perhaps describe some influences in how we developed the environment over the past four years or so. Two general points should be mentioned, namely the user interface, and the simulation model.

User Interface

In her description of how *The Sims Online* was developed as a game, the designer Chris Trottier cited two important factors. The first she called 'design by accretion' (Cieniawa, 2003). At first the simulation exists as a mass of separate ideas and components. Gradually these begin to be pieced together. This is precisely what we did in the early days of the Ardcalloch development. But the simulation as it then existed was relatively crude, and if development were to stop there, then the process of learning would have been difficult and problematic for students. Instead, what we did each year was collect feedback, note problems and engage in what Trottier calls 'tuned emergence' – the balancing of components, rules, scenarios and much else. This fine-tuning is an essential element of MUVE design and for us it happens every year once student activities are over.

There are further conceptions about simulations that we needed to bear in mind. These were summarised quite usefully by Don Hopkins in his report of a talk by Will Wright (the designer of *SimCity* and other major games) given to Terry Winograd's Interface class at Stanford.[13] For Wright, there were a number of key features to game design that required to be integrated: the simulation model, the game play, the user interface, and the user's model. The latter two points were of interest to us in our simulation. By the term 'user interface' Wright means something deeper than the mere collection of buttons, links, functionality and so on. He is really referring to the virtual interface with the real world. Thus in *SimCity* the end product is not

> the shallow model of the city running in the computer. More importantly, it's the deeper model of the real world, and the intuitive understanding of complex dynamic systems, that people learn from playing it, in the context of everything else about a city that they already know. In that sense, *SimCity*, *SimEarth*, and *SimAnt* are quite educational, since they implant useful models in their users' minds.

Compare this to the situation of students in the virtual firms. They have tools they can use in their new professional environment, such as diary, task manager, collaborative communication tools and the like. This environment teaches them not merely about the value of such tools in the professional workspace, but how such tools mediate and change the relationships within the firm, between firms and others and between firm and client.

Simulation Model

Simulation, though, is not reality. In Borges' famous short story, the ambitious map of the realm is contiguous with the realm – it is the same size and stretches over the land. In the case of SimCity, if the same thing happened the simulation would *be* the city. In terms of our virtual firms, the simulation is obviously not reality. Our students are not real trainees any more than Ardcalloch is a real town – though many of them will be. But the tension between simulation and reality is always there. Students explore the environment of the map. They click on websites to discover how much detail there is and how deep the simulacrum actually runs – and they discover how shallow it is. This is not an admission of failure. What matters, as Will Wright points out, is the sensitivity of the design team to the gap between reality and simulation. In Hopkins' account,

> Some educators have asked Maxis to make SimCity expose more about the actual simulation itself, instead of hiding its inner workings from the user. They want to see how it works and what it depends on, so it is less of a game, and more educational. But what's really going on inside is not as realistic as they would want to believe: because of

---

13 See Hopkins (2002). For an update on many of the issues discussed by Hopkins, see Ondrejka (2006, pp. 158–79).

its nature as a game, and the constraint that it must run on low end home computers, it tries to fool people into thinking it's doing more than it really is, by taking advantage of the knowledge and expectations people already have about how a city is supposed to work. Implication is more efficient than simulation. (Hopkins, 2002)

Hopkins reports Wright as giving this as an example:

> Then there was the oil company who wanted 'Sim Refinery', so you could use it to lay out oil tanker ports and petroleum storage and piping systems, because they thought that it would give their employees useful experience in toxic waste disaster management, in the same way *SimCity* gives kids useful experience in being the mayor of a city. They didn't realize that the real lessons of *SimCity* are much more subtle than teaching people how to be good mayors. But the oil company hoped they could use it to teach any other lessons on their agenda just by plugging in a new set of graphics, a few rules, and a bunch of disasters.

Simulation is a subtle art, involving implication as well as overt statement. The same problems arose in the environment of Ardcalloch. For example, the number of citizen characters needed to be higher than the relative handful of roles needed for individual transactions. We therefore created a list of around 330 names, Ardcalloch street addresses and ADeX digital mail addresses which are used in the transactions set within the town. Only a few of the names appear in any particular firm's case-load and the sheer anonymity lends the list the sense of a body of strangers necessary for the illusion of an urban community. Novelists have long realised that they could use this device in writing about the city. As Walter Benjamin observed of Balzac's novels, with some astonishment, 'the number of supernumeraries runs to five hundred persons. Five hundred of his characters appear episodically without being integrated in the action' (Benjamin, 1999, p. 536 [Q4a, 5]).

What we supply in the transactional environment is an outline background, the firm environment, and scenarios where a variety of transactions can be carried out. But the crucial difference is in attempting to limit the educational experience. As Wright points out, it is indeed crude and unrealistic to expect a company's work force all to learn the same points from such a simulation. They can expect a minimum benchmark of learning, but inevitably their learning will be different. Nor is this different from the most mechanistic and shallow of MCQs: individual learning will always differ, sometimes quite profoundly. In this sense, learning within a simulation environment has the capacity to be at one and the same time a similar experience for all learners, and yet a profoundly different learning experience, depending on many different vectors such as prior experience, knowledge, motivation, collaborative skills and the like.

There is another, more general point here, though. Wright's words are of a piece with the approach taken by reader-response theorists to the interpretation of meaning, such as Rosenblatt, Iser and Jauss.[14] For these theorists, meaning derives from the relationship between reader and text and cultural context, and therefore – much as in music production – the gaps or spaces in the narrative or form are as important as the information that is there on the page. Meaning is thus shaped not by information *per se*, but by the absence of information and what readers do when faced with such a gap. This is a profound point for all game and simulation designers. An example of this point arises from the rules underlying the simulation transactions. The rules are rarely as apparent as they might appear at first glance. A personal injury pre-litigation negotiation transaction, for example, is highly a highly complex transaction to map out because some of the rules (for example, disclosure of evidence from one party to another, sharing of evidence, negotiation conventions, communications with client and other professionals, ethics, and so on) are not always clear in practice, however they might appear in theory and often such matters require to be negotiated between parties. For a transactional designer, one of the key design issues is which rules should be made explicit within the simulation and which rules should be left as absences, unspoken, to be discovered and negotiated by students.

Much more could be said of our use and implementation of the general virtual community itself. But enough has been given to give a sense of why we began this experiment and how we went about it. While it is useful in itself to learn how such a transactional environment could be developed, it is set out here as background information for the next section of this chapter, where we shall describe in some detail the transactions, teaching and learning that took place in this environment.

Development of the Transactional Learning Environment (TLE)

Personal Injury (PI) Negotiation Transaction: Background

The transaction itself has been described in detail elsewhere and will therefore be only briefly described here.[15] The aim of the transaction is an agreed settlement between student firms, one set representing the client who has been injured at work, while another set represents the insurer. The rules of the transaction

---

14 Also termed 'reception aesthetics'. See for instance Rosenblatt (1978), Iser (1978) and Jauss (1982). The movement involved many other literary critics and developed sub-schools within itself – for instance the Constance School of Iser, Jauss and others, based at University of Constance. The concept of the absence or gap was specifically developed by Iser, adapting Roman Ingaarden's concept of the indeterminacies of meaning. Rosenblatt, originally a professor of education at Columbia, was much influenced by John Dewey's concept of transactional meaning creation, as can be seen from the subtitle of her influential text.

15 See for example Maharg (2001b, pp. 345–60); Maharg and Paliwala (2002).

state that student work is assessed on four evidence-bases: fact-finding in the virtual community, legal research, construction of negotiation strategy and performance of the strategy, and communications. There is no binding rule that students must reach a negotiated settlement with the other side; only that they should make all efforts to so do. Both sides are given minimal information at the start of the transaction (some documents, and the firm representing the injured claimant has an initial video interview) and need to construct the factual basis of their case by corresponding with over 20 businesses, institutions and citizens in Ardcalloch. Behind these characters is a body of trained postgraduates, trainees and practitioners who feed information in real-time and in character on request and who can also enter to guide students as a 'PI senior partner'.

Each year the transaction lasts for around 12 weeks. During that time there are no formal classes except for initial and general feedback lectures. The absence of formal academic classes is, of course, deliberate. There are alternative forms of face-to-face contact with staff. Students can attend voluntary 'surgeries' in their firms with a PI practitioner if they wish; and nearer the time of face-to-face negotiation with the other side they can discuss their legal research and negotiation strategy with a negotiation tutor – in effect, adaptations of salon and masterclass learning that were discussed in Chapter 2 with reference to the Kodàly Method.

Supporting the students throughout the process is a range of textual resources that are carefully planned and placed within the online environment – weblinks to general PI information on the intranet, FAQs specific to the transaction, a week-by-week overview of the transaction's stages, separate discussion forums for claimant firms and defender firms, while there are correspondence files on firm websites, as well as confidential deal rooms for negotiation with their opposite firm. The PI facilitators are themselves supported by a library of template documents for each transaction (differing in names, types of injury and other details), a forum on which to discuss problematic information requests or situations; and they can also monitor all intra-firm communications on the student firm pages (see Figure 7.6). This diagram represents the communications and resources matrix of the transaction (note that Practice Management will be dealt with in the next chapter).

With this complex structure we are attempting to support the complexity of the students' educational experiences. It is by no means approaching the complexity of the logs in *World of Warcraft* noted in Chapter 6, but it is beginning to support the sophistication of students' educational experiences online. Such multi-layered communication channels are essential to learning and being within the simulated world. They enable students to have, for instance, 'long conversations' about learning (Mercer, 1995, pp. 70–71).[16]

---

16 The idea that we have short extracts or bursts of conversation which we carry with us to a greater or lesser extent over a period of time is a normal, if generally unregarded, feature of conversation. We do not remember word for word, but carry with us a sense of what was said, with episodic chunks being remembered. Mercer applies this concept to

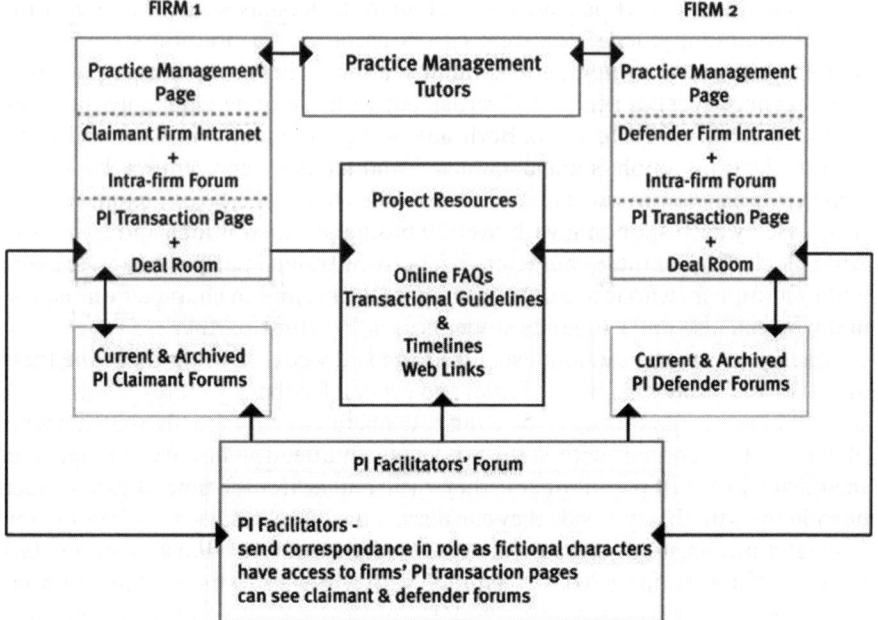

Figure 7.6   Personal Injury transaction communication lines

All of this is crucial to the process of negotiation, which is similarly a form of long conversation based heavily on memory and expectation. There is, in experienced negotiators, the gestalt of a negotiation: the repertoire of moves, plans, shifts, communication choices, interpersonal sensings and much more that go to make up the dance of negotiation. Throughout this, memory and expectation are crucial components against which the negotiator is always testing the present transaction. For our students, this gestalt was a developing one. Their conversation with each other in their firms, with the other side, and with fictional sources in the virtual community was composed largely of the formal dance of letters and documents. Students themselves largely choreographed this dance, both within their firms and between them. The negotiation process was itself a negotiation, this time of meaning, as students pieced together the practical elements of the incident. For instance, the facts of the incident required to be interpreted on many levels: witness statements, medical reports, and the like. In other words,

---

learning, noting that, like conversations, learning depends on references to past and future: it relies on memory and expectation or anticipation. We would hold, from our experience in simulation learning, that it is vital to give students the tools with which to manage such a long conversation about learning, with themselves, other students they are working with and tutors, across spans of time and across different transactions. The communications and resources matrix set out here represents our attempt to do just that.

information was negotiable itself[17] (see Barnes and Todd, 1977, at Mercer, 1995, p. 94). Moreover, students require to take categories from the sub-areas of the discipline – contributory negligence, DSS benefit payments – and apply them to others' complicated and always unfinished narratives. In this sense they are practising the use of legal categories to interrogate the relevance and quality of claims, evidence and hypotheses made by others and to do so they need to reach their own collaborative decisions and understandings.

Examples of Situated Learning

What we have in this project is an example of situated learning. Every year there are numerous examples of situated learning created by students which demonstrate not merely that they learn how to carry out a legal transaction, but that in the process they learn the values and ethics of professional practice, and at a deep level. Two examples will suffice.

Example 1

A student from a virtual firm that represented the insurers (that is, they were the defenders or defendants) in the Personal Injury transaction wrote to the Managing Director of Melville Welding, where the accident that was the basis of the pursuer's claim took place. As a PI facilitator for this firm, one of my responsibilities was to answer mail in real-time and in character. I replied in the character of John Rutherford, who is a no-nonsense MD of the firm and who was glad to get rid of the injured employee whom he regarded as a poor worker. Over the course of six weeks we became quite friendly in our respective roles and the student lawyer entered into the role play by referring in his letters to playing golf in the local club, and so on, to which I responded in kind. Student lawyer and businessman were developing trust in an interesting way.

Towards the transaction deadline (20 December), the student wrote Rutherford a letter asking if he minded granting access to a specialist Health and Safety consultant employed by the pursuer's solicitors to assess and analyse the status of the grinding equipment upon which the accident had occurred, but only after 20 December (that is, after the transaction was due to finish). I wrote back in character, quite open to this suggestion, but let it be known to the student that my diary and workflows on the shop floor could accommodate an earlier date and that I was quite amenable to this – what did he want to do? The student was now in the situation of effectively asking the client to lie in the hope of achieving a better settlement. I then sent a memo to the firm in my character as firm PI

---

17 And learning becomes negotiable, too, in the best sense. Mercer (1995, p. 94), quoting Barnes and Todd (1977, p. 127), notes the effect of this. The passage is worth quoting in full: 'Our point is that to place the responsibility in the learners' hands changes the nature of that learning by requiring them to negotiate their own criteria of relevance and truth. If schooling is to prepare young people for responsible adult life, such learning has an important place in the repertoire of social relationships which teachers must have at their disposal.'

senior partner, reminding the firm in very general terms of the need to manage risk appropriately, be aware of ethical circumstances and so on that may arise in the course of the transactions. I then waited to see what would happen.

In this situation we can see the usefulness of the transaction as a tool for enhancing ethical awareness in students. The scenario has its own ethical points embedded in documents, but this ethical situation arose out of the student's enthusiasm to exclude the other side from obtaining useful evidence and to do the best for his client. It arose from the process of document exchange and the relationship that had been built up between the anonymous information source as characters, and the student. In this we can see the advantage of detailed and realistic virtual communities. The situation arose, almost unawares, as many ethical situations often do, and the student now had to make a decision. What was he going to do? Would he send the letter that John Rutherford would provide most willingly? Or would he rethink his strategy as regards provision of information to the other side?

In the event, he did not send the letter. It may be, of course, that the fact that a senior partner pointed out to him the ethics of his action was enough to warn him off. But the very fact that he did not send the letter is a decision that he made: the situation was created by the student within the scenario and only partly shaped by me. It arose from the communications flow within the transaction and would not have arisen had the student merely learned *about* ethics and the transaction. Moreover, this is 'just-in-time' knowledge, not 'just-in-case' knowledge, of the sort Gee analysed and which was summarised in Chapter 6.

Example 2

One year, two firms were unable to settle. Prior to this, there had been problems in the process: firm B was adamant that there was no case to answer, while firm A was frustrated with the lack of progress over a number of weeks.[18] The firms agreed to a meeting, at the end of which a fairly low settlement figure of just above £6,000 was left on the table, with both firms reverting to their principals for final agreement. Firm A reported back to the claimant who asked for the figure could be increased to £7,000, which he would accept.

Firm A acknowledged and responded to the other side. Firm B responded, answering a point raised about time constraints and, since the counter-offer bore no relation to the points discussed at the face-to-face meeting, alleging unprofessional behaviour. Firm A's even lengthier reply hotly denied such behaviour, raising in turn points of behaviour on the part of firm B they considered 'unhelpful' and 'insulting'. With that, the correspondence between the two firms broke down entirely.

The whole correspondence (too long to quote here) is fascinating because it reveals many things about the course of the negotiation and the attitude

---

18 'Firm A' is acting for the claimant, while 'firm B' are the insurer's legal agents. Names have of course been removed to preserve anonymity.

of the negotiators. We can trace the gradual breakdown of trust through the communications. The monetary difference between the positions was not great, but the distance between the firms in terms of willingness to deal with each other was much greater and appeared to blind them to the best interests of their respective clients. This came about because of their commitment to the play rather than to the client. Clifford Geertz describes what might be seen as a similar situation in his famous anthropological study of Balinese cock-fighting, noting the huge sums of money that would be wagered on the outcome, and calling this 'deep play', where 'more is at stake than material gain: namely esteem, honour, dignity, respect – in a word, status' (Geertz, 1973).[19]

Such deep play calls up those very qualities that Barnett lamented as being absent from contemporary higher education and that Ferguson named to his class as the qualities they should aspire to. The simulation drew students into investing time and energy into fact-gathering, practical legal research and thinking about negotiation strategy, and created a powerful incentive for them to represent their clients to the best of their ability. The power of this was recognised by one of the pursuers, who commented to me on his client's painful acknowledgement of defeat,

> As you probably know, we've got a reply from the client and notwithstanding the fact that I know it's completely artificial, I feel gutted for him![20]

The situation had much wider implications, though, particularly as regards the resolution of the transaction. The PI transaction actually encourages students to become personally involved in their work on behalf of clients and others; but to be aware, too, of the nature of such personal involvement within a professional arena. There is also, too, the potential to analyse critically rather than merely reproduce the discourse of professionalism – what does it mean to work within an adversarial system of justice and retain 'personal honour'?

The lack of a settlement was not the end of the transaction – there was too much unfinished business, and raw feelings on both sides. The impasse between the two firms also presented staff with a quandary: what should we do in these circumstances to bring closure to the transaction? Two options presented themselves:

1) *Do nothing*
   Judge the firms on the evidence of the four criteria. Ignore their deteriorating situation.
2) *Force the firms to come to agreement*
   Compel them to a meeting in which an agreed settlement would be reached.

---

19 We might note in passing Ferguson's emphasis to his students on the need to learn about qualities such as 'personal honour' (Chapter 4).

20 Quoted with student permission.

Neither option was particularly helpful. The first would treat the transaction as an academic exercise where feelings did not really count – what mattered was whether both sides had fulfilled assessment criteria. The objectivity of the four-criteria assessment seemed to be false in the circumstances and more was required. Both firms would probably have passed; but the quarrel had soured the relationship between them and something needed to be done about this. On the other hand, forcing the firms to come to the table to negotiate yet again was wholly unrealistic and meant that staff imposed settlement in a parental way upon the firms. Option 1 seemed like negligence, while option 2 seemed oppressive.

A third option presented itself to us as the only way out of this dilemma. I asked each firm if it would enter a mediation process and they agreed to this. The mediation was carried out by a Visiting Professor to the GGSL, trained and highly experienced in mediation. Mediation appeared the best option for a number of reasons. First, it provided the possibility of realistic closure to the legal dispute. Second, it took account of the emotional and personal aspects of the failed negotiation process – the intimate dimensions of ethical practice explored in Chapter 4. Third, it was a neutral learning ground in which, in a positive environment, both sides could come to a complex understanding of why the negotiation had failed and their part in this failure. In this sense, it became an extension of the collaborative learning methods used in the transaction, and was a way that students could explore the social processes that contributed to the breakdown of the negotiation (Lea and Rogers, 2003). As Lea and Rogers point out, such matters are highly sensitive and involve students in the analysis of their own changing identities as they move from being students to being lawyers.

Just as identity was a key element in the play of avatars, so identity is a key issue here in negotiation, and not only in simulated negotiations carried out in legal education. Dezalay and Garth (1996, chs 1 and 2), for instance, show convincingly that in international business arbitration, the field of the informal, settlement-oriented system was governed by networks of practitioners known to each other and identified as key players by other lawyers and professionals. Who we are, how we play out those selfhoods in the interests of ideals, institutions, careers, employers and clients are all crucial issues in the formation of a personal legal identity. They were certainly central to the failure of the above negotiation. Yet they currently figure hardly at all in the formal assessment of skills and knowledge at the professional end of legal education – a point that will be explored in more depth in the next chapter.

Over the seven years the transaction has been running to date we have collected a substantial amount of qualitative data from students, which we use to improve the resources and environment every year. It is clear from some of the feedback that students could be involved in what is called 'thrashing' – 'the extended application of heuristics at an impasse that have a low probability of resolving that impasse' (Lewis et al., 1993, p. 195).[21] This is quite different from goal-oriented and productive inquiry, which either leads to the conclusion that further evidence is required or that a solution can be reached to the impasse in a number of steps. Thrashing involves random searching for information, whether in fact or in law, and generally happened because students found that none of their heuristics or negotiation plan strategies could move them on. And yet there is a difference between what one might regard as aimless thrashing and more sophisticated 'threshing'. This happened when students were unsure of the information that might result, but framed their communications so as to be open-ended and catch what there might be. The information would then often be sifted and threshed and issues arising would be added to the growing layers of legally-relevant information.

What we have here, interestingly, is students doing two things. They can logically plan out what their strategy is or they can put themselves in a situation where they know they have little knowledge and then have to work out a strategy from that move – situations strikingly similar to that of forward and backward thinking described in Chapter 1.[22] Student comment reflected this – for example, one member of the firm commented thus on the process of mediation that ended this transaction:

> the mediator forced the firm to be realistic – this meant that there was no opportunity for avoiding issues or playing games. The fact that the firm had no idea what the pursuers expected meant that we were forced to make a fair offer and point scoring exercises were successfully avoided. It also emphasised the fact that what was important was the client.

Having to face the issue that they had 'no idea what the pursuers expected' led them to engage in more positive and client-oriented methods of fact-finding and negotiation.

Private Client

As a number of educationalists point out, there is a paradox at the heart of the constructivist enterprise. Some version of authenticity is essential to a constructivist transaction, but this authenticity needs to be designed into the transaction.

---

21 Lewis et al. also give a useful history of discovery learning in twentieth-century American education.

22 Cf. Lee Shulman's distinction between thinking and acting, as told by James Rhem (2002): 'Shulman recounted how a wise head in medicine had explained to him that a surgeon acts in order to know what to think while an internist thinks in order to know how to act … the anecdote underscored the point he'd already previewed, that 'performance' or 'commitment' can (and quite appropriately may) precede 'understanding and knowledge.'

Authentic reality is therefore simulated. The paradox has led some commentators to argue that such work is a delusion: there can be no real authenticity in such a simulation (Terwilliger, 1997, pp. 24–7). Others call for a more detailed definition of what constitutes validity in constructivist projects (Schneuwly and Dolz, 1997, pp. 27–40). Whatever view one takes of this, it is doubtful whether the issue can be resolved on a general plane: it is probably best solved constantly within cycles of project planning, implementation and review (Tochon, 2000, pp. 331–59).

All aspects of such projects are careful constructions, even the spaces. Recall the analogies with music and silence, language and absence in Chapter 2: the same is true of the creation of transactions, where spaces or absences need to be built into the structure, as we shall see in the description of this transaction.[23]

Transactional Background

In the Diploma curriculum, 'Private Client' is that subject dealing with transactions such as the inheritance of property after death, the winding up of a deceased client's estate, and the drafting of wills. The subject currently consists of no lectures but a series of tutorials over the course of approximately 15 weeks. It was redesigned in 1999 for the joint GGSL Diploma; and after consultation with tutors we focused on the following four assessment points:

1) drafting a will;
2) drafting an initial writ;
3) composing letters to other professionals to ingather and evaluate the deceased's estate;
4) dealing with inheritance tax arising from the deceased's estate.

In the first year, we held these assessments as open-book examinations. However, it became clear after the marking of these assessments that open-book assessment was not particularly appropriate for the tasks in hand. Students could score as much as 80 per cent or more in the assignments, but could fail particular elements of it in such a way that the documents would be regarded by practitioners as seriously flawed documents in certain respects – the wording of particular clauses or the omission of key phrases or clauses, for example.

One response to this would be to mark particular drafting faults as 'red light' faults, that is, errors so severe that students would fail as a result of making them, and to highlight this to students in classes before the assessment. However, the attitude that this would probably engender amongst students would not have been helpful. 'Red lighting' has the effect of focusing student attention on specifics to the detriment of the whole. Students would probably become anxious about small, albeit important, elements of drafting, when we wanted them to consider

---

23 And of course note the parallel with reader-response criticism alluded to earlier in this chapter at pp. 199–200.

the context of the document and the document as a whole, as well as its detail (Cheltenham and Mutch, 2004).

In more detail, though, there are three more reasons why we discovered that open-book assessment and a 'red lighting' approach to drafting skills might not be the best approach:

1) As we have already seen in Chapters 1 and 2, rhetorical theory and research into writing in law schools gives us excellent evidence for holding that student and trainee composition can be significantly improved if law schools focus on the process of writing, rather than the product alone. This is true of professional writing as well. It is of course necessary to teach students the key points of legal difficulty in a document. However if a 'red lighting' approach to the assessment of drafting skills is taken, students may focus on these to the detriment of other points. Moreover, their understanding of process and their enactment of that process in the assessment becomes skewed.

2) A legal document is rarely drafted in isolation. It is frequently part of a set of documents that follow on in a process of exchange, with the client, with court administrators or other personnel, or with other professionals, including other lawyers. Sometimes the test of a good piece of drafting is how it is carried out in this context. Which decisions are made about choices and why? If students are to learn how a transaction can be carried out in its entirety, they need to learn this process-thinking about a transaction. The foundation of such thinking is knowledge of which documents are drafted and in which order. Open-book drafting assessment can of course accommodate this by incorporating assessment of document flow (for example, by way of multiple-choice or objective questions), but this is not quite the same as using this knowledge within a drafting task. Such assessment actually separates factual knowledge of process from the process of writing. By contrast, the principles of transactional learning require that procedures of legal process and drafting be carried out as authentically as possible in assessment tasks.

3) Drafting is almost always conducted in an informational environment. Any document exists within a web of information that must be sought before the document can be properly drafted. Some of this is fact-based and therefore easy to discover (but of course by no means trivial). Discovery, though, is only part of the process. Students also need to learn to interpret a document, store it and be able to retrieve it for the drafting task. Some of it is interpretive by nature – what the client wants to happen, how this translates into legal practice, and so on. Information-seeking is actually part of the drafting process, just as much as it is part of the process of drafting academic essays and dissertations. Open-book examinations cannot replicate this process – indeed, they deny it by often giving students the details that they would otherwise need to have discovered for themselves. The student's role in information-discovery and retrieval is thus impoverished by an emphasis on *product* at the expense of *process*.

4) An open-book assessment is nearer the reality of practice than a closed-book examination, but it is still an unnatural environment. It is defended on the basis that it puts students under the same time-pressures as many of them are under when they are drafting in firms. This is true to an extent, but actually it minimises those pressures because, in the period of time allotted for the assessment, students concentrate on nothing but the task in hand. In an office environment there are many tasks in hand that may need to be done and which will impinge upon the drafting task. The open-book assessment brackets the task and removes it from the reality of lived experience in the office, and the pressures that accumulate around the task.[24] Drafting tasks are difficult because of such pressures. One of the reasons for poor execution is that the students or trainees do not learn to set aside time to concentrate on the task in hand, having got to the position where all relevant information has been obtained for the drafting task and where they are ready to draft the document.

Transactional Life-cycle

Instead of an open-book approach and a focus on 'red-lighting', therefore, we decided to use the virtual learning environment of Ardcalloch as both a learning and assessment tool and to turn the open book examination into a form of coursework. The four assessment tasks would be strung together as a transactional narrative, which is what they are in practice. This is a strategic and development move that we found ourselves making again and again throughout the transactional process. Its effect on staff was considerable, altering roles and tasks. For course designers it involved liaison with solicitors in practice and others in identification of those forms of practice relevant to the transaction and analysis of them to determine how they might be used within a transaction.

For teaching staff it involved shifting the alignment of teaching and resources from forms of academic learning to workshop and coursework forms. The transaction became in effect the central pillar around which the rest of the course revolved; and this was the case whether the transaction was an open-field transaction, as was Personal Injury, or a more bounded-field transaction, as was Private Client (more on this terminology below). For administrative staff, there was a shift, too, in the way that assessment results were communicated to them. Clearly they needed a way in which they could receive the results of assessment as and when the assessment was completed and any updates. It became clear to us throughout the process of designing the administrative environment that the liaison between tutors and administration staff was crucial. Administrative environments needed to include the following information:

• transaction completion dates;

---

24 This is of course one of the key points raised by the literature on situated learning – see Wenger, 1998, particularly ch. 2.

- merit, competent and not yet competent status;
- prizewinners.

After the completion of the transaction, we engaged in reviews, not only with the students but also with staff and with administrative and ICT development staff. Many suggestions for improvement from teaching staff were implemented, although of course not all were possible.

The general structure of the lifecycle of development in this transaction applies to the design and development of most transactions. It is represented in Figure 7.7 (though obviously some of the detail is specific to Private Client). This is an indication of the general activities involved in transactional planning.[25]

The Private Client Transaction

The transaction begins with a memo from a senior partner to the four trainees in the firm, asking them to complete the winding up of an intestate estate, and giving the necessary details. The students are then required to draft and lodge an initial writ to begin the transaction. They know from their tutorials the details that should comprise the writ (though, of course, the details of the scenarios do not replicate the templates they are given in tutorials – students must adapt the template to their own scenario). There are deadlines for each of the assessments that students know in advance so that they can therefore plan their work. They have all the information that they need at the start of the transaction that would normally be available to them in the real life transaction. They also need to gather information from characters or institutions in Ardcalloch, particularly when they in-gather the estate and value the deceased's estate.

Each firm is given a different scenario. All scenarios are effectively built around the same generic narrative – deceased dies intestate and brother or sister arrives at the office with a collection of his or her estate – bank books, bills, share certificates, etc. This meant that we needed to create 64 different scenarios. In order to manage the detail of this, we created each scenario as a database of details drawing upon the central scenario. In planning this, we resorted to laying out the scenario as a matrix. What we have, in effect, is a cascade of variables across the scenarios which creates every scenario as a unique set of data. To an extent, therefore, we can detect direct plagiarism across firms.

At the same time, we wanted to leverage knowledge between members of the firms. As with all such transactions, the work of the firm itself is assessed rather than that of the individual four members of the firm. Each individual therefore needs to cooperate with others and there must be evidence that they have agreed each assessed document before it is submitted. In this way, we try to maximise learning within the group and ensure that they have the experience of working

---

25   It is, of course, not a learning plan or a taxonomy. For more general frameworks of this nature, see Laurillard (2002) and Conole and Oliver (1998), pp. 4–16.

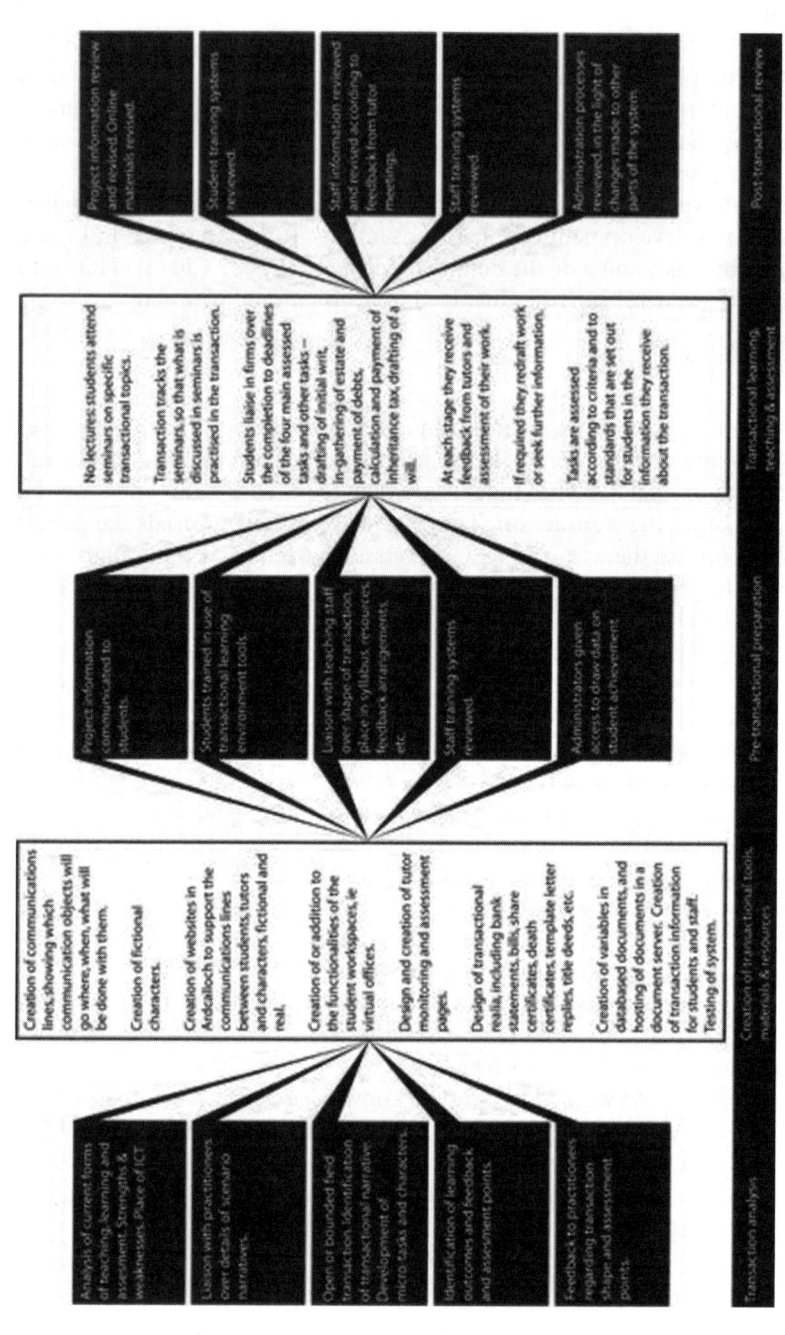

Figure 7.7 Transactional life-cycle development chart

Note: This is based upon the Private Client transaction, but contains many developmental activities generic to all transactions.

on a legal transaction as part of team, with each person taking responsibility for part of a transaction. It is, of course, a form of collaborative learning within the firm, as with all the transactional learning environment projects. However, as in the other transactions, the students determine how the tasks will be carried out. They do so on the basis of three contexts: task process, relevant information and time pressures. Each of these three contexts needs to be managed within the firm and they need to be managed in the overall context of personal relationships within the firm as well. Thus, in task process they need to be aware of the legal process surrounding the task. They also need to gather the relevant information before they can complete the task. At the very least they need to be aware of the information that is required and why it is necessary. They also need to plan the drafting of the document within the other time pressures that they have on the course, so that they can multi-task within the firm and within their own individual preparation for examinations, other assessments, tutorial preparation and the like.

After the transaction had run for the first year we needed to improve a number of aspects of the overall learning environment:

- the environment was poorly integrated with tutorial work and assessments;
- students were uncertain about online role-play – this was important, because we were relying upon e-role-play for students to develop their identities as lawyers;
- the differences between the PI transaction and Private Client transaction were not made apparent to the students. During the PI transaction, students are immersed in their roles. However, the Private Client transaction relies much more on traditional courseware assessment points throughout the curriculum. There is thus less immersion, all the more so because there was less communication with fictional characters and institutions in Ardcalloch and because tutors played a key role in marking assignments as the transaction moved through the semester.

Once these problems were dealt with, student feedback about the transaction as a form of learning and assessment was impressive:

- 'I am confident that the skills I have learned in this class will be invaluable in my traineeship.'
- 'Effective in that it [the transaction] made me more aware of practising and the implications of doing so.'

There is a substantial amount of research work to be carried out on virtual environments such as the two simulations described above. For example:

1) The nature of dialogues, between members of firms, between firms and between firms and tutors needs to be investigated in depth.

2) While it is possible to assess students according to fairly general criteria based on competence evidence, there are criteria that can be drawn from practice as regards communication with which we could refine the tools of analysis.[26] There is, after all, evidence that students can fail to understand the deep causal models of behaviour within a simulation, precisely because they are led to focus on mere manipulation of the objects in the simulation environment (Twigger et al., 1991, pp. 144–55*)*.[27]

3) The role of the tutor-discussants on the PI negotiation transaction discussion forum is clearly to mediate knowledge about the transaction, both as it is played out within the GGSL and more importantly within legal practice. This suggests a transmission model of education, in the midst of what is supposed to be a constructivist transaction. Instead, I would argue that the tutor-discussants perform a critical function, in helping students to resolve practice issues. They have, as Laurillard would put it, an *adaptive* mediating role. But this being so, which dialogues are best at bringing about engagement, understanding and change?

In addition, we are constructing a matrix for what we term 'open-field' transactions, as opposed to 'bounded-field' transactions. These terms are the poles of a spectrum within which we can create transactional spaces. Their characteristics are set out at Figure 7.8 (see below). There is, though, a deeper meaning to the field concept. Real-life transactions happen in what we might regard as a field – a tiny microcosm of Bourdieu's vast social field, with its *habitus* – ways in which thoughts and actions become ingrained or 'habituated', and thus gradually invisible and difficult to analyse –its *méconaissance* or misrecognition and its *sens pratique* – the sense of being there within a practice (Bourdieu and Passeron, 1977, p. 171).[28] Through the process of developing the detail of a transaction for a simulation, the designer must engage in detail with this field and can, if he or she wishes, focus on and expose aspects of the *habitus* to students at the very moment it has begun to take shape for them.[29]

---

26 For an example from the field of medical education, see Lingard et al. (2002).

27 This of course is analogous to discussions of phenomenographical literature, where researchers analysed forms of interventions in student understanding of text, and the effect it had on learning.

28 *Méconaissance* is both lack of awareness and deliberate misunderstanding, in the sense that agents work within the grid of a field and choose to understand their perceptions in terms of the grid – they may indeed perceive their understanding as the only rational choice, the natural way to understand a phenomenon.

29 Many others have advocated this form of cultural awareness-raising. Gramsci's hegemonic analysis, for instance, is at times close to Bourdieu's commentary on how dominant classes maintain their position in society through their acquisition and management of both material and symbolic resources. Cultural awareness-raising that uses simulation as the tool of analysis is, however, unusual – unless of course one includes instances such as Boal's Forum Theatre, etc. discussed above.

		Bounded field ie transaction tends to...	Open field ie transaction tends to...
1	Learning outcomes (LOs) & assessment	Precise learning outcomes, with simulation tasks based closely on outcomes – pre-defined LOs	Bodies of evidence required to be produced to bench-mark standards, but less emphasis on pre-specified outcomes
2	Alignment with traditional learning & teaching methods	Teaching is aligned with tasks and outcomes, often according to an academic structure, eg lecture–seminar; learning is heavily 'pushed' by curriculum structure	Teaching is provided where needed according to learners' needs, often according to a professional, just-in-time learning structure; learning is 'pulled' by learners
3	Operational model	Linear domain procedures, eg predictable document chain – more operationally predictable	More varied, open or diffuse domain procedures, eg transactional guidelines but no specific document chain – less operationally predictable
4	Student outputs	Specific documents, drafted to specific standards, eg initial writ; fixed or correct versions expected as student output	Procedures that involve a variety of documentation, or documents that cannot be specified easily in advance, eg negotiated agreements; various versions acceptable
5	Resources	Resources are tied closely to tasks and learning outcomes – highly model driven	Simulation resources are not linked to tasks; learner needs to structure transaction through interactive querying of resources – highly learner driven

Figure 7.8   Characteristics of bounded-field and open-field transactions

Summary

The Ardcalloch transactional experiments are by no means the only simulations in recent legal education. The negotiation project between the EDHEC Business School in France and International Economic Law LLB students at Warwick, and the first year undergraduate module in Contracts at Lancaster are initiatives that show how successful and powerful simulation can be when implemented effectively (Maharg and Paliwala, 2002, pp. 96–7 and Bloxham and Armitrage, 2003). In the Diploma in Legal Practice, transactional learning is being implemented not merely in one module, but in stages across an entire curriculum, and therefore faces the large-scale implementation problems associated with such a project – problems and solutions we shall consider in the next chapter.

But can the transactional environment of a professional and postgraduate course be adapted to undergraduate law programmes? It might be argued that the

Personal Injury and Private Client transactions discussed above were designed for and implemented within a postgraduate professional practice course, and therefore are incompatible with the aims of undergraduate modules. Professional education is sometimes seen as having different educational aims to that of undergraduate education. Certainly, in terms of the types of skills and knowledge that are taught and how they are *currently* taught the two are quite different.

But the design work of Bloxham and Armitage (2003) and Barton and McKellar (1998) shows that simulations can be used effectively in undergraduate curricula. In addition, I would add that transactional learning theory is as relevant to undergraduate as it is to postgraduate legal education – indeed, that even the most apparently conceptual subjects in the legal curriculum can, at least in part, be taught, learned and assessed using variations of transactional learning. The basis for this claim lies in educational models which can, indeed *must*, be adapted for both. Essential to our task of implementation is the body of transactional theory that is put into practice in the virtual environment, and which is for us an essential guide to actions in the virtual world.[30] Well before Bloom's Taxonomy it has been axiomatic that the development and integration of skill, knowledge and values is one of the chief aims of education (Bloom, 1956). It may be appropriate to focus at times on either skill or knowledge in the course of a programme of study; but one of the overall aims of any educational strategy should be to give students opportunities to practise such integration. Contemporary educationalists of Higher Education emphasise this aspect of the learning process (Biggs, 2003; Ramsden, 1992; Laurillard, 2002). We are already adapting our approach for undergraduate education – for example, in a new problem-based induction course for first year students which is integrated across study guides, tutorials, video lectures and which takes into account the social aspects of learning through collaborative work.

Our approach is being adapted not only to undergraduate learning but also to legal learning across jurisdictions as well (Maharg and Muntjewerff, 2003). In the academic year 2005/6 we ran a simulation between GGSL law students on the Diploma and business students in Erasmus University, Rotterdam for the first time, based on a scenario that ran on the platform of our sister project in the Netherlands, Sieberdam. The transaction involved two small boatyards, in Sieberdam and Ardcalloch, and centred on an international contract, the focus of which was intellectual property upon a design for yachts. The potential for such trans-jurisdictional, transdisciplinary and transnational simulation learning is, of course, immense.[31]

---

30 Transactional learning theory is still in its early stages of construction and its robustness can only be developed by fieldwork and theory-building. It is not the only body of theory we use on the Diploma. In our construction of multimedia online resources, for example, we use cognitive feedback theory that is more appropriate to the teaching and learning environment and student use of the resources.

31 For information on Sieberdam, see http://tinyurl.com/27vw7p.

But how were students supported during these curriculum-wide transactions? How did we ensure that collaborative learning was truly collaborative? What changed in the curriculum when the transactional environment was planned to be embedded throughout it? These and other questions will be answered in the next chapter.

Chapter 8

Relational Objects: Transactions, Professionalism, E-mergence

> But there is another way of thinking, one that stresses making the virtual and the real more permeable to each other. We don't have to reject life on the screen, but we don't have to treat it as an alternative life either. Virtual personae can be a resource for self-reflection and self-transformation. ... Like the anthropologist returning home from a foreign culture, the voyager in virtuality can return to the real world better able to understand what about it is arbitrary and can be changed.
>
> (Turkle, 1996, p. 57)

In the last chapter we saw how a sophisticated simulation environment can be designed to facilitate learning. The transactional learning environment raises many questions, precisely because it operates within an overtly transformational agenda. How good is the quality of the work that students produce? What do students learn better or worse in such an environment compared to more traditional environments? How do students work collaboratively to such a degree in this environment? If this method has ambitions to support an entire curriculum, how do student and staff methods of working change from that required in a course of study that takes a more traditional approach to academic or professional education? What do these changes mean for staff roles, workloads and work patterns? This chapter sets out to answer some of these questions, and in particular, how this approach changes both student work patterns and staff patterns of engagement with students. Collaborative work, at every level, is the key: between students, between staff and students, and between disciplinary specialisms. To set the context, I shall start by describing some aspects of curriculum design, then how firms are constructed and how students work together within their virtual firms.

Curriculum Design: Speed and Topography

Transactional learning requires as much careful plotting within the curriculum as does problem-based learning.[1] It is essential to chart how a simulation will relate to other simulations on a course, not just to avoid choke-points on

---

1   See Barrows and Tamblyn (1980) and Boud and Feletti (1991).

assessment deadlines or to align with learning outcomes, but to ensure that the simulations integrate with each other in the curriculum. All transactions consist of sequenced events that contain nested elements. Some, such as Conveyancing, consist of document flows and interactions that are highly order-dependent. Others, such as Personal Injury, contain a series of interactive mini-sequences that can be enacted in a number of different ways and at different occasions by students. A firm, for instance, may wish confidential health information about its client. It may want to gather such information at any point in the transaction, but before it can do so, it must first obtain a mandate to do so from its client.[2] Sometimes parts of a simulation can be played in parallel. For example, in Private Client the ingathering of the estate can proceed while students begin to absorb how the estate information will be represented in an IHT200 form (the IR form used in the UK to pay death duties). Within themselves, then, simulations consist of nested elements that can be transacted linearly (as with Conveyancing) or in parallel. The more nested elements there are and the more parallelism there is, the more complex the simulated environment becomes for students to understand and play, and the more complex it is for staff to design and administer. If nested elements can be transacted in a variety of manoeuvres, then – as we saw in the previous chapter – the more 'open' is the simulation. If the nested elements must be played out in a strict order, then the simulation is said to be highly 'bounded'.

This is of course true of the wider context of the whole programme of study – see Figure 8.1. As represented there, the Diploma curriculum as it currently exists in 2006/7 consists of nested transactions, which are played out in parallel. The simulations start with an open-field project, PI Negotiation, together with another firm project, namely the assessment for Tax, which consists of a firm's presentation to the entire tutorial group on the tax options open to a client, given the client's circumstances. Both transactions start the firms working at a fairly gentle transactional pace (that is, students have considerable latitude in deciding when they carry out specific tasks). Private Client has more deadlines, and the pace quickens. In Conveyancing, the rate of complexity increases again: not only does this type of transaction move more quickly from one document to the next, but students need to deal with two parallel transactions – purchase and sale. Like Conveyancing, the Civil Court Action is a fairly fast-moving transaction, with swift document exchange and drafting tasks to be undertaken in relatively short timescales.

Speed of transaction is something that is almost never dealt with in traditional professional learning, yet it is of the essence of a transaction. Increased speed involves more cognitive effort, puts more pressure on the firm and leaves less room for error while increasing the risk of error. By introducing transactional speed as a variable we are introducing one of the key characteristics of legal practice and

---

2   Elements of this procedure may be repeated if the firm seeks health information from a general practitioner and also a consultant surgeon in a hospital.

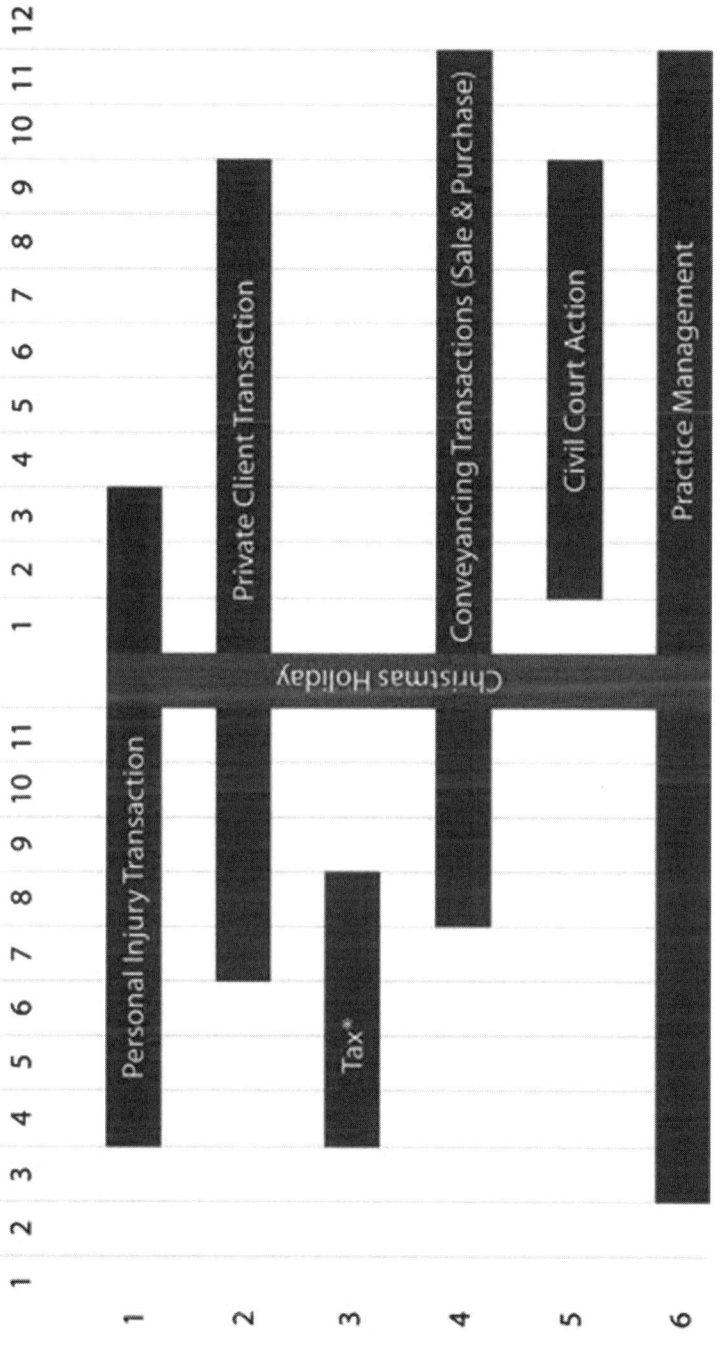

Figure 8.1 Chronology of transactions within the Diploma curriculum (2006/7)

Note: *Firm-based learning and assessment, but not online.

giving students the opportunity, within the safe environment of the transactional learning environment (TLE), to learn to cope with the practice complexities it introduces. This can only be done via highly experiential means. Gee pointed this out as regards learning complex online games (see Chapter 6, p. 177, where he compared the language of instruction in a game's instruction booklet to the game itself): the same is true of transactional learning.

This planned activity is essential to the success of a simulation, in much the same way that Gee pointed out that careful introduction of novice players to levels of games was important to the players' ongoing success. The same is true of educational simulations, and the induction activities we plan for student firms. We introduce them to their firms using supervised and then unsupervised sandbox activities. Learners find their own levels of competence within the environment, and if they need further help then they can attend back-up sessions.

The two-dimensional metaphor of the open or bounded field, however, does not alone do justice to either the planning of resources by staff or the use of resources by students within the simulation field. Students carry out the transaction by using resources and objects within the field. The topographical distribution of objects therefore requires careful planning and is one of the most time-consuming phases of the design process. Ideally they must be as available or hidden as they would be in the real world. If they are not immediately to-hand for students then we try to replicate the process by which students would obtain them in the real world.

Two examples will serve to illustrate the importance of this. First, in the Personal Injury transaction one of the aims is to help students to question and clarify the facts that they come across or are given by clients or witnesses or expert witnesses. Early in the transaction, for instance, the defender firms are given a set of photographs in the insurance company's report which show a flight of stairs, with the unstated presumption that this flight was the locus of the accident in which an employee tripped and fell. The claimant's firm is sent photos too, but of an entirely different flight of stairs, taken by the claimant himself.[3] The firms are not alerted to the discrepancy. They discover this for themselves in the fact-finding stages of the transaction if they are playing cooperatively with each other, at which point they can resolve the situation quite easily. If they are playing competitively and refuse to share resources, then they will probably discover the discrepancy at a later stage of the negotiation, at which point the error is more serious and problematic to resolve – particularly if they have instructed specialist reports on the stairs – but not impossibly so. The strategy behind this is to let students appreciate the value of cooperative negotiation, as well as confirming facts key to their case. As such, it represents an ideological value that the simulation designers attach to this view of negotiation. We could, of course, have made a different point – for example, by embedding within a document a

---

3   The situation is not unknown in such cases: it is difficult to pin down the exact location of a flight of steps, though essential to do so.

detail that was highly personal and damaging to a client's case, and should not be shared with the other side.

Second, we try to place transactional resources so that they may exhibit the same meaning or randomness that would attend their existence in the real world. This means that, where appropriate, we try to surround objects with the network of meanings or noise that would accrete around them in the real world. In the Personal Injury transaction. for instance, some witnesses will be helpful and/or amenable; others will be unhelpful and/or brusque – all will give meaningful and relatively irrelevant information and within case guidelines it is in the hands of the mentor to decide how to play that aspect of the case. To take an example of implicit meaning, if in the Private Client transaction objects from the deceased's estate need to be valued, the valuation comes from a website that looks as if it is a local auction site and the documents match the look and feel of the site. The same point applies to the provision of irrelevant information. Whatever information is given to students, they need to make decisions about whether (and if so when) they attend to it, thus pushing it to the foreground of the transaction, or whether they leave it in the background, or ignore it entirely. Students thus practise the process not only of fact gathering, but fact prioritisation and interpretation, as well as corroboration of the critical facts.

The realia of the transaction thus begin to take on a 3D effect: no longer are resources simply flat and uninteresting representations of data. They become objects in a *depth of field*, to adopt a photographic metaphor.[4] In this and many other ways, the TLE supports complexity.[5] As we have seen in Chapter 6, MUVE players dislike single-decision games and flat, uninteresting decision-topographies. They want polyphonic environments, supported by content-rich resources, tools, databases, FAQs, online forums and networks that can contribute to that richness. The TLE is created to facilitate the move from a curriculum in which memorised knowledge is the focus of teaching and assessment, to one where action in a situated environment is the engine of learning and assessment.

Virtual Firm Construction

Virtual firms are constructed by choosing at random four students, with only one exception to the randomness rule. The majority of our 280 or so students come from either Glasgow or Strathclyde University Law Schools. The two streams arrive knowing very little of each other, and we use the virtual firm concept as an opportunity to extend friendships and to help students to get to know each other and network in what is a relatively small jurisdiction. Two students, therefore, are chosen from Strathclyde University and two from Glasgow University Law School,

---

4   For more information on this, see Barton and Maharg (2006, pp. 139–41).

5   Note the difference in this regard between a TLE and a learning management system (LMS), which performs largely administrative functions.

though sometimes one is a student from a law school elsewhere in Scotland. The students will probably be relative strangers to each at the outset of the year. This affects the dialogic relationships that form within the group. The phenomenon has been observed in online game literature, where games are played by strangers who meet online – the VATSIM community, discussed in Chapter 6 (p. 179) is one such example. What is interesting in the online game is that first, the software code does not provide the dramatic interest in the game, whether well-controlled approaches and landings, or near misses, etc. It is the gamers themselves who create interest. Second, the community itself provides the social 'glue' and the interest of the game for strangers. Indeed it is provides the game's dynamic qualities: '[some] players, pursuing their own agenda, buffeted by their own peculiarities and accidents, are more likely to create the vitality of the real world than even the most inventive programmer' (McCracken, 2006).

Within the Diploma we counteract the indifference of strangers by likewise emphasising two points. First, that *everyone* to do with the Diploma is held together in a self-selecting matrix whose grid is composed of the warp of legal professionalism, and the weft of legal ethics. This is the ground of our purpose on the course, and all interactions within the firm must be carried out with that in mind (it is discussed in more detail below). Second, the members of the firm either pass or fail assessments not individually but *as a firm*. In other words, there is a necessity for them to overcome their strangeness and form a team of players in order to carry out transactions, and the basis for this relationship of intimate strangers lies in ethical behaviour and professionalism. The curriculum rules thus rely upon the social nature of learning, and the firms' leveraging of each other's skills and strengths in order to learn. The virtual firm treats students as citizens of the republic of legal learning, rather than individuals or employees only, and asks that they practise civic behaviour within this context. We encourage this by setting them to work on team-building tasks in the Foundation Course, before they are introduced to their virtual firm environment. These consist of legal problem-solving activities, jointly undertaken work in performative skills (interviewing, negotiation, advocacy) and professional legal research. They are then introduced to their virtual firms in activities that mirror the description in Chapter 6 of the careful introductions designed by commercial games designers. They work first of all on supervised sandbox activities, then unsupervised. Each virtual firm also draws up a partnership document that firm members sign up to, declaring the work patterns they will undertake on the course, and the characteristics of those working practices. Importantly, they agree a set of at least four values selected from a set of 30 or so to represent the agreed core values of the partnership. This provides a baseline document for the firm's collaborative work, and can provide a useful measure of experiential development.

This practice is based on research into other disciplines and instances of their intra- and co-professionality (Lingard et al., 2002).[6] The construction of identity – which is a key element of the simulations, since the simulations bridge academic into professional learning – was a critical element in another subject, called Practice Management.

Practice Management

Practice Management is the name of a subject prescribed by the Law Society on the Diploma. It deals with topics such as client care, time management, law as a business, risk management and the like, and as defined by the Society's learning objectives and materials it functions as a baseline introduction to these concepts and processes. The first year that we taught this course, we found the subject problematic, not merely because of the highly situated nature of the material (which really required experience of office practice) but also because of the lack of a theory base underpinning the topics. In the GGSL our early attempts to teach it as a separate subject failed. It was not until we realised that the subject could become a meta-narrative for the other simulations that we began to learn how to teach and assess it.

For this reason, therefore, over a two-year period we re-aligned the timetable and re-wrote the content of the course to service the online projects. Now, students learn time management by practising it using the tools we provide. Risk management is practised within the firms' own work procedures and relations. Each firm is assigned a Practice Management tutor who meets to discuss the subject topics and the work of the firm. Students thus manage their 'practice' (that is, the firm) by managing their individual practice and their relations with others in the firm. As a professional domain, Practice Management deals with much more than individual relations within a firm, but we embed learning about management concepts within the arena of personal experience deriving from coaching and the virtual firm experience.[7]

After the first year it became clear from student and staff feedback that email communications between Practice Manager and students were insufficiently focused for the tasks we were setting the Practice Managers and that we needed to create communication channels between Practice Manager and students that were not provided by conventional VLE or other generic LMS systems. Each

---

6   As Lingard et al. point out, '"Construction of the other" in this sense refers to the process by which we perceive and implicitly categorise or form impressions about those with whom we come into contact, particularly early in social relations. ... For novices (as for any newcomer into a complex environment), such constructions assist in the organization and management of what appears at first to be social chaos' (p. 729). Also influential were Senge (1994) and Westwood (2000).

7   A number of practitioner texts emphasise the importance of this approach. See for example Maister (2005).

firm website now has a page where a student can log in to either an activity or a personal log. Students are required to use the activity log to note every piece of work undertaken within the virtual firm. In the activity log, which is available only to the individual and the Practice Manager, students note the date, time and duration of activity, in addition to noting the category of transaction and the detail of the task undertaken. In this way we have a record of work undertaken both on- and offline. By contrast the purpose of the personal log is to serve as a space for reflection on learning. Though not compulsory, many students use it regularly and report the value of this reflective activity. It is also a confidential communication channel between student and Practice Manager. We assess student performance in Practice Management by attendance at Practice Management seminars and a 1,500 word reflective practice report which is based upon the two tools of activity log and personal log that students use throughout the Diploma.

Partly as a result of these information flows and partly because of their new mediatory roles, Practice Management tutors now function less as tutors and much more as Practice Managers who perform the realistic role of trainee supervisor of the transactional tasks that the firm is required to carry out. To help with this transformation, the practitioner-tutors were given training sessions in *coaching* students rather than tutoring them. The role is akin to that of the masters in the architecture master classes described by Donald Schon.[8] The role of the Practice Manager means that he or she does not comment on the substantive detail of the transactions (that is the domain of tutors or other professionals), but instead focuses on identifying the practice management issues arising within the transactional projects and commenting upon the *process* by which the transaction is carried out by the firm: who does what, how, by when; the quality of the work; the ability of the firm to work together as a productive unit, and so on. The tutor is aided in this by peer- and self-assessment online forms, in which all firm members rate each other's activities on a weekly basis, in terms of quality and quantity and by access to the 'Trainee Noticeboard' in the firm – effectively a discussion forum for the four members of the firm and their Practice Manager.

Practice Management is thus a meta-narrative that underpins the simulations. The topics of risk, time, teamworking are those personal and organisation qualities that the Law Society wishes to see as the focus of the subject. Such qualities, however, are highly disputed. The activity log, for instance, can be perceived as a form of oversight that is oppressive: a form of panopticon, an embodiment of the chilling transparency of technology, and therefore the subjugation of students to the post-Fordist employment economy. That many law firms use such technologies to track employee efficiencies and bill clients and in much more sophisticated ways than we use it is of course no adequate reason why it should

---

8   See Schön (1987). See also Westwood (2004), p. 10: 'professionals, as they develop through their careers, are expected to bring on and teach younger professionals the "tools of their trade". All of this requires the ability to coach and mentor people, rather than tell people what to do.'

be used. A better reason is that the activity log enables students to develop trust in each other's work patterns, to develop a community of work, based around patterns of engagement that were determined by the group and set out in the firm's minutes as well as their partnership agreement. Seen in this context the activity log is merely one device amongst others for creating and assuring trust and confidence in the group, as well as managing conflict, and a tool that can be used in discussions.

The Practice Management system thus is completely integrated with the transactional learning environment and works to encourage and monitor the work of the firm. There are, though, fundamental issues of equity that are raised by the system, regardless of how well it may work in practice. We can appreciate these if we turn to the nearest analogy, namely 'griefing' in online games. Griefing is the term given to deliberate misbehaviour or destructive play carried out to distress other players. Even in a game such as *World of Warcraft* or *EverQuest*, where play is both collaborative (within guilds, for instance) and destructive (in that avatars can be wantonly maimed and killed), there are rules and conventions governing the play. Much of it is actually governed by social conventions and ethics.[9] In our TLE we aim to structure the 'play' so that students are aware of the rules – assessment criteria, links to professional practice, and so on – but also learn by adoption of conventions. Students become aware of this early on when, in the sandbox activities, the sessions are structured so that they teach each other and learn from each other. In this way we try to persuade students to adopt procedures and ways of working that are inherently sound practice (the adoption of notes to file, meeting minutes, for example) and ethical – honesty as regards the record of work performed; a sense of collaborative conscience regarding the quality of work through self- and peer-assessment, and the like. For this reason we emphasise connectivity, collaboration, the necessity to keep in touch with each other in the firm, and we signal this to students by placing a calendar, task tool and discussion forum on the firm intranet front page.[10]

This is the case within firms, but we encourage the same between firms too. Scotland is a small jurisdiction and of the 500 or so entrants to the profession each year between 40–50 per cent enter through the GGSL Diploma programme. It makes sense for students to network with each other from the start and to begin to discover how to relate to each on a professional level. They cannot know everyone on the course, but even on the level of 'familiar strangers' they can begin to map

---

9 Steinkuehler gives a good example from her experience of play as an elf in *Lineage*, on a mithril hunt. She was taught, inter alia, the social convention of *not* accompanying other elves (because each elf is hunting mithril). She was also taught the ethics of behaviour, for instance not stealing mithril dropped by elves. There are other examples in Yee (2006), quoted in Chapter 6. These conventions, often based upon an underlying ethic of collaborative play, are rarely made explicit at this level, are often taught by one gamer to another, and underlie the more explicit rules of the game as embodied in the EULA.

10 Though we welcome students using other media and channels – mobile texting is a popular alternative.

out the levels of intimacy they wish to have with their peers. The phrase 'familiar strangers' refers to Stanley Milgram's 1972 essay on the concept, which followed in the early tradition of urban psychology and analysed the relationship between ourselves and those strangers in the city whom we regularly observe but with whom we have no direct relations.[11] Milgram's study expresses well the type of baseline relationship between students on a course of study of the size of the Diploma, where it is impossible for all students to know each other, but where there are levels of intimacy built upon such familiarity. It expresses the sense of purpose that underlies even the most baseline familiar stranger relationship: all students on the Diploma are there because they wish to become lawyers in Scotland in much the same way as Milgram's study cohort of commuters at a suburban train station focused on people who were present at locations to travel to work in the city. Milgram's study pointed up the importance of place to such encounters and the mental linkages we make to familiar strangers and specific locales.

Whether or not Milgram's buffer state of familiar strangers can be replicated online, it is true that the new state of communicative being, namely online presence, helps facilitate the move from complete stranger to familiar stranger to acquaintance. It may make the bond more porous and this is interesting from an educational point of view. Barton and Westwood are presently working on the correlation between the use made of online communicational and personal organisational tools such as discussion forum, calendar, task organisers, etc, and the success of the firms, both as working entities and in their assessments.[12] We shall examine this line of research further, below.

Teamworking

As will be clear by now, collaborative learning is an essential element of our TLE and our approach to professional learning. The concept of teamworking, though, has been criticised recently in some sociological literature. In a powerful critique of corporate capitalism and its effects on career and occupational security, Richard Sennett has described the erosion of personal freedom via the 'expressants of flexible capitalism', and he identifies the concepts of teamworking and networking as partly responsible for the corrosion of character (Sennett, 1998). Sennett sees teamworking as an expression of workplace uncertainty (1998, p. 31) in an

11   For information on Milgram's Familiar Stranger project and a mobile and wireless update of it, see The Familiar Stranger Project: Anxiety, Comfort and Play, at http://berkeley.intel-research.net/paulos/research/familiarstranger/.

12   This work is ongoing and on file with the authors Barton and Westwood. It is generally well documented that networked learning has the capability to shift the focus from teacher- to learner-centred activities. As Levin and Thurston (1996) reported in their review, students who were involved in such learning could produce better quality writing, had the facilities to work better in teams and produced better problem-solving heuristics and thinking strategies.

economic climate where capitalism requires ever increasingly shorter returns on investment. Such anxious flexibility, according to Sennett, corrodes careers, loyalty, trust and mutual commitment, and the emphasis on teamworking ethics serves both to deepen and gloss over this uncertainty.

It may, though, be too much of a generalisation to say, as Sennett does, that character is being corroded by such workplace practices as teamworking. As Hughes points out, character is also 'being transformed, enchanted, rather than corroded, within some, but by no means all, sectors of the contemporary workplace' (Hughes, 2005, p. 620). While it is undeniable that the rhetoric of management 'attempts to disguise power in the new economy by making the worker believe he or she is a self-directing agent' (Sennett, 1998, p. 173), it is also true that Weber's iron cage is no longer quite as imprisoning as it was in early twentieth-century Fordist economies, with their hierarchical industrial monoliths and the 'institutional shelters' of large bureaucratic organisations.[13]

Others have different views. Where Sennett sees freedom and teams as masks for their opposites, Giddens sees in such flexibility a freedom for individuals to shape and sustain a narrative of identity (Giddens, 1991b). Sennett also takes a fairly narrow view of what team production actually involves, focusing on relatively traditional capitalist exchanges. But a method of production such as teamworking also relies on motives that have little to do with employment relations or workplace organisation. As Benkler has observed of the arena of digital capitalism, peer production can be a new mode of collaboration, one where individuals participate in joint production in return for status within or beyond the team (Benkler, 2002).[14] Others, such as Hardt and Negri (2000), point to the changing relationships within the structure of capital:

> today we participate in a more radical and profound commonality than has ever been experienced in the history of capitalism. The fact is that we participate in a productive world made up of communication and social networks, interactive services, and common languages. Our economic and social reality is defined less by the material objects that are made and consumed than by co-produced services and relationships.

---

13 Hans Pruijt (2002) makes this point well in his article comparing anti-Tayloristic and neo-Tayloristic practices in workplace teamworking, particularly with reference to the 'cosmetic autonomy' of teamworking. For other applications of Sennett's approach, see Collier (2004) and Bradney (2006).

14 Though Lessig has rightly warned us against sites that appear to allow collaborative activity, but which in fact do the opposite: 'There's an important distinction developing among "user generated content" sites – the distinction between sites that permit "true sharing" and those that permit only what I'll call "fake sharing". A "true sharing" site doesn't try to exercise ultimate control over the content it serves. It permits, in other words, content to move as users choose. A '"fake sharing" site, by contrast, gives you tools to make seem as if there's sharing, but in fact, all the tools drive traffic and control back to a single site' (Lessig Blog, http://lessig.org/blog/archives/003570.shtml).

Producing increasingly means constructing co-operation and communicative commonalities.[15]

The fluidity of relationships, the dislocated professional communities so characteristic of late capitalism, the contested nature of professionalism and co-professionality – all these are, within an educational context, reasons for the adoption not of superficial teamworking activities, or what might be termed *inauthentic* teamworking practices (more of this below), but of deep and sustained teamwork. There are strong educational reasons for this, too. There is much research to suggest that, properly designed, collaborative work can increase student learning.[16] Activity theory, situated learning and other approaches to social learning emphasise the distribution of knowledge and expertise across nodes of professional activity.[17] Practice theorists similarly argue that practices are the 'source and carrier of meaning, language and normativity' and therefore the analysis of practices cannot be extricated from the social context which creates such meaning (Schatzki et al., 2001, pp. 1–14 and Barnes, 2001 pp. 17–18). Collaborative and discursive constructions of tasks are key activities for professionals. For students such constructions are essential as alternatives to the individualised, competitive mastery of specific areas of legal knowledge which constitutes much (though by no means all) of their previous experience of legal education. The importance of such relationships for learning cannot be underestimated – see for example Wells' studies of dialogic enquiry (1999), and Mercer's work (already discussed in Chapter 2 – 1995) on types of talk, Edwards (2005) on communities, Edwards and Mackenzie (2005, 2006) on social context and identity shifts and, further back, the work of Leont'ev (1979) on how collective activity shapes material and conceptual objects All these and many more bodies

---

15 Also cited in Bowrey (2005, p. 100). I do not agree with the conclusions Bowrey reaches in this chapter, though I agree with her general conclusion that, while '[l]aw creates and denies possibilities of community', globalisation has created new 'legal spaces' that 'offer sites for our participation, compliance and resistance' (p. 199). One such is the remarkable network of resistance to the Blackboard patent, with sites currently at No Edu Patent http://noedupatents.org/, online petition http://www.boycottblackboard.org/index.php?view=1, and especially the Wikipedia entry http://en.wikipedia.org/wiki/History_of_virtual_learning_environments which, prior to Blackboard's announcement of their patent grant, was a backwater site, little more than a stub. Since then, in the collaborative effort to identify 'prior art' before 1999, it has become one of the most sophisticated Wikipedia entries.

16 See for example Benbunan-Fich and Hiltz (1999). The key, of course, is the design and development of intervention and feedback processes. As Laurillard points out (2002, p. 105), '[f]or learning to take place, the core structure of the conversational framework must remain intact in some form: the dialogue must take place somewhere, the actions must happen somewhere, even if it is all done inside the student's head'.

17   And not only professions – as we saw in Chapter 1, trading zones are essential to many areas of modern science. See also Knorr-Cetina (1998).

of research point to the necessity – it is as strong as that – for much more social learning in our learning institutions.

In teamworking, Sennett points out, power struggles remain but authority is either deliberately obscured, or masked by team activities. The team thus contributes to domination because there appears to be no overall responsibility. This is certainly true of some versions of teamworking, but by no means all. Indeed it could be said that such manipulation of group processes contributes to forms of inauthentic group interaction, where the group act out either the narcissistic relations of the group or the oppressive power dynamic forced upon it.[18] While Sennett's version of teamworking can undoubtedly apply to specific areas of industry and commerce, we need to identify how, within an educational context, social learning actually occurs and how best to support it. In our virtual firms of four students, for instance, there is no senior partner. Each student takes a turn at leading a transaction and being responsible for the organisation of this work among the group. It may appear as if we have Sennett's classic situation of responsibility without power in a team, but in fact there is responsibility present: the team members are responsible to each other, since the team is awarded an assessment mark in high-stakes assessment *as a group* and not individually. And there is an overt power relation present, in that the Practice Manager is an authority figure as well as a coach and encourager through the reporting mechanisms of activity and personal logs, self- and peer-assessment and seminars.[19]

High- and middle-order theory on the subject of collaboration can only take us so far. On the subject of legal education and teamworking we do not need *grands récits* but *petits récits*, narratives of experience and the types of experiences that arise from situational and temporal actions, the recording and analysis of which can create meaning while avoiding the homogeneity of the *grands récits*.[20] Detailed empirical research on collaboration within online games is rare enough; but in online educational simulations it is rare indeed.

Such research is already being undertaken in the GGSL. Barton and Westwood (2006) have carried out analyses of the Practice Management reflective reports of the entire year group. Reflective learning reports are a way to enable team members to take the long view of their collective work, and to evaluate group performance

---

18 For an acute analysis of the narcissism of such groups, see Sennett (1978).

19 I have argued against Sennett's strictures on the power dynamic of teamworking being applied *tout court* to teamworking; but it has to be said that they did apply to our early versions of the firms' teamworking, where the relations between Practice Manager and virtual firm were much more loosely defined, and there was consequent dissatisfaction as regards the locus of responsibility within the firms and the programme of study.

20 There are of course many studies of teamworking in the workplace, some of which support Sennett's theory of character corrosion, others not. See for instance Appelbaum et al. (2000) and Kuhlmann and Schumann (2001).

– for example, the formalisation of rules, effect of leader rotation, and so on.[21] They coded the themes of each student's reflective report double-blind, then plotted them in a grid where the X axis was low learning > high learning and the Y axis was low trust > high trust (see Figure 8.2). They named their quadrants Dysfunctional Firm (low learning, low trust), Legal Eagles (high learning, low trust), Friendly Societies (low learning, high trust) and Learning Communities (high learning, high trust). Their grid reveals the characteristics of successful and less successful firms, including criteria such as culture, approach to tasks, relationships and work styles. They show also how even when a firm collaborated well together, student collaborative work could be performative without being transformative. In other words, the group can perform a transaction without adequately understanding what is happening or why, either within the transaction's procedures or within the team's processes, while these are taking place.[22]

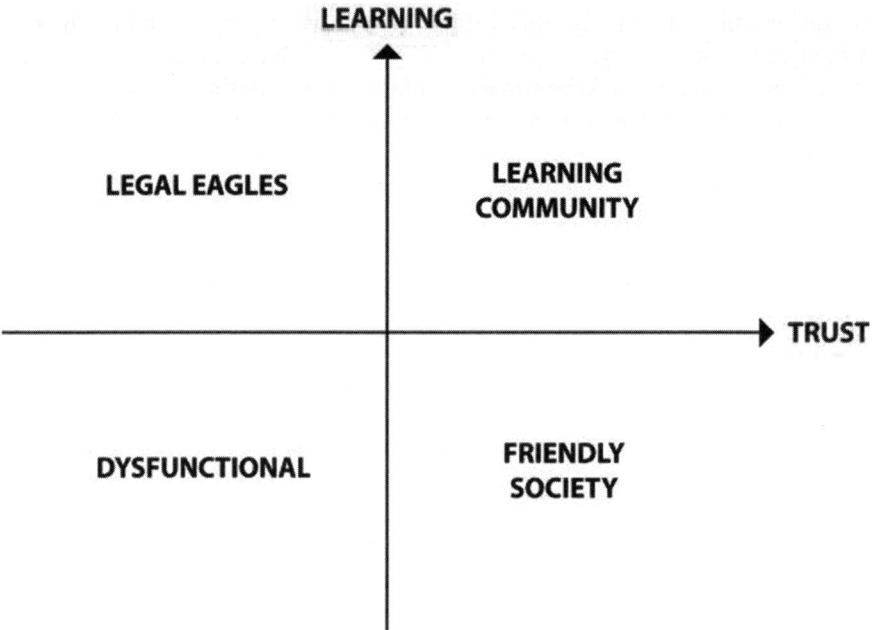

Figure 8.2   Barton and Westwood's matrix of trust and learning within student firms

---

21 For an interesting analysis of this in the workplace see Barker (1993).

22 This is an interesting parallel to the work carried out on collaborative talk, where friendly talk and good relations were not necessarily productive of effective learning.

The Barton and Westwood grid is one way of representing firm work. Their axes grew out of the themes they observed, but were also representative of the relationship between trust and learning. Their research showed what an important role trust plays in collaborative work.[23]

When we compare their grid to that of Bartle, discussed in Chapter 6, there are a number of interesting comparisons.

1) Their grid is derived from a substantial body of empirical data and is therefore dynamic, altering each year they test the cohort reflective reports and dependent upon the multi-factorial environment and culture of the Diploma. Bartle's quadrants are static descriptors of types of MUVE players

2) The categories are by no means an exact mapping, but they are close enough to suggest parallels between approaches taken by game players and our students in simulations. In particular 'Socialisers' and 'Friendly Societies' are almost identical. 'Learning communities' probably contains elements of both 'Achievers' and 'Explorers'.

3) Bartle's quadrant measures static qualities which he takes to be mutually exclusive. Thus an explorer cannot also be a killer or an achiever.[24] By contrast, Barton and Westwood's quadrants are plotting areas to measure each firm's overall quality of practice as reported by the reflective reports and evidenced by peer- and self-feedback, and the activity logs. This data was used to analyse a firm's culture, its approach to tasks, its internal relationships and its work styles. But – and this is perhaps the most important point about their research – it was implicit in Barton and Westwood's research that firms could change their dynamics and could be influenced to move between quadrants. For this reason the grids were used as tools to help students achieve the best learning experience and to help staff identify the types of support that would help firms move to the top-right, 'learning community' quadrant.

Barton and Westwood's work presents an absorbing insight into the ways in which social and collaborative learning can enhance learning about professionalism and legal transactions. In successful firms (top right-hand quadrant), the collaborative environment was a powerful engine of conceptual change. Participants committed to views of pieces of work; they discussed detail and strategy, pulling together information from books, web, tutorials and each other to create conceptual knowledge. Their work created 'social capital' that led to further initiative and collaboration.[25] By contrast, dysfunctional firm teamwork (lower left-hand quadrant) was 'jarring', there were 'tantrums', and as Johnson

---

23 Their findings correlate well with those of other researchers. On group identity and self-identity see, for instance, McConnell (2005).

24 Yee's research, though, has contradicted Bartle in this respect – see Chapter 6, p. 179.

25 See Cohen and Prusack (2001), cited by Barton and Westwood.

and Johnson point out, 'distrust creates destructive conflict among members [of the firm]' (Ginsburg, 2002, pp. 516–22).[26]

Their results are supported by research carried out in PBL. In a study on student perspectives on PBL collaborative work, for instance, Cockrell et al. (2000) discovered that the groupings facilitated students' sense of ownership of their knowledge and learning. In addition they observed that leadership within groups moved fluidly from student to student as a result of many different factors. This supports our early decision to give students control of the collaborative process and to appoint a 'Transaction Manager' within the firm who would be responsible for leading work on any specific transaction.

The role of the Practice Manager (PM) in all this was crucial. A good Practice Manager could guide a firm having problems and discuss the firm's problems in the light of legal practice issues. However, as always on the Diploma, our Practice Managers were practitioner-tutors. Many of them had greater or lesser experience of tutoring and workshop facilitation, but almost none of them had had experience of coaching very small groups of students. The first set of results from the Barton and Westwood survey in 2004 identified further PM training as a priority in increasing the numbers of firms in the top-right quadrant. This was carried out, along with a number of other 'hard' and 'soft' implementations – teamworking activities in the Foundation Course, a 'Values Activity' (where firms discuss and set their values), drafting of a firm's partnership agreement, embodying those values, self- and peer-assessment tools mentioned earlier and a formal mediation process. All this served to make the nature of both the quality and quantity of work within the firm as transparent as possible to the members of the firm and the PM. This has helped students in the firm to track the quality of the firm both individually and as a unit, and in the high trust firms facilitated the development of that trust. Did all this work to improve student performance, however? It is too early to say, but first indications from the dataset at time of writing reveal an increase in the numbers of student firms in the top-right quadrant.

Professionalism and E-mergence

Some students found that their experience of the course suffered because of personal or financial circumstances that arose while they were on the course and, while our primary duty was to the welfare of the students, we were also required to assess their competence in the transactions. What could we do, though, with that other category, the few proven defaulters within firms? In this situation much depends on how the context that is created on a course by its value-systems

---

26 In addition, there also occurred within these firms the marginalisation of members. As Wenger (1998, p. 208) pointed out, such practices lead to feelings of 'powerlessness, vulnerability, narrowness, marginality'.

operates to discourage students from defaulting in the first place; and then making clear the gravity of the situation if it persists. This arises from research carried out in the medical field, not so much in the field of competence, but in that of professionalism.

There is a fairly substantial body of literature which indicates that whereas competence may be useful as threshold standards for developing-trainee and early-career assessment, the most useful standards of assessment are those of professionalism. Papadakis et al., for instance, set out to determine if medical students who demonstrated unprofessional conduct in medical school were more likely to be disciplined by their State Board. Their study set out possible correlative factors, including gender, grade point average, Medical College Admission scores, school grades, National Board of Medical Examiner Part 1 scores and negative excerpts from evaluation forms. The study subjects were alumni graduating between 1943 and 1989. They revealed correlations between unprofessional behaviour at medical school, and practitioners who had been disciplined by their profession. As they reported,

> We found that UCSF, School of Medicine students who received comments regarding unprofessional behavior were more than twice as likely to be disciplined by the Medical Board of California when they become practicing physicians than were students without such comments. The more traditional measures of medical school performance, such as grades and passing scores on national standardised tests, did not identify students who later had disciplinary problems as practicing physicians. (Papadakis et al., 2004b, pp. 244–79; 2004a, pp. 1100–106)

This is not the only study to produce such results. Other studies have focused on the part that professionals can play in being role models for students. Kenny et al. outline the practical consequences of a new emphasis on professionalism as character formation (Kenny, 2003, pp. 1203–10). Misch has argued for the appointment of what he calls 'humanism "connoisseurs"' to the medical curriculum, namely staff specially trained to give feedback on qualities such as empathy, compassion, integrity and respect, 'while evaluating physicians' behaviors as an integrated, cohesive whole' (Misch, 2002, pp. 489–95).[27]

Other studies have focused on the view that students have of professionalism. One study by Ginsburg et al., using a grounded-theory approach, considered the gradual development of medical students' views of professionalism by documenting the students' reports of what they perceived as professional lapses. The authors reported that

> [s]ix critical 'issues' emerged: communicative violations (to or about patients or other health care professionals); role resistance (individuals chafing against constraints or expectations of their perceived roles); objectification of patients (ignoring patients or

---

27 The concept of connoisseurship has something of a lineage in this literature. See Eisner (1990).

treating patients as vehicles for learning); accountability (to colleagues or patients, including avoiding patients, failing to disclose information, or failing to treat appropriately); physical harm (to patients or others); and crossfire (being put in the middle of a struggle between superiors). (2002, p. 516)

The authors concluded that the critical issues students reported did not 'map easily onto standard, abstract definitions of professionalism'. They concluded that such incongruence should be addressed by curriculum designers if the gap between 'traditional taxonomies and students' perceptions of professionalism' were to be bridged (Ginsburg et al., 2002, pp. 516–22).

Such findings are mirrored by concern in the medical literature as a whole, which is characterised by a shift from measurement of competencies and academic achievement to professionalism and qualities associated with that. As Jordan J. Cohen, President of the Association of American Medical Colleges put it,

academic medicine must … address some current realities within medical education, such as the admission process (where at present there is a tendency to overemphasize indices of academic achievement and underemphasize the personal characteristics sought in applicants) and the acculturation process in medical school (which can often dehumanize students and convert idealistic ones into cynics). (Cohen, 2001, pp. 475–80)

In another study, Brownwell and Coté set out to determine senior residents' views on the meaning of professionalism. Among their findings, they discovered that their total subjects (*n* = 258)

listed 1,052 attributes they associated with professionalism. The three most common attributes, all listed by more than 100 respondents, were respect, competence, and empathy. The respondents had learned the most about professionalism from observing role models, they rated the quantity and quality of teaching about it positively, and they felt comfortable explaining professionalism to a junior resident (Brownwell and Coté, 2001, p. 734).

Compare this to what two researchers have conceptualised as a dichotomy in North American medical education between explicit commitment to 'traditional values of doctoring – empathy, compassion and altruism' and 'tacit commitment to behaviors grounded in an ethic of detachment, self-interest and objectivity' (Coulehan and Williams, 2001). What was of interest to Coulehan and Williams is how medical students and young physicians responded to this dichotomy. Some of them 're-conceptualise themselves primarily as technicians and narrow their professional identities to an ethic of competence, thus adopting the tacit values and discarding the explicit professionalism'. A second group enacted 'non-reflective professionalism' that is manifested by treating patients as 'objects of technical services (medical care)'. A third group seemed to be 'immunised' against tacit values, in the process internalising and developing professional virtue. Factors that helped to bring about this process included personal characteristics such as belief systems, and features of the medical school such as courses in communication skills, medical ethics, and social issues in medicine.

All of this literature is pertinent to legal education, not just to experiential learning and professional education, but to undergraduate education as well. A course such as Practice Management cannot perform as a meta-narrative, as described above, unless it examines professionalism and treats the ethical and the performative as integrated with, and essential to, each other. If there is a core to the recent developments in the literature of professionalism, it is this integration – an integration that, like the ethical broken middle, is a challenge to both staff and students to return to the ground of experience. For if our students could not comprehend this crucial link between the ethical and the performative, then we had failed in the whole transactional enterprise. If they understood it, but failed to enact it, then this was a serious comment on their professionality that deserved to be noted.

Enough will have been said in Chapter 7 on the subject of professionalism to show that transactional learning is a fertile process for the development of professionalism. When combined with the procedures involved in a subject such as Practice Management transactional learning becomes a powerful learning environment applicable to most professions and most discourses within professions. What happens is in fact a process we call 'e-mergence' – simultaneously a merging within the electronic domain of communications and data, and the emergence of learning from the distribution of information and the engagement of learners with that information. In the process, the learning environment becomes a relational object – a means by which students negotiate the relationships within the firm and their own understanding of professionalism, and has the possibility of becoming an evocative object with which one thinks.[28] It also entails a process of curriculum design which has significant implications for the future of staff work patterns in HE.

Changing Patterns of Staff Engagement

How do transactional projects change staff work patterns? They do so in profound ways. The normal pattern of academic teaching involves writing lectures, planning tutorials, updating legal content and occasionally methods of teaching and facilitation, within the assumed boundaries of a system of education structured around events such as lectures, tutorials, coursework, examinations and a reasonably settled pattern of administration associated with these events. There is a strongly linear character to a course designed in this way, expressed in concepts such as Biggs' constructive alignment of teaching and assessment (Biggs, 1999, 2003). I am not suggesting that Biggs' concept is limited only to the metaphor of

---

28 See Turkle (2005 and 2007).

a line (the implications and the research are far richer than that); but the linear progression of the curriculum – literally the race – is embedded so deeply in our educational system that we rarely think to question it.

There are different ways of designing learning, though. Lave and Wenger (1991) give us a radical alternative, a description of legitimate peripheral design: the circles upon circles, with the learner, peripheral at first, moving ever closer to the expert centre of the circles. Our own metaphor is perhaps best described as a spiral and it affects the way staff work in the following ways.

Pre-transaction Design-intensive Work

A transactional project differs fundamentally from traditional teaching in the time that is given to design of transaction and subtasks, so that students work off resources which include staff, but where staff are only one of many resources to be used in a 'just-in-time' fashion. Pre-progamme design work thus increases considerably for staff, and includes the tasks of:

1) narrative and events creation;
2) development of micro-tasks (who will do what when, why and how will they know it), characters and communication lines;
3) placing of feedback lines and assessment points within the transaction;
4) sourcing or writing, digital placing and testing of resources.

Feedback and Assessment

During the transaction, feedback and assessment cycles govern interaction of staff with students and much depends on the form of curriculum: whether it is entirely distance-learning, or face-to-face teaching events blended with transactional work; whether student work is collaborative or singleton; whether a simulation lasts for three highly-intensive days, or for three months.[29] In this model it is as important for staff to step into the background as it is for them to come forward to help. At the design stage they are involved in creating not just paths through the transaction for students, but clearings where students can stop, consider which way to go, rest, reflect. Staff may step forward into the clearing, or may not: the design is the crucial element. Models such as Laurillard's conversational design, or LAMS, or indeed most others can help, but they by no means exhaust the possibilities of learning design.

In addition, the design of the transaction – whether it is open-field or bounded-field – affects staff interaction. The Personal Injury transaction, for example, is

---

29 In conversation with Suzanne Fine, International Head of Training at Linklaters, she described her three-day intensive transactional simulation, which had been designed for newly-qualified lawyers when she was at Lovells.

open-field, with real-time information given to 70 firms of students by a group of seven postgraduates, trainees and practitioners, who are trained in mentoring and character-portrayal and who function online as a community, helping each other with problems and documents and working under the direction of a practitioner (Charles Hennessy) and myself. In addition to managing two forums during the project, Charles and I were also present on the mentor forum. There were, you will recall from the previous chapter, almost no formal classes in the accepted sense: an introductory lecture, a final feedback lecture, voluntary face-to-face 'masterclass' sessions – small, intense workshops – with experienced practitioners who negotiated regularly as part of their working lives.

Post-transaction Reflection

Whatever the form of the transaction, and in addition to assessment of tasks, it is essential that staff engage with at least some students in reflection on what was achieved in the transaction, and what can be taken forward to the next iteration, or the next transaction. They also need to review the transaction, both structure and content and revise it for the next iteration.

Summary

The process of weaving the Practice Management subject into the transactions continues. It has involved us in a complete re-evaluation of the way in which the subject is taught, and how it can function within the curriculum as a lynchpin for the entire programme of study. Originally envisaged as a traditional course structure with a lecture series, seminars and an examination assessment, the course now comprises an introductory workshop where the 'grid' of firm characteristics are discussed, and team-building activities carried out; a series of firm meetings over the course of the year that integrates the experience of the firm and transactions with the content of the Practice Management subject, and an assessment that includes work on the formal content of the subject and the submission of logs to Practice Management tutors throughout the course of the year. In other words, the Practice Management course has been gradually transformed in its detail and structure by its merging with the transactional learning environment, and has in turn enhanced the student experience within the environment.

Can we improve upon the quality of collaborative work within and between firms? Undoubtedly – we have really only begun to understand what happens when such deep collaborative work over the course of an academic year is undertaken within a transactional environment that takes seriously the distributive nature of knowledge generation across the curriculum. ICT has a role to play in this. Three examples will suffice:

1) History flow tools can show the revisions of various firm member contributions to a document, rather like the edition history in a wiki.
2) The second example is based upon the idea of 'glanceability', that is, the development of social network analysis tools that can represent the work of a firm to itself in more detailed granularity.[30]
3) The development of an e-portfolio environment that will seamlessly fuse with both Practice Management and the transactional learning environment and enable students to take their achievements, learning, learning tools, knowledge and information networks with them into traineeship.

Would these tools help firms to develop the quality of their communication? We cannot predict that. But it is interesting that the latest results collated by Barton and Westwood appear to show that those firms who used the existing online tools more than others were the firms who performed best in transactions – not just by the measure of assessment marks, but in their placing within the matrix.[31]

More importantly, the tools of communication can involve communication outside the virtual firms. One application provides an inspiring example from the school community, namely *Radiowaves*. This is a network of school radio stations on which young people can publish their own music, communicate about music and enter music competitions.[32] It has its equivalent in Ardcalloch, where law firms can enter a project where they provide e-bulletins for their clients on a shared 'public access' website (that is, public within Ardcalloch) called ALIAS – Ardcalloch Legal Information and Advisory Service. In this way they practise client-based communication skills (writing to specific client groups, for instance), role-playing, collaborative activity and professional legal research. The activity can be developed in so many ways – client–relations management, community outreach, government communications, client education, clinic dissemination.[33] It is yet another activity that grows from the basic simulation engine of Ardcalloch, one that is not explicitly transactionally-based but which is a further development of the simulation concept. Not everything is achievable: it has taken us almost seven years to reach the stage we are at in the GGSL. But while we may be limited

---

30 http://www.ambientdevices.com/cat/index.html.

31 Unpublished as yet; private conversation with Karen Barton. Research data is on file with Barton.

32 As Boyes (2006) points out student self-reporting demonstrated impressive learning gains – 84 per cent learned about teamwork, 76 per cent considered themselves better at collaborative learning, 73 per cent thought they were better at decision-making and taking responsibility. See Boyes (2006, pp. 22–3).

33 For example we have noticed from working with several large law firms in IT and multimedia that the dual concept of dynamic client seminars and compliance education can be problematic. One way round this is to give trainees experience not only in client-based writing activities such as e-bulletins, but to train them in the design and delivery of various models of client-facing training activities, for instance compliance training.

by many constraints in our use of ICT – financial, time, pre-existing curriculum design – if we are limited in our imagination, nothing can be achieved.

Chapter 9

Multimedia and the Docuverse of Law: Learning and the Representation of Knowledge

The docuverse is but one slice through this virtual reality, on the axis of media, at the point marked 'text.' Here lies the dream of the universal library – every word ever recorded knit together in a mosaic of knowledge, just waiting for the holy command to bring it forth. This is the ultimate manifestation of a primal will to closure. The move to cyberspace reifies, as Benedikt has noted, the age-old desire for the Heavenly City, 'its radiance like a most rare jewel' (*Revelation* 21:9). After coming so far, we still find ourselves looking for an Eden, a Xanadu, no less fervently than before.

(Keep, McLaughlin and Parmer, 2000)

Introduction

The last two chapters have described, inter alia, how ICT can facilitate transactional learning in legal education across an entire curriculum. Such learning depends, as we have seen, not just on doing transactions but on the quality and depth of support from staff and the student collaborative environment built around the transaction. The process also depends on the placing of digital resources around a transaction so that students can use materials to guide their learning within a transaction. This chapter explores the design, implementation and use of such digital resources to support transactional learning. It involved the creation of resources that would not merely enable students to understand law conceptually, but would enable them effectively to transfer that learning to practical, transactional activities. Transfer of learning is always difficult for students, as well as problematic for curriculum designers; but it is essential if a transformational curriculum is to be achieved.

This is particularly true of areas where students have no or very little substantive knowledge. There are some areas of the Diploma curriculum where students have no almost no basic existing legal knowledge to draw upon and where resources such as small-scale webpages cannot encompass the extent of the information that students need to negotiate. Two key subjects where this is the case are Criminal Court Practice and Civil Court Practice. In Scotland, many students do not study procedural or adjectival law in their undergraduate LLB and therefore modules in both procedural knowledge and relevant advocacy and plea-drafting skills are mandated by the Law Society of Scotland as part of the Diploma curriculum.[1]

In the past both classes had been organised around traditional curriculum lines, with sets of formal lectures on criminal and civil procedure, seminars based largely on skills acquisition, and end-of-year examinations on procedural knowledge. Following Barnett, Eraut and many others who rightly criticise the invidious separation of theory and practice, we decided to redesign the modules to merge conceptual, skills-based and attitudinal learning as much as possible. In Civil Court Practice, therefore, we carried out a three-year plan that has gradually been transforming the subject. In the first year (2003/4) we created a set of online and CD resources that replaced entirely both the Criminal and Civil face-to-face lecture series. These resources included texts, graphics and multimedia units on plea drafting and advocacy structured around video lectures. In the second and third years (2004/5, 2005/6), in a two-stage implementation, we created within Civil Court Practice the transactional Civil Court Action (CCA), the background to which has been partly described in the last two chapters.[2] This chapter will focus on the resource base that largely replaced the Criminal and Civil lecture series, namely the set of online and CD resources. I shall describe the Civil Court Practice resources – especially the video lectures – and explore some of the theoretical context, the implementation of the video lectures, some of the responses from students to our innovation, and I shall then sketch out the development of such tools in the next five years or so.

It may seem perverse to take as an item for analysis something that is often seen as a cheap substitute for a highly traditional form of teaching.[3] But if video lectures were only talking heads they would be tedious and would be perceived by students as poor substitutes (however accessible) for lectures. From our work over the past three years it has nevertheless become clear to us that video lectures, when used in appropriate virtual learning environments, can do more than provide cheap

---

1   See http://www.lawscot.org.uk/training/Diploma.aspx.

2   The CCA was written by Karen Barton and Patricia McKellar. Technical design and implementation was carried out by Scott Walker and Michael Hughes of the Learning Technologies Development Unit, within the GGSL.

3   At first glance video lectures seem to be the digital equivalent of Paulo Freire's famous banking analogy: 'Narration (with the teacher as narrator) leads the students to memorise mechanically the narrated content. Worse still, it turns them into "containers", into receptables to be filled by the teacher. The more completely he fills the receptacles, the better a teacher he is. [...] Education thus becomes an act of depositing, in which the students are depositories and the teacher the depositor. Instead of communication, the teacher issues communiqués and 'makes deposits' which the students patiently receive, memorise and repeat. This is the "banking" concept of education, in which the scope of action allowed to the students extends only as far as receiving, filing, and storing the deposits' (Friere, 1996, pp. 52–3). However as we shall see, the reality of student use was quite different.

lectures on the web. The profoundly different medium of the web transforms the student experience of learning. Such claims are not new, of course: the media of radio, TV and video were in their turns expected to do something similar when first introduced but, in the UK at least, have had relatively little impact on learning in HE. Learning with e-resources, however, is different in a number of respects.[4] Put simply, the relative ease with which audio, video and text can be spliced, the accessibility of information and the environment within which knowledge can be constructed is significantly different from the experience, *la durée*, as Bergson has it, of paperworld study environments.

Our interest in video lectures goes back over four years.[5] In that time we have completed over 30 separate projects, spanning both undergraduate and postgraduate legal education and ranging from one-off lectures to entire modules.[6] Video elements were already being experimented with in different learning projects – in our intranet and in the virtual firms that we used in the virtual town of Ardcalloch. We had already begun the process of working with video in our Foundation Course multimedia CD and we had learned how to use videotape excerpts, in combination with on-screen text, to enhance student learning over a variety of professional legal skills. We knew both from extensive student feedback on this course and the literature that the combination of on-screen text and video was a powerful learning tool in the acquisition of professional legal skills.[7] But could the environment be adapted to enhance the acquisition of more conceptual and rule-based knowledge and facilitate its transfer to transactional projects?

The first video lectures were single interventions – simple video windows containing talking heads which were synchronised to static PowerPoint slides.

---

4   As Garrison and Anderson (2003, p. 7) put it, 'electronic communications technologies, with their multiple media text, visual, voice and their capacity to extend interaction over time and distance, are transforming teaching and learning'.

5   As we saw in Chapter 5, the graphical tradition in legal learning is an ancient one. In the US, Alfred Reed's report on law schools (cited in Stevens, 1978, p. 110, n.79) contains an entertaining description of early AV in US legal education: 'Unhampered by scholastic tradition, [Mr X] has devised a new method of legal instruction, rendered possible by his ingenious discovery that legal definitions can be printed on pieces of celluloid with an ordinary typewriter. Throwing these definitions on a screen by the aid of a magic lantern, he supplemented these exhibitions, held two evenings a week, by running comment, and so appealed to eye and ear at once. Strangers, in the town of M. [California], making a round of the moving picture houses, took in his show along with the rest, thus establishing the value of this pedagogic innovation. At intervals, typed sheets, containing such questions as 'Define the difference between a nuncupative and an oleographic (sic) will' were distributed as tests to the students' (Reed, 1928, p. 73, n.2).

6   In addition the LTDU also act as consultants to others wishing to use this technology. For example our code and consultancy based upon it was the basis for the development of the College of Law's i-tutorial initiative on their LPC.

7   See Maharg (2001a).

It soon became clear that we needed to rethink the environment, which could become crowded and confusing. We were also aware that we needed to redesign the complex interface between video and resources, for the early video lectures were highly monologic, with meagre resources surrounding them. In other words, we were gradually moving from a presenter-centred event to a user-centred event, where more control was given over to the user and where the sophistication of the interface matched the complexity of other learning events in the module, for example, seminars or the transactional project, as these built up over the course of the syllabus. We learned many valuable lessons from the early video lectures, but we were aware that there was still a lot to learn. This was particularly true because while there is a rich and growing literature on the development of multimedia, there is little in the way of substantial research on the use of video lectures. As Baecker has pointed out, video lectures have generally been seen as a fairly uninteresting element of the learning environment and 'typically viewed as an ephemeral one-way broadcast medium' (Baecker et al., 2003, p. 896; see also Baecker, 2003).[8] We were interested in investigating the use of video lectures as part of an integrated study tool, where images and text are used to provide what we hoped would be a flexible and powerful environment for study. With the initiation of two large-scale video lecture projects in Civil and Criminal Procedure in the Diploma in Legal Practice the opportunity was presented us to research the use made of the video lectures by students.[9]

Research Literature and Design

A literature search revealed research on video lectures, but surprisingly little directly relevant research into video lecture design and usage in legal education.[10] Video lectures have been used, but there has been little commentary on its design or on the effects it has had on learning and teaching, or on assessment results. That such research is required is beyond question: the video lecture is not, as some have termed it, a talking head on the web. It is a completely different communicational

---

8   See also Knowledge Media Design Unit at the University of Toronto, and his homepage at http://kmdi.utoronto.ca/rmb/.

9   For more detail on the methodologies used in the project, see our longer paper at www.ggsl.strath.ac.uk/ltdu/research. This paper also provides much more analysis and feedback on issues such as accessibility and management of resources, forms of learning adopted by students and the like. It also contains in an appendix a list of all video lecture projects then carried out with the Glasgow Graduate School of Law (the list has since extended considerably).

10   Searches were conducted using ERIC (1990–2004); and the Multimedia Research Bibliography at University of Sydney (http://www.iml.uts.edu.au/learnteach/resources/pubs/mmpubs.html).

environment, where perception, language, meaning and memory are affected by many different factors (Baggaley, 1980).[11]

Even more important is the general issue of whether there is any evidence that specific forms of hypermedia or multimedia can improve student learning. The evidence appears to be conflicting, not just because the question of 'improvement' is a complex one but also because the conditions under which multimedia applications are developed and used, and the comparators against which they are rated by researchers, are different in each study. The meta-analysis of research findings by Dillon and Gabbard concluded that benefits from using multimedia are limited, although they did note that the power of multimedia to scaffold knowledge and cue it for the less able student is a strong advantage (Dillon and Gabbard, 1998).[12] The meta-analysis by Liao presented conflicting evidence, with a majority of studies proving that multimedia can be more effective than traditional instruction (Liao, 1999). However a sizeable minority of the studies (10 out of 35) showed the opposite. Mousavi, Lowe and Sweller (1995), for instance, claim that the presentation of difficult concepts to learners in both auditory and visual modes can enhance learning more than if the information is presented in one mode only.[13] A year later, a further and more detailed meta-analysis by Liao, this time of 46 studies, confirmed his earlier conclusion but cautioned that the form of multimedia and the form of traditional instruction being compared is critical to any evaluation of learning gain.

The most recent studies relevant to video lectures stemmed from medical education (Martin, 1999; Maggs, 2001). A review of the medical literature post-1979 conducted by Wofford et al. (2001) concluded that a computer-based lecture 'should be no less effective than a traditional lecture', while acknowledging the

---

11 Baggaley, for instance, has shown that small differences in camera angles (horizontal and vertical) and shot can have quite significant effects on our perception of the speaker and what is said by him or her.

12 They highlighted three conclusions:

1) hypermedia is useful where users have specific tasks that require searching through lengthy or multiple information sources;

2) increased learner control over access and use is differentially helpful to learners according to their abilities and learning styles;

3) the interaction of learner style and hypermedia environment could account for the confusing results in studies. What seemed to be important was that the explicit cueing that could be built into hypermedia aided passive learners, while deep processing learners benefited from exploring and using the extensive resources available in such applications (p. 349).

13 This was confirmed by Mayer, but only for a small group of users with little prior knowledge of the content to be learned and high visual abilities. Nevertheless it points to interesting findings regarding the place of dual channel presentation of information. Note that their propositions are one set amongst a number of design theories useful in the design and implementation of any multimedia learning environment.

'difficulty of randomised controlled trials and true comparison groups in testing that effectiveness' (p. 466).[14]

Our research project took account of these studies; but comparisons with what might be termed more 'traditional' forms of instruction were not the aim of the project. Instead, we aimed to investigate:

1) the *variation* in student learning;
2) the *quality* of student learning on the two procedural courses.

The aims were of course influenced by the project methodology, which was phenomenographic in nature. We tracked variation and quality in learning using the following instruments:

- selection of 11 students to track closely throughout the year;
- students filled in and submitted weekly logs when they used the resources;
- focus group discussion late in semester one;
- individual interviews in early/mid semester two and post-examination;
- questionnaire issued to the group of students;
- end-of-year evaluation data derived from whole-year cohort.

Qualitative responses were coded into themes by two raters, with relatively high inter-rater reliability (70 per cent). Over 100 pages of qualitative data were collected – too much to discuss in depth here. Instead, I shall highlight a number of the themes that arose, and comment on them. Before this, however, I shall give a brief description of the learning environment and its design process.

Design of the Video Learning Environment

There is, of course, a substantial body of research into multimedia design and the basic assumptions and principles of best practice.[15] Three widely-accepted assumptions underpinned our work: first, the dual channel assumption (that there are two separate information processing channels – visual/pictorial and auditory/verbal); second, our limited capacity for cognition through each channel; and

---

14 This finding was confirmed by other studies. Williams et al. (2001) found no difference in knowledge acquisition after testing two groups of students, one learning from a structured lecture and the other from a computer-based learning application. Spickard et al. (2002) concluded that an online lecture is a 'feasible, efficient and effective method to teach students'. In a later trial Spickard et al. (2004) confirmed the learning value of audio-feed with PowerPoint slides within an online lecture environment.

15 For some of the principles arising from this research, see Paivio (1986), Chandler and Sweller (1991), Sweller (1988) and Sweller et al. (2001). For cognitive load theory, see Sweller (1988 and 1994). For multimedia theory, see Mayer (1997), Mayer and Moreno (2000) and Moreno and Mayer (2000).

third, that learning is an active process in which the learner processes information, integrates it with prior knowledge and experience and uses it to form expectations about future information.[16] Following on from these are a number of design principles to enable more effective learning:

1) *multimedia*: use of multiple representations of information, for example, pictures as well as text;
2) *contiguity*: information sources should be close to each other on the page or screen, both in space and time;
3) *redundancy*: information that is repeated unnecessarily tends to inhibit learning;
4) *modality*: pictorial cues + spoken narrations tend to increase learning than pictorial cues + on-screen texts;
5) *signalling*: coherent structuring of information, containing clear signals to the user;
6) *interactivity*: students can interact with and control the resources to be learned;
7) *personalisation*: users learn more effectively in a conversational milieu than in a more formal learning event;
8) *pre-training*: users should be given brief training in the use of the application;
9) *adaptivity*: user traits should be considered in the design of multimedia resources, including such factors as prior knowledge and working memory.[17]

These principles are standard and accepted across the industry, but many aspects of them are still the focus of fundamental research, as we shall see. They are useful guides to basic practice but, where justified, we have departed from them in our larger aim of supporting the learning that students require to carry out if they are to understand civil procedure as a set of interlocking concepts, rules and events and therefore the procedure involved in the transactional project.

More specifically, our environment had to take into account two key requirements. First, the substantive complexity of civil procedure had to be presented coherently. Second, the environment needed to provide students with different ways of accessing, understanding and memorising the materials to be learned. As Tulving pointed out, retrieval cues need to be provided along with the information that is being learned (here, semantic knowledge) if learning resources are to be effective (Tulving, 1972).[18] The problem for us was to provide information structures that could do both (Clark, 1998). In the first phase of the design process

---

16 See for example Mayer and Moreno (2003).

17 For references to most of them in practice, see Mayer (2001), Clark and Feldon (2005) and Bodemer et al. (2004)), all of whom reference versions of this list.

18 Semantic knowledge is the function of long-term memory to store knowledge of facts and concepts as well as the meaning of words.

we aimed to support learning in tutorials, and to enable students to gain a basic understanding of forms of civil procedures in the Sheriff Court in Scotland. We planned out 'levels' of information: at the core of the application was the video lecture, with succeeding layers of information (see Figure 9.1). Within each layer, information was clustered on the contiguity and adaptivity principles mentioned above: which information would a user be likely to reach for and to what purpose. Such decisions inevitably involved us thinking about the tasks that users would undertake (bearing in mind their role-play assessments in advocacy, their plea-drafting examination and their examination in conceptual understanding of civil procedure).[19] The design followed best practice in human–computer interface design but we were also concerned that the interface should be elegant and pleasing to the eye as well as usable.[20] The process began around nine months before the start of the academic year in which the video lectures would be used. The environment we subsequently created was available both on CD and online on GGSL computers. Students were still required to attend a series of 10 weekly seminars in groups of approximately 12–15.

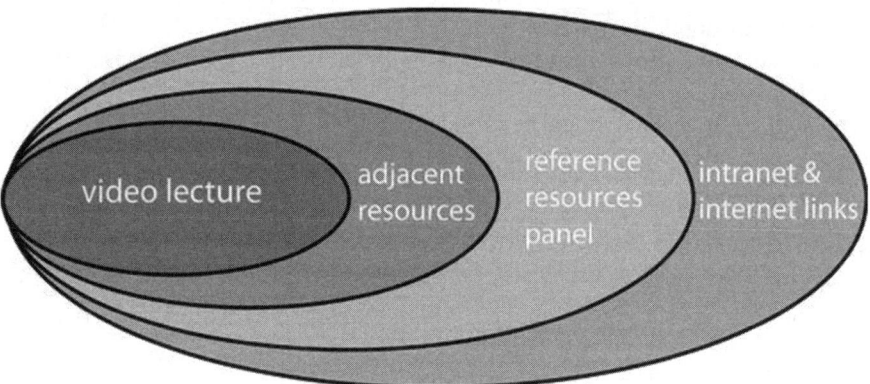

Figure 9.1   Information layers in the video lecture environment

---

19 Note that at this stage, the CCA transaction had not yet been implemented. The transaction was planned and implemented in the following 18 months.

20 This process included consideration of artistic elements such as relationship between background and foreground, fonts, colour, shape, overall look and feel and much else. Students would be spending a fair amount of their time looking at the screen and we wanted the interface to be restful, inviting and cool. See Thalheimer (2004).

Civil Court Practice Video Lecture Environment

When students open the CD or webpage to enter the video lecture learning environment they are given a menu of options:

- *video lectures*: this includes not only the video lectures but also the external resources;
- *handbook*: the students are given an online copy of the handbook they receive in paper copy form with the CD;
- *advocacy multimedia unit*: this unit shows the student how to approach court hearings through role play and short activities;
- *drafting multimedia unit*: this unit takes the students through the process of drafting the initiating document in a civil court action and gives the students the opportunity to practice the skills themselves;
- *assessment*: this section gives students information on the assessment for the module together with interactive objective questions for formative assessment.

Figure 9.2 shows a typical video lecture page for Civil Procedure. The environment includes: the talking head; synchronised downloadable PowerPoint slides (which include text, images, diagrams and other imported materials); volume control; section headings linked to the speaker and slides, lecture number and the ability to return to the complete lecture contents menu; the length of time the lecture will take; and a timeline which allows the students to scroll through the lecture to particular points.

Students can listen, pause and review a video lecture as often as they like. Each video lecture was deliberately split up into appropriate section lengths according to topic. Video lectures allowed us to move away from the traditional 50 minute slot into divisions based upon topic and subtopic hierarchies: one lecture is only 20 minutes long while another stretches to two hours and is subdivided into eight mini lectures. In Figure 9.2, for instance, users can search the section categories; and they can use the timeline at the bottom of the page, for scanning within a category.[21] They can thus access the video lectures systematically or they can use the timeline as a form of speculative searching or 'bricolage' (Turkle, 1995).

Students are also able to access an external resources menu from the 'information' icon to the right of the video window. This will draw a panel over

---

21 For the role of categories in searching, see 'Strategies for Categorising Categories'. Available online at: http://world.std.com/%7Euieweb/Articles/strategies_categories.htm. Timelines are obviously useful devices for video lectures, but they are also excellent textual designs. For a general introduction to the field of data representation see Friendly and Dennis. For detailed exposition of the medieval background (outlined in Friendly and Dennis) see also Carruthers (1998).

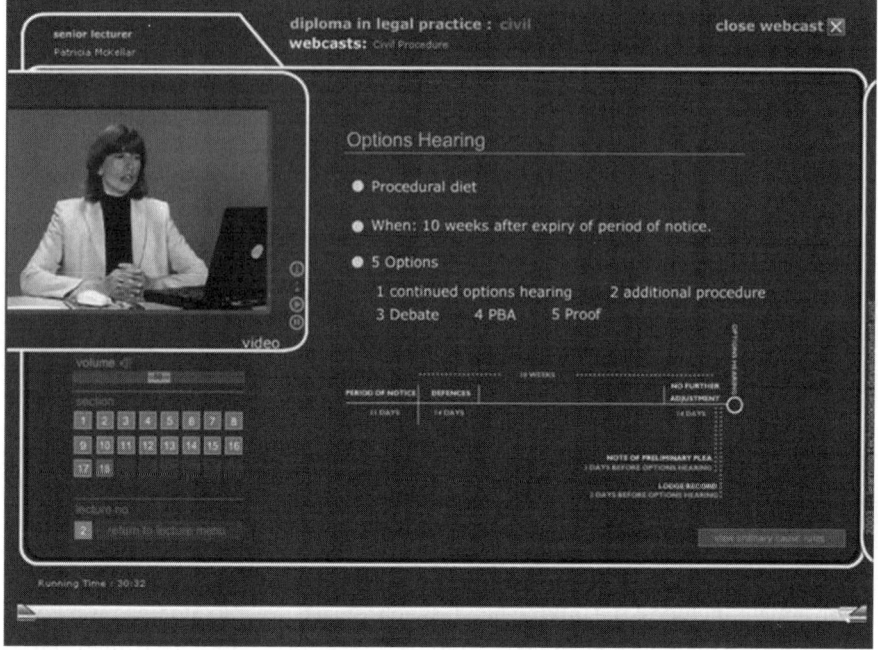

Figure 9.2   Main Civil Court Practice: video lecture page

the full screen which can be accessed while the speaker is talking or while the video is paused. This page's menu includes:

- *web links*: this takes students to the webpage for the course which contains a list of relevant websites that can be constantly updated by the technical support staff. There is a discussion forum for the course on the webpage;
- *statutes*: a full list of the statutes referred to in the course as weblinks or pdf files;
- *Ordinary Cause Rules*: full text of the main statutory rules;
- *bullet-point slides*: these are downloadable;
- *cases*: a list of all the cases referred to in the lectures and many others;
- *Westlaw*: a link to the authentication page;
- *BAILII*: (British and Irish Legal Information Institute);
- *documentation*: the documentation is subdivided into the different court procedures covered and includes the statutory templates together with examples of style documents. There are also photographs of items not readily reproduced in digital format and a flowchart.

So far we have outlined the general background to the video lecture initiatives. We shall now consider some of the data we received from the research project participants under a number of the themes that arose from their data.

Integration of Resources

The literature has shown convincingly that dual-encoding of information (for example, by video and text) can enable more effective learning than single-channel encoding, for example, text. But in order for any video lecture environment to work effectively there must be a convergence of all resources – the sense of well-organised, seamless knowledge management that supports cognitive development. The theme itself is an ancient one, as we have seen in Chapter 5, where integration of image and text was important to the act of reading and understanding. The integration need not only be of text and image but of other genres and channels as well.[22] In addition, however, grandiose the Wagnerian analogy might be, there is about well-designed multimedia a sense of complex and interweaving *leitmotif* in visual design, placing of graphics, organisation of text, control of textual register, interweaving of sound and video and much else.

Matching task to environment is critical and we had to take account of user purpose as well.[23] As we struggled with this, it became clear that there were deeper issues involved. The design task circled around not just navigational principles, but informational and indeed epistemological issues. As Dillon and Vaughan point out, the typical navigation metaphor of multimedia design actually 'sheds no light' on how students create a 'map of semantic space'; nor does it clarify the real heart of the issue, namely how to help users integrate information design with semantic knowledge (Dillon and Vaughan, 1998). In order to do so, users need to develop what they do almost without thinking when they read texts – namely, construct a sense of the informational structure of the environment. The key to this is what Dillon and Vaughan call 'shape' – the development within the user of a sense of

---

22 See for example Richard Wagner's early essay, 'The Artwork of the Future' (1849), where he discusses his concept of the *Gesamtkunstwerk*, 'Total Artwork', that combines song, orchestral music, poetry, visual art and dance into one experience. For him, opera was the form most suitable for this type of experience. For F.T. Marinetti writing his Futurist Manifesto in 1916, it was cinema that held the promise of integrating all arts into one form. In the early 1970s, for Alan Kay working at Xerox PARC (Palo Alto Research Center), the first PC, called the Dynabook, would provide text, animation, images, sound – hypermedia. See the interesting exhibition of Jordan and Packer (2000) (though rather bizarrely the exhibits start at Cro-Magnon cave paintings and leap to Wagner, missing out all intervening cultural episodes).

23 The variables involved in this design activity are quite complex; and to accommodate them we adopted an evolutionary approach to the environment. We have built as best we can for particular user purposes, and the following year's integration takes account of the previous year's project data. For a discussion of evolutionary approaches, see Spool (2002).

genre, a developing sense of informational schema that is part knowing the types of information present and part knowing where the information is, and how it links up. The rhetorical structure of the information thus needs to offer cues for retrieval of information, as Tulving pointed out. Indeed, we can take Tulving's conclusions a step further and say that students needed cues to find and retrieve information in the environment, as well as retrieving items from memory.

Genre is a good metaphor for design principles of the textual resources within the environment, but it does not quite address the problems presented by a video lecture. Unlike a book, a video lecture is performative and dynamic in the sense that it moves through time. As a result, there are aspects of it that are simply not defined by genre-modelling. Instead, it is more fruitful to think of at least the video lecture elements as a film-script. Our narrative was civil procedure – a conceptual narrative, based on the chronology of the trial process. It was both a cinematographic representation of knowledge and a textual display. The problem, as with all filmic narratives, is the decision regarding how much information needs to be available to the viewer or user. It is as impossible to show all information to the user at once as it is to shoot a scene in a film without some objects being occluded by others within view. Such occlusion is a necessary part of our perception of reality and a necessary part of learning knowledge for the learner, so as to focus on what is to be learned.

We tried to find a balance where resources were easily accessible but not intrusive. If the screen becomes too busy, the relative proportions of any single knowledge object become confused amidst the mass of information. Resources should be present without being invasive, and their positioning became an important issue for us. Certain aspects of this gave us more problems than others. For example, students welcomed visual aids and prompts which gave them an overall picture of the procedure – a form of aerial perspective shot:

> what would be most useful to me is a map of how these procedures actually work. I still can't see, I can't absolutely visualise the situation in which you would go to a proof before answer as compared to a debate. That's not absolutely clear to me yet. I think I just need to see that written down.[24]

What was interesting about this and other comments was that there was already in the resources section a comprehensive flow chart of civil procedure. Some students – like the one quoted above – never found it. Other students became aware of the flow chart through other routes:

> I took [the flow chart] to tutorials actually and quite a lot of people noted and [said] 'Where did you get that?'

---

24 All student comments quoted with permission.

Clearly, we needed to re-think the integration of this particular resource. In analysis of the feedback it became clear that there were also more profound issues of how new knowledge was assimilated into prior structures – a point we shall address later in the chapter.

For most of the students we tracked, though, the integration of seminar, video lectures and textbook worked well:

> I think … the Civil video lectures are linked well to the tutorials and I feel they also link well to [the core textbook] because …there's a lot to grasp with procedure especially if you are not used to it and you do need it reinforced …what is good is that I feel that they do link up.

Some of the civil tutors made good use of the video lectures within the tutorials:

> every week [the tutor] pulled out the small manual and said you have to watch 3, 4 and 5 so we knew exactly for next week he was going to be discussing video lectures 3, 4 and 5, for example. […] The system works if it's followed.

Some tutors, though, were not as diligent in this respect:

> [Our] civil tutor was completely unaware of what we doing. At the start of every class we had to tell him what we had covered. There was a lot of repetition, like he was going over a lot of what we had already covered in the video lecture instead of maybe explaining stuff a bit further that we were having difficulty with.'

> I would have liked my Civil tutor to have had more contact with the lecturer or my Civil tutor to have watched the video lecture and Criminal as well. A kind of lack of 'joined-up-ness'.

The issue was a serious one, for it was clear from student feedback that transfer of learning from video lecture to transaction was easier if tutors were able to point up the links. This issue of integration was discussed with tutors at the end-of-course meeting. One solution considered was a set of online Q&As, with feedback linking directly to specific video lectures – a resource that we have since designed and implemented. Another one was a set of short questions to be available for tutors to discuss with students at the start of tutorials. Tutors also suggested that, in order to assist students see the link between lectures and tutorials, a short period could be set aside at various points to review procedure examination questions. Not only would these activities assist in integrating the video environment with the face-to-face seminars but they would also serve as a prompt for students to watch the video lectures.

Flexibility and Portability of Use

The single most attractive feature of the video lectures was their flexible nature and ease of access. In our project group of 11 even the single student who would have preferred face-to-face lectures accepted that video lectures had this advantage. As one student put it,

> I find it a hassle coming in [to the GGSL] to study. Apart from train times, which are pretty unreliable from where I stay it's just I study a lot better at home. I can get up early and study all day and go to my work and come back and study so I used it at home.

When asked to think about whether they might use the video lecture environment in their traineeships, most students considered the portability of the resource to be of significant benefit:

> It's great. When I start work in September I can take the CD with me and if there is anything they ask me that I am not sure about then I know where to check and that's super cos, you know, when you look at you own lecture notes eight months later *I* don't even know what [they say] never mind what it is supposed to mean. So it's great to have that as a tool I can use for coming years. I never expected anything like that.

> Video lectures are excellent because you can go back to them oh my goodness what was the procedure for the options hearing? Of course there are books you can do that but [the environment] is a very student friendly environment and doesn't assume a particularly high level of knowledge.

> You know, after the summer holidays I kinda wonder how much of this I'm going to remember. It could be a year down the line before I'm ever doing any Civil Court work and a lot of that will be forgotten. And it will be good to have that to go back to and be reminded, just again, even from just a confidence point of view, of the sort of way the court cases are carried out, even if it is just that. Then again video lectures are excellent because you can go back to them … 'What was the procedure for the Options Hearing?'.

> When I go on and do my traineeship you've got those materials there and it is not a case of finding the box under the bed where your lecture notes were stored 6 months previously … I have got something I can take into work with me and use on the computer. So it has been more than just a set of lectures it is a whole resource I can use for other things.

Students recognised the problem of updating but still saw the CD as an excellent resource:

> if you had a feature on the CD that linked up to the Internet that would be great because if I am watching that in a year's time there might be changes that have happened.

Presence and Absence

Social Presence and Image

There is a considerable literature on the subject of social presence in electronic teaching learning, but the great majority of it focuses on the social factors in techniques such as tele- or video-conferencing, discussion forums, largely in the context of online distance-education.[25] A number of researchers have developed tools to measure social presence.[26] The concept is still a contested one, though, and it would therefore be useful to define what precisely we mean when we talk about social presence within a video lecture. Rourke et al. (2001) considered the subject, starting with Mehrabian's concept of 'immediacy', which he defined as 'those communication behaviours that enhance closeness to and nonverbal interaction with another'. Note that Mehrabian defines enhancement of communication by means of two factors – 'closeness' and 'nonverbal interaction'. We shall see that even in a pre-recorded video lecture, where there are no synchronous or asynchronous modes of communication associated with the video lecture, these two elements were important, and had an effect on student attitude to the two environments.

Nonverbal Interaction: The Conversation with the Camera

Even within the highly restricted context of the video lecture talking head – and perhaps because of it – nonverbal elements of the speaker's behaviour are heightened. Camera angles – horizontal and vertical – affect viewer perception. A low angle (looking up at the subject from below) tends to make the subject look powerful or dominating. When combined with a full-frontal presentation of the subject's face and steady gaze, the effect can be intimidating, even though the subject does not intend this (McCain et al., 1977).[27] Camera angle can even have an effect on a viewer's memory for pictorial events (Kraft, 1987).[28] We discovered much of this for ourselves when we experimented with the early video lectures prior to the full-course video lecture environments.

---

25 The classic early study on social presence was Short et al. (1976). Their work is based on the premise of one-to-one communications, but their work is important for video lectures to the extent that it emphasised the contribution of the visual image to social presence. For work on social presence in email, see Sproull and Keisler (1991) and Gunawardena and Zittle (1997). For an update on Short et al. in the field of teleconferencing, see Egido (1990). For a more recent review of research, see Williams (1997)

26 See, for example, Tu (2002).

27 See also Mandell and Shaw (1973). For a general survey of the research, see Messaris (1997). For an interesting application of rhetorical reading of images, see Kress and van Leeuwen (1996).

28 Note that this study focused on memory for pictorial events, rather than for textual events.

In addition to camera angle, eye-gaze, tone of voice, diction, relative speed of delivery, attitude of head and shoulders to the camera and dress all have an effect upon the viewer, as students pointed out. When asked what it was they liked about the presentation style of the civil procedure presenter (Patricia McKellar), they often drew attention not just to her style of talking but her way of structuring knowledge in her manner of delivery. They thought her delivery 'natural' and equated it with conversational ease:

> Patricia's [presentation] felt more real, obviously not reading from notes. […] [it] was a lot easier because there was a lot more fill-in words and so it was much easier to follow.

She achieved this because her presentation technique appeared unscripted, she frequently used second-person address, she varied facial expression depending on the content of the point she was making and her gaze wandered briefly from the camera and returned to it, as can happen in real-life conversation and rarely occurs when, for instance, newsreaders read the news.[29] In other words her presence humanised not only the subject matter but also the medium.[30]

Closeness

Was there an 'affective response' by the students to the video lecture presenters? The phrase is used by Rourke et al. (2001) to describe qualities such as 'warmth, affiliation, attraction, openness'. Rourke et al. point out that according to filtered-cues theorists these qualities are reduced in text-based environments, but attain a higher profile when they are embodied within expressive images of people.[31] At least half of the students were affected by the images of the video lecture presenters they had in front of them. One student put it thus:

> … it's always there and it's not just a text or a book that you have got because it is someone else sitting there talking to you. It's kind of comforting in a way as well, because they know what they are talking about, you can't misread it.

One student referred in particular to the aural quality of presence:

---

29 Take for instance the start of the third video lecture: 'Hello, welcome to lecture three in the Civil Procedure lecture series. Today we're going to be looking at the Options Hearing but let's look first at how we got here. You'll remember that we drafted up our Initial Writ, you'll remember that the Initial Writ had a principal copy and a service copy ….' Pronouns such as 'we', 'you' are used in a conversational style that actually discusses a fairly abstract list of documents and procedures.

30 For further evidence of this, see Bancroft (1995).

31 See, for example, Christenson and Menzel (1998).

I think that intonation as well was really important to me. Just reading something, you can read it, but the intonation I found really helpful. That was why I did go back over not just my own notes [for the exam] but actually watch it again because there is emphasis in important places and that is so important. Also you don't want to end up completely isolated with no … I know video lectures are not very interactive anyway but they are much more interactive than reading a script.

The personal effect of lecturers and tutors on students can be a powerful determinant of learning. Such 'closeness' had an interesting effect on methods of study and what might be termed the affective context of study. Another student referred to a lecturer in another subject and how she associated the materials for that subject with the lecturer:

… his voice was ringing through my ears and every time I'm studying I'm thinking about him. It is a good thing that you can see the face on the screen [in the procedure video lectures] because when I am reading my notes and things like that you can hear them in my head and the way they say things and stuff like that.

A student commented on the variety of ways of learning that the civil video lecture could give rise to:

It's like a different way of learning, like if you hear it and then you write it down and then you read it back. Then you learn something in three different ways.

When asked about watching and listening, this student replied as follows:

Interviewer: Would it have made any difference to you if you hadn't actually seen the person and you had only heard what they were saying […]?
Student: Strange, but I probably hardly looked at it [the video lecture image] because I was writing notes anyway … But I don't know … it just seems quite nice having a person there.

When asked about social presence, the student acknowledged its importance to her:

Yes, but it seems a bit strange because there is no real reason for it when you are not really looking that much [at the video window].

It is indeed strange, but it is nevertheless clear that, for a number of students, social presence as represented by the video window did matter to them when they were studying.[32]

---

32   Social presence as linked to video image is still a controversial issue. Our conclusions here contradict some of the literature, and support other findings. In one study while there was no perceived advantage to social presence across a number of different applications (video-based, audio-based and textual), nevertheless there were a number of interesting

Memory and Knowledge Objects: Intensive Study for Examinations

Curriculum Context and Knowledge Objects

If social presence matters, then curriculum context matters even more. The video environment was designed to be viewed and used in a study context, within a structure of seminars, assessment requirements (both transactional and skills assessment as well as examination) and other subjects within the Diploma. As such, we were interested in how students moved from isolated memory of individual video lectures to a more structured conceptual understanding of legal procedure and how the video lecture environment had affected that process. As research on learning points out, students need to undergo this process in traditional lecture series if they are to arrive at a coherent and structured sense of the materials to be learned.

There is a considerable body of work on the relation of memory to consciousness and how memory, learning and understanding can be best facilitated. However, much of the early work was conducted with a laboratory setting and it is difficult to relate much of this research to real-world learning by students within university settings. So much depends on the integration of different factors within situations: the experience of a tutor, the way teaching is implemented, how resources are used and so on. These factors can often skew statistically-calibrated laboratory research results.[33]

Nevertheless, within the field of cognitive psychology there are directions in research that are useful indicators as to how students understand and memorise information. In Chapter 2 (p. 77) I described briefly the work of Tulving (1972; 1985) and Conway et al. (1997) and how certain forms of learning could facilitate the 'remember-to-know' shift. Their findings were substantiated by Herbert and Burt (2004) who used Biggs' SOLO taxonomy (structure of observed learning outcome) to assess the content and structure of student knowledge.[34] In their experiment, they hypothesised that '[t]he greater the amount of remembering experienced early in learning, the more likely it is that the shift to knowing will occur'. Their results confirmed that how students experience resources affects long-term retention of conceptual knowledge (Herbert and Burt, 2004; see also Herbert and Burt, 2001 and 2003).

For Herbert and Burt there were clear indicators arising from the research as to design principles for the design of teaching materials that would facilitate the shift

---

findings regarding social presence: '[t]he higher the degree of social presence perceived by the student, the higher the level of satisfaction with the computer-based instruction; the higher the degree of social presence perceived by the student the higher the level of motivation toward the computer-based instruction' (Steffey, 2001).

33 See, for example, McKeachie (1990).

34 See Biggs and Collis (1982). The taxonomy can be used to differentiate between memory and knowledge in student understanding.

to knowing. It was also clear that those students who set out from the start of their study to remember more from lectures tended to create better schemes of structured knowledge later in their learning: they shifted successfully from episodic memory to semantic memory of information. In an earlier study, Herbert and Burt (1999) paralleled their findings with those of the literature on deep and surface learning, aligning the successful students' remember-to-know shift with deep learning, and surface learning with an incomplete or poorly executed shift. As we shall see below, this is supported quite independently in the phenomenographical literature.

Knowledge Objects

In their classic phenomenographical study entitled 'Knowledge Objects: Understandings Constituted through Intensive Study', Entwistle and Marton interviewed 11 undergraduate science students about their methods of study leading up to their final examinations (1994).[35] The metaphor of a knowledge object is, they suggest, a way of 'describing aspects of memory processes and understanding which is not reductionist': '[t]he structure of a knowledge object is not a way of acting appropriately in a familiar situation, it is a way of making sense of personal experiences of learning and studying' (Entwistle and Marton, 1994, pp. 174–5).[36] As Entwistle and Marton describe it, a knowledge object for students is a form of understanding legitimated within a particular disciplinary community, 'a tightly integrated "bundle" of ideas and related information and experience', in which

> the nature of the knowledge object formed will depend crucially on the range of material incorporated, the effort put into thinking about that material, and the frameworks within which the knowledge object is developed. (Entwistle and Marton, 1994, pp. 174–5)

There are four characteristics of knowledge objects:

---

35 See also Entwistle and Entwistle (2003). In this latter article the linkage of forms of intention (deep, surface) to specific studying processes is made overtly. I would argue for a similar complexity in the studying techniques adopted by students in the video lecture environments. It is interesting to note that Dewey expressed a similar notion in his concept of 'idea artefacts' – *LW*, 16, pp. 326–7; 330).

36 This concept parallels different approaches to learning and the structure of knowledge. Berardi-Coletta et al. (1995) for instance, conducted studies on the role of metacognition in problem-solving, and concluded that 'process-oriented [i.e. metacognitive] participants consistently form[ed] more sophisticated problem representations and develop[ed] more complex strategies' (1995, p. 207). For them, the process of verbalisation was not the source of better problem-solving so much as the metacognitive processing involved in the effort to produce explanations. Curiously enough, there are a number of parallels between the phenomenographical approach to knowledge objects and Sherry Turkle's concept of 'evocative objects' with which we think.

1) the student's awareness of a closely-integrated body of knowledge;
2) the quasi-sensory representation (often visual) of this corpus;
3) a movement from unfocused and episodic remembering to much more detailed and coherent knowing;
4) structure of the knowledge object itself.[37]

However, a knowledge object is not merely the product of cognitive processes. There are also experiential entities and qualities that are brought into being within an ever-shifting social and a disciplinary horizon. Entwistle and Marton describe this phenomenological awareness well, quoting Donaldson:

> We may know in a variety of ways characterised by differing degrees of awareness. Some kinds of knowledge are in the light of full awareness. Others are in the shadows, on the edge of the bright circle. Knowledge on the fringe of consciousness ... is always ready to move to the centre. It is accessible to us, even if we don't attend to it.[38]

Did the video lecture environment facilitate the remember-to-know shift? Did it enable students to construct knowledge objects? These were key issues for us, for if the environment could not help students in these processes, it would not be able to facilitate transfer of learning to the CCA transaction. The format of the examination, of course, influenced student study patterns. The CD and web environment were not going to be available to students in the open-book examinations and only certain annotated texts were allowed into the examinations. Students were given notice of this and asked to prepare notes from the CD or online video lectures in any form that they wanted. One of our concerns was that students would be uncertain how to do this, and that this would affect the process of intensive study, and the formation of knowledge objects. Within this context, what we discovered was the surprising and delightful range of objects created by students within the horizon of the video lecture environment, in order to make comprehensible and memorable the subject of procedural law. These included use of visual and aural channels, graphics, text and other media.

At the start of the process of intensive study, most students found that having the actual words of the lecture that they could review a source of comfort. One compared it to the situation in a face-to-face lecture where she would have had only her own lecture notes:

---

37 In a similar study that confirmed the earlier findings, Entwistle and Entwistle warned against a too easy identification of rote learning with shallow learning. As they put it, 'The analysis showed that the distinction between "understanding" and "memorising" is not easy to delineate, with "committing to memory" and "rote learning of details" both contributing to the production of a knowledge object. The findings warn against too ready a linkage of intention to any specific process in student learning: a deep intention can involve rote memorisation, while a surface approach at university level will include understanding, even if it is reproduced from lecture notes' (Entwistle and Entwistle, 2003).

38 Ibid., p.175, quoting Donaldson (1992).

Yes the way the words on the page can become a miasma and you can think 'Oh how do I get back into this' but [when using the video lecture] you can just sit and you can hear and – that is what I was trying to say about not taking notes. Sometimes you can just sit and you can listen to what they are trying to describe.

Immersion was essential to at least half the students in our study, and it seemed that the video lecture environment encouraged them to immerse themselves in it according to their preferred approaches to learning.

I would come in, in the morning and watch a load of them in one day. I would just sort of hammer my way through lots and lots of them. I just found that much easier to do rather than – I think I just learn things much better if I immerse in them. I am not very good at kind of incremental learning where I build upon it and go – 'Oh yes that rings a bell from last week.' So I did the whole Civil and Criminal video lectures in two days.

Another student explained how she constructed her knowledge objects through the process of revising over time according to subject:

I did Civil and Criminal a wee bit differently. Criminal, I just sat down and hammered through them all at once. I sat with my statute books, marking all the relevant points and annotating them as I went along and that was basically all I did. I didn't look at any other materials it was just me and the CD ROM. For Civil, I sat going through them one at a time and then would go on and read the relevant chapters in the Hennessy book and sort of annotate, not at the same time but at a different point and sort of try and let it soak in a bit more. Because I think Civil is a bit more complicated it is more than just marking a book up, you are trying to remember the stuff a bit more. Obviously you are trying to remember stuff for Criminal but [in civil procedure] everything is more complex.

Annotation formed a key part of knowledge object construction. One student noted how the process of reviewing the video lectures made annotation and memorising easier:

I would say, for Criminal, I would just put the video lecture on and would be sitting watching it and as [the presenter] went along and was mentioning sections I would be sitting with my statute book annotating the parts and highlight them and then he would mention cases to do with it and I would mark them in. I don't think it was anything more complex than that. Obviously because it was revision, you had watched them before. You didn't feel you needed the same level of concentration as you would when you watched them first time round. You were able to sit there marking away and listening to him. I felt that I was doing something else, that the information was still going in, and I was learning it as I was going along. It was much better than sitting with a set of lecture notes and trying to revise that way. I have often found going back to the lecture notes and I can't remember what I meant when I wrote something down and I think, 'What was the lecturer's point?' and can't remember, and you end up going back to books and that sort of thing.

Another student spoke about how she used the video lectures alongside other resources, annotating the resources:

> I would probably try and do two lectures at a time, just to have a target. I always do that. Then I would sit with the Civil, I would just go through it and mark off the Ordinary Cause Rules. Anything that wasn't in the rules that I thought I needed to know I would just scribble at the side and then sit and write things down. I would write it down until I knew it straight off my head. If there was something about preparation that we spoke about in the lectures that wasn't in the Statute Book I would go to Charles Hennessy's book and read it there. I didn't expect to have to use it in the exam but just that I knew it was there – you know, the things you had to take into the proof and things like that.

Another commented on the usefulness of the focused set of resources within the video lecture environment:

> Before, [i.e. on the undergraduate LLB course] I felt that the resources were scattered everywhere. You would have so many books, you had to refer to lecture notes, handouts you had been given. You spent a lot of time trying to pull all your resources into one set of notes that you could refer to so that you weren't constantly reading that chapter, that set of notes and trying to put it all together. [In the video lecture environment] [a]ll your information was together. Obviously for Civil you would have Hennessy's book to look at as well but you had your video lecture and your book and that was it more or less. Again Hennessy's book was only adding to it or going over material that you had already done on the video lecture. It encompassed everything that you needed you know I felt. Maybe you should have been doing a lot wider reading but I felt that was enough for me.

Within procedural law, most students felt the need to be able to reproduce overview and detail. Students realised how the video lectures could help in this regard:

> I just watched them the day before to re-orientate myself within the whole thing and the structure of it and certainly that helped me and the exam picked up what I had learned from the video lecture.

Video lecture note-taking was always going to be very different from taking notes at lectures. The procedures that students adopted varied considerably. Some felt safer creating sets of what were akin to traditional lecture notes:

> I think I am happier doing it pen and paper. I guess, I have written shorthand, rather than typed shorthand, so I think I would rather write and I can write quicker. But not everyone will be the same as that.

> When I did the first few I was writing absolutely everything out and I hadn't really – because quite a lot of people were looking at the screen and were writing down what was on the screen and working their notes around that. I wasn't doing that I was writing

everything out and that took ages. So it was like well I'll just write down what's on the screen and then write my own notes.'

Some took notes on the computer, using MS Word. When asked about the writing styles they adopted, students revealed that they used a variety of methods:

Bullet points and headings, just kind of try and base it around the headings you've got and then expand like make my own notes from what the lecturers are saying.

The PowerPoint style of bulleted information points did not suit all students:

Maybe it is just me, but I found it quite hard to work from the PowerPoint slide presentation that was on the lecture slides. It highlights what [the presenter] was saying – so it is quite difficult then to think back and think what context was it in or what was the first part of that sentence or what was the last few words of the sentence. There was one point where I thought I can't remember if that flows on from the thing above so I started to draw arrows on to it to make sure that I knew the sentence was one and it flowed rather than thinking of things as distinct parts as bullet points.

This points to ways in which we can improve the environment. But the issue has deeper resonances. These responses show that formation of knowledge-objects is a deeply personal moment and occurs best when a student is using the environment rather as one might gaze through a window at a scene beyond it. There is a degree of transparency associated with the object of gaze, but also a degree of awareness that one is focusing on the object through the glass. The use of technology is never as simple a matter as complete immersion or complete transparency. The balance is a fine one and if there needs to be too much attention given to the technology of communication (the window itself), then the construction of knowledge objects is interrupted.

As will be clear from the above interview data, students were using the video lecture environments in quite different ways. Examples included use of *two* computers by some students, different time planning, different forms of reading and listening and the use of the video lecture as a mnemonic. Was there any discernable pattern to the approaches they took to their study? As we reflected on the themes of the interviews and other project data it became clear that there were amongst the project students what one might regard as two polar attitudes towards the video lectures – we call them paperworld student and e-world student.

Paperworld Student
The first was characterised by student A. He did not like using the video lectures and would have preferred face-to-face lectures. He did not use any of the learning tools in the environment and engaged as little as possible with the resources on the CD and online. Where possible, he used books instead of electronic resources, for example, paper-based case and statute collections. He took verbatim notes from the video lectures so that he had a set of notes that most closely resembled

what he regarded as a good set of lecture-notes and did not listen to them again. He then worked on these notes in the way that he had always worked with his lecture notes, by reducing them to more easily comprehensible and memorisable structures on paper. He used WestLaw, but only to get a set of leading cases on paper. He viewed the multimedia units and found them helpful. The biggest improvement in his eyes would be a transcript of the video lectures that he could print out, and thus avoid listening to the video lectures themselves (this was later provided for all students).

E-world Student
This pole was characterised by student B. She was very happy using the environments, made full using of the learning tools and used online information where she could, including all the information resources. She used a word processor to type up her notes or printed out the information in the resource panel to the right of the video lecture and added written notes to these. She studied for the examination by viewing and reviewing the video lectures and using printed out word-processed notes. She used the 'speak-fast' button and many of the navigational aids.[39] She viewed the multimedia and liked it. Her suggested improvements included sorting one of the bugs she had detected in the software and adding more functionality, for example, an .mp3 download of the lectures and the addition of functionality to the flowchart of civil actions so that students could obtain more information from it.

These two polar positions, though useful in characterising different approaches to the electronic environment, should probably be seen as pathologies of study techniques within the environment. The great majority of students ranged in the spectrum between A and B, more often towards e-world student than paperworld student. When one student was asked if she typed out information from the video lectures, she replied:

> No, I like writing – I have seen people sitting typing but I don't know how I could do that because I have done it [i.e. taken written notes] for four years – just sat writing. I can't study from type either. I like studying from my own handwriting as well so I just knew that would make it much easier.

This sounds like a paperworld student; but the same student used the video lectures extensively for revision and felt happy using the environment. Another student, asked about the effects that the video lecture environments had upon her learning, described this mid-spectrum position in a way that summarised other students' positions well:

> If you look at it as being a different study technique of sitting in front of a computer then yes [i.e. it was a different study technique that was being adopted when using the

---

39 An embedded function in the Windows Media Player, whereby one can speed up or slow down the rate at which video-data is presented.

environment]. But it was basically the same processes that you were going through but it was more condensed because to you didn't have this really big pooling exercise going on of trying to get all your information together. I mean the information is together so you were just sitting and working through the information the same as I would have done with anything else. I would have sat and annotated a statute book before but it would have been a longer process to trying to get all the information together to see what points needed to be annotated.

What was interesting was how each of the students came in quite different ways to an accommodation within the environment. They used it in unique ways to dovetail with their traditional forms of examination study – or, to look at it from the other side, they extended their study repertoire into the electronic domain. The quality of attention to such a space was vital, as students made clear. Without exception it was clear from both the pre- and the post-exam interviews that they were giving careful consideration to the process of preparing for the procedure exams as well as the forms of attention needed at each stage and for different knowledge objects. In fact, it might be said that students themselves, when aware of the type of examination they would sit, used the environment in quite different ways that suited their modes of study. Nor should we be surprised at this. At a fairly deep level of theory, it could be said, as constructivists do, that learning rarely happens in individuals alone, but in the complex interaction between individuals and previous knowledge and the distributed tools within their learning environment. Jean Lave, for example, in her studies of Liberian tailor apprenticeships and other subjects, has drawn upon the phenomenological concept that human thinking and action in the world are so inextricably bound up with each other that what we understand by the concept 'mind' can only be understood within the context of social organisation. But cognition is not only in the 'situated contexts' analysed by Lave and Wenger (1991).[40] It is also distributed around us in the form of real objects and teleological concepts with which we understand the world and its real and conceptual structures. Indeed, it is a general observation of cognitive psychology that most productive learning happens when the material distribution of resources within any context closely supports a student's learning structures without dictating how a knowledge object should be learned.

Quality of Learning

Quality of the learning experience is crucial: the critical question for us, after all, was did the video lecture environment help students to learn procedural law effectively? Quality of learning is almost inevitably a comparative process, not an absolute. Students compare their way of learning in one environment with that in another subject, module, programme, learning environment, and so on. Such

---

40 See Lave and Wenger (1991) and Wenger (1998).

feedback can be useful, but we wanted to know if, at the subjective level, students could tell us whether the environment had helped or hindered their study for the examinations. We were aware, of course, of the skewing effect of affordance – namely, the notion that if students have poor resources in one channel or medium, they will compensate by learning what they need to learn from another. We did not ask students whether in their opinion they *would* have studied more effectively with face-to-face lectures than with the VLE, since this would be asking them to compare their actual experience with an unknown variable (the face-to-face lectures they did not have) in an area of law that was entirely unknown to them. Such a triangulation would give us relatively meaningless information. Instead, we asked students about the quality of their learning while they used the video lecture environment by asking them whether, in retrospect, the video lectures had helped or hindered their revision for exams. With only two exceptions, all of them thought that the environment had enhanced their processes of learning.[41] One student described it thus:

Interviewer: Did you think the video lecture environment helped or hindered your study for the exams?
Student: It definitely helped.

Another was quite emphatic about the effect that the environment had had on the quality of her learning:

Interviewer: Do you think the video lecture environment helped or hindered your study for the exams?
Student: Definitely helped. It was very, very positive. I know some people have complained that they found it hard to work and all the rest of it. But I just thought in comparison – I have sat four years of exams before I came here, I am an expert as far as exams are concerned, and this has really, was two of the easiest exams I have sat, in terms of revision for them. I felt that I came in well prepared – maybe my results will show that this was not the case! I definitely felt that I was really learning the material. I understood it better.

Another revealed in her language how familiar she had become with the environment, and how much the v had become a part of her study environment:

Helped, definitely helped, being able to flick around. Just right before the exam I actually went back and watched one particular lecture on fast speed again for half an

---

41 The simple statistics from our questionnaire amply confirmed this. For example, when the larger body of students who responded to the Civil Procedure class questionnaire was asked what they thought of the video learning environment as a learning tool, 17 thought it excellent, 41 very good, 42 good, 37 reasonable, 9 not very good, 14 poor, with two giving no response (N = 162).

hour and was lucky one of the things came up. It was all there and I just sort of blasted through it one more time because I thought I am not absolutely sure.

Two students were neutral because they had used the video lectures to take notes during the semester, and did not use the video lectures again in their revision for the examination. One of these students had no computer at home. She lived on the outskirts of Glasgow and did not want to travel in to the GGSL to study, preferring to study at home. She explicitly planned her semester time so that she could revise from paper-based notes. When asked if she found that this had disadvantaged her, she replied

Student: I probably should have planned for it more because I would have liked to have done that, but that was my own fault, so ... I mean, the day I came in and watched the video lecture, it was just the one Criminal [lecture], I was thinking, 'Gosh, this is good', because as soon as you hear something it is not going to go out of your head.
Interviewer: When you say it was good, what do you mean?
Student: It's just like I knew what he was going to be saying ... It makes more sense when you are doing it for another time. You kind of understood it because you had looked at the statutes and know what they are talking about as opposed to the first time when you don't really know.
Interviewer: [...] Your advice to students who are coming next year would be ...?
Student: View the video lectures twice and especially during your study session. But the thing is, it is time-consuming and some people just don't have that amount of time to do it.

Quality of learning and available time are always issues for students, as they were for this student, who had no home computer and for whom two hours' round trip travel to the GGSL was not perceived at the time to be a useful option. She had planned her study time in detail but, almost by chance, had discovered that the video lecture environment could have been more useful in intensive study than she reckoned. Nevertheless, she had come to a realisation that e-learning could be a significant enhancer of learning, in surprising, unbidden ways. Her words are quite profound: they indicate an openness to experience on her part and a willingness to acknowledge that e-learning could help her understand the law as much as traditional forms of learning.

Next Steps

The use of resources such as these and on this scale is not unique, but it is still relatively unusual in legal education. With the use of blogs, podcasts and other forms of social software described in Chapter 6, together with the introduction of personalised learning systems, the practice will become more common in legal education in the future. For us in the GGSL, it became clear on reviewing the data and the emerging themes from student feedback that the process of knowledge construction and review carried out by students was a highly complex one in which students made many subtle alterations to their normal study practice in order to accommodate the new learning environment, its richness and constraints. The context of information and its retrieval and the situativity created by tasks both heavily influenced the process and product of knowledge generation. It was clear to us that learning could be improved by the development of more task-specific tools. Learners working from paper resources often switch between affordances so as to create for themselves the granularity of knowledge required for a task or an assessment. Lecture notes, for example, may give an overview of a topic, but a published text will give more detail: a practitioner text will give yet more detail and students will switch between these resources to achieve the detail they feel might be necessary.

In the subsequent two years my colleagues Karen Barton and Patricia McKellar created the CCA transaction, which was dependent in many ways upon the resources around it such as the video lectures discussed here and the multimedia units on advocacy and plea-drafting. It became clear to us then that the digital domain was successful because, in addition to being an information-rich environment, it was focused upon the needs of students at a particular stage in the development of professional knowledge and skill. If the concept were to be extended to other users such as trainees or practitioners, however, would we need to create another set of resources for these audiences, with all the work that this would entail?

Once again, the digital domain provided a solution. We could give learners *multiple views* of information, which would be appropriate to the needs of specific categories of learners – Diploma students encountering civil procedure for the first time and needing to be aware of it in a transaction and learn it for open-book examinations; trainees requiring to review it to understand the contents of litigation files while they were in a civil litigation seat; practitioners wishing to review specific forms of procedure for pleadings drafting or court appearances. Information, in other words, could be structured around the type of tasks that learners were required to perform.

We therefore drew up three different knowledge views: presentational, structural and transactional, which include navigational and content management tools. Note that, from an educational perspective, this is not a taxonomy. What we are describing are different, equally valid, overlapping views of knowledge and learning. Use of the views depends on the user purpose and task in hand, and extent of prior knowledge and confidence in handling the resources. The first view already exists as the current video lecture environment. The second and third are still in the process of construction. The three views are set out in more detail below (see Figure 9.3 for a summary).[42]

---

42 Extracted from a GGSL Internal Working Paper authored by Barton, McKellar, Maharg, and on file with the author.

	Presentational view	Structural view	Transactional view
Functionality...	1 Video lectures 2 Resource base, including PowerPoint slides, documentation, cases, statutes, MCQs, etc.	1 Flowchart 2 Rollover on each node, containing summary of node information 3 Links to Presentational and Transactional views	1 Multimedia unit and document workflow, with drafting tools, video 2 Links to Presentational and Transactional views
Typical user purposes	1 Initial familiarisation with concepts and rules 2 highly structured and teacher-centred learning 3 use of resources to create learning objects	1 Gain an overview of the structure of legal procedure 2 Identify possible options or directions in procedure 3 Take notes that can be attached to the flowchart	1 Prepare for pleadings 2 Prepare for advocacy 3 Prepare for actual drafting or court appearance 4 liaise with virtual firm or others in the transaction
Supports...	1 Broad chronology of Sheriff Court procedure 2 Detailed knowledge of concepts and rules 3 Global set of resources.	1 Overview of legal process based upon a flowchart 2 Quick access to forms of hearings 3 Global set of resources.	1 Detailed understanding and analysis of specific forms of procedure 2 Quick access to forms of court events 3 Global set of resources, attached to a multimedia unit or document workflow
Personalised functionalities	1 Bookmarking 2 Notetaking	1 Bookmarking 2 Notetaking	1 Bookmarking 2 Notetaking 3 personalised case notes tools

Figure 9.3   Knowledge views of Civil Court Practice

1) *Presentational view*

   Basically the functionality of the video lectures as discussed here. A number of different presentation events linked closely to a set of resources. Students come to an understanding of the concepts by moving chronologically – as if through all the issues of a general court action – and in a fashion determined by the presentation and the course designer, even though they may move freely within the presentation and its rich resource base. Flexibility of use will always be bounded, but in this view learning is guided from one presentation to the next so that the user comes to a conceptual understanding of what the elements of civil procedure actually are and how they fit together into larger forms of court process. The series of presentations fit the design of the curriculum.

2) *Structural view*

Where conceptual knowledge in the presentational view is represented by the linear presentations of the video lectures, in the structural view students will be able to select for themselves and access specific elements of the presentation that deal in detail with a particular concept. The view will be represented by a flow chart with nodes representing particular application of knowledge to specific circumstances in the flow of a case. If a user clicks on an 'Options Hearing' node for instance, the structure of the flow chart will alter so that, in an animation, a number of other resources will be drawn down to the node. Moving towards it will be the video lectures associated with it, any multimedia units demonstrating court performance, the set of court forms and documents associated with the action and any drafting tools that may aid the drafting of written pleadings. This view is more student-centred, allowing construction of knowledge: that is, students building and amending their own structures or schemata from direct interaction with the model or schema provided.

3) *Transactional view*

As we saw in Chapter 8, transactions are not just sequenced events: they also contain nested elements that can be transacted linearly or in parallel. In order to make this view accessible within transactions, knowledge components will be embedded within an actual legal transaction represented either by a workflow of documents or by a multimedia unit if there is any court or tribunal advocacy to be presented. The relevant components could be available chronologically as the specific transaction progresses, and will support learners' understanding of the pleadings, advocacy, and general significance of the court process that they are viewing. In addition, since this is essentially a practitioner tool, we would investigate the creation of a personalised learning tool which would allow users to capture relevant cases or procedural notes and to share these – effectively social software for legal practitioners, where users would be able to share legal information as one might share photographs, for instance, in an application such as Flickr.[43]

Note that with the addition of the transactional column, the use of multimedia and video becomes much more social. It becomes, indeed, the fully-operational model of cognitive presence, teacher presence and social presence envisaged by Garrison et al. (2000, pp. 87–105) and which, as they freely admit, is derived

---

43 The trans-media use of information in this way has always been experimented with. Pictures, as Carruthers reminds us, were an integral part of the page for a medieval audience, for whom mnemonic reading was crucial, as we saw in Chapter 5. In the modern era, Benjamin made a similar point: 'Couldn't an exciting film be made from the map of Paris? From the unfolding of its various aspects in temporal succession? From the compression of a centuries-long movement of streets, boulevards, arcades and squares into the space of half an hour?' (Benjamin, 1999). Benjamin was right, and reality is catching up with his early twentieth century vision – see for instance the work of the MASA group on this project, at http:www.masa-sci.com.

from Dewey's practical inquiry model. Thus does transactional learning come full circle, returning to its conceptual source.

It would be tempting to see this revised application as a workflow, where we tell students to view in Presentation mode, then understand the flowchart, then do the transaction, as if there is neat staircase of simple > complex that we want students to tread. But this would be to mistake one of the central themes that emerged from student responses in our research, which is that context powerfully mediates knowledge at all levels. There is no staircase: like the celebrated instance of Dale's Cone of Experience, this is a plausible but misleading fiction.[44] There is knowledge learned purposefully and the closer the alignment of knowledge-learning tools to purpose and prior knowledge, the easier it is for learners to transform information into knowledge.[45] It was clear from our research that students used a variety of methods to transform knowledge in this way and that these were not the result of uncertainty in a relatively new medium and context, but were the product of choices, aligned to purpose. They were attentive to many different cues and this enabled them to navigate the tasks of knowledge generation.[46]

---

44 For information on Dale's Cone of Experience, see Molinda (2003, pp. 472–3).

45 See, for example, the statements of students above who wanted to use the flowchart quite early in the process of knowledge formation. Another instance of this is the comment by e-world student who observed that she would have liked to have been able to download the video lecture to her iPod. In future iterations of the video lecture environment we shall enable this. It has already been incorporated into video lecture environments in other modules, for example, Evidence.

46   As Suchman (1987) points out, the 'situation of action is … an inexhaustibly rich resource', and our research by no means exhausts the richness of the situation students were in. Further research on many aspects of their study patterns is required.

Part 3 Conclusion:
Simulation and Transformation

> One possibility is that people are going to do what people always do with a new communication technology: use it in ways never intended or foreseen by its inventors, to turn old social codes inside out and make new kinds of communities possible. CMC [computer-mediated communication] will change us, and change our culture, the way telephones and televisions and cheap video cameras changed us – by altering the way we perceive and communicate.
>
> Rheingold (1992)

One view of the last four chapters is that it represents one law school's pet project. Who *needs* all this technology? Why change, and so much of it?[1] The simple if unsatisfactory answer is, look around you – your watch or your phone, your washing machine or car, the global financial and communications networks that saturate most aspects of our lives – all rely upon digital technology to a greater or lesser extent. Why should we not use educationally what is so much a part of our personal, social and commercial world? Viewed thus, the last four chapters present less a collection of digital tools than an attempt to create a learning ecology that matches the complexity of the technology existing outside the law school, an ecology that will change the way students learn in the way that Rheingold describes above.[2]

But there are other answers to these questions, and three in particular are relevant here. First is our conviction – nothing less – that at a time when corporate versions of learning environments are being sold as solutions to the perennial problems that technology creates for Higher Education, a discipline must maintain control of the intellectual and pedagogical forms by which it enacts and reproduces itself; that it should determine which forms of education are essential to its being in the world. In Chapter 5 we saw one solution adopted by medieval scholarly communities. In practical terms in our culture, active learning should be structured upon the intellectual tasks required by disciplines. Resources, in turn, need to be structured around such tasks. As Chapter 9 illustrates, information should be

---

1   Particularly since, to judge from the conclusions of some high-level studies, it would seem that e-learning has failed to emerge as a significant force in educational change. See Centre for Educational Research and Innovation (2005).

2   As Nardi and O'Day (1999, p. 51) put it, '[c]hange in an ecology is systemic' and like an ecology it is never in a state of complete stasis: it changes ceaselessly. How is change brought about? Through staff feedback and student feedback, in iterative loops, as technological decisions are implemented and integrated with local values, aims, attitudes.

structured around the type of tasks that learners are required to perform. The proposition that task profoundly influences knowledge structure is nothing new: the literatures on situated learning and the information sciences tell us so.[3] But these insights have yet to be embedded in any widespread way within the digital learning designs used in legal education, where the use of technology largely involves word processing, legal databases and LMSs.

Secondly, what drives the development of the technologies described here is the conviction that individual learners should have much more control over, and personal investment in, their environment. Pea describes the problem well: '[in everyday life] we intentionally design distributed intelligence into our environment. The culture of schools, however, is one that de-emphasizes this design process in favour of "individual, tool-free cognition"' (Pea, 1993, p. 49). For this reason, students have been co-designers with us in the process of personalising their learning. Green et al. (2005, p. 5) put it precisely: "the logic of education systems should be reversed so that it is the system that conforms to the learner, rather than the learner to the system'. This process involves designing disciplinary intelligence within an environment so that it facilitates variation in learning, but also emphasises learning from experience. This is partially evident in the way that students are tested and evaluated. Consider the physical outputs of classroom activity (tests, essays, projects, reports). Such objects are powerful knowledge artefacts, yet they are rarely treated that way. Typically, they are submitted to staff for evaluation and either archived or returned to students. In neither case are they likely to be referred to again. Thus, 'while students go through the motions of creating new artefacts, they fail to reap the benefits of actually using these objects as cognitive tools' (Hewitt and Scardamalia, 1998, p. 77). Such a process is the antithesis of Stenhouse's approach to education, as well as Dewey's approach to democratic inquiry, and for students makes the process of defining and understanding and using knowledge objects all the more difficult. Part 3 of this book therefore offers a new approach to learning and assessment, where there is more learner control, more authenticity in assessment, and more use and re-use of assessment objects.

Thirdly is the conviction that while many aspects of the liberal approach to legal education are essential to the philosophical core of the curriculum, that approach is still insufficiently active in its engagement with the world. We have taken a Pragmatist approach to the use of technology, where students learn by understanding from, acting within, and critiquing the forms of engagement that lawyers use in the world. In transactional environments, authenticity becomes a

---

3   See for example, Lucy Suchman's (1987, p. 57) observations on the practical objectivity of situations: for her and other ethnomethodologists 'the notion that we act in response to an objectively given social world is replaced by the assumption that our everyday social practices render the world publicly available and mutually intelligible'. For an example from information sciences, see Jain (2006).

key issue.[4] The Pragmatist equation can also be inverted: if law students are using transactional simulation as a form of learning, what is to stop lawyers from doing so, too? What effect might this have on future forms of situated learning for law students? And with access to information on the power of simulation learning such as this at our disposal, why are we not using transactional learning to embed ethical education within professional practice?[5] Nor is this reversible equation limited to law: it applies, I would hold, to every profession. Other professions have managed the reversibility of this equation better than law, notably medicine and architecture.

All the innovations described in this section have been carried out within one course in one institution, namely the Diploma in Legal Practice. I would like to say that what had hitherto been a largely traditional, indeed conservative, course by the standards of professional education in the late 1990s has been transformed by these and other innovations. However this would be to deny the complexity of the process of change, and to overstate the rate of change. Some aspects of the curriculum have changed little by comparison in the last six years. Nevertheless, it is worth noting that the innovations have transformed those subjects in the Diploma where they have been applied, and reshaped the way we teach professionalism at a profound level within the course.

How could this come about? It could do so because a small number of academics were given the opportunity to research, design, experiment with and implement innovative forms of learning with practitioners and technologists. They implemented projects with the consent of the corps of tutor-practitioners; and behind the implementations lay a coherent, evolving vision of learning that guided the innovations.[6] The course has become a trading zone between educationalists, practitioners, technologists. Indeed, the Diploma is in many ways a laboratory for experiments in professional education. In this sense it is not too presumptuous

---

4   See, for example, Anneta and Holmes (2006). The authors investigate the use of a 3D online world for distance-learning in which students adopt avatars. Their results suggested that student avatars provided a 'sense of presence that is the catalyst for community and learning'. It is significant that their research is based upon the principles elaborated by Garrison and Anderson (particularly the sense of presence), which in turn were derived from Dewey.

5   Webb discussed this general approach (1998) citing Macfarlane (1997), pp. 440, 443. See also Boon (2002) and Freamon (1997)

6   Detailed acknowledgments are due: to Karen Barton and Patricia McKellar who were responsible for the Virtual Court Action; Patricia also wrote and co-designed with Maharg the video lecture environment; Leo Martin designed and wrote the Conveyancing Purchase and Sale projects; Maharg co-designed the original Private Client project with Beth Hamilton who wrote materials with Private Client tutors, revised by Karen Barton; Karen and Fiona Westwood designed the Practice Management environment; and the PI environment was designed by Maharg and Charles Hennessy – Charles wrote successive scenarios. In each project the applications design and web design was undertaken by LTDU, variously Scott Walker, David Sams, Michael Hughes and others.

to say that we have been inspired by the idea of Dewey's Chicago Laboratory School and other experimental schools, and by a process of educational inquiry that is ground-up and experiential in its method and theory.

There are some taxonomies of learning that describe aspects of our practice, but none of them entirely fit the concepts of transactional learning we try to implement.[7] Perhaps the closest guides to transaction-shaping are aesthetic. One could for instance apply Dewey's set of six 'formal conditions of aesthetic form' – the conditions of continuity, cumulation, conservation, tension, anticipation and fulfilment.[8] There is strong continuity of knowledge, sensed in cumulation. Conservation – ever a resonant term for Dewey – applies not just to knowledge, but to sensings, skills, attitudes, values. But in addition there is a sense of transformation, exhibited in tension with the first three values, and the dialogue with the future that is innate in the sense of anticipation. Or, as pointed out in Chapter 7, one could look to Boal's Forum Theatre for another aesthetic, which pre-supposes an audience committed to thinking about the simulated reality of the stage, and then engaging in it.

Where will this experiment go in the future? The use of constructivist and situated learning methods using ICT rests on a fast-developing body of educational theory about the nature of communication, dialogue, learning and understanding, as we saw in Part 1. Much of this theory derives from pre-existing models and research, and from disciplinary traditions that are at least several centuries old: it is not radically new. But in the GGSL transactional experiment there are two new elements: first, the scale of the experiment and secondly, related to that, the changed situation in which teachers and learning designers in the GGSL now find themselves. Both points require more comment.

The scale of the transactional curriculum in the Diploma goes beyond most experiments in ICT. Normally, a module or a section of modules is the focus for innovation. The remainder of modules and the overall structure of a curriculum remains largely the same; and if there is a curriculum theory, it is largely the default of liberal or vocational model.[9] As I have argued in this book, we need

---

7   As Lee Shulman has cautioned us, taxonomies are taxis: they take us where we want to go, we pay our dues and get on with what we came to do. They are heuristics: 'They help us to think more clearly about what we're doing, and they afford us a language through which we can exchange ideas and dilemmas. They point to the mutually interdependent facets of an educated person's life of mind, of emotion, and of action. They are powerful in these ways as long as we don't take them too seriously, as long as we don't transform mnemonic into dogma or heuristic into orthodoxy' (Shulman, 2002).

8   *LW*, 10, pp. 143–4. This will be dealt with in detail in a future publication – I mention it here as an example of how close to aesthetic form is the structure of a transactional project.

9   The exception to this, of course, is the use of VLEs in intranets, such as Blackboard or WebCT. But even here, the use of VLEs varies across subjects according to the module or subject leader's interest and predilection, subject of course to departmental or faculty guidelines.

to think beyond the invidious divide of the liberal and the vocational models. In the GGSL Diploma we intend to introduce transactional learning into every subject, so that modules are built around transactions, and the entire curriculum becomes a simulation environment, where most resources – people, printed and digital resources – point toward and support the transactions, which are assessment as well as learning and teaching spaces. The curriculum is thus based upon an educational philosophy that is intellectually coherent, pragmatic, ethical and social, – one that is flexible enough to allow for essential variation within different sub-disciplinary fields (as we saw in the examples of open and bounded transactions in Chapters 7 and 8), and reflexive enough to encourage critique of law in society. Curriculum change, though, is a long-term process. We are still in process, both in our development of theory and practice.

Even so, we have found that the curriculum transformation taking place changes the nature of staff activities fairly substantially. The creation of projects within Ardcalloch is a major undertaking, in terms of time and expense and effort. There are pay-offs, in that in subsequent years it is much easier to create and assemble the resources, and if the transactions are well-designed, for some time after only minor updating is required (assuming law in the area does not substantially change). As a result, academic staff on the Diploma have found that their job specification and satisfaction-level has changed: overall, less teaching, more design work, more support for flexible learning and the creation of more targeted and authentic assessment activities. It is highly rewarding, both intellectually and emotionally.

The change in type of activities also led us to a deep re-appraisal not just of role and function of staff within the GGSL, but of the technological forward-planning and therefore the financial and strategic management of the School itself. It is clear to those of us involved in it that transactional learning creates the potential for interdisciplinary collaboration across the faculties of an institution, and between and among disciplines at other institutions, both nationally and internationally. The potential is astonishing. Other disciplines have pointed the way in this regard – business simulation games, for instance.[10] To achieve this there is a need for national and international collaboration on:

1) *Successful educational design work*

This implies not just design of an activity within a module, but financial planning, the planning of design time for staff, integration of tradition with innovation, activities across different curricula and across different law schools; and across jurisdictions.

---

10 See for instance Capsim Management Simulations at http://www.capsim.com/; SimPort, http://www.simport.eu/, which was originally created as a simulation of the creation of a port over a 30-year period, and is now used as a business and management simulation tool.

2) *Communication of aims*

It was crucial to the success of the transactional environment (including resources such as video lectures) that students saw it primarily as a *learning* environment. As research shows, when students perceive the principal aim of an environment is to support learning rather than deliver information to them or assess them, then they are more likely to engage in meaningful learning (Trigwell and Ashwin, 2006, pp. 243–58). The same is true of communication of aims to staff, administrators, part-time tutors or adjunct professors, and senior management officers.

3) *Relation of theory to practice*

The development of the concept of transactional learning could not have taken place if those of us contributing to it had not placed ourselves deliberately in the empty quarter of Stokes' quadrant, discussed in Chapter 2. The theory draws upon pure basic research, is in part both use-inspired basic research and pure applied research; but it aims to move beyond contemporary practice into transformative practice. In the process, staff need to consider which approaches are useful in which contexts, both disciplinary and institutional.[11] This is, in effect, an evolutionary approach to the implementation of theory into practice.[12]

4) *Development of communities of practice*

Theory can inspire individuals and groups, but as Dewey understood in the Chicago Laboratory School and Columbia's Teachers College, little is achieved in education without the collaborative work of a community of practice. Such a community will always re-interpret and re-fashion theory to local circumstances, and create of it new forms of practice: in this way, the community becomes transformative itself: regenerative, rather than merely replicative.

5) *Co-operative funding*

Our experience is that use of the web for the building of communities, both fictional and actual, does work. However there is no question but that, at this stage of web application building at least, the process is resource-intensive. Almost nothing in the last four chapters could have come about without the GGSL's Learning Technologies Development Unit (LTDU), the development wing of which currently consists of two applications developers and two web and graphics designers, all of them under the direction of our Learning Technologies Development Officer, Scott Walker. The Unit would not have existed without the merging of the two graduate schools of Glasgow and Strathclyde universities. Even then, a case had to be made, based on educational as well as financial grounds, that there should be a Unit dedicated to the production and maintenance of ICT resources. This included not just the

---

11 What Mercer (2000) calls a process of 'interthink'.

12 For a good example of this approach, which discusses the methodology, see Cooke (2002).

creation, expansion and maintenance of the virtual community, but video lecture and multimedia resources as well. LTDU is now an essential, core function of the Diploma. Its work is proof that law schools can seize control of their future by combining resources and working for mutual benefit.

The GGSL is committed to local, national and international collaboration, and is currently leading a project called SIMPLE (simulations for professional learning). Funded by JISC and UKCLE, and in partnership with Futurelab, this project will create the second iteration of the transactional environment for professional learning – an open-source, open-standards transactional learning environment, free at point-of-use – and will engage in large-scale evaluation of the implementation of this environment. Our project is, at the time of writing, implementing the environment across a number of disciplines within the University of Strathclyde and five other law schools and, over the course of two years, will evaluate student learning and the staff experience within the environment and disseminate the results of the evaluations.[13] Thereafter the SIMPLE transactional environment will be available generally to HE and FE. The project will:

- provide a highly innovative learning environment for professional learning across a wide range of disciplines;
- through the evaluation of application design and implementation, enhance our knowledge of aspects of successful simulation and mobile learning;
- via the cross-curricular implementation within an institution, be a springboard for further and wider implementations across curricula and institutions in HE and FE.[14] We also intend to create a community of practice around the applications toolset and its associated literatures – transactional guidelines, case studies, and the like.

The project is ambitious (anything less does not do justice to the transformative power of transactional learning), but any attempt to change culture needs to be ready to deal with the range of attitudes that exist toward simulation learning as a method. In her analysis of online behaviour in multi-user dungeons (MUDs), Turkle defined three attitudes towards simulations. The first was 'simulation denial', where users simply refuse to acknowledge that simulations can adequately represent reality. The second, 'simulation resignation', describes the attitudes of

---

13 The law schools of the universities of Glamorgan, Glasgow, Stirling, Warwick, West of England. Note that most of the transactional projects from these law schools are undergraduate: we aim to prove that SIMPLE can be used as effectively in undergraduate as in postgraduate legal education.

14 For more information on this see our project website, http://tinyurl.com/2ys7hh, and the JISC project web page at http://www.jisc.ac.uk/whatwedo/programmes/elearning_innovation/eli_simple.aspx.

those who work with simulations, but recognise the implicit limitations of the system. The third, though, is more interesting:

> [t]his would take the cultural pervasiveness of simulation as a challenge to develop a more sophisticated social criticism. This new criticism would not lump all simulations together, but would discriminate among them. It would take as its goal the development of simulations that actually help players challenge the model's built-in assumptions. This new criticism would try to use simulation as a means of consciousness-raising. (Turkle, 1995)

The last phrase above is redolent of Dewey's inquiry-based learning, of Kilpatrick's project-based learning, and Stenhouse's approach to learning.[15] Turkle's view of the psychology and power relations implicit in simulation learning is prescient and indicates how simulations could be used not only in professional programmes of study, but in undergraduate legal modules too.

For such consciousness-raising inevitably involves ethics. The truth is that, *au fond*, every online environment, every MUVE game, contains assumptions about how a particular society ought to operate; and the game embodies and plays out its implicit theories. To take a fairly extreme example, the MUVE *Grand Theft Auto III* is infamous for its violence, abuse of women, and glorification of organised crime in which players need to participate if they are to proceed in the game. As Reynolds (2002) points out in its defence, it is also full of postmodern irony about urban attitudes. Nevertheless, the Hooker Cheat seems to embody most of the game's attitudes to society's norms – the player picks up a prostitute, pays for virtual sex, then kills the prostitute before she can walk away with the player's money. As Reynolds points out, the virtue ethics approach to moral judgements made on the game actually enables us to see that the game is not necessarily as innately evil as it is described: as a player one is not forced to ride with the prostitute or have sex with her, or kill her. These are choices made by the player. However, as Reynolds candidly admits, the choices are stripped down starkly: within the game and its values there are no consequences except good things for the player who successfully plays the Hooker Cheat. His comment is of course based on a consequentialist approach to ethical choices. Consequences apart, freedom from social norms in Liberty City also implies freedom from moral and ethical norms – a fundamental approach that is an essential ethical choice made in code by the designers, and to which players assent, as if agreeing to a hidden terms of service agreement, when they enter the world and play the game.

Ardcalloch itself has been constructed as a space for law students, lawyers and legal ethical values to be played out. But virtue ethics exist in many forms, and surface in myriad ethical problems within an urban space and professional networks. If Ardcalloch is to be a site of such competing discourses it needs

---

15 Note, though, as Tanner points out, that Kilpatrick's project-based approach to the curriculum differed significantly from Dewey's earlier 'activities', with their 'occupational themes'. See Tanner, 1997, pp. 85–7.

to be richer – used beyond the GGSL and for many more purposes, and more multivarious in its detail. This is an aim of the SIMPLE project. But above all it needs to accommodate the operation of free will. The Hooker Cheat is code; and as Lessig has reminded us, code defines the architecture of the online world. But if code were to circumscribe the limits of action so that users could choose only from a limited set of options once they were in a situation (as above, do nothing or do evil) that constructed situation would be a morally compromised one – for the purposes of education, a much less effective tool; for the purposes of ethical learning, a positively dangerous one. Malign intent and griefing in professional behaviour should be an option in Ardcalloch, and is, as we saw in Chapters 7 and 8 – in the student firms, and in the virtual communications. But there is also the potential for the full play of virtuous action, and for the consequences of virtuous and malign or criminal actions and norms to be played out and explored – in the simulated world, in the real curriculum, before students as trainees become immersed in real-world professional activity. In this sense, a transactional simulation can be a rich and powerful environment for ethical learning.

Elective Affinities: Experience, Ethics, Technology, Collaboration

I believe that the community's duty to education is, therefore, its paramount moral duty. ... [T]hrough education society can formulate its own purposes, can organize its own means and resources, and thus shape itself with definiteness and economy in the direction in which it wishes to move.

Dewey (*EW*, 5, p. 94)

Spaces have values.

Lessig (1999, p. 64)

Conclusion

This final chapter takes heed of Bourdieu's timely admonition that we should not 'fall into the trap of offering a programme' (Bourdieu, 1998, p. 56). A general programme of action, a development plan – these are rarely applicable to specific local circumstances. If we are to take the lessons of situationists, phenomenologists and pragmatists, we should perhaps advocate methods rather than plans.[1]

I said in the Introduction that my approach was sympathetic to a pragmatist approach to legal education and strongly influenced by John Dewey. All of the approaches described in Parts 1 and 3 are aligned on this perspective. My interpretation of the failure of realist experiments in Chapter 4 also contributes to this perspective. But in general terms, what might pragmatist legal education look like, and how could it transform legal education? We can begin to think about this by taking as a definition of contemporary legal education William Twining's admirably concise – and over 25 years later, still relevant – summary of the scene:

In all Western societies law schools are typically in a tug of war between three aspirations: to be accepted as full members of the community of higher learning; to be relatively detached, but nonetheless engaged, critics and censors of law in society; and to be service-institutions for a profession which is itself caught between noble

---

1   Compare also the position of the blogger who deliberately has no hosted blog listed on the blogdex, but who instead comment-blogs on other blogs, leaving a conceptual trail across the internet. See Rothenberg (2003).

ideals, lucrative service of powerful interests and unromantic cleaning up of society's messes.[2]

Twining describes the triple bind we find ourselves in. Where might we start with this situation? A strong pragmatism would probably plan to start with the last phrase – with society's messes. What are they, who are involved, what are the contributing problems, how are lawyers involved in them, how can students begin to understand the causes and effects in their complexity? Next, and working back, their 'cleaning up' resolution, via clinic, placement and other forms of experiential learning we have not yet really considered – solutions for whom, when, and under what conditions? At the same time one could analyse the source and nature of those 'powerful interests', the noble as well as ignoble ideals, and so on – moving, in other words, from situated practice to critical framing. In general, a pragmatist programme of study would start with situated practice – the experience of law in society – not a case-dialogue about this, nor the resumption of client or victim narratives into the formal discourse of judgment and due process, not even an educational taxonomy of skills and knowledge components, but the mess itself. Such a programme of study would enable students and staff to achieve critical framing by moving between legal analysis and the social situation in a to-fro motion.

This approach is nothing new: problem-based learning is one version of it. How might we better understand it and operationalise it as a method? The following are observations as to how we might begin to transform our educational practice in four key areas: experience, ethics, technology, collaboration.

Experience

Perhaps the first thing we ought to do is stop using the phrase 'teach them to think like lawyers'. As Rhode pointed out, all too often this means teaching students to think like law professors (Rhode, 2000, p. 36). After half a century of legal educational and jurisprudential research and comment there is no concept in this phrase that will stand scrutiny for long. We need to subject it to post mortem examination, before burying it, preferably in the same lair as the black-letter tradition.[3]

More seriously, experiential learning is the foundation for the development both of professionalism and a commitment to democratic behaviour, whether in clinic, simulation or some other method. But as Dewey realised, commitment to democracy means embodying that commitment in the educational forms and

---

2   Twining (1982, p. 2) quoted in Boon and Levin (1999, p. 154).

3   Some may be more hopeful of resurrecting the corpse – Moran (2003), after all, has performed miracles with the 'reasonable person'. But the prognosis is not good – the phrase has shown no vital signs for some time now.

values we use everyday within education. Ralph Sleeper makes this point well: what mattered for Dewey in all human activity, he observed, was 'the emergence of logical forms from *the practice of inquiry*' (Sleeper, 1986, p. 202, my emphasis). Dewey's radical form of pragmatism was profoundly democratic because deep within its experiential method, his pragmatism possessed a 'ground-map whereby [social] inequities could be identified and diagnosed, as well as a method for resolving them' (p. 202). It is also a map for educational transformation, as radical now as it was over a century ago in the Chicago Laboratory School and as relevant to us as it was to the realist experiments at Columbia.

How might we embed such experiential experiments in our curricula? Following Latour's interpretation of Pasteur (outlined in Chapter 2) and the example of Dewey's Laboratory School, our law schools should be our labs. This is what we have tried to do on the Diploma in Legal Practice in the GGSL: it is one of our key guiding principles. We need to engage in small-scale radical pilots, leading to larger trials, paying careful attention to how the contexts of law school, other disciplines, traineeship, legal community and the wider social community among many vectors affect our implementations. This is one way in which transformation can be brought about. It requires constant attention to emergent experiences and also (to adopt the forceful words of Garfinkel) to the vexed problem of 'the practical objectivity and practical observability of practical actions and practical reasoning' (Garfinkel, 1991, p. 11).

The primacy of experiential learning has long been recognised in other disciplines, and acted upon. As the recent Carnegie Foundation report on legal education in the US has re-asserted, we need to return to the fundamentals of such experiential learning, and learn from other professions, other disciplines.[4] The authors point out that we still tend to view learning 'in an *additive* way, not an integrative way' (2007, p. 9) when what we need is deep re-consideration of the curriculum so that students can move freely 'back and forth between understanding and enactment, experience and analysis' (2007, p. 10):

> [i]f legal education were serious about such a goal, it would require a bolder, more integrated approach that would build on its strengths and address its most serious limitations. In pursuing such a goal, law schools could also benefit from the approaches used in education of physicians, teachers, nurses, engineers and clergy, as well as from research on learning. (2007, p. 6)

This of course has implications for the teaching and learning of ethical behaviour:

---

4   See Sullivan et al. (2007). The report was published in full in late February 2007, just after this text went to print, and therefore I rely on the extensive 16-page summary provided on the Carnegie Foundation's website. The report is based of course upon legal education in US and Canadian law schools, but it contains many perceptive comments on legal education that most mixed and common law jurisdictions could learn from.

[i]n their all-consuming first year [of the JD degree], students are told to set aside their desire for justice. They are warned not to let their moral concerns or compassion for the people in the cases they discuss cloud their legal analyses ... The fact that moral concerns are reintroduced only haphazardly conveys a cynical impression of the law that is rarely intended. (2007, p. 8)

Ethics

Towards the end of Chapter 8 I outlined how professionalism could be explored and learned within the transactional learning environment. Other professions have for some time now set about embedding the learning and practice of professionalism in their schools. David Stern, for instance, has argued – rightly I think – that the lists of values that describe what a profession regards as professionalism are insufficient because this implies a dialogue of practitioner with static, individuated qualities or values. Rather, professionalism lies in a much more dynamic ethical encounter, in the *negotiation of the conflict* of those static values, and in the management of that conflict (Ginsburg and Stern, 2004; Stern, 2006).

The idea takes us back to Ferguson's position, negotiated in tension between the Stoic virtue tradition and the commercial values of contemporary Scotland. To define what our ethical values are, we must look beyond regulatory codes to the analysis of the broken middle, the fundamental relationship between ethics and law, and enact that relationship within the law school. It is, as we saw, a negotiation of the boundaries of the soul and the city, and their perennial anxiety. And as we saw in the first case study of Chapter 1 ('Representations of Law'), where there is no space for such negotiation, there can be little ethical learning worthy of the name. In Chapter 2, though, we saw the negotiation of values played out between student and role-playing standardised client in an arena where client-centredness was key. In Chapters 7 and 8 we encountered narratives of ethical learning that arose from simulations where students learned not merely about the surface procedures of legal transactions, but about the deeper transactions: the complex passages between ethics and law, between collaborative relationships, and the anxieties of personal identity in moving into a professional cadre. In such simulations – a form of situated learning – there is the possibility of seamless learning between the levels of transaction, which enables students to practise professionalism and encounter the ethical relation experientially (Breger et al., 2004).

Ethics and experiential learning are inseparable. For Barnett, Ferguson and Rose, an education that was not ethical in its basis was no education at all. As Rose makes clear from her autobiographical *Love's Work*, ethically challenging education is often inspirational in its effects, because it entails personal commitment, by staff as well as students – and when it is lacking, education can be perceived as a form of lifeless *anomie* (Rose, 1995, pp. 129–34).

Dewey, as ever the acute observer of educational values in society, pointed out the role of the teacher as inspirer, whose role was undeniably social:

> Whatever he as a teacher effectively does, he does as a person; and he does with and towards persons. His methods, like his aims … are practical, are social, are ethical, are anything you please – save merely psychical. (Cantor and Schomberg, 2002, p. 6)

We can see this at work historically in the work of educationalists such as Dewey, Stenhouse and others, in the work of contemporary educationalists such as Linden West and Barnett and in constructivists, situated theorists, clinicians and many others. The work of Engeström is a good example of how radical we must be. For him, the landscape of learning at work is changing significantly and he calls for 'transformative, horizontal and subterranean' change, where education is 'embedded within work, and yet transcends it, bringing in tools for theorizing work and for constructing zones of proximal development' (Engeström, 2002).[5] Transformations, of course, do not happen overnight. The sort of change envisaged by Engeström and others can only happen with the consent of the community. But is there not an ethical duty upon us to re-appraise our own role within our own community with regard to transformative change?

Our condition is described by Lessig in *Code and Other Laws of Cyberspace*. There, he defined two types of constitutions: the codifying constitution, which 'tries to preserve something essential from the constitutional or legal culture in which it is is enacted'; and the transformative constitution, which 'tries to change something essential in the constitutional or legal culture in which it is enacted' (Lessig, 1999, pp. 213–14). The codifying regime has its 'moment of self-affirmation'; the transformative is 'haunted with self-doubt' and is the more difficult to realise. One cannot exist without the other. In our practice as law teachers we need both and often find ourselves in the broken middle between them, but we have to admit to ourselves that the codifying mode is much the easier default mode for living. Its structures are implicit and for those in position and power life is just that much easier. And so this book argues for the transformation of legal education, for the revolutionary moment and for acting upon the awareness, deep within ourselves, that many aspects of the *status quo* are no longer defensible and that we need to work for further transformation, using whatever tools are at our disposal. Which leads us to ask which tools *are* at our disposal, and whose tools are they?

---

5   Again, Dewey, this time from an essay entitled 'Ethical Principles Underlying Education'· '[w]e need to translate the moral into the actual conditions and working forces of our community life, and into the impulses and habits which make up the doing of the individual' (*EW*, 5, p. 83).

Technology

Part 3 explored a body of practice and theory coalescing around the concept of transactional learning. It represents one attempt to negotiate imaginatively the educational problems of agency, free will and identity and to navigate between the poles of centralisation/decentralisation, the academy and legal practice, community and individual and the like: the Part 3 Conclusion takes a broad view of this whole endeavour. But the e-mergence of technology and transactional learning also has a deeper political and ethical purpose. Two accounts illustrate this. After the 2004 terrorist bombings in Madrid, popular opinion was mobilised against the government at a critical juncture just before an election by the use of blogs and mobile phones, to organise street demonstrations in Madrid and in other cities across Spain. Ignacio Escolar, a journalist and blogger at the centre of events, described it as follows:

> Almost spontaneously, more than four thousand people went out to support a call to protest that had gone out only hours before. By means of SMS message chains, blogs, electronic mail and discussion forums on the web the demonstrators were aware that people were massing. If 23 February 1981 was the 'night of the transistors', 13 March 2004 was the night of the web and activists.[6]

Escolar rightly points up the way in which the new communication channels, in the hands not of powerful media conglomerates or politicians but the people themselves, enabled the organisation of protest at short notice and thereby affected the political process of the election. Nor was the event in Madrid an isolated example of this phenomenon. The same pattern has occurred in elections in Kenya and South Korea.[7] Howard Rheingold's concept of the 'smart mob',

---

6   Also reported in *The Guardian* (March 2004). My translation. Spanish text at: http://www.escolar.net/, 19 March 2004, entitled 'Tecnologia y Movimientos': 'De forma casi espontánea, más de cuatro mil personas salieron a la calle para respaldar una protesta que había sido convocada apenas unas horas antes. Los manifestantes supieron de la concentración mediante una cadena de mensajes SMS, a través de los blogs, del correo electrónico y de los foros de la Red. Si el 23F fue la noche de los transistores, el 13M fue la de Internet y los móviles'. The 'night of the transistors' refers to the occasion in 1981 when a military officer attempted a coup in the Spanish parliament and, in the absence of TV cameras, many people listened to their radios to find out what their political future might be. In a posting of 30 March, Escolar summarised the debate that has surrounded his claim (http://www.escolar.net/MT/archives/2004_03.html) and admits that more traditional media such as radio may have played a part. Neverthless, the increased volume of text messages and eyewitness evidence quoted by Escolar, Javier Candeira and others do reveal that SMS and other web media played a significant role in mobilising demonstrators. See http://www.escolar.net/MT/archives/000638.html.

7   One of the first signs of this was Steven Clift's posting to the Democracies Online Newswire (4 November 2002), commenting on the use of cellphones by politicians in the South Korean elections of 2002, and quoting an article by York (2002). Regarding the

quoted by Escolar, is descriptive and predictive of the events that occurred in Spain.[8] With such technology at their disposal, people have the tools to become not just passive, anxious consumers of information (the night of the transistors) but active and determined participators in a political process.

Escolar's account, of course, belongs to a genre of the sublime – the thrilling account of the cyberhacker and cyberprotester, and all those out in force against globalised capital at WTO and elsewhere. But as Dewey would have agreed, there are telling democratic issues for both students and teachers here. Technology has profoundly affected the history and use of ideas, not just in the substance of the idea but also in how ideas are enacted in society. Where the printing press revolutionised the spread of ideas in the fifteenth century, it helped to revolutionise society. Where printed posters were used in great numbers during the French Revolution, together with the huge increase in genres and quantity of print products, the speed of production served to overwhelm *ancien régime* channels and restraints.[9] What is interesting about the SMS and web revolutions in the Madrid demonstrations is that they are, in effect, creating and re-affirming what E.P. Thompson, in his analysis of eighteenth century British riots, called the 'moral economy' of the crowd (Thompson, 1971). In the Madrid demonstrations technology was used to bring about social action on moral grounds in the face of democratic regulation (regarding the ban on political demonstrations just prior to an election). In a sense, then, the cultural situation is the reverse of the late

---

Kenyan elections of 2002, Clift cites Gologo (2002) on cellphone use and distribution during the election.

8   As Rheingold (2003, pp. 146–7) summarises the concept here, a 'smart mob' emerges when 'communication and computing technologies amplify human talents for cooperation. The impacts of smart mob technology already appear to be both beneficial and destructive, used by some of its earliest adopters to support democracy and by others to coordinate terrorist attacks. The technologies that are beginning to make smart mobs possible are mobile communication devices and pervasive computing – inexpensive microprocessors embedded in everyday objects and environments'.

9   Before the 1789 revolution in Paris, there were around 60 newspapers throughout France. As Schama points out, there followed an explosion of communication genres, both in type and quantity, following the overthrow of censorship (Schama, 1989, p. 180). By the middle of 1792, for instance, there were around 500 newspapers in Paris alone. Many of them were short-lived, with tiny circulations. But what is remarkable is the explosion of communication channels as well as the sheer increase in volume – newspapers and gazettes with a huge range of formats and tone; subscription journals; and illustrated literature such as almanacs, copies of speeches, prints, engravings and the like. The sales figures also point to a remarkable literacy among the general population. As Schama remarks, 'literacy rates in late eighteenth-century France were much higher than in the late twentieth-century United States' (1989, p. 180) and it was this literacy that, through the media of posters, brochures, reviews, journals, almanacs, fantasy novels, pornography and non-fiction of many kinds, fed the appetite of the people, in Paris and beyond, for information about the political and cultural events of the Revolution. For information on the power of the press, see Censer (1976). For a fine study of almanacs, see Welschinger (1884).

eighteenth, early nineteenth century: where 200 years ago innovating technology often disrupted moral economies, in the twenty-first century wireless and web-based communication channels may serve to facilitate and sustain such a sense of collective values.[10]

Contrast this account of technology-as-liberation with a quite different story of technology use. The power of technology to disseminate and persuade is very much a concern to governments in China and Saudi Arabia, amongst others, where free speech on internet websites, blogs and discussion boards is explicitly censored. In the case of China, censorship was effected over the course of several years, with the highly public collusion of Yahoo!, Google, Microsoft and other major corporations.[11] Information on human rights, Tibetan independence, Tiananmen Square, Taiwan and other 'sensitive' issues simply does not appear in the .cn domain: it has been airbrushed from that sector of the internet in a much more effective form of censorship than the *ancien régime* ever achieved. In this account, technology is unquestionably used to oppressive ends (Zittrain and Edelman, 2003 and Zittrain and Palfrey, 2005).

These two stories are polar opposites: the daily use of technologies by millions of us in common law jurisdictions lies somewhere on a spectrum between these two poles.[12] But as the research in the field of e-democracy begins to mature, one of the key questions for technologists and policy-makers is whether the internet can be used as a deliberative mode of communication for the construction of participatory democracy in the public sphere, as that sphere has been constructed by Arendt and others.[13] As Benkler has observed:

> A genuine shift in the way we produce the information environment that we occupy as individual agents, as citizens, as culturally embedded creatures, and as social beings goes to the core of our basic liberal commitments. (Benkler, 2006, p. 464)

These issues – democratic, ethical, political and rhetorical – require much more of our attention in legal education. Over the past few decades we have generally accepted the technology made available to us by our institutions and large corporations, or if we are uninterested in the matter, we have ignored it. We can no longer either accept or ignore it: we need to use it to transform our ways of working with our students, with society and with each other. Part 3 is a case study

---

10 See also Noveck (2006, pp. 257–82) for a description and analysis of civic cyberspace initiatives and concepts.

11 See http://en.wikipedia.org/wiki/Google_China for information on China; and the *New York Times*, 23 April 2006, http://tinyurl.com/re2cn; and http://www.internationalrelations.house.gov/,

12 They are versions of the Janus-face of technology, noted by, among others, Castells (2000). For an analysis of this and e-governance and learning, see Paliwala (2005).

13 Buchstein observes that 'viewed in terms of contemporary democratic theory, the positive qualities attributed to the Internet strikingly resemble the Habermasian unrestricted public sphere' (1997, pp. 248–63, quoted in Agre, 2003).

in the transformation of the curriculum using technology. There are many other ways technology could be used – to facilitate student clinics, for instance, which would benefit hugely from practice management software adapted for their precise purposes and educational aims, based on careful analysis and specification of what students needed when and how, to support and share their learning within the community of the clinic. If students have placements with NGOs or as in-house trainees, how can technology support their work? Another instance is the provision of a form of online record of student activity that can be carried into their futures – an e-portfolio of their lives and learning experiences.

The internet can also be used to extend and deepen intellectual debate in society and law schools have a place to play in the development of this. Hitherto, most law schools have largely used technology as repositories for information in the form of VLEs and MLEs. Occasionally there is discussion forum use, but on the whole, as Jos Boys has pointed out with regard to MLEs generally, technology is used to mimic traditional forms of university administration, teaching, learning and assessment.[14] Yet we have seen in the discussion of rhetorical theory and medieval text the huge potential for the web to be a space for collaboration and sharing within our networked communications society. Such a genre of communication is potentially a widening of access to new forms of speech and writing that can contribute to a historically new form of public sphere. The Berkman Center for Internet and Society at Harvard Law School, for instance, has developed in their Openlaw project an Annotation Engine which, used with Twiki pages and collaborative forums, serves as the basis for

> an experiment in crafting legal argument in an open forum [in order to] develop arguments, draft pleadings, and edit briefs in public, online. Non-lawyers and lawyers alike are invited to join the process by adding thoughts to the 'brainstorm' outlines, drafting and commenting on drafts in progress, and suggesting reference sources.[15]

The Cairns Project is another such attempt to use the web in order to facilitate public discourse on politics, the law and other issues.[16] We need many more such

---

14 Not for the first time, as we saw in Chapter 5 with regard to incunables. As a result, the interpretation of the model of what a MLE could be (since there are many conflicting models of the environment) becomes seriously degraded to limited portal concerns. What have always been regarded as separate systems of learning services – registry services, archival services, library functions, learning interfaces – still remain so in the MLE, and the key opportunity for change, organisationally and technically, is lost. Indeed, Boys argues that 'the portal approach is taking hold *precisely because it enables institutions to avoid difficult questions about how they organise themselves*' (my emphasis, Boys, 2002, quoted in Maharg and Muntjewerff, 2002, pp. 310–11). It is of course an example of *méconnaissance*, Bourdieu's description of the deliberate misrecognition by agents (1977, p. 6).

15 See Berkman Centre for Internet and Society, Openlaw, at http://cyber.law.harvard.edu/openlaw/.

16 See Cairns Project (2007).

narratives of internet activity, where justice and democratic and participative practices and legal education are facilitated by technologies that, in one way or another, have the potential to transform lives.

Given the huge cost and culture change implications of all this, what can be done to bring it about?

Collaboration

Collaborative student learning is scarcely new: throughout this book I have argued that we need more of it and more of a research focus on how it can enhance learning within legal education. But I would also argue that there is insufficient collaboration between teachers, law schools and the profession, and in four areas in particular.

First, and at a policy level, we need to work with policy-makers to ensure that HE policy is aligned to its avowed intentions and that those intentions are what we deem to be best for academic practice and the profession. In the UK, for instance, there is evidence that the RAE (Research Assessment Exercise) has served to lower the already low status of teaching and learning in universities, at a time when other Funding Council initiatives, for example, HE Academy, are attempting to do the opposite (Trowler et al., 2005).

Secondly, academic and professional legal educational programmes need to integrate much more than any previous reports and consultation papers in the common law jurisdictions have acknowledged.[17] There is much educational innovation and experimentation that takes place in the profession which would be of use to academic programmes; the reverse is also true; and there is probably insufficient knowledge on both sides as to how legal education and training has changed markedly in the last few decades in universities and in the profession. As Dewey put it in an essay on culture and professionalism in education,

> [f]undamentally we are co-workers. The more theoretical studies do not attain their highest development until they find some application in human life, contributing indirectly at least to human freedom and well being, while the more practical studies cannot reach their highest practicality save as they are animated by a disinterested spirit of inquiry. (*MW*, 15, p. 197)

Thirdly, academic programmes need to collaborate with other groupings within society. We need to be more interdisciplinary in our educational work with other professions, other disciplines. We need much more in the way of interdisciplinary trading zones between institutions instead of competition, much more creativity

---

17 The recent Carnegie Foundation summary report makes the same point (2007, pp. 10–12).

and diversity, rather than conformity, of educational structures.[18] Our cherished Rutlands and Rummidges must alter and become collaborative hubs of partnerships between law schools, civic groupings and law schools, the profession and law schools, and law schools and other professions, and this collaboration should extend internationally as well.[19] The GGSL is an example, being a collaboration between the law schools of the universities of Glasgow and Strathclyde, where partnership is at the core of what we do, but even this sort of collaboration is only the merest of beginnings. As a discipline we could do, and must, much better and essential to this change is institutional leadership and global foresight.[20]

Fourthly, we need to develop an open-access culture to our pedagogy and our materials, similar to that adopted by the MIT OpenCourseWare Initiative and, in the UK, the Open University's OpenLearn Initiative.[21] We also need to develop theory and procedures that will support such interdisciplinary and inter-institutional initiatives. As Shulman pointed out, the 'signature pedagogies'

---

18 To facilitate this, we need to develop research structures. The LLM at Warwick Law School is a good start in this direction. We need to take it further by, for example, developing a PhD programme with strong links to practice. Shulman et al. (2006) have made a strong case for two types of doctoral programmes for education graduates – the PhD programme and the PPD, the Professional Practice Doctorate – each of them open to postgraduate students, academics, practitioners. They draw the comparison with the similar medical differentiation between the biomedical PhD and the MD and present a strong case for the PPD. I would add administrators to the pool of potential candidates, for such job specifications have changed and are liable to change significantly in the near future under the impact of more technological implementation. Susskind's application of the concept of 'disintermediation' is one example of the types of processes that will occur.

19 Which in one sense is what Twining has called for. See also Jones (1997). Galison, discussing the MIT Radiation Laboratory, pointed out that its creation as a trading zone was 'an epistemic matter *and* ... a physical location', thus revealing the scale of the difficulty involved (Galison, 1997, p. 830).

20 International groupings have been formed of course for some time now: Universitas and IARU are current examples – see http://www.universitas21.com/ and http://www.iaruni.org/. Such high-level international consortia have had mixed success, as Beerkens (2004, p. 258) points out. I do not deny that there are many complex issues of autonomy and independence to be negotiated. But I argue here for much lower level and embedded consortia between disciplines and schools around projects that are of mutual benefit – as Beerkens says,

'it is clear that cooperation in fields where it is seen as an inherent part of academia is more likely to be the standard than when cooperation is moulded on a business-like model. The cooperation that places emphasis on cross-cultural exchange and intercultural learning for students and staff is still most successful, at least in the higher education consortia in this study' (p. 266).

21 For the MIT OCW Initiative, see http://ocw.mit.edu/index.html; the Open University's OpenLearn initiative can be found at http://openlearn.open.ac.uk/. Note that OpenLearn has available for users a 'remix' function and (as befits a second generation OCW initiative) is generally more interactive. For a discussion of open learning initiatives, see Brodie (2006), pp. 885–98.

of disciplines are critical to their practice.[22] But pedagogies can be improved, refreshed, transformed by careful graftings and transplants from other disciplines and the professions. The SIMPLE project, described in the Conclusion to Part 3, is one example of a learning environment, formed in one law school's trading zone, that will soon be open to all; the Standardised Client Initiative (Chapter 2) is another, where the project resources are freely available from the Initiative's blog.[23] Swifter transformation can be brought about by the sharing of best practice and resources among us all.

As we saw in Chapter 1, Galison proved that for collaborative inquiry and activity to take place between disciplines, there needs to be at least a set of procedures – a syntax, as it were. Transactional learning is one such. It turns away from self-referential learning outcomes, is future- and society-oriented in its concern for the *consequences* of legal theory and action. But transactional learning and pragmatic educational theory is only one version of what might be construed as effective theory and practice. As I said in the Introduction, this book exists as an invitation to readers to create such theory and practice from the rich historical traditions and contemporary variations within both legal education and education, wherever we find it and however it may be applied to our own local situations. If this book has contributed to this process it will have served its purpose.

Experience, ethics, technology, collaboration: this is not a programme, but an array of elective affinities within which transformation can take place. The title of Goethe's extraordinary novel, published late in his long life (*Elective Affinities*, 1809), referred to the theory that the chemical properties of certain materials bond with each other. Goethe applied the metaphor to human relationships of love and desire in the novel, creating portraits not just of affinity and attraction, but of resistance and separation, too. On another view, Goethe brings together science and experience, moral duty over against desire and many other dualities.

Teaching is an elective affinity. Like love, we are called into it, irresistibly. It is not egotistical, is based on dialogue with others. Its stories compel us back to the dialogue with ourselves, with students, other teachers, those around us and the ghosts of many others stretching back decades and centuries. But in a deeper sense, just as cyberspace is a metaphor so too is the idea of teaching. Both are fictions. There is no cyberspace, no teaching: there is simply communication and learning in all its forms or there is nothing; what the best of our working lives consist of, when all other metaphors and conditions melt away. As a poet and lawyer once put it:

Phoebus is dead, ephebe. But Phoebus was
A name for something that never could be named.
There was a project for the sun and is.

---

22 As he puts it, 'if different disciplines value particular forms of evidence and argument, narrative and explanation, then their pedagogies should reflect the same forms of representation and exposition'. See Foreword, p. vi of Huber and Morreale (2002).

23   See http://zeugma.typepad.com/sci.

There is a project for the sun. The sun
Must bear no name, gold flourisher, but be
In the difficulty of what it is to be.[24]

Notes Toward a Supreme Fiction: The Silken Keyboard

He had been told that when looking for a good oracle it was best to find the oracle that other oracles went to, but he was shut. There was a sign by the entrance saying, 'I just don't know any more. Try next door, but that's just a suggestion, not formal oracular advice'.

(Adams, 1993, p. 73)

From the window in her flat, Anna watched the torn storm clouds blow in from the west along the river, trailing curtains of rain across the city.[25] She sipped her coffee, thinking abstractedly as she often did that weather and place and character intersected, like music. If only her work could do that. A beep from behind her and she turned back to the table and touched the heavy silk oblong, connecting to the world beyond her window, her biodata read, her person and personality, whatever that was, joining the streaming millions of others.[26] In the air around her, faces

---

24 'Notes Toward a Supreme Fiction', Stevens, 1978, p. 381.

25 Acknowledgements: to Nabokov's *Pale Fire*, where the interest is in the footnotes, not the text; to Alasdair Gray, whose *Lanark* contains a self-referential Epilogue confessing many plagiarisms woven into that brilliantly original novel; to Avrom Sherr's (2000) incisive account of the near future; to Boaventura de Souza Santos, ch. 3 of whose *Toward a New Common Sense* consists of two chapters, facing each other: 'The Law of the Oppressed: The Construction and Reproduction of Legality in Pasargada' (verso) and 'Relationships Among Perceptions that we call Identity: Doing Research in Rio's Squatter Settlements' (recto); and to Abdul Paliwala's (2001) inspiring account of student Maria. Six years on, we are still catching up with his future vision.

26 Anna's desktop is rather different to those on our computers. It isn't a desktop so much as a holographic display in front of and around her, and designs custom content for her entire life. Her learning is part of every other activity and boundaries between real and virtual are so blurred that the idea of separate categorisation would appear inexplicable to her. As one early commentator on this epistemological shift put it (quoting a movie, *The Matrix*), 'There is no spoon. There are only social relations mediated by richly rendered communications platforms. The question of "who should own this spoon:" should be understood as a question about what we want the social relations using the platform to be like' (Benkler, 2006, pp. 180–86).

In this way her whole computing environment is part simulation, part real life, and part very high-level programming environment. All her peers have a similar application, and in her learning life she is assessed at the end of her traineeship in part on the way she thinks creatively about the whole environment she uses online. Though perhaps 'online' is exactly the wrong word to use, since everything around her, including her clothes, the furniture, kitchen utensils, etc are part of the Grid. The concept of ubiquitous computing is so ubiquitous that she no longer thinks of it as computing, merely as a form of consciousness,

smiled and beckoned her into their portals, but she ignored them. She spoke one word, 'Ardcalloch', and was taken to the virtual town's portal.[27] The weather there was pretty stormy, raining spattering the streets as it blew in from the river.[28]

---

an innate connectedness. Her grandparents could tell her of the days when there was no Grid, just paper and telephones, and later there were pagers, cell phones, laptops, PDAs (how did folk keep track of their lives with so many gizmos?); but it was hard to imagine such bewilderingly diverse environments. Anna accesses, drafts, alters, transfers, shares, manages sharing policies, saves and deletes data with an ease and mobility that is almost unimaginable to earlier generations. Consequently, the formal divisions between applications, interfaces and devices simply do not exist as mental constructs. Anna creates the flexible multimodal interfaces she wants. She carries around no model of cyberspace any more than we have a model of a telephone exchange when we pick up the phone. She has no need. In a world of near-invisible cameras, nano-sensors, micro-tracking devices, embedded bio- and RDF-tags and global positioning system chips she has everything she needs literally at her fingertips and in her voice. Privacy regulation has grown apace to control this exponential increase in the creation and storage of data, and is now a substantial arm of government.

She is, though, a bit of a retro-freak, so she likes the idea of connecting to something that sounds as if it belongs to late twentieth-century sci-fi, when most of her contemporaries have comms sewn into the fabric of jackets and intelligent computers far more powerful than our own PCs the size of a button . The silken oblong is a hugely powerful computer, highly geo-context aware and contains in its woven intelligence a representation of a keyboard – a piano keyboard – which she has customised to adapt to chordal gestures (she also uses it to play music, at which point she can surround herself with a noise-cancelling pod). It powers itself, like all such devices, *via* solar power and electromagnetic induction technology (electric toothbrushes were an early application in the last century) built into furniture, floors and walls.

27 The town is fictional, and one of the most ancient of the internet applications, having been developed in the early years of the century by, among others, an eccentric legal academic who, colleagues recalled, preferred the reality of legal fictions to the fiction of legal realities. The webcams show a virtual environment such as can currently be created in applications such as Active Worlds – but immensely more real, and evolving in real time. The environment is peopled by training events, citizens of the fictional world, and so forth. Its hugely complex algorithms connect it to the real world around it. In history, politics, economics, culture, entertainment, topography and climate it shares the surrounding zoosphere. Anna can enter it and walk around its streets, its buildings, catch a tram, meet others within it (both human avatars and bots or robots – more of these below) and so on. It is a playground, a living space, working space, learning space. Or she can view it as if through a camera, which is what she is doing now, to save time.

28 The link between typical west of Scotland weather and virtual worlds is not coincidental. As was pointed out in *The Economist*, 20 April 2006, 'Wonders of the Metaverse', 'Unlike earlier generations of video games, which appealed mainly to narrow demographic groups, *Second Life* is popular with women as well as with men, and with middle-aged people as well as teenagers. If there is a trend, Mr Rosedale [CEO, *Second Life*] says, it is perhaps that *Second Life* does best in places with bad weather, fast broadband connections and unexciting entertainment options. He considers British suburbs an excellent growth market'.

But wait. She zoomed in on a building site near the docks.[29] Her VF was acting for the project consortium there.[30] There didn't seem to have been much progress with the demolition of the small warehouse on the site. She paused, froze the image, then spoke: 'Active files, Construction, Project Data, 3-D deadlines, 31.3.47'.[31] The documents appeared, dissolved and then reformed as a hologram of the architect's three-dimensional representation of how the work should have progressed to date, data-displays integrated with the 3D building. She was right. When she touched the plan as it hung in the air before her the updated architect's plans resolved into images of a warehouse demolished, a cleared site

---

29 Zooming over actual topographies was already a commercial reality as early as 2004 – see http://www.keyhole.com/. She zooms by pointing her finger or hand towards the holograph image matrix, which recognises gesture-based interaction.

30 VF – Virtual Firm. All law students in the recently-formed Law School of Scotland are assigned to virtual training firms, each of which is attached to a real firm. Their transactions are modelled as closely as possible on actual transactions. Trainees work on the transactions negotiated between them, the firm and the university. Anna is currently working on Construction Law, Property and Litigation, with specialist arbitration options in Health Care.

31 Voice recognition authenticating software syncs with her biodata readings to give her access to her VF files without need for further security clearance. The software employs 'software agents' (autonomous entities that can proactively process information in distributed digital environments), which are ubiquitous in all organisational structures – police, government, healthcare, education, and so on. The avatar is based on a much more sophisticated version of this technology, with a model of space and cyberspace equivalent to our own. Here the software robot processes information silently for the user (unless there is a need to dialogue) and in collaboration with other software agents with whom it has been designed to collaborate. It collects information, knows how and when to present it, can summarise it, find elaborated versions of the information, check the integrity of the information and check its own integrity and those of other agents. It can perform complex version-control tasks, and can operate in closed information systems (for example, healthcare patient records within Ardcalloch, if it has authority), semi-open (for example, electronic auctions) and open information systems. When it fails, it can analyse its actions and report to AgentDomain. It self-heals if injured. If fatally damaged, it suicides. There was major litigation in the 2020s on the subject of agents which established that a simple 'bot' such as the one described above, was a *res* not *persona*. There is, however, an ongoing debate that the most advanced forms of avatars (much more complex than Vikki – see below) are approaching the status of sentient being, and should accordingly be treated as a human being.

Students and trainees are not the only ones with software agents, of course. As one of the first articles on the Semantic Web, way back in the early years of the century put it, 'Teacher agents will track professional interests of teachers relating to their field of subject expertise, developments in new pedagogies with active evaluation and testing of pedagogical interventions. Teacher agents will assist teachers in routine marking tasks, record keeping, and document control for assessments requiring manual effort' (Anderson and Whitelocke, 2004).

By 2047 they are common in every area of society. The Legal Resources course teaches students how to set up and fine-tune an agent for legal research.

and automatic diggers waiting to dig the founds of the office building in a corner of the site. She checked back to the webcam image. Nothing of this appeared: the warehouse stood there, obstinate, derelict, black in the rain. She paused: what should she do? She quickly sent a note to her supervisor to let her know.[32] She also made a note on the file to investigate later with Alastair, one of the three trainee architects in the virtual architecture firm in charge of the project.[33] Or maybe there was a Planning problem had come up that she ought to know about before Planning Control in Ardcalloch got their teeth into it.[34] She remembered that Neil was in the Legal Dept there – perhaps he could be persuaded to let her know if there were problems with the documentation for the new development.[35] Basic facts first, then the research.

Meanwhile there was the international deal for Global Construction. She checked the file. No action for two days. Two days! She chorded the keyboard and her avatar appeared, welcomed her warmly, and scanned her face for details of mood.[36] 'Hi there, Vikki, she said neutrally. 'I want to talk to John.'

---

32 Anna doesn't yet know it, but this is the start of one her most important challenges to date. Her supervisor has just gone on holiday and Anna is going to have to handle the situation with builders, subcontractors and local authority. An important completed building consent has not been lodged by the subcontractor, who has also neglected to inform the building contractor, and consequently the work is now falling behind schedule. How will she deal with this situation? Does she have the legal and business acumen, skills and initiative to deal with it successfully? She will argue, with good reason, that since the consent software automatically informs contractors of upcoming deadlines and counts down the days to consent day, then the obligation lies with the contractor. The contractor will hotly deny liability, pointing to the sub-contractor and trade custom and practice.

33 The School of Architecture uses Ardcalloch for simulations of building projects and site planning. The Ardcalloch Educational Infrastructure Committee, which oversees all educational projects in the town, allows only a certain number of building projects each year.

34 Planning is under the control of trainee public administrators, who of course are in touch with their Legal Department in Ardcalloch.

35 Neil is a friend who knew Anna from their Foundation Course. He is about to be put in rather a tricky professional situation by Anna, and his tutor in Debrief will be interested to know how he responds to this.

36 Early agents, constructed in the 2000s, were based upon AI algorithms derived from the communications protocols of pilots and air traffic controllers. They were not successful. Only when agents were programmed on the more tacit procedures in codes of social etiquette did they become usable, able to allow for prediction and emotion in conversation, and take into account differences in language, culture and behaviour. See Miller (2004, pp. 30–34); and Lester et al. (2000, pp. 123–54). Tracking and understanding conversation was for long a holy grail of the telecommunications industries, and breakthroughs in natural language analysis took place a decade later. See Patch (2004). Sophisticated agents can cause problems for students, who can alter the appearance of the agent. Some students dislike them, some fall in love with them – such issues are dealt with in Debrief. See Patch (2004) and Yu et al. (2004). Thus does life imitate art: in Philip K. Dick's novel

'He's busy, Anna', said Vikki.[37]

'It's urgent.'

Instantly the scene dissolved and one of her student law firm partners appeared. 'Hi John – how did you get on with Gobal Construction's team yesterday?'

John glanced briefly to Anna before returning his gaze slightly to the side and over her shoulder. The path continued along the steep ridge up to the sky-line, heavily wooded on either side. Not a good place to stop, exposed to ambush, when the scouts had already seen movement ahead.[38]

'OK. They're cool about the damages clause, but want more time to think about the arbitration stuff.'

'You mean they don't want to go ahead with the contract?'

Shapes among the trees to the left. 'Well, not just yet. I think it was the arbitration clause.' Off the path, quick, into the brushwood. He signalled to Euan McPherson, and the highlanders dropped to the ground, working back towards the trees at the edge of Lake Champlain. Should get a message back to the main body, a mile or so back.

'But the arbitration stuff is pretty standard. Did you did tell them about the deadline the Malaysian firm gave us?'[39]

The shadows resolved into flitting warriors. 'Yeah, but they weren't having it. Said they'd need to think about the ... the Selangor rules?'

Anna frowned; she knew nothing about this. Surely John could have...? She called her avatar whom she knew would be listening in, ever-watchful, until she was dismissed.

'Vikki, get me a copy of the Selangor rules, will you?'

Vikki appeared, then hesitated. 'Do you want the Professional Practice Rules of the Selangor Bar, the Selangor Cricket Club Rules or the Selangor Club rules?'

Do Androids Dream of Electric Sheep? the hero Deckard, who hunts androids, falls in love with the near-perfect android Rachael and begins to wonder if he too is an android.

37 John has signed he should not be disturbed but can be available. He could, if he wanted, be completely unavailable to Vikki or any other avatar.

38 John is play-gaming. Anna has appeared in the landscape around him, though she is of course unaware that she has dropped into deep forest and swamp. It's impolite – people only do this when they're in a hurry to talk. Anna has used her avatar to drop into the game, instead of leaving a message for John that she wanted to speak.

39 Global, a client of John and Anna's firm, are constructing an office block for a Malaysian media corporation (law students from a university in Kuala Lumpur act for them) on land owned by a CyberJaya property company, which is represented by a virtual firm from an Australian university. Anna and John have already done a lot of background work on this contract. Much of the tuition they received in their Transsystemia Law class was relevant to this type of global transaction. In fact, they both acknowledged this in Debrief, wondering how it was possible to be trained in just one jurisdictional practice, and be able to act in several cross-jurisdictional transactions, as they do here. Private International Law used to be the medium of such classes, or sometimes Conflict of Laws, but neither focused anthropologically on common problems in law. See Strauss (2006)

Anna checked the habitual thought about the literalness of the recent avatar-issue for a moment – actually, the media corporation people would probably belong to the Selangor Club, and it might be no bad thing to get a little background on that.[40]

'Selangor Club rules and the Bar rules please. Put them in the KL file' She glanced back to John.

'OK John. John.'

The edge to her voice did it.[41] John froze the game, and dragged his eyes away from the looming trees. He'd need all his attention if the patrol were not to be wiped out.[42]

'Sorry. All yours.'

---

40   Anna is following good practice as explored in her Global Justice class, where she studied amongst other options Tiv justice, judicial reasoning in family law in the Gayo Highlands of Central Aceh, Indonesia, and organised crime in Taiwanese business. She is well aware that law is local knowledge, never more so than in global business (see Geertz, 1989, p. 215), and is putting that knowledge to use in this transaction. She has studied the business background to the deal; but this is an interesting lead which will help her understand the nature of business dealing in KL.

41   There is an edge to the relationship, too. Anna controls, initiates. John plays the subordinate. Anna likes the high-profile role, John prefers the cool laidback style. But she irritates him nevertheless, and it's something he's not really come to terms with.

42   John has made the mistake of play-gaming when he should have been work-gaming. The firm does not discourage this activity, but it makes it clear they monitor his performance in it if he indulges in firm time. When he returns to the game his patrol will be ambushed and several, including himself, killed by Iroquois warriors. Several weeks' worth of experience in deep-forest warfare as George Farquharson, lieutenant of the 42nd Highland Regiment, will be erased from his record. Had he prepared more closely by scanning information in background texts such as *Sketches of the Character, Manners and Present State of the Highlanders of Scotland; with details of The Military Service of The Highland Regiments*, by Major-General David Stewart, vols I and II (1825), Edinburgh, he might have been better prepared for the encounter (these and many other texts are part of the game's realia library). Will he learn the lesson for his legal career? His supervisor will be discussing this with him in Debrief, during which the supervisor will quote Donald Schön: 'the situations of practice are not problems to be solved but problematic situations characterized by uncertainty, disorder, and indeterminacy' (Schön, 1987, pp. 14–16) and ask him to compare his performance in the eighteenth-century French and Indian Wars with his performance in the VF. It will be an uncomfortable meeting. It is of course the point that was made long ago in the last century, and is now taken as axiomatic: 'In order to become expert learners, students must develop some of the same insights as the psychologist into the demands of the learning situation. They must learn about their own cognitive characteristics, their available learning strategies, the demands of various learning tasks and the inherent structure of the material. They must tailor their activities finely to the competing demands of all these forces in order to become flexible and effective learners' (Brown et al., 1981, pp. 16–17). Others in the early twenty-first century pointed out the relationship between behaviour in online play and behaviour at work, and how the first could be an indicator of the second: Brown and Thomas (2006).

'I think we need to discuss what's happening with this transaction. I got an email to say that the construction crew will be ready to start on the founds in Cyberjaya in a week's time. Every day we lose after that, we're going to lose money The way I see it we've got to persuade the Melbourne firm there's not a problem with the arbitration clause. They've *got* to accept that.'

'Yeah, I'll get in touch. Might not be easy.'

'I know, but if we don't then the contract's way behind and we've a lot of explaining to do in Debrief. This is the last transaction for me before I graduate, and I don't want to muck it up when there's a job in the firm hanging on it.'

'Where?'

'Lisbon Clinic. Six month secondment.'

'So you're not staying in Glasgow then.'

'Fed up with the rain.[43] Listen, I'll have another look at the contract. Could you contact me when you've talked to them?'

'Sure.'

OK, see ya.' His image dissolved.

The problem with play-game learning, she thought, as she turned to the window again, was boundaries.[44] Not with work–sim learning, there was a definite space there, and if sometimes you weren't sure what was real and what wasn't, after a while it didn't matter. After all, the firm she belonged to was both a real firm and learning space, not only for her but for everyone else. The Final Debrief and its procedures and checks were the only things that separated her from the profession.[45] She remembered her mother telling her of her own legal education. You sat in lecture theatres for years, took notes from someone who stood up and talked at you for an hour at a time. Anna visited a reconstruction of one when she was on a school trip. So slow. Everyone copying notes down at the same pace. Convoy pace. Now, she had transactions to complete, reports, briefings, critiques,

---

43   The effects of global warming are being felt in every aspect of the UK economy. Ever since the early years of the century the weather patterns in the west of Britain have become steadily more unpredictable. Warm winters, hot summers in the early years gradually gave way to colder and stormier climate change as the Gulf Stream began to fade under pressure from colder currents down the Labrador coast as the polar ice-cap melted.

44   Something John is yet to negotiate in his own life.

45   The Final Debrief is only one of a long series of Debriefs. To mark the special occasion, it is held in one of the University of Scotland's ancient buildings and takes place in front of a panel of nine, from university and the profession. Anna will sit in a chair called the Blackstone Chair, a Jacobean copy of a earlier medieval Chair, whose name derived not from the black marble square set into the seat of the chair but from the medieval practice (which went back to the University of Paris in the twelfth century) of notifying students of their success (on which they were given a little white stone) or failure (a black stone) at the end of the oral examination. She will undergo an oral examination not too far removed in form from the medieval provenance of the Blackstone Chair, but very different in content.

theory seminars, procedure labs and post-transactional debriefs with academics, senior partners, some of whom were academics, and other professionals and lay people. It was like the university mountaineering club she was part of, in between work – alpine-style ascents, light, seizing the moment and weather, not cumbersome expedition learning, just like the exams she'd heard about, great halls hushed quiet, her mother telling her about the essays they wrote. Essays ... She enjoyed Montaigne in the Foundations Programme but who could reproduce the wit and the style? 'If I study, 'tis for no other science that what treats of the knowledge of myself, and instructs me how to die and how to live well'.[46]

No, the problem was the boundaries with others in the firm. She spoke to the file then reviewed her comment to ensure it was balanced. She amended, then again. It wasn't that she didn't trust John, or maybe she didn't, but it had more to do with her wanting to do it all herself, just to be sure. Be careful, she'd been told in Debriefs: let go more. She called up the file and spent the next 40 minutes with the arbitration clause, researching it, reading the two sets of rules, annotating digitally, linking to other files and documents and leaving it for John.[47]

Final issue: the housing association. She spoke: Active files, Purchase, 11 Mackenzie Street, Ardoch'.[48] She opened the final entry, reviewed it, then entered Ardcalloch HA: 'Clare Riadan'.[49] Clare's familiar face met her. 'How's things Clare.'

---

46 Quoting de Montaigne (1952, p. 194), one of the texts in her 'Renaissance Politics and the Personal Style' class.

47 ... who will of course interpret this as interference and resent it – he feels she talks to him as if he were her avatar ... Should she have done this work, or left it entirely for John, who has already carried out a substantial portion of the work to an adequate standard? Final Debrief will focus on this amongst other issues.

48 This is a block in the area of Ardoch, a conservation area within Ardcalloch. It consists of an experiment designed in the 1890s by Patrick Geddes, who was employed by Ardcalloch Municipal Council to come up with an answer to problems of poor housing and social welfare. It consisted of a planned living environment of smallholdings and tenements, a unique answer to the problems of suburbs and inner-city tenemental living in Scottish cities – in effect, Scotland's first garden suburb. However, there was a debate as to whether the Council's Conservation Plan for the area precluded bodies such as the HA from owning property within the area. Anna presented the HA's case before the sheriff in Ardcalloch Sheriff Court, and won the case for the HA.

49 Clare is a student studying a course on Housing Development and Management. Her portfolio includes the management of a tenement block in Rankeillor and this development project in Ardoch (over which she is liaising with Alistair, the architecture student). She engaged Anna as her legal agent for the acquisition of the block, dealing with issues such as sitting tenants (all of them 'avies' or avatars), purchase, etc. A property company (in effect another set of students studying land management courses) owned half the block and the negotiation over acquisition has not been an easy one. Anna's law school – the Law School of Scotland – contains several dozen clinics which offer multidisciplinary practice opportunities for students to practise, ranging from the largest global law firms to the smallest local providers of legal services, to public services, law clinics and in-house

'Pretty good. You got news for me?'

'Yes, and it's the best. They've accepted our offer for the tenement block with accelerated entry.'

'Fantastic news Anna!'

'– and you've got the smallholding as well.'

'That's just brilliant. So what's next?'

'Well I need some documents signed by your HA Director – I have his details, so I'll write him and enclose the documents with guidance on signing.'

Anna paused. 'What are you going to be doing next with the block?'

'The Rehab Plan's nearly finished. We're working with Henderson Gould Architects on the design –'

'— Oh I know one of them – Alastair, he's pretty good.'

'Yeah, we've had a couple of meetings already and he's come up with some really good plans for two- and three-bedroom flats using basically the same shell. And now that we've got the block we're going to arrange Clerk of Works adverts and interviews as well – students from James Watt University and elsewhere I think – that'll be my first employment stuff, so I'll need some advice on employment procedures nearer the time. Is that part of your remit?'

'No, but I'd like it to be. That's where I want to be heading, career-wise. I'll discuss with my supervisor and get back to you.'

'That's great. Listen, I'm late for a briefing – can we meet up tonight at the bar?'

'Sure – eight o'clock ok for you?'

'Great – see you then.'

Anna edited and linked their conversation to the file, prepared and sent the documents to Clare's Director, then sent a note about employment electives to

---

lawyering. (The Law School is a more radical version of the International Legal Centre proposed by Twining as long ago as 1995.) Clare is sponsored by the Strathclyde Housing Association, which is a community-based association in Glasgow; and in addition to supervised law students providing legal advice and assistance at all levels as an essential part of their own law course, the law school also provides free legal training to the Association and support for sim training in their housing courses. Law students are thus involved in the creation of training materials for other disciplines, professions and occupations. They perform this as an integral part of their course and in the Foundation stage are taught how to create resource-based learning, sim-based training, and how to develop the use of avatars. They do this in conjunction with law staff and educationalists, who monitor and sign off on the results.

Clare is on Level 2 of her course. Once she has successfully dealt with the simulation at this level, she moves on to a more sophisticated set of issues and problems in Glasgow and elsewhere, and her meetings with mentors will become briefer and more complex. Like Anna, when she moves into level 3 she will find it difficult at times to discern what is real and what is not. But her mentor has reassured her that such issues, which tended to be seen in the past of problems of metaphysics, or language games, are now simply regarded as experiential and phenomenological data. Her Philosophy mentor, of course, disagrees.

her supervisor. She had other stuff to research, but it could wait. She played a chord, and the bright displays in front of her shimmered and melted into thin air. She folded up the silken keyboard and put it in her bag. Time to go.

References

Manuscript Sources

Ferguson, A. (1733–93) Papers of Professor Adam Ferguson, Edinburgh University Library, Special Collections, GB237, Coll–138.
Stone, H.F. (1911–1924) Papers, William Butler Library, Columbia University, Ms. Coll. Stone, Special Collections.

Secondary Sources

Adams, D. (1993) *Mostly Harmless* (London, Pan Macmillan).
Agre, P. (2002) Cyberspace as American culture, *Science as Culture*, 11(2), pp. 171–189.
Agre, P. (2003) *Information and Institutional Change: The Case of Digital Libraries* (Cambridge, MA, MIT Press).
Albanese, M.A. (1993) Problem based learning: a review of literature on its outcomes and implementation issues, *Academic Medicine: Journal of the Association of American Medical Colleges*, 68(1), pp. 52–81.
Aleman, A.M.A. (2006) Latino demographics, democratic individuality, and educational accountability: a Pragmatist's view, *Educational Researcher*, 35(7), pp. 25–31.
Alexander, T. (1987) *John Dewey's Theory of Art, Experience and Nature: The Horizons of Feeling* (Albany, State University of New York Press).
Althusser, L. and Balibar, E. (1970) *Reading Capital*, translator B. Brewster (London, Verso).
always_black (2006) Bow, nigger, in: K. Salen and E. Zimmerman (eds) *The Games Design Reader. A Rules of Play Anthology* (Cambridge, MA, MIT Press).
Amos, E. and White, M.J. (1998) Teaching tools: Problem-based learning, *Nurse Educator*, 23(2), pp. 11–14.
Anderson, S., Murray, L. and Maharg, P. (2003) Minority and Social Diversity in Scotland, Report to the Scottish Executive. Available at http://www.scotland. gov.uk/Publications/2003/03/16713/19581. Accessed 27/02/07.
Anderson, T. and Whitelock, D. (2004) The educational semantic web: visioning and practicing the future of education, *Journal of Interactive Media in Education* (Special Issue), 1 (Introduction). Available at http://www-jime. open.ac.uk/2004/1. Accessed 27/02/07.
Anncta, L.A. and Holmes, S. (2006) Creating presence and community in a synchronous virtual learning environment using avatars, *International Journal*

of Instructional Technology and Distance Learning, 3(8). Available at http://www.itdl.org/Journal/Aug_06/article03.htm. Accessed 27/02/07.

Appelbaum, E.T., Bailey, T., Berg, P. and Kalleberg, A. (2000) *Manufacturing Advantage: Why High Performance Work Systems Pay Off* (Ithaca, NY, ILR Press).

Arendt, H. (1958) *The Human Condition* (Chicago, IL, University of Chicago Press).

Aristotle (2002) *Nicomachean Ethics*, S. Broadie (ed.) trans. C. Rowe (Oxford, Oxford University Press).

Armstrong, I. (2000) *The Radical Aesthetic* (Oxford, Blackwell Publishers).

Bacchetti, R. and Ehrlich, T. (2006) *Reconnecting Education and Foundations. Turning Good Intentions into Educational Capital* (San Francisco, Jossey-Bass Publishers).

Baecker, R.M. [no date] Home page. Available at http://kmdi.utoronto.ca/rmb/. Accessed 27/02/07.

Baecker, R.M. (2003) A principled design for scalable internet visual communications with rich media, interactivity, and structured archives, *Proceedings of the 2003 Conference of the Centre for Advanced Studies on Collaborative Research* (Toronto, Ontario) 16–29. Available at The ACM Digital Library, http://portal.acm.org/citation.cfm?id=961327anddl=ACMandcoll=andCFID=15151515andCFTOKEN=6184618. Accessed 16/03/07.

Baecker, R.M., Moore, G. and Zijdemans, A. (2003) Re-inventing the lecture. Webcasting made interactive. *HCI International 2003*, June 2003, Lawrence Erlbaum Associates, Volume 1, pp. 896–900.

Baggaley, J. (1980) *Psychology of the TV Image* (Westmead, Gower).

Balkin, J. (2005) Virtual liberty: freedom to design and freedom to play in virtual worlds, *Virginia Law Review*, 90(8), pp. 2043–98.

Balkin, J. and Levinson, S. (1999) Interpreting law and music: performance notes on 'The Banjo Serenader' and 'The Lying Crowd of Jews', *Cardozo Law Review*, 20, pp. 1531–72.

Balkin, J.M. and Levinson, S. (2006) Law and the humanities: an uneasy relationship, *Yale Journal of Law and the Humanities*, 18, pp. 155–87.

Bancroft, W.J. (1995) Research in nonverbal communication and its relationship to pedagogy and suggestopedia, ERIC Document Reproduction Service No. ED 3844 243.

Bankowski, Z. (1991) Analogical reasoning and legal institutions, in: Z. Bankowski (ed.) *Legal Knowledge and Analogy: Fragments of Legal Epistemology Hermeneutics and Linguistics* (Amsterdam, Kluwer).

Banks, S.P. Ge, G. and Baker, J. (1991) Intercultural encounters and miscommunication, in: N. Coupland and H. Giles (eds) *'Miscommunication' and Problematic Talk* (London, Sage).

Bann, S. (1989) The sense of the past: image, text, and object in the formation of historical consciousness in nineteenth-century Britain, in: H. Aram Veeser (ed.) *The New Historicism* (London and New York, Routledge).

Barker, J. (1993) Tightening the iron cage: concertive control in self-managing teams, *Administrative Science Quarterly*, 38, pp. 408–37.

Barnes, B. (2001). Practice as collective action, in: T.R. Schatzki, K. Knorr Cetina and E. von Savigny (eds) *The Practice Turn in Contemporary Theory*, pp. 17–28 (London, Routledge).

Barnes, D. and Todd, F. (1977) *Communication and Learning in Small Groups* (London, Routledge and Kegan Paul).

Barnett, R. (1994) *The Limits of Competence. Knowledge, Higher Education and Society* (Buckingham, Society for Research into Higher Education, Open University).

Barnett, R. (1999) *Realizing the University in an Age of Supercomplexity* (Buckingham, Open University Press).

Barr, R. and Tagg, J. (1995) From teaching to learning: a new paradigm for undergraduate education, *Change*, 27(6), pp. 12–25.

Barrows, H.S. (1987) *Simulated (Standardized) Patients and Other Human Simulations* (Chapel Hill, NC, Health Sciences Consortium).

Barrows, H.S. and Tamblyn, R. (1980) *Problem-based Learning: An Approach to Medical Education* (New York, Springer Publishing Company).

Barthes, R. (1970) *S/Z*, trans. R. Miller (New York, Hill and Wang).

Bartle, R.A. (1999) Hearts, clubs, diamonds, spades: players who suit muds. Available at http://www.mud.co.uk/richard/hcds.html. Accessed 27/02/07.

Bartle, R.A. (2003) *Designing Virtual Worlds* (Berkeley, CA, New Riders Publishing).

Bartle, R.A. (2005) Contradictions. Available at http://terranova.blogs.com/ terra_nova/2005/06/contradictions_.html. Accessed 16/03/07.

Barton, K. and McKellar, P. (1998) The virtual court action: procedural facilitation in law, *ALT-J*, 6(1), pp. 87–94.

Barton, K. and Westwood, F. (2006) From student to trainee practitioner – a study of team working as a learning experience, *Web Journal of Current Legal Issues*, 3. Available at http://webjcli.ncl.ac.uk/2006/issue3/barton-westwood3. html. Accessed 27/02/07.

Barton, K. and Maharg, P. (2006) E-Simulations in the Wild: Interdisciplinary Research, Design and Implementation, in: C. Aldrich, D. Gibson and M. Prensky (eds) *Games and Simulations in Online Learning: Research and Development Frameworks* (Hershey, PENN, Information Science Publishing).

Barton, K., Cunningham, C.D., Jones, G.T. and Maharg, P. (2006) What clients think: standardized clients and the assessment of communicative competence, *Clinical Law Review*, 13(1), pp. 1–65.

Barton, K., Bloxham, S., McKellar, P. and Maharg, P. [no date] Zeugma: legal education, technology, rhetoric, legal theory blog. Available at http://zeugma. typepad.com/. Accessed 27/02/07.

Barton, K., Cunningham, C., Ker, J., Maharg, P. and Slorach, S. [no date] Standardised Client Initiative blog. Available at http://zeugma.typepad.com/ sci. Accessed 27/02/07.

Bass, R. (1999) The scholarship of teaching: what's the problem? Inventio, 1(1). Available at http://www.doiiit.gmu.edu/Archives/feb98/randybass_1A.htm. Accessed 27/02/07.

Baudrillard, J. (1988) *Jean Baudrillard, Selected Writings*, M. Poster (ed.) (Stanford, CA, Stanford University Press).

Becher, T. (1989) *Academic Tribes and Territories: Intellectual Enquiry and Culture of Disciplines* (Buckingham, Society for Research into Higher Education, Open University).

Beck, K. and Beddle, M. (2001) Manifesto for agile software development. Available at http://www.agilemanifesto.org/. Accessed 27/02/07.

Beer, G. (1983) *Darwin's Plots: Evolutionary Narrative in Darwin, George Eliot, and Nineteenth-Century Fiction* (London, Routledge and Kegan Paul).

Beer, G. (1995) *Open Fields: Science in Cultural Encounter* (Oxford, Oxford University Press).

Beerkens, H.J.J.G. (2004) Global Opportunities and Institutional Embeddedness: Higher Education Consortia in Europe and Southeast Asia (unpublished thesis, University of Twente). Available at http://www.beerkens.info/files/phd. pdf. Accessed 27/02/07.

Bell, M. (2001) Online role-play: anonymity, engagement and risk, *Education Media International*, 38(4), pp. 251–60.

Benbassat, J. and Baumal, R. (2002) A step-wise role playing approach for teaching patient counselling skills to medical students, *Patient Education and Counseling*, 46(2), pp. 147–53.

Benbunan-Fich, R. and Hiltz, S.R. (1999) Impacts of asynchronous learning networks on individual and group problem solving: a field experiment. *Group Decision and Negotiation*, 8(5), pp. 409–26

Benjamin, W. (1999) *The Arcades Project*, trans. H. Eiland and K. McLaughlin (Cambridge, MA, The Belknap Press).

Benkler, Y. (2002) Coase's Penguin, or Linux and the nature of the firm, *Yale Law Journal*, 112(3), pp. 369–446

Benkler, Y. (2006) *The Wealth of Networks. How Social Production Transforms Markets and Freedom* (New Haven, CT and London, Yale University Press).

Benkler, Y. (2006) There is no spoon, in: J.M. Balkin and B.S. Noveck (eds) *The State of Play. Law, Games, and Virtual Worlds* (New York, New York University Press).

Bennet, N., Dunne, E. and Carre, C. (2000) *Skills Development in Higher Education and Employment* (Buckingham, Society for Research into Higher Education, Open University Press).

Berardi-Coletta, B., Dominowski, R.L., Buyer, L.S. and Rellinger, E.R. (1995) Metacognition and problem solving: a process-oriented approach, *Journal of Experimental Psychology Learning: Memory and Cognition*, 21(1), pp. 205–23.

Bergman, P. (2003) Reflections on US clinical legal education, *International Journal of the Legal Profession*, 10(1), 109–21.

Bergus, G.R., Chapman, G.B., Gjerde, C. and Elstein, A.S. (1995) Clinical reasoning about new symptoms despite pre-existing disease: sources of error and order effects, *Family Medicine*, 27(5), pp. 314–20.

Berners-Lee, T., Hendler, J. and Lassila, O. (2001) The semantic web, *Scientific American*, 284(5), pp. 34–43.

Bernstein, D. (1998) Putting the focus on student learning, in: P. Hutchings (ed.) *The Course Portfolio: How Faculty Can Examine Their Teaching to Advance Practice and Improve Student Learning* (Washington, DC, American Association for Higher Education).

Bhandari, J. (2006) Empirical Methods, Law and Econ Prof Blog. Available at http://lawprofessors.typepad.com/law_econ/2006/09/empirical_metho.html. Accessed 16/03/07.

Bhatia, V. (1993) *Analysing Genre: Language Use in Professional Settings* (London, Longman Publishers).

Biesta, G.J. and Burbules, N.C. (2003) *Pragmatism and Educational Research* (Boulder, CO, Rowman and Littlefield Publishers).

Biggs, J. (1999) T*eaching for Quality Learning at University* (Buckingham, Society for Research into Higher Education, Open University Press).

Biggs, J. (2003) Aligning teaching and assessing to course objectives, Teaching and Learning in Higher Education: New Trends and Innovations (Portugal, University of Aveira). Available at http://event.ua.pt/iched/main/invcom/p182.pdf. Accessed 27/02/07.

Biggs, J.B. and Collis, K.F. (1982) *Evaluating the Quality of Learning: The SOLO Taxonomy* (New York, Academic Press).

Bijker, W.E. (1995) *Of Bicycles, Bakelites and Bulbs. Toward a Theory of Sociotechnical Change* (Cambridge, MA, MIT Press).

Bijker, W.E. (2001) Social Construction of Technology, in: N.J. Smelser and P.B. Baltes (eds) *International Encyclopedia of the Social and Behavioral Sciences*, vol. 23 (Oxford, Elsevier Sciences Ltd).

Bijker, W.E. and Wiebe, E. (2002) The Oosterschelde storm surge barrier. A test case for Dutch water technology, *Management, and Politics, Technology and Culture*, 43, pp. 569–84

Bikson, T.K. and Eveland, J.D. (1990) The interplay of work group structures and computer support, in: J. Galegher, C. Egido and R. Kraut (eds) *Intellectual Teamwork* (Hillsdale, NJ, Lawrence Erlbaum).

Bilimoria, D. (2000) A new scholarship of teaching and learning: an agenda for management education scholarship, *Journal of Management Education*, 24(6), pp. 704–7.

Birks, P. (1994) The historical context, in: P. Birks (ed.) *Reviewing Legal Education* (Oxford, Oxford University Press).

Bischoff, W.R., Bisconer, S.W., Kooker, B.M. and Woods, L.C. (1996) Transactional distance and interactive television in the distance education of health professionals, *The American Journal of Distance Education*, 10(3), pp. 4–19.

Blackburn, T. (2003) Simulator-based learning for obstetric anaesthesia ASME Conference. Available at http://www.uni-mainz.de/FB/Medizin/Anaesthesie/SESAM/Downloads/Abstracts%202003.pdf. Accessed 27/02/07.

Blake, R.L., Hosokawa, M.C. and Riley, S. (2000) Student performances on step 1 and step 2 of the United States medical licensing examination following implementation of a problem based learning curriculum, *Academic Medicine*, 75(1), pp. 66–70.

Blasi, G.L. (1995) What lawyers know: lawyering expertise, cognitive science, and the functions of theory, *Journal of Legal Education*, 45(3), pp. 313–98.

Bleakley, A. (2006) Broadening conception of learning in medical education: the message from teamworking, *Medical Education* 40(2), pp. 150–57.

Bleakley, A., Farrow, R., Gould, D. and Marshall, R. (2003) Learning how to see: doctors making judgements in the visual domain, *Journal of Workplace Learning*, 15(7/8), pp. 301–6.

Bloom, B.S. (1956) *Taxonomy of Educational Objectives: The Classification of Educational Goals: Handbook I* (New York, Toronto, Longman).

Bloxham, S.M. and Armitage, S. (2003) What a LUVLE way to learn law, *International Review of Law Computers and Technology*, 17(1), pp. 39–50.

Blumberg, P. and Michael, J.A. (1992) Development of self-directed learning behaviors in a partially teacher directed problem based learning curriculum, *Teaching and Learning in Medicine*, 4(1), pp. 3–8.

Boal, A. (1998) *Theatre of the Oppressed* (New York, TCG Publishers).

Bodemer, R., Ploetzner, I., Feuerlein and Spada, H. (2004) The active integration of information during learning with dynamic and interactive visualisations, *Learning and Instruction*, 14(3), pp. 325–41.

Böhm, A., Davis, T., Meares, D. and Pearce, D. (2002) *Global Student Mobility 2025: Forecasts of the Global Demand for International Higher Education* (Melbourne, IDP Education).

Bonaventura (1882–1902) *Opera Omnia*, Collegium a S. Bonaventura (eds), 10 vols (Florence, Quaracchi).

Book, B. Moving beyond the game: social virtual worlds. Available at http://www.virtualworldsreview.com. Accessed 27/02/07.

Boon, A. (2002) Ethics in legal education and training: four reports, three jurisdictions and a prospectus, *Legal Ethics*, 5(1/2), pp. 34–67.

Boon, A. (2005) From public service to service industry: the impact of socialization and work on the motivation and values of lawyers, *International Journal of the Legal Profession*, 12(2), pp. 229–60.

Boon, A., and Levin, J. (1999) *The Ethics and Conduct of Lawyers in England and Wales* (Oxford, Hart Publishing).

Bordage, G. and Lemieux, M. (1991) Semantic structures and diagnostic thinking of experts and novices, *Academic Medicine*, 66(9, Supplement), pp. S70–72.

Boud, D. and Feletti, G.I. (1991) *The Challenge of Problem-Based Learning* (London, Kogan Page).

Bourdieu, P. (1977) *Outline of a Theory of Practice*, trans. R. Nice (Cambridge, Cambridge University Press).

Bourdieu, P. (1990) *In Other Words: Essays Towards a Reflexive Sociology*, trans. M. Adamson (Stanford, CA, Stanford University Press).

Bourdieu, P. (1998) *Acts of Resistance: Against the Tyranny of the Market*, trans. R. Nice (New York, The New Press).

Bourdieu, P. and Passeron, J.-C. (1977) *Reproduction in Education Society and Culture*, trans. R. Nice (Beverly Hills, CA, Sage).

Bourdieu, P., Passeron, J.-C. and de Saint Martin, M. (1994) *Academic Discourse: Linguistic Misunderstanding and Professorial Power*, trans. R. Teese (Cambridge, Polity Press).

Bowrey, K. (2005) *Law and Internet Cultures* (Cambridge, Cambridge University Press).

Boycott Blackboard Petition. Available at http://www.boycottblackboard.org/index.php?view=1. Accessed 16/03/07.

Boyes, L.C. (2006) Evaluation of the Radio Waves Project, in: M. Owen, L. Grant, S. and K. Facer (eds) *Opening Education. Social Software and Learning* (Bristol, Futurelab).

Boys, J. (2002) Managed learning environments, joined up systems and the problems of organisational change. Available at http://www.tinyurl.com/2bpofr. Accessed 28/02/07.

Bradney, A. (1999) Liberalising legal education, in: F. Cownie (ed.) *The Law School: Global Issues, Local Questions* (Aldershot, Dartmouth Publishing).

Bradney, A. (2003) *Conversations, Choices and Chances* (Oxford, Hart Publishing).

Bradney, A. (2006) Teamworking and the LLB, Society of Legal Scholars Annual Conference, 6–7 September, University of Keele.

Bradney, A. and Cownie, F. (2000) British university law schools in the twenty-first century, in: D. Hayton (ed.) *Law's Future(s). British Legal Developments in the 21st Century* (Oxford, Hart Publishing).

Bransford, J.D., Franks, J.J., Vye, N.J. and Sherwood, R.D. (1989) New approaches to instruction: because wisdom can't be told, in: S.V.A. Ortony (ed.) *Similarity and Analogical Reasoning* (New York, Cambridge University Press).

Brecht, B. (1957) Alienation effects in Chinese acting, in: J. Willett (ed.) *Brecht on Theater* (New York, Hill and Wang).

Brecht, B. (1998) *Collected Short Stories*, trans. Y. Kapp, H. Rorrison and A. Tatlow (New York, Arcade Publishing).

Brecht, B. (1999) Theatre for learning: in *Brecht Sourcebook*, trans. E. Anderson, ed. C. Martin, H. Bial (London, Routledge).

Breger, M.L., Calabrese, G.M. and Hughes, T.A. (2004) Teaching professionalism in context: insights from students, clients, adversaries and judges, *South Carolina Law Review*, 55, pp. 303–47.

Brodie, M.T. (2006) Open access in law teaching: a new approach to legal education, *Lewis and Clark Law Review*, 10(4), pp. 885–98.

Bronwell, K.A. (2001) Senior residents' views on the meaning of professionalism and how they learn about it, *Academic Medicine*, 76(7), pp. 734–7.

Brown, A.L., Campione, J.C. and Day, J.D. (1981) Learning to learn: on training students to learn from texts, *Educational Researcher*, 10(2), pp. 14–21.

Brown, J.S. and Thomas, D. (2006) You play *World of Warcraft*? You're hired! *Wired*, April. Available at http://www.wired.com/wired/archive/14.04/learn.html. Accessed 27/02/07.

Brownell, A.K.W. and Côté, L. (2001) Senior residents' views on the meaning of professionalism, and how they learn about it, *Academic Medicine*, 76(7), pp. 734–7.

Brownsword, R. (1996) Where are all the law schools going? *The Law Teacher*, 30(1), pp. 1–27.

Brownsword, R. (1999) Law schools for lawyers, citizens and people, in: F. Cownie (ed.) *The Law School: Global Issues, Local Questions* (Aldershot, Dartmouth Publishing).

Buchstein, H. (1997) Bytes that bite: The Internet and deliberative democracy, Constellations 4(2), pp. 248–63.

Bulmer, M. (1984) *The Chicago School of Sociology: Institutionalization, Diversity, and the Rise of Sociological Research* (Chicago, IL, University of Chicago Press).

Burbules, N. and Callister, T. (2000) *Watch IT: The Risks and Promises of Information Technologies for Education* (Boulder, CO, Westview Press).

Bush, V. (1945) As we may think, *Atlantic Monthly*, 176, pp. 101–8.

Butterfield, S. (2005) An article complaining about 'social software', Sylloge Blog. Available at http://www.sylloge.com. Accessed 27/02/07.

Cairns: the First Amendment, democratic design and civic innovation for the digital age. Blog. Available at http://www.nyls.edu/pages/2150.asp. Accessed 27/02/07.

Cantor, N. and Schomberg, S. (2002) What we want students to learn: cultivating playfulness and responsibility in a liberal education, *Change Magazine*, 34(5), 47–9.

Cardozo, B.N. (1921) *The Nature of the Judicial Process* (New Haven, CT, Yale University Press).

Carey, J. (1999) *The Faber Book of Utopias* (London, Faber and Faber).

Carlquist, J. (2004) Medieval manuscripts, hypertext and reading. Visions of digital editions, *Literary and Linguistic Computing*, 19(1), pp. 105–18.

Carnegie Foundation for the Advancement of Teaching. Available at http://www.carnegiefoundation.org. Accessed 27/02/07.

Carnochan, B. (1993) *The Battleground of the Curriculum: Liberal Education and American Experience* (Stanford, CA, Stanford University Press).

Carruthers, M. (1990) *The Book of Memory. A Study of Memory in Medieval Literature. Cambridge Studies in Medieval Literature* (Cambridge, Cambridge University Press).

Carruthers, M. (1998) *The Craft of Thought. Meditation, Rhetoric and the Making of Images* (Cambridge, Cambridge University Press).

Castells, M. (2000) *The Rise of the Network Society*, vol. 1 (Oxford, Blackwell Publishing).

Castronova, E. (2001) Virtual worlds: a first-hand account of market and society on the cyberian frontier. Available at CESifo Working Paper Series No. 618 http://ssrn.com/abstract=294828. Accessed 27/02/07.

Castronova, E. (2003a) Home Page. Available at http://mypage.in.edu/Ncastro/home.html. Accessed 27/02/07.

Castronova, E. (2003b) The price of 'man' and 'woman': a hedonic pricing model of avatar attributes in a synthetic world. Available at http://papers.ssrn.com/sol3/papers.cfm?abstract_id=415043. Accessed 27/02/07.

Castronova, E. (2004) Insta-Globalization, Terranova blog. Available at http://terranova.blogs.com/terra_nova/2004/04/instaglobalizat.html#mor. Accessed 27/02/07.

Cavers, D.F. (1943) In advocacy of the problem method, *Columbia Law Review*, 43, pp. 449–61.

Censer (1976) *Prelude to Power: Parisian Radical Press, 1789–91* (Baltimore, MD The Johns Hopkins University Press).

Centre for Educational Research and Innovation (2005) *E-learning in Tertiary Education: Where Do We Stand?* (Paris, OECD Publications). Available at http://new.sourceoecd.org/education/9264009205. Accessed 27/02/07.

Cerquiglini, B. (1999) *In Praise of the Variant: A Critical History of Philology*, trans. B. Wing (Baltimore, MD, The Johns Hopkins University Press).

Chandler, P. and Sweller, J. (1991) Cognitive load theory and the fomat of instruction, *Cognition and Instruction*, 8(4), pp. 293–332.

Chandler, S. and Rowbotham, P. (2005) Putting ethics into practice, Vocational Teachers Forum V, http://www.ukcle.ac.uk/resources/vtf/chandler.html. Accessed 27/02/07

Chapman, J. (2005) Why teach legal ethics to undergraduates?, *Legal Ethics*, 5(1/2), pp. 68–89.

Chase, A. (1979) Birth of the modern law school, *American Journal of Legal History*, 23(4), pp. 329–48.

Cheltenham, J. and Mutch (2004) 'Traffic lights' and responsibility to the profession, Vocational Teachers Forum III, UK Centre for Legal Education, www.ukcle.ac.uk/resources/vtf/cheltenham.html. Accessed 27/02/07.

Chen, Y.-J. and Willits, F.K. (1998) A path analysis of the concepts in Moore's theory of transactional distance in a videoconferencing learning environment,

Journal of Distance Education. Available at http://cade.athabascau.ca/vol13.2/ chen.html. Accessed 27/02/07.

Chicago Arts Partnerships in Education (2007). Available at www.capeweb.org. Accessed 27/02/07.

Choksy, L. (1999) *The Kodály Method II: Comprehensive Music Education* (Upper Saddle River, NJ, Prentice Hall).

Christensen, L.M. (2006) Going back to kindergarten: applying the principles of Waldorf education to create ethical attorneys. Available at http://ssrn.com/ abstract=899218. Accessed 27/02/07.

Christensen, L.M. (2007) Legal reading and success in law school: an empirical study, University of St Thomas Legal Studies Research Paper, No 06–29. Available at http://papers.ssrn.com/abstract=924650. Accessed 27/02/07.

Christenson, L.J. and Menzel, K. (1998) The linear relationship between student reports of teacher immediacy behaviours and perceptions of state motivation, and of cognitive, affective and behavioural learning, *Communication Education*, 47(1), pp. 82–90

Chung, W., Chen, H., Chaboya, L.G., O'Toole, C. and Atabakhsh, H. (2005) Evaluating event visualization: a usability study of COPLINK spatio-temporal visualizer, *International Journal of Human-Computer Studies*, 62, pp. 127–57.

Cieniawa, L. (2003) Chris Trottier (Sims Online) Q and A. Available at http:// www.armchairempire.com/Interviews/chris-trottier-the-sims.htm. Accessed 27/02/07.

Claessen, H.F.A. and Boshuizen, H.P.A. (1985) Recall of medical information by students and doctors, *Medical Education*, 19(1), pp. 61–7.

Clanchy, M. (1993) *From Memory to Written Record: England 1066–1307* (Oxford, Blackwell Publishing).

Clark, R.C. (1998) Authorware, multimedia, and instructional methods. Available at http://www.macromedia.com/support/authorware/basics/instruct/. Accessed 27/02/07.

Clark, R.E. and Feldon, D.F. (2005) Five common but questionable principles of multimedia learning, in: R.E. Mayer (ed.) *Cambridge Handbook of Multimedia Learning* (Cambridge, Cambridge University Press).

Clegg, S., Hudson, A. and Steel, J. (2003) The emperor's new clothes: globalization and e-learning in higher education, *British Journal of Sociology of Education*, 24(1), pp. 39–52.

Coates, T. (2003) My working definition of social software. Plasticbag.org blog. Available at http://tinyurl.com/2xdcre. Accessed 27/02/07.

Cockburn, A. and McKeachie, B. (2004) Evaluating spatial memory in two and three dimensions, *International Journal of Human-Computer Studies*, 61(3), pp. 359–73.

Cockrell, K.S., Caplow, J.A.H. and Donaldson, J.F. (2000) A context for learning: collaborative groups in the problem based learning environment, *Review of Higher Education*, 23(3), pp. 347–63.

Cohen, D. and Prusack, L. (2001) I*n Good Company. How Social Capital Makes Organizations Work* (Boston, MA, Harvard Business School Press).

Cohen, J.J. (2002) Our compact with tomorrow's doctors, *Academic Medicine*, 77(6), pp. 475–80.

Cole, M., Gay, J. and Sharp, D. (1971) *The Cultural Context of Learning and Thinking* (New York, Basic Books).

Collier, R (2004) 'We're all socio-legal now?' Legal education, scholarship and the global knowledge economy – reflections on the UK experience, *Sydney Law Review*, 26(4), pp 503–37.

Colliver, J.A. (2000) Effectiveness of PBL curricula: research and theory, *Academic Medicine*, 75(3), pp. 259–66.

Conole, G. and Oliver, M. (1998) A pedagogical framework for embedding C and IT into the curriculum, *ALT-J*, 6(2), pp. 4–16.

Conway, M.A., Gardiner, J.M., Perfect, T.J., Anderson, S.J. and Cohen, G.M. (1997) Changes in memory awareness during learning: the acquisition of knowledge by psychology undergraduates, *Journal of Experimental Psychology: General*, 126(4), pp. 393–413.

Cooke, J. (2002) The role of dialogue in computer-based learning and observing learning: an evolutionary approach to theory, *Journal of Interactive Media in Education*, 5. Available at http://www-jime.open.ac.uk/2002/5/cook-02-5-01. html. Accessed 27/02/07.

Cooke, M., Irby, D.M., Sullivan, W. and Ludmerer, K.M. (2006) American medical education 100 years after the Flexner Report, *The New England Journal of Medicine*, 335(13), pp. 1339–44.

Cooper, M. and Holzman, M. (1985) Talking about protocols, *College Composition and Communication*, 34(3), pp. 31–5.

Corcos, C.A. (1997) Presuming innocence: Alan Pakula and Scott Turow take on the great American legal fiction, *Oklahoma City University Law Review*, 22(1), pp. 129–66.

Corns, T.N. (2000) The early modern search engine: indices, title pages, marginalia and contents, in: N. Rhodes and J. Sawday (eds) *The Renaissance Computer. Knowledge Technology in the First Age of Print* (London and New York, Routledge).

Coulehan, J. and Williams, P.C. (2001) Vanquishing virtue: the impact of medical education, *Academic Medicine*, 76(6), pp. 598–605.

Coupland, N., Giles, H. and Wiemann, J. (1991) *'Miscommunication' and Problematic Talk* (London, Sage Publications).

Cownie, F. (2000) The importance of theory in law teaching, *International Journal of the Legal Profession*, 7(3), pp. 225–38.

Cox, B. (1999) Achieving intercultural communication through computerized business simulation/games, *Simulation and Gaming*, 31(1), pp. 38–50.

Creative Partnerships UK (2007). Available at www.creative-partnerships.com. Accessed 27/02/07.

Creme, P. and Lea, M. (1998) Student writing: challenging the myths, *Proceedings of the 5th Annual Writing Development in Higher Education Conference* 1998 CALS, April (University of Reading).

Crook, C. (1994) *Computers and the Collaborative Experience of Learning* (London, Routledge).

Cubrilovic, N. (2007) Yahoo! launches Pipes, TechCrunch blog. Available at http://www.techcrunch.com/2007/02/07/yahoo-launches-pipes/. Accessed 27/02/07.

Cunningham, C.D. (no date) Home Page. Available at http://law.gsu.edu/ccunningham/. Accessed 27/02/07.

Cunningham, C.D. (1992) The lawyer as translator, representation as text: towards an ethnography of legal discourse, *Cornell Law Review*, 77(6), pp. 1298–387.

Cunningham, C.D. (1999) Evaluating effective lawyer-client communication: an international project moving from research to reform, *Fordham Law Review*, 67(5), pp. 1959–86.

Currie, B. (1951) The materials of law study, Parts 1 and 2, *Journal of Legal Education*, 3, pp. 331–83.

Currie, B. (1955) The materials of law study, Part 3, *Journal of Legal Education*, 8, pp. 1–78.

Curtis, D. (2006) Everything I wanted to know about teaching law school I learned from being a kindergarten teacher: ethics in the law school classroom, *Brigham Young University Education and Law Review*, 2, pp. 47–83.

Cutler, C. and Hay, I. (2000) 'Club Dread': applying and refining an issues-based role play on environment, economy, and culture, *Journal of Geography in Higher Education*, 24(2), pp. 179–97.

Dahllof, U. (1991) Towards a new model for the evaluation of teaching, in: Dahllof, U., Harris, J., Shattock, M., Staropoli, A. and Veld, R. (eds) D*iscussions of Education in Higher Education* (London, Jessica Kingsley).

Dalrymple, J. [Viscount Stair] (1981) *The Institutions of the Law of Scotland: Deduced from its Originals, and Collated with the Civil, Canon and Feudal Laws, and with the Customs of Neighbouring Nations in IV Books*, ed. D.M. Walker (Edinburgh, University Presses of Edinburgh and Glasgow).

Daly, R.A. (1924) *Law Teachers' Manual of the Analysis of Cases and the Use of Law Books*, 2nd edn (St Paul, MN, West).

Dator, J. (1999) Utopian coursework, in: J. Carey (ed.) *The Faber Book of Utopias* (London, Faber and Faber).

Davidson, D. (1982) On the very idea of a conceptual scheme, in: M. Krausz and J.W. Meiland (eds) *Relativism: Cognitive and Moral* (Notre Dame, IN, University of Notre Dame Press).

Davie, G. (1961) *The Democratic Intellect* (Edinburgh, Edinburgh University Press).

Deegan, D.H. (1995) Exploring individual differences among novices reading in a specific domain: the case of law, *Reading Research Quarterly*, 30(2), pp. 154–70.

Delgado, R. (2001) Official elitism or institutional self interest? 10 reasons why UC-Davis should abandon the LSAT (and why other good law schools should follow suit), *U.C. Davis Law Review*, 34(3), pp. 593–614.

Dellaportas, S., Cooper, B.J. and Leung, P. (2006) Measuring moral judgement and the implications of cooperative education and rule-based learning, *Accounting and Finance*, 46(1), pp. 53–70.

Deliberative Democracy E-Bulletin (2006) Posting 8. Available at http://www.deliberative-democracy.net/ebulletin/20060425.shtml. Accessed 27/02/07.

Delwiche, A. (2006) Massively multiplayer online games (MMOs) in the new media classroom, *Journal of Educational Technology and Society*, 9(3), pp. 160–72.

Designing virtual worlds: the web site. Available at http://www.mud.co.uk/dvw/bibliography.html. Accessed 16/03/07.

Dewey, J. (1969–72) *The Early Works of John Dewey, 1882–1898*, ed. J.A. Boydston (Carbondale, IL, Southern Illinois University Press).

Dewey, J. (1976–83) *The Middle Works, 1899–1924*, ed. J.A. Boydston (Carbondale, IL, Southern Illinois University Press).

Dewey, J. (1981) *The Later Works, 1925–1953*, ed. J.A. Boydston (Carbondale, IL, Southern Illinois University Press).

Dezalay, Y. and Garth, B.G. (1996) *Dealing in Virtue. International Commercial Arbitration and the Construction of a Transnational Legal Order* (Chicago and London, University of Chicago Press).

Diamantes, T. and Williams, M. (1999) Using a game format to teach national education standards to aspiring school administrators, *Education*, 119(4), pp. 727–30.

Dibbell, J. Play money: diary of a dubious proposition. Available at http://www.juliandibbell.com/playmoney/. Accessed 27/02/07.

Dibbell, J. Serfing the web: Black Snow Interactive and the world's first virtual sweat shop. Available at http://www.juliandibbell.com/texts/blacksnow.html. Accessed 27/02/07.

Dibbell, J. (2003) Weblog. Available at http://www.juliandibbell.com/texts/index.html. Accessed 27/02/07.

Dick, P.K. (1999) *Do Androids Dream of Electric Sheep?* (London, Millennium).

Dillon, A. and Gabbard, R. (1998) Hypermedia as an educational technology: a review of the quantitative research literature on learner comprehension, control and style, *Review of Educational Research*, 68(3), pp. 322–49.

Dillon, A. and Vaughan, M. (1997) 'It's the journey and the destination': shape and the emergent property of genre in evaluating digital documents, *New Review of Multimedia and Hypermedia*, 3, pp. 91–106.

Dillon, P. (2004) Trajectories and tensions in the theory of information and communication technology in education, *British Journal of Educational Studies*, 52(2), pp. 138–50.

DiPardo, A. (1994) Stimulated recall in research on writing. An antidote to 'I don't know, it was fine', in: P. Smagorinsky (ed.) *Speaking about Writing: Reflections on Research Methodology* (London and Thousand Oaks, CA, Sage).

Donaldson, M. (1992) *Human Minds: An Exploration* (London, Allen Lane, Penguin Press).

Doris, J.M. (2002) *Lack of Character. Personality and Moral Behavior* (Cambridge, Cambridge University Press).

Drew, S. (1998) Students' perceptions of their learning outcomes, *Teaching in Higher Education*, 3(2), pp. 197–217.

Dreyfus, H.L. and Dreyfus, S.E. (1986) *Mind over Machine: The Power of Human Intuition and Expertise in the Era of the Computer* (Oxford, Blackwell Publishing).

Ducheneaut, N., Yee, N., Nickell, E. and Moore, R. (2006) Alone together? Exploring the social dynamics of massively multiplayer online games, *Human Factors in Computing Systems*, CHI 2006, pp. 407–16.

Duffy, T.M. and Cunningham, D.J. (1996) Constructivism: implications for the design and delivery of instruction, in: D.H. Jonassen (ed.) *Handbook of Research for Educational Communications and Technology* (New York, Simon and Schuster Macmillan).

Duggan, C. (1961) *Twelfth-Century Decretal Collections* (London, Athlone Press).

Duxbury, N. (1995) *Patterns of American Jurisprudence* (Oxford, Clarendon).

Dwyer, J. (1987) *Virtuous Discourse: Sensibility and Community in Late Eighteenth Century Scotland* (Edinburgh, John Donald Publishers).

Eagles, J.M., Calder, S.A., Nicoll, K.S. and Walker, L.G. (2001) A comparison of real patients, simulated patients and videotape interview in teaching medical students about alcohol misuse, *Medical Teacher*, 23(5), pp. 490–93.

Economist, The (2006) It's the links, stupid. Available at http://www.economist.com/surveys/displaystory.cfm?story_id=6794172. Accessed 27/02/07.

Eck, R. van (2007) Building artificially intelligent learning games, in: D. Gibson and M. Prensky (eds) *Games and Simulations in Online Learning: Research and Development Frameworks* (Hershey, PA, Information Science Publishing).

Edwards, A. (2005) Let's get beyond community and practice: the many meanings of learning by participating, *The Curriculum Journal*, 16(1), pp. 53–69.

Edwards, A. and Mackenzie, L. (2005) Steps toward participation: the social support of lifelong learning trajectories, *International Journal of Lifelong Education*, 24(4), pp. 282–302.

Edwards, A. and MacKenzie, L. (2006) Identity shifts in informal learning trajectories, in: B. van Oers, E. Elbers, R. van der Veer and W. Wardekker (eds) *The Transformation of Learning* (Cambridge, Cambridge University Press).

Edwards, P. (2006) The shell game: who is responsible for the overuse of the LSAT in law school admissions? *St John's Law Review*, 80(1), 153–66. Available at http://tinyurl.com/336v4r. Accessed 27/02/07.

Egido, C. (1990) Teleconferencing as a technology to support co-operative work: its possibilities and limitations, in: J. Galegher, R.E. Kruatt and C. Edigo (eds) *Intellectual Teamwork: Social and Technological Foundations of Co-operative Work* (Hillsdale, NJ, Lawrence Erlbaum Associates).

Ehninger, D. (1968) On systems of rhetoric, *Philosophy and Rhetoric*, 1, pp. 131–44.

Einon, G. (1995) *Information Technology and Society: A Reader* (London, Open University Press).

Eisenstaedt, R. (1990) Problem-based learning: Cognitive retention and cohort traits of randomly selected participants and decliners, *Academic Medicine*, 65(9), pp. 511–12.

Eisner, E.W. (1990) *The Enlightened Eye: Qualitative Inquiry and the Enhancement of Educational Practice* (New York, Macmillan).

Eliot, T.S. (1963) 'The Waste Land', *Collected Poems 1909–1962* (London, Faber and Faber).

Elkins, J.R. (1985) *Rites de passage*: law students 'telling their lives', *Journal of Legal Education*, 3(1), pp. 27–55.

Ellerman, D.P. (1995) *Cultural Trespassing as a Way of Life: Essays in Philosophy, Economics and Mathematics* (London, Rowman and Littlefield Publishers).

Engelbart, D.C. (1988) *The Augmented Knowledge Workshop* (New York, SEM Press).

Engeström, Y. (2002) The new language of learning at work. Available at http://tinyurl.com/336v4r. Accessed 27/02/07.

Entwistle, N. (1995) The use of research on student learning in quality assessment, in: G. Gibbs (ed.) *Improving Student Learning Through Assessment and Evaluation* (Oxford, Oxford Centre for Staff Development).

Entwistle, N. and Entwistle, D. (2003) Preparing for examinations: the interplay of memorising and understanding, and the development of knowledge objects, *Higher Education Research and Development*, 22(1), pp. 19–41.

Entwistle, N. and Marton, F. (1994) Knowledge objects: understandings constituted through intensive academic study, *British Journal of Educational Psychology*, 64(1), pp. 161–78.

Eriksson, B. (1993) The first formulation of sociology: a discursive innovation of the eighteenth century, *Archives-Européenes-de-Sociologie*, 34(2), pp. 251–76.

Erlanger, H., Garth, B., Larson, J., Mertz, E., Nourse, V. and Wilkins, D. (2005) Is it time for a new Legal Realism? *Wisconsin Law Review*, 2, pp. 335–63.

Evans, A. and Palermo, J. (2003) Australian law students' perceptions of their values: interim results in the first year – 2001 – of a three year empirical assessment, *Legal Ethics*, 5(1/2), pp. 103–17.

Fairfield, J. (2005) Virtual property, *Boston University Law Review*, 85, p. 1047.

Farrow, F. and Norman, G. (2003) The effectiveness of PBL: the debate continues. Is meta-analysis helpful? *Medical Education*, 37(12), pp. 1131–2.

Feitelson, J. and Stefik, M.J. (1977) A case study of the reasoning in a genetics experiment, Heuristic Programming Project Report, HPP–77–18 (Working Paper), May 1977.

Felstiner, W. and Sarat, A. (1992) Enactments of power: negotiating reality and responsibility in lawyer-client interactions, *Cornell Law Review*, 77, pp. 1447–98.

Ferguson, A. (1769, 1978) *Institutes of Moral Philosophy* (New York, Garland Publishing Company).

Ferguson, A. (1792) *Principles of Moral and Political Science: Being Chiefly a Retrospect of Lectures Delivered in the College of Edinburgh, in Two Volumes* (Edinburgh, Strathan and Cadell).

Ferscha, A. and Mattern, F. (2004) *Pervasive Computing Second International Conference*, PERVASIVE 2004 (Linz/Vienna, Austria).

Fish, S. (1989) Being interdisciplinary is so very hard to do, *Profession*, 89, pp. 15–22.

Fish, S.E. (1981) *Is There a Text in This Class? The Authority of Interpretive Communities* (Cambridge, MA, Harvard University Press).

Fitzgerald, F.S. (2000) *The Great Gatsby* (London, Penguin Books).

Fitzgerald, M., Crowley, T., Greenhouse, P., Probert, C. and Horner, P. (2003) Teaching sexual history taking to medical students and examining it: experience in one medical school and a national survey, *Medical Education*, 37(2), pp. 94–8.

Fleishman, S. (1990) Philology, linguistics and the discourse of the medieval text, *Speculum*, 65, pp. 19–37.

Flexner, A. (1910) *Medical Education in the United States and Canada: A Report to the Carnegie Foundation for the Advancement of Teaching* (New York, Carnegie Foundation for the Advancement of Teaching).

Flexner, A. (1925) *Medical Education: A Comparative Study* (New York, Macmillan).

[No author] Flight Simulator. Available at http://www.microsoft.com/games/flightsimulator/. Accessed 27/02/07.

Flower, L. (1994) *The Construction of Negotiated Meaning: A Social Cognitive Theory of Writing* (Carbondale, IL, Southern Illinois Press).

Flower, L. (2003) Talking across difference: Intercultural rhetoric and the search for situated knowledge, *College Composition and Communication*, 55(1), pp. 38–68.

Flower, L. and Hayes, J.R. (1981) A cognitive process theory of writing, *College Composition and Communication*, 32(1), pp. 365–87.

Flower, L. and Hayes, J.R. (1984) Images, plans, and prose: The representation of meaning in writing, *Written Communication*, 1, pp. 120–60.

Flower, L. and Hayes, J.R. (1985) Response to Marilyn Cooper and Michael Holzman, 'Talking about Protocols', *College Composition and Communication*, 36(1), pp. 94–7.

Flower, L. and Hayes, J.R. (1989) Cognition, context, and theory building, *College Composition and Communication*, 40(3), pp. 282–311.

Flower, L., Higgins, L. and Long, E. (2000) *Learning to Rival. A Literate Practice for Intercultural Inquiry* (Mahwah, NJ, Lawrence Erlbaum Associates).

Foreign Office Architects (1995–2002) Models of the Prize – winning project Yokohama International Port Terminal. Available at http://www.arcspace.com/architects/foreign_office/yokohama/yokohama_index.htm. Accessed 27/02/07.

Forrest, F.C., Taylor, M.A., Postlethwaite, K. and Aspinall, R. (2002) Use of a high-fidelity simulator to develop testing of the technical performance of novice anaesthetists, *British Journal of Anaesthesiology*, 88(3), pp. 338–44.

Forrest, F.C., Grimes, S. and Postlethwaite, K. (2003) Does debriefing novice anaesthetists after simulator practice improve technical performance in the first three months of training? ASME 2003 Conference. Available at http://tinyurl.com/2o5cuy. Accessed 27/02/07.

Foucault, M. (1988) *Politics, Philosophy, Culture: Interviews and Other Writings 1977–84*, trans. A. Sheridan (London, Routledge).

Francis, A.M. and McDonald, I.W. (2006) Preferential treatment, social justice, and the part-time law student – the case for the value-added part-time law degree, *Journal of Law and Society*, 33(1), pp. 92–108.

Frasca, G. (2001) Videogames of the oppressed: videogames as a means for critical thinking and debate. Available at http://www.ludology.org/articles/thesis/FrascaThesis/. Accessed 28/02/07.

Freamon, B.K. (1997) Action research for justice in Newark, New Jersey, in: J. Cooper and L.G. Trubek (eds) *Educating for Justice: Social Values and Legal Education* (Dartmouth, Ashgate).

Freitas, S. de (2006) Learning in immersive worlds. a review of game-based learning. JISC Report Available at http://tinyurl.com/2ukvwl. Accessed 27/02/07.

Friendly, M. and Dennis, D.J. (no date) Milestones in the history of thematic cartography, statistical graphics and data representation, an illustrated chronology of innovations. Available at http://www.math.yorku.ca/SCS/Gallery/milestone/. Accessed 27/02/07.

Friends Reunited. Available at http://www.friendsreunited.co.uk/?li=f. Accessed 19/03/07.

Friendster. Available at http://www.friendster.com/. Accessed 19/03/07.

Freire, P. (1996) *Pedagogy of the Oppressed*, trans. M.B. Ramos (London, Penguin).

Futurelab. Available at http://futurelab.org.uk. Accessed 27/02/07.

Gabbert, F., Memon, A., Allan, K. and Wright, D. (2004) Say it to my face: examining the effects of socially encountered misinformation, *Legal and Criminological Psychology*, 9(2), pp. 215–27.

Gadamer, H.-G. (1975) *Truth and Method*, trans. W. Glen-Doepel, translation eds G. Barden and J. Cumming, (London, Sheed and Ward).

Galison, P. (1987) *How Experiments End* (Chicago, IL, University of Chicago Press).

Galison, P. (1997) *Image and Logic: A Material Culture of Microphysics* (Chicago, IL, University of Chicago Press).

Galison, P. (1997) *Relativism: Cognitive and Moral* (Notre Dame, IN, University of Notre Dame Press).

Galison, P. and Jones, C. (1995) Centripetal and centrifugal architectures: laboratory and studio. Discussion 2, in: C.C. Davidson (ed.) *Anyplace* (Cambridge, MA, MIT Press).

Gardener, H. and Mansilla, V.B. (2003) Assessing interdisciplinary work at the frontier: an empirical exploration of 'symptoms of quality'. Available at http://www.pz.harvard.edu/interdisciplinary/pdf/AssessingSymptoms.pdf. Accessed 27/02/07.

Gardner, H. (1985) *The Mind's New Science: A History of the Cognitive Revolution* (New York, Basic Books).

Gardner, P.J. (2003) A role for the business attorney in the twenty-first century: adding value to the client's enterprise in the knowledge economy, *Marquette Intellectual Property Review*, 17(7), pp. 39–77.

Garfinkel, H. (1991) Respecification: evidence for locally produced, naturally accountable phenomena of order, logic, reason, meaning, method, etc. in and as of the essential haecceity of immortal ordinary society (I) – an announcement of studies, in: G. Button (ed.) *Ethnomethodology and the Human Sciences* (Cambridge, Cambridge University Press).

Garrison, D.R. (1995) Deweyan pragmatism and the epistemology of contemporary social constructivism, *American Educational Research Journal*, 25(6), pp. 716–40.

Garrison, D.R. (2000) Theoretical challenges for distance education in the 21st century: a shift from structural to transactional issues, *International Review of Research in Open and Distance Learning*. Available at http://www.irrodl. org/content/v1.1/randy.html. Accessed 27/02/07.

Garrison, D.R. and Archer, W. (2000) *A Transactional Perspective on Teaching and Learning: A Framework for Adult and Higher Education* (Oxford, Pergamon Press).

Garrison, D.R. and Archer, W. (2003) *E-Learning in the Twenty-first Century. A Framework for Research and Practice* (London and New York, RoutledgeFalmer).

Garrison, D.R., Anderson, T. and Archer, W. (2000) Critical inquiry in a text-based environment: computer conferencing in higher education, *The Internet and Higher Education*, 2(2/3), pp. 87–105.

Garrison, D.R., Anderson, T. and Archer, W. (2001) Critical thinking, cognitive presence, and computer conferencing in distance education, *American Journal of Distance Education*, 15(1), pp. 7–23.

Garrison, J. (2006) The 'permanent deposit' of Hegelian thought in Dewey's theory of inquiry, *Educational Theory*, 56(1), pp. 1–37.

Geddes, P. (1904) *City Development: A Study of Parks, Gardens, and Culture Institutes A Report to the Carnegie Dunfermline Trust* (Edinburgh, Geddes and Co.).

Gee, J.P. (1996) *Social Linguistics and Literacies: Ideology in Discourses* (New York, RoutledgeFalmer).

Gee, J.P. (2004) *Situated Language and Learning. A Critique of Traditional Schooling* (New York and London, Routledge).

Geertz, C. (1973) *The Interpretation of Cultures* (New York, Basic Books).

Geertz, C. (1989) *Local Knowledge* (New York, Basic Books).

Genes Reunited. Available at http://www.genesreunited.co.uk/genesreunited.asp?wci=yourhome. Accessed 19/03/007.

Giddens, A. (1984) *The Constitution of Society: Outline of the Theory of Structuration* (Cambridge, Polity Press).

Giddens, A. (1991a) M*odernity and Identity* (Stanford, CA, Stanford University Press).

Giddens, A. (1991b) *Modernity and Self-Identity. Self and Society in Late Modern Age* (Cambridge, Polity Press).

Gilson, R.J. (1984) Value creation by business lawyers: legal skills and asset pricing, *Yale Law Journal*, 94(2), pp. 239–313.

Gilson, R.J. and Mnookin, R.H. (1995) Foreword: business lawyers and value creation for clients, *Oregon Law Review*, 74(1), pp. 8–10.

Ginsburg, S. (2002) The anatomy of the professional lapse: bridging the gap between traditional frameworks and students' perceptions, *Academic Medicine*, 77(6), pp. 516–522.

Ginsburg, S., and Stern, D. (2004) The professionalism movement: behaviors are the key to progress, *The American Journal of Bioethics*, 4(2), pp. 14–15.

Ginsburg, S., Regehr, G., Hatala, R., McNaughton, N., Frohna, A., Hodges, B., Lingard, L. and Stern, D. (2000) Context, conflict, and resolution: a new conceptual framework for evaluating professionalism, *Academic Medicine*, 75(10 Supplement), pp. S6–11.

Glaser, H., Alani, H., Carr, L., Chapman, S., Ciravegna, F., Dingli, A., Gibbins, N., Harris, S., Schraefel, M.C. and Shadbolt, N. (2004) *The Semantic Web: Research and Applications First European Semantic Web Symposium*, ESWS May 2004 Proceedings, 417–32 (Heraklion, Greece).

Glassman, M. (2001) Dewey and Vygotsky: society, experience, and inquiry in educational practice, *Educational Researcher*, 30(4), pp. 3–14.

Goffman, E. (1959) *The Presentation of Self in Everyday Life* (Garden City, New York, Doubleday).

Goffman, E. (1967) *Interaction Ritual* (New York, Pantheon).

Gologo, C. (2002) Role of ICTs and Kenya elections. Available at http://www. mail-archive.com/do-wire@tc.umn.edu/msg00587.html. Accessed 27/02/07.

Goodrich, P. (1990a) *Languages of Law: From Logics of Memory to Nomadic Masks* (London, Weidenfeld and Nicolson).

Goodrich, P. (1990b) We orators, *Modern Law Review*, 53(4), pp. 546–63.

Goodrich, P. (1996) Of Blackstone's Tower: Metaphors of Distance and Histories of the English Law School, in: P. Birks (ed.) *What are Law Schools For?* Vol 2: *Pressing Problems in the Law* (Oxford, Oxford University Press).

Goody, J. and Watt, I. (1963) *The Consequences of Literacy, in: J. Goody (ed.) Literacy in Traditional Societies* (Cambridge, Cambridge University Press).

Gordon, R.W. (1995) The case for (and against) Harvard, *Michigan Law Review*, 93(6), pp. 1231–60.

Gould, H. and Tobochnik, J. (1996) *An Introduction to Computer Simulation Methods: Applications to Physical Systems, 2/E* (Boston, Addison-Wesley).

Gould, S.J. (1977) *Ontogeny and Phylogeny* (Cambridge, MA, Belknap-Harvard University Press).

Graham, S. (2004) The cybercities reader, in: R.T. LeGates and F. Stout (eds) *The Routledge Urban Reader Series* (New York, Routledge).

Graham, W.S. (1979) *W.S. Graham. Collected Poems 1942–1977* (London, Faber and Faber).

Grant, J.L. (1929) The single standard in grading, *Columbia Law Review*, 29(7), pp. 920–55.

Gratian (1993) *Gratian: The Treatise on Laws with the Ordinary Gloss*, trans. A. Thompson and J. Gordley (Washington, DC, The Catholic University of America Press).

Gredler, M.E. (1996) Games and simulations and their relationships to learning, in: D.H. Jonassen (ed.) *Handbook of Research on Educational Communications and Technology*, 2nd edn (Mahwah, NJ, Lawrence Erlbaum).

Green, D.H. (1994) *Medieval Listening and Reading: The Primary Reception of German Literature 800–1300* (Cambridge, Cambridge University Press).

Green, H., Facer, K., Rudd, T., Dillon, P. and Humphreys, P. (2005) Personalization and Digital Technologies. Available at: www.futurelab.org.uk/research/ personalisation/report_01.htm. Accessed 27/02/07.

Greenfield, P. (1983) Review of the psychology of literacy, *Harvard Educational Review*, 53(3), pp. 216–20.

Gunawardena, C.N. and Zittle, F.J. (1997) Social presence as a predictor of satisfaction within a computer-mediated conferencing environment, *American Journal of Distance Education*, 11(3), pp. 8–26.

Gunsalus, C.K. and Beckett, J.S. (2006) Playing doctor, playing lawyer: interdisciplinary simulations. Available at SSRN Paper Collection, at http:// ssrn.com/abstract = 879750. Accessed 27/02/07.

Haakonssen, K. (1990) Natural law and moral realism: the Scottish synthesis, in: M.A. Stewart (ed.) *Studies in the Philosophy of the Scottish Enlightenment* (Oxford, Clarendon Press).

Haas, C. and Flower, L. (1988) Rhetorical reading strategies and the construction of meaning, *College Composition and Communication*, 39(2), pp. 167–83.

Hacking, I. (2004) The complacent disciplinarian. Available at http://www.interdisciplines.org/interdisciplinarity/papers/7/1#_1. Accessed 27/02/07.

Haggis, T. (2003) Constructing images of ourselves? A critical investigation into approaches to learning' research in Higher Education, *British Educational Research Journal*, 29(1), pp. 89–104.

Halliday, M.A.K. (1978) *Language as Social Semiotic* (London, Edward Arnold).

Hamel, C.F.R. de (1984) *Glossed Books of the Bible and the Origins of the Paris Booktrade* (Woodbridge and Wolfeboro, NH, Boydell and Brewer).

Hamel, C.F.R. de (1986) *A History of Illuminated Manuscripts* (London, Phaidon Press).

Hardt, M. and Negri, A. (2000) *Empire* (Cambridge, Cambridge University Press).

Hardt, M. and Negri, A. (2005) *Law and Internet Cultures* (New York, Cambridge University Press).

Hartley, J. and Chesworth, K. (1998) What difficulties do first-year students find in essay writing? Some results from a questionnaire study, in: P. Thompson (ed.), *Proceedings of the 5th Annual Writing Development in Higher Education Conference*, Academic Writing Development in Higher Education Conference, Centre for Applied Language Studies, April.

Haskins, C.H. (1923) *The Rise of the Universities* (New York, Henry Holt).

[No author] Harvard Law School News. HLS faculty unanimously approves first-year curricular reform. Available at http://www.law.harvard.edu/news/2006/10/06_curriculum.php. Accessed 15/03/07.

Havelock, E. (1963) *Preface to Plato* (Cambridge, Cambridge University Press).

Havelock, E. (1976) *Origins of Western Literacy* (Toronto, OISE Press).

Hayes, T. (2004) A good judge is hard to find: an essay on legal realism and law school casebooks, *Journal of Legal Education*, 54(2), pp. 216–22.

Hearn, J. (2000) *Scotland: National Identity and Liberal Culture* (Edinburgh, Polygon).

Heath, E. and Merolle, V. (2007) *Adam Ferguson: History, Progress and Human Nature* (London, Pickering and Chatto).

Heath, E. and Merolle, V. (2008, forthcoming) *Adam Ferguson: Philosophy, Politics, Society* (London, Pickering and Chatto).

Heim, M. (1987) *Electric Language: A Philosophical Study of Word Processing* (New Haven, CT, Yale University Press).

Henderson, B. (2006) Leiter on New Legal Realism. Available at http://www.elsblog.org/the_empirical_legal_studi/2006/06/leiter_on_new_L.html. Accessed on 16/03/07.

Henderson, W.D. (2004) The LSAT, law school exams, and meritocracy: the surprising and undertheorized role of test-taking speed, *Texas Law Review*, 82(4), pp. 975–1052.

Herbert, D.M.B. (1999) Remembering and knowing: the student learning experience. HERDSA Annual International Conference, 1999. Available at http://www.herdsa.org.au/branches/vic/Cornerstones/pdf/Herbert.PDF. Accessed 27/02/07.

Herbert, D.M.B. and Burt, J.S. (2001) Memory awareness and schematisation: learning in the university context, *Applied Cognitive Psychology*, 15(6), pp. 617–37.

Herbert, D.M.B. and Burt, J.S. (2003) The effects of different review opportunities on schematisation of knowledge, *Learning and Instruction*, 13(1), pp. 73–92.

Herbert, D.M.B. and Burt, J.S. (2004) What do students remember? Episodic memory and the development of schematization, *Applied Cognitive Psychology*, 18(1), pp. 77–88.

Hewitt, J. and Scardamalia, M. (1996) Design principles for the support of distributed processes, *Educational Psychology Review*, 10(1), pp. 75–95.

Hildebrand, D. (2003) *Beyond Realism and Antirealism: John Dewey and the Neopragmatists* (Nashville, TN, Vanderbilt University Press).

Hill, L. (2006) *The Passionate Society. The Social, Political and Moral Thought of Adam Ferguson, International Archives of the History of Ideas* (Dordrecht, Springer).

Hilsdon, J. (1998) Awareness of language on a BA programme, *Proceedings of the 15th Annual Writing Development in Higher Education Conference*. Available at http://www.rdg.ac.uk/AcaDepts/cl/CALS/wdhe98/hilsdon.html. Accessed 28/02/07.

Hiltz, S.R., Coppola, N., Rotter, N., Turoff, M. and Benbunan-Fich, R. (2000) Measuring the importance of collaborative learning for the effectiveness of ALN: a multi-measure, multi-method approach, *Journal of Asynchronous Learning Networks*, 4(2). Available at http://www.sloan-c.org/publications/jdn/v4n2/index.asp. Accessed 27/02/07.

Hmelo, C. and Day, R. (1999) Contextualized questioning to scaffold learning from simulations, *Computers and Education*, 32(2), pp. 151–64.

Hmelo, C., Gotterer, G.S. and Bransford, J.D. (1997) A theory-driven approach to assessing the cognitive effects of PBL, *Instructional Science*, 25(6), pp. 387–408.

Hope, L., Memon, A. and McGeorge, P. (2004) Understanding pre-trial publicity: predecisional distortion of evidence by mock jurors, *Journal of Experimental Psychology: Applied*, 10(2), pp. 111–19.

Hopkins, D. (2002) Designing user interfaces to simulation games. Available at http://www.donhopkins.com/drupal/node/9. Accessed 01/03/07.

Hopkins, D. and Ruddock, J. (eds) (1985) *Research as a Basis for Teaching: Readings from the Work of Lawrence Stenhouse* (Oxford, Heinemann Educational Publishers).

Horwitz, M. (1992) *The Transformation of American Law* (New York, Oxford University Press).

Houlahan, M. and Tacka, P. (1998) *Zoltán Kodály: A Guide to Research. Garland Reference Library of the Humanities, Composer Resource Manuals*, vol. 44 (New York, Garland Publishers).

Huber, M.T. and Morreale, S.P. (2002) *Disciplinary Styles in the Scholarship of Teaching and Learning: Exploring Common Ground* (Washington, DC, American Association for Higher Education and the Carnegie Foundation for the Advancement of Teaching).

Hughes, J. (2005) Bring emotion to work: emotional intelligence, employee resistance and the reinvention of character, *Work, Employment and Society*, 19(3), pp. 603–20.

Hunt, A. (1978) *The Sociological Movement in Law* (London, Macmillan).

Hunter, D. (2002) Philippic.com, *California Law Review*, 90(2), pp. 611–70.

Hutcheson, F. (1969–90) *Collected Works of Francis Hutcheson*, 7 vols (Hildesheim, Olms).

Hutchinson, A. (1999) Beyond black-letterism: ethics in law and legal education, *The Law Teacher*, 33(3), pp. 301–9.

[No author] Intensive Writing Model. Available at http://writing.umn.edu/tww/policy/index.htm. Accessed 19/03/07.

[No author] Interdisciplines. Available at http://www.interdisciplines.org/. Accessed 27/02/07.

Isaacs, N. (1923) How lawyers think, *Columbia Law Review*, 23(6), pp. 555–63.

Iser, W. (1978) *The Act of Reading* (Baltimore, MD, The Johns Hopkins University Press).

Ivanic, R. (1998) *Writing and Identity* (Amsterdam, John Benjamins).

[No author] IVIMEDS. Available at http://www.ivimeds.org/. Accessed 16/03/07.

Jackson, P. (1968) *Life in Classrooms* (New York, Holt, Rinehart, and Winston).

Jacobson, A.J. (1989) Autopoietic law: the new science of Niklas Luhmann, *Michigan Law Review*, 87(6), pp. 1647–89.

Jain, J. (2006) Bypassing and WAPing: reconfiguring timetables for 'real-time' mobility, in: M. Sheller and J. Urry (eds) *Mobile Technologies of the City* (London, Routledge).

Jardine, L. (1996) *Worldly Goods: A New History of the Renaissance* (London, Macmillan).

Jauss, H.R. (1982) *Toward an Aesthetic of Reception*, trans. T. Bahti (Minneapolis, University of Minnesota Press).

Johnson, D. (ed.) (1991) *Building and Using Hypertext Systems in the Practice of Law, in: From Yellow Pads to Computers – Transforming your Law Practice with a Computer* (New York, American Bar Association).

Johnson, D.R. and Post, D. (1996) Law and borders – the rise of law in cyberspace, *Stanford Law Review*, 48(5), pp. 1367–75.

Johnson, S. (1999) *Interface Culture: How New Technology Transforms the Way We Create and Communicate* (San Francisco, CA, Harper).

Johnson, S. (2005) *Everything Bad is Good for You* (New York, Penguin).

Jonçich, G.M. (1968) *The Sane Positivist: A Biography of Edward L. Thorndike* (Middletown, CT, Wesleyan University Press).

Jones, H.F. (1957) Edwin Wilhite Patterson: man and ideas, *Columbia Law Review*, 57(5), pp. 607–23.

Jones, P.G. (1997) The growing need for community legal education, in: J. Cooper and L.G. Trubek (eds) *Educating for Justice: Social Values and Legal Education* (Aldershot, Dartmouth).

Jordan, K. and Packer, R. (2000) Multimedia: from Wagner to virtual reality. Available at http://www.artmuseum.net/w2vr/contents.html. Accessed 27/02/07.

Jordanova, L.J. (1986) *Languages of Nature: Critical Essays on Science and Literature* (London, Free Association).

[No author] Kazaa. Available at http://www.kazaa.com/us/index.htm. Accessed 19/03/07.

Keep, C., McLaughlin, T. and Parmer, R. (2000) The electronic labyrinth. Available at http://www3.iath.virginia.edu/elab/hfl0158.html. Accessed 27/02/07.

Kenny, N.P. (2003) Role modeling in physicians' professional formation: reconsidering an essential but untapped educational strategy, *Academic Medicine*, 78(12), pp. 1203–10.

Ker, J., Mole, L. and Bradley, P. (2003) Early introduction to interprofessional learning: a simulated ward environment, *Medical Education*, 37(3), pp. 248–55.

Ker, J.S., Ramsay, J., Hogg, G., Dewar, G. and Ambrose, L. (2005) Medical use of standardized patients, Learning in Law Initiative Conference 2005. Available at http://zeugma.typepad.com/LILI2005.pdf. Accessed 27/02/07.

Kettler, D. (2005) *Adam Ferguson*: Biography, 2nd edn (New Brunswick, NJ and London, Transaction Publishers).

Kidder, W.C. (2001) Comment: does the LSAT mirror or magnify racial and ethnic differences in educational attainment? A study of equally achieving 'elite' college students, *California Law Review*, 89(4), pp. 1055–124.

Kilpatrick, W.H. (1918) The project method, *Teachers College Record*, 19, pp. 319–355.

Kimball, B. (1999) 'Warn students that I entertain heretical opinions which they are not to take as law': the inception of case method teaching in the classrooms of the early C.C. Langdell, *Law and History Review*, 17(1), pp. 57–141.

Kirschenbaum, M. (2003) Kirschenbaum's blog. Available at http://www.otal.umd.edu/~mgk/blog/archives/000215.html. Accessed 27/02/07.

Kliebard, H.M. (2004) *The Struggle for the American Curriculum 1893–1958* (New York and London, RoutledgeFalmer).

Klein, J.T. (1993) Blurring, cracking, and crossing: permeation and the fracturing of discipline, in: E. Messer-Davidow, D.R. Shumway and D.J. Sylvan (eds)

Knowledges: Historical and Critical Studies in Disciplinarity (Charlottesville, VA, University Press of Virginia).

Knorr-Cetina, K. (1998) *Epistemic Cultures: How Sciences Make Knowledge* (Cambridge, MA, Harvard University Press).

[No author] Knowledge Media Design Unit (Toronto, University of Toronto). Available at http://kmdi.utoronto.ca/?docID=Documents/2/2. htmlanddb=kmdi. Accessed 27/02/07.

[No author] The British Kodály Academy. Available at http://www. britishkodalyacademy.org/about_kodaly.htm. Accessed 27/02/07.

Kohlberg, L. (1969) Stage and sequence: the cognitive-developmental approach to socialization, in: D.A. Goslin (ed.) *Handbook of Socialization Theory and Research* (Chicago, IL, Rand McNally).

Kohlberg, L. (1981) *Essays on Moral Development, Volume I: The Philosophy of Moral Development* (San Francisco, Harper and Row).

Kohlberg, L., Levine, C. and Hewer, A. (1983) *Moral Stages: A Current Formulation and a Response to Critics* (New York, Karger, Basel).

Konefsky, S.J. (1946) *Chief Justice Stone and the Supreme Court* (New York, Macmillan).

Koschmann, T. (2000) The physiological and the social in the psychologies of Dewey and Thorndike: the matter of habit, in: B. Fishman and S. O'Connor-Divelbiss (eds) *Fourth International Conference of the Learning Sciences* (Mahwah, NJ, Lawrence Erlbaum Associates).

Koschmann, T. (2001) A third metaphor for learning: toward a Deweyan form of transactional inquiry, in: S. Carver and D. Klahr (eds) *Cognition and Instruction: 25 Years of Progress* (Mahwah, NJ, Lawrence Erlbaum Associates).

Koschmann, T. (2003) CSCL, argumentation, and Deweyan inquiry in: J. Andriessen, M. Baker and D. Suthers (eds) *Arguing to Learn: Confronting Cognitions in Computer-Supported Collaborative Learning Environments* (Amsterdam, Kluwer Academic Publishers).

Koschmann, T. (2006) Tools of termlessness: technology, educational reform, and Deweyan inquiry. Available at http://edaff.siumed.edu/tk/articles/UNESCO. pdf. Accessed 27/02/07.

Koster, R. (2004) Online world timeline. Available at http://www.legendmud.org/ raph/gaming/mudtimeline.html. Accessed 27/02/07.

Kraft, R.N. (1987) The influence of camera angle on comprehension and retention of pictorial events, *Memory and Cognition*, 15(4), pp. 291–307.

Kreiger, S.H. (2004) Domain knowledge and the teaching of creative legal problem solving, *Clinical Law Review*, 11(1), pp. 149–207.

Kress, G. (1988) *Linguistic Processes in Sociocultural Practice* (Oxford, Oxford University Press).

Kress, G. (1997) *Before Writing: Rethinking the Paths to Literacy* (London, Routledge).

Kress, G. (2000) A curriculum for the future, *Cambridge Journal of Education*, 30(1), pp. 133–45.

Kress, G. and Leeuwen, T. van (1996) *Reading Images: The Grammar of Visual Design* (London, Routledge).

Krieger, L. (2002) Institutional denial about the dark side of law school, and fresh empirical guidance for constructively breaking the silence, *Journal of Legal Education*, 52(1–2), pp. 112–29.

Kritz, M.M. (2006) *Globalisation and Internationalisation of Tertiary Education*. Final Report submitted to the United Nations Population Division. Available at http://tinyurl.com/3cw8vk. Accessed 27/02/07.

Kruse, K.R. (2005) Lawyers, justice, and the challenge of moral pluralism, *Minnesota Law Review*, 90(2), pp. 389–458.

Kuhlmann, M. and Schumann, M. (2001) What's left of workers' solidarity? Workplace innovation and workers' attitude towards the firm, in: S.P. Vallas (ed.) *The Transformation of Work* (Amsterdam, JAI).

Lageman, E.C. (1989) The plural worlds of educational research, *History of Education Quarterly*, 29(2), pp. 185–214.

Lambton, C. (2006) Voices of change. Available at http://www.nycos.co.uk/press_articles.htm#BBCMusicMagazine. Accessed 27/02/07.

Landow, G.P. (1992) *Hypertext: The Convergence of Contemporary Critical Theory and Technology* (Baltimore, MD and London, The Johns Hopkins University Press). Available at www.landow.com. Accessed 27/02/07.

Landow, G.P. (1994) *What's a Critic to Do? Critical Theory in the Age of Hypertext* (Baltimore, MD, The Johns Hopkins University Press).

Langdell, C.C. (1879) *A Selection of Cases on the Law of Contracts*, 2nd edn (Boston, MA, Little, Brown).

Langdell, C.C. (1887) Teaching law as a science, *American Law Review*, 21(1), pp. 123–5.

Langsam, D.M. (1998) Case study 5: a course portfolio for midcareer reflection, in: P. Hutchings (ed.) *The Course Portfolio: How Faculty Can Examine Their Teaching to Advance Practice and Improve Student Learning* (Washington, DC, American Association for Higher Education).

Lanham, R. (1993) *The Electronic Word: Democracy, Technology and the Arts* (Chicago, IL, University of Chicago Press).

Lastowka, G.F. and Hunter, D. (2004) The laws of the virtual worlds, *California Law Review*, 92(1), pp. 1–74.

Latour, B. (1983) *Give Me a Laboratory and I Will Raise the World* (London, Sage).

Latour, B. (1987) *Science in Action: How to Follow Scientists and Engineers Through Society* (Cambridge, MA, Harvard University Press).

Latour, B. and Woolgar, S. (1979) *Laboratory Life: the Social Construction of Scientific Facts* (Los Angeles, CA and London, Sage).

Laurillard, D. (1992) Learning through collaborative computer simulations, *British Journal of Educational Technology*, 23(3), pp. 164–71.

Laurillard, D. (2002) *Rethinking University Teaching: A Conversational Framework for the Effective Use of Learning Technologies* (London, Routledge).

Lavaux, S. and Riche, F. (2001) (Un)plug building (TourEDF). Available at http://www.architecture.it/hp/copertina/19/default.htm Accessed 27/02/07.

Lave, J. and Wenger, E. (1991) *Situated Learning: Legitimate Peripheral Participation* (Cambridge, Cambridge University Press).

[No author] Law Society of Scotland. Available at http://www.lawscot.org.uk. Accessed 27/02/07.

Le Brun, M. and Johnson, R. (1994) *The Quiet (R)evolution: Improving Student Learning in Law* (North Ryde, NSW, Law Book Company).

Lea, M. and Rogers, P. (2003) Social processes in electronic teamwork: the central issue of identity, in: A. Haslam, D. van Knippenberg, M. Platow and N. Ellemers (eds) *Social Identity at Work: Developing Theory for Organizational Practice* (Philadelphia, PA, Taylor and Francis).

Lea, M. and Stierer, B. (2000) *Student Writing in Higher Education* (Buckingham, Society for Research into Higher Education and Open University Press).

Leclercq, J. (1961) *Love of Learning and the Desire for God* (New York, Fordham University Press).

Lefebvre, H. (1991) *The Production of Space*, trans. D. Nicholson-Smith (Oxford, Blackwell Publishing).

Leiter, B. (no date) The so-called New Legal Realism project. Brian Leiter's Law School Reports, Brian Leiter's Law School Reports. Available at http://leiterlawschool.typepad.com/leiter/2006/06/the_socalled_ne.html. Accessed 27/02/07.

Leiter, B. (2006) Introduction: from Legal Realism to naturalized jurisprudence. Available at SSRN: http://ssrn.com/abstract=926079. Accessed 27/02/07.

Lemonnier, P. (1993) *Technological Choices. Transformation in Material Cultures Since the Neolithic* (London, Routledge).

Lenoir, T. (1997) *Instituting Science: The Cultural Production of Scientific Disciplines. Writing Science Series* (Stanford, CA, Stanford University Press).

Leont'ev, A.N. (1979) *Activity, Consciousness, and Personality* (Englewood Cliffs, NJ, Prentice-Hall).

Leont'ev, A.N. (1981) The problem of activity in psychology, in: J. Wertsch (ed.) *The Concept of Activity in Soviet Psychology* (Armonk, NY, Sharpe).

Lessig, L. Lessig Blog. Available at http://lessig.org/blog/archives/003570.shtml. Accessed 27/02/07.

Lessig, L. (1999) *Code and Other Laws of Cyberspace* (New York, Basic Books).

Lessig, L. (2006) *Code Version 2.0* (New York, Basic Books).

Lessig, L. (2003) Creators in *Second Life*. Available at http://www.lessig.org/blog/archives/001577.shtml. Accessed 27/02/07.

Lester, J.C., Towns, S.G., Callaway, C.B., Voerman, J.L. and Fitzgerald, P.J. (2000) *Deictic and Emotive Communication in Animated Pedagogical Agents* (Cambridge MA, MIT Press).

Levin, J. and Boon, A. (1999) *The Ethics and Conduct of Lawyers in England and Wales* (Oxford, Hart Publishing).

Levin, J. and Thurston, C. (1996) Educational electronic networks: a review of research and development, *Educational Leadership*, 54(3), pp. 46–50.

Levine, G. (1988) *Darwin and the Novelists: Patterns of Science in Victorian Fiction* (Cambridge, MA, Harvard University Press).

Levinson, S. and Balkin, J.M. (1991) Law, music, and other performing arts, *University of Pennsylvania Law Review*, 139(6), pp. 1597–658.

Lewis, M.W., Bishay, M, McArthur, D. and Chou, J. (1993) Supporting discovery learning in mathematics: design and analysis of an exploration environment and inquiry activities, *Instructional Science* 21(6), pp. 473–88.

Liao, Y.C. (1999) Effects of hypermedia on students' achievement: a meta-analysis, *Journal of Educational Multimedia and Hypermedia*, 8(3), pp. 255–77.

Lieux, E.M. (1996) A comparative study of learning in lecture versus problem based format, *About Teaching*, 50 (Spring). Available at http://www.udel.edu/pbl/cte/spr96-nutr.html. Accessed 27/2/07.

Lillis, T. and Grainger, K. (1998) Exploring the socio-discursive space of higher education: focus on student-tutor talk. Education-line. Available at http://www.leeds.ac.uk/educol/documents/000000686.htm. Accessed 27/02/07.

Lingard, L. (2004) Expert and trainee determinations of rhetorical relevance in referral and consultation letters, *Medical Education*, 38(2), pp. 168–76.

Lingard, L., Reznick, R., DeVito, I. and Espin, S. (2002) Forming professional identities on the health care team: discursive constructions of the 'other' in the operating room, *Medical Education*, 36(8), pp. 728–34.

Llewellyn, K. (1930) Realistic jurisprudence – the next step, *Columbia Law Review*, 30(4), pp. 431–65.

Llewellyn, K. (1960) *The Common Law Tradition – Deciding Appeals* (Boston, MA and Toronto, Little, Brown).

Losowsky, A. (2004) A 21st-century protest, *The Guardian*. Available at http://www.guardian.co.uk/online/story/0,3605,1176738,00.html. Accessed 27/02/07.

Lucas, U., Cox, P., Croudace, C. and Milford, P. (2004) 'Who writes this stuff?': students' perceptions of their skills development, *Teaching in Higher Education*, 9(1), pp. 55–68.

Luff, I. (2000) 'I've been in the Reichstag': rethinking roleplay, *Teaching History*, 100, pp. 8–17.

Luhmann, N. (1982) Autopoesis, handlung und kommunikative verständigung, *Zeitschrift für Soziologie*, 11(4), pp. 366–79.

Lundeberg, M.A. (1987) Metacognitive aspects of reading comprehension: studying understanding in legal case analysis, *Reading Research Quarterly*, 22(4), pp. 407–32.

Lyons, J. (1972) Formal analysis of communicative processes, in: R.A. Hinde (ed.) *Nonverbal Communication* (Cambridge, Cambridge University Press).

Lyotard, J.F. (1984) *Postmodern Condition. A Report on Knowledge* (Manchester, Manchester University Press).

MacCormick, N. (1994) *Legal Reasoning and Legal Theory* (Oxford, Clarendon Press).

MacDonald, B. (1999) *Doctor Honoris Causa Address* (Valladolid, University of Valladolid).

MacFarlane, J. (1997) The legal skills movement ten years on: triumph or compromise?, *Journal of Law and Society*, 24(3), pp. 440–43.

MacIntyre, A. (1985) *After Virtue: A Study in Moral Theory* (London, Duckworth).

MacKenzie, D. (1990) *Inventing Accuracy. A Historical Sociology of Nuclear Missile Guidance* (Cambridge, MA, MIT Press).

Maclean, I. (1992) *Interpretation and Meaning in the Renaissance: The Case of Law* (Cambridge, Cambridge University Press).

MacLure, M. and Pettigrew, M. (1997) The press, public knowledge and education (East Anglia, Centre for Applied Research Education University of East Anglia). Available at http://www.uea.ac.uk/care/research/press.html. Accessed 27/02/07.

MacLure, M. and Stronach, I. (1993) Great accidents in history: vocationalist innovations, the National Curriculum and pupil identity, in: J. Wellington (ed.) *The Work Related Curriculum* (London, Kogan Page).

Maggs, E. (2001) Creating law school review videos and slides and putting them on the internet (Pittsburgh, University of Pittsburgh School of Law). Available at http://jurist.law.pitt.edu/lessons/lessept01.htm. Accessed 27/02/07.

Maharg, P. (2000a) 'Context cues cognition': writing, rhetoric and legal argumentation, in: S. Mitchell and R. Andrew (eds) *Learning to Argue in Higher Education* (London, Boynton/Cook, Heinemann).

Maharg, P. (2000b) Rogers, constructivism and jurisprudence: educational critique and the legal curriculum, *International Journal of the Legal Profession*, 7(3), pp. 189–204.

Maharg, P. (2001a) Legal skills and multimedia: enhancing student learning, Learning in Law Initiative Conference, UKCLE, University of Warwick. Available at http://www.ukcle.ac.uk/interact/lili/2001/maharg.html. Accessed 01/03/07.

Maharg, P. (2001b) Negotiating the web: legal skills learning in a virtual community, *International Review of Law, Computers and Technology*, 15(3), pp. 345–60.

Maharg, P. (2002) Agile methods in the development of web-based teaching, learning and assessment. Internal Working Paper 11, Learning Technologies Development Unit, Glasgow Graduate School of Law.

Maharg, P. (2004) Virtual communities on the web: transactional learning and teaching, in: A. Vedder (ed.) *Aan het Werk met ICT in het Academisch Onderwijs* (Nijmegen, Wolf Legal Publishers).

Maharg, P. (2006) On the edge: ICT and the transformation of professional legal learning, *Web Journal of Current Legal Issues*, 3. Available at http://webjcli. ncl.ac.uk/2006/issue3/maharg3.html. Accessed 27/02/07.

Maharg, P. and Muntjewerff, A. (2002) Through a screen darkly: electronic legal education in Europe, *The Law Teacher*, 36(3), pp. 307–32.

Maharg, P. and Muntjewerff, A. (2005) Editorial: legal education and information and communications technology, *The Law Teacher*, 39(1), pp. iv–vi.

Maharg, P. and Paliwala, A. (2002) Negotiating the learning process with electronic resources, in: R. Burridge, K. Hinett, A. Paliwala and T. Varnava (eds) *Effective Learning and Teaching in Law* (London, Kogan Page).

Maister, D. (2005) A great coach in action. Available at http://davidmaister.com/ articles/1/40/. Accessed 01/03/07.

[No author] making of modern law: a mirror on society, The. Online database, Available at http://tinyurl.com/2qfhex. Accessed 27/02/07.

Malone, M.A. (2003) Lines blur between art and medicine in new course, Stanford, CA News Report. Available at http://news-service.stanford.edu/news/2003/ february19/artmed.html. Accessed 19/03/07.

Mandell, L.M. and Shaw, D.L. (1973) Judging people in the news – unconsciously: effect of camera angle and bodily activity, *Journal of Broadcasting*, 17, pp. 353–62.

Mansilla, V.B. and Gardener, H. (2003) Assessing interdisciplinary work at the frontier. An empirical exploration of symptoms of quality, *Rethinking Interdisciplinarity*. Available at http://www.interdisciplines.org/ interdisciplinarity/papers/6. Accessed 01/03/07.

Marchionini, G. (1991) Psychological dimensions of user-computer interface. Available at http://www.ericfacility.net/ericdigests/ed337203.html. Accessed 27/02/07.

Martin, C. and Bial, H. (eds) (2000) *Brecht Sourcebook*, trans. E. Anderson (London, Routledge).

Martin, P.W. (1999) Distance learning: the LII's experience and future plans. Available at http://www.law.cornell.edu/background/distance/liidistance.htm. Accessed 27/02/07.

Martin, T. (1995) Tom Martin's Journal for his 'Herodotus Class using Perseus' in the spring term of 1995 at Holy Cross. Available at http://vanth.perseus. tufts.edu/classes/TMHerodotus.95s.html. Accessed 03/03/07.

Marton, F. (1976) On non-verbatim learning, IV: some theoretical and methodological notes, *Scandinavian Journal of Psychology*, 17, pp. 125–8.

Marton, F. and Booth, S. (1997) *Learning and Awareness* (Mahwah, NJ, Lawrence Erlbaum Associates).

Maturana, H.R. (1981) Autopoesis, in: M. Zeleny (ed.) *Autopoesis, A Theory of Living Organization* (North-Holland, Elsevier).

Matyka, M. [no date] Computer simulations in physics. Available at http://panoramix.ift.uni.wroc.pl/~maq/eng/. Accessed 27/02/07.

Matyka, M. [no date] The Hubble volume simulations. Available at http://www.physics.lsa.umich.edu/hubble-volume/. Accessed 27/02/07.

Mautner, T. (1993) *Francis Hutcheson: Two Texts on Human Nature* (Cambridge, Cambridge University Press).

Mayer, R. (1997) Multimedia learning: are we asking the right questions?, *Educational Psychologist*, 32(1), pp. 1–19.

Mayer, R. (2001) *Multimedia Learning* (New York, Cambridge University Press).

Mayer, R. and Moreno, R. (2000) A split attention effect in multimedia learning: evidence for dual processing systems in working memory, Journal of *Educational Psychology*, 90(2), pp. 312–30.

Mayer, R. and Moreno, R. (2003) Nine ways to reduce cognitive load in multimedia learning, *Educational Psychologist*, 38(1), pp. 43–52.

McCain, T.A., Chilberg, J. and Wakshlag, J. (1997) The effect of camera angle on source credibility and attraction, *Journal of Broadcasting* (21), pp. 35–46.

McConnell, D. (2005) Examining the dynamics of networked e-learning groups and communities, *Studies in Higher Education*, 30(1), pp. 25–32.

McCracken, G. (2006) How virtual worlds discovered dynamism. This Blog Sits at the Intersection of Anthropology and Economics. Available at http://www.cultureby.com/trilogy/2006/05/how_virtual_wor.html. Accessed 27/02/07.

McCraken, G. (2006) How virtual worlds discovered dynamism. Available at http://www.cultureby.com/trilogy/2006/05/how_virtual_wor.html. Accessed 27/02/07.

McGrew, W.C. (1992) *Chimpanzee Material Culture. Implications for Human Evolution* (Cambridge, Cambridge University Press).

McKeachie, W.J. (1990) Research on college teaching: The historical background, *Journal of Educational Psychology*, 82(2), pp. 189–200.

McKendree, J., Reader, W. and Hammond, N. (1995) The 'homeopathic fallacy' in learning from hypertext, *Interactions*, 2(3), pp. 74–82.

McMillan, J.H. and Schumacher, S. (1984) *Research in Education: A Conceptual Introduction* (Boston, Little Brown).

Memon, A. and Bull, R. (2001) *Handbook of the Psychology of Interviewing* (Chichester, Wiley).

Memon, A., Hope, L. and Bull, R. (2003) Exposure duration: effects on eyewitness accuracy and confidence, *British Journal of Psychology*, 94(3), pp. 339–54.

Menand, L. (2001) *The Metaphysical Club: A Story of Ideas in America* (New York, Farrar, Straus and Giroux).

Mercer, N. (1995, repr. 1998) *The Guided Construction of Knowledge: Talk Amongst Teachers and Learners* (London, Multilingual Matters).

Mercer, N. (2000) *Words and Minds: How We Use Language to Think Together* (London, Routledge).

Mertz, E. (2006) My take on New Legal Realism, *Empirical Legal Studies* blog. Available at http://www.elsblog.org/the_empirical_legal_studi/2006/06/my_take_on_new_.html. Accessed 27/02/07.

Messaris, P. (1997) *Visual Persuasion: The Role of Images in Advertising* (London, Sage).

Mignon, C. (1998) Post-tenure review: a case study of a course portfolio within a personnel file, in: P. Hutchings (ed.) *The Course Portfolio: How Faculty Can Examine Their Teaching To Advance Practice and Improve Student Learning* (Washington, DC, American Association for Higher Education).

Milgram, S. [no date] The Familiar Stranger Project: Anxiety, Comfort and Play. Available at http://berkeley.intel-research.net/paulos/research/familiarstranger/. Accessed 16/03/07.

Miller, C.A. (2004) Human-computer etiquette: managing expectations with intentional agents, *Communications of the Association for Computing Machinery*, 47(4), pp. 30–33.

Misch, D. (2002) Evaluating physicians' professionalism and humanism: the case for humanism 'connoisseurs', *Academic Medicine*, 77(6), pp. 489–95.

[No author] MIT Open Courseware Initiative [no date]. Available at http://ocw.mit.edu/index.html. Accessed 27/02/07.

Molinda, M. (2003) Cone of experience, in: A. Kovalchick and K. Dawson (eds) *Educational Technology: An Encyclopedia* (Santa Barbara, CA, ABC-Clio).

Montaigne, M.E. de. (1952) *The Essays of Michel Eyquem de Montaigne*, ed. W. Carew Hazlitt (London, William Benton).

Moore, J. (1990) The two systems of Francis Hutcheson: on the origins of the Scottish enlightenment, in: M.A. Stewart (ed.) *Studies in the Philosophy of the Scottish Enlightenment* (Oxford, Clarendon Press).

Moore, J. and Campbell, T.D. (1982) *Francis Hutcheson: 'Father' of the Scottish Enlightenment* (Edinburgh, John Donald).

Moore, M. and Kearsley, G. (1996) *Distance Education: A Systems View* (Boston, MA, Wadsworth Publishing).

Moore, M.G. (1993) *Theory of Transactional Distance, Theoretical Principles of Distance Education*, ed. D. Keegan (London, Routledge).

Moore, U. and Callahan, C.C. (1943) *Law and Learning Theory: A Study in Legal Control* (New Haven, CT, The Yale Law Journal Company).

Moorehead, R., Paterson, A. and Sherr, A. (2003) What clients know: client perspectives and legal competence, *International Journal of the Legal Profession*, 10(1), pp. 5–33.

Moran, M. (2003) *Rethinking the Reasonable Person. An Egalitarian Reconstruction of the Objective Standard* (Oxford, Oxford University Press).

Moreno, R. and Mayer, R. (2000) A coherence effect in multimedia learning: the case for minimizing irrelevant sounds in the design of multimedia instructional messages, *Journal of Educational Psychology*, 92(1), pp. 117–25.

Morissette, Y.M. (2002) McGill's integrated civil and common law program, *Journal of Legal Education*, 52(1), pp. 12–28.

Morrissey, T.E. (1989) The art of teaching and learning law: a late medieval tract, in: L. Brockliss (ed.) *History of Universities*, vol. VIII (Oxford, Oxford University Press).

Moss, B. (2000) The use of large-group roleplay techniques in social work education, *Social Work Education*, 19(5), pp. 471–83.

Moss, B. (2002) Review article, *Social Work Education*, 21(5), pp. 597–601.

Mousavi, S., Lowe, R. and Sweller, J. (1995) Reducing cognitive load by mixing auditory and visual presentation modes, *Journal of Educational Psychology*, 87(2), pp. 319–34.

Mulligan, J. and Patrovsky, B. (2003) *Developing Online Games: An Insider's Guide* (Berkeley, CA, Pearson Education).

[No author] Napster. Available at http://www.napster.co.uk/. Accessed 19/03/07.

Nardi, B.A. (1996) *Context and Consciousness: Activity Theory and Human-Computer Interaction* (Cambridge, MA, The MIT Press).

Nardi, B.A. and O'Day, V. (1999) *Information Ecologies. Using Technology with Heart* (Cambridge, MA, The MIT Press).

Nelson, T.H. (1965) A file structure for the complex, the changing, and the indeterminate, in: Association of Computing Machinery, *Proceedings of the 20th National Conference* (New York, Association for Computing Machinery), pp. 84–100.

Nerhot, P. (1991) *Legal Knowledge and Analogy: Fragments of Legal Epistemology, Hermeneutics and Linguistics* (London, Kluwer Academic Publishers).

Nesson, C. (2006) A proposal summary, CyberLaw wiki. Available at http://tinyurl.com/3y368l. Accessed 27/02/07.

Nesson, C., Nesson, R. and Koo, G. (2006) CyberOne: law in the court of public opinion. Available at http://blogs.law.harvard.edu/cyberone/administration/course-description. Accessed 16/03/07.

Neva, P. (2006) Comment. Terranove blog. Available at http://tinyurl.com/2v7btq. Accessed 16/03/07.

[No author] New Legal Realism blog. Available at http://www.newlegalrealism.org. Accessed 16/03/07.

New London Group (1996) A pedagogy of multiliteracies: designing social futures, *Harvard Educational Review*, 66(1), pp. 60–92.

Newble, D.I. and Clarke, R.M. (1986) The approaches to learning of students in a traditional and in an innovative problem-based medical school, *Medical Education*, 20(4), pp. 267–73.

Newman, M. (2001) A pilot systematic review and meta-analysis on the effectiveness of problem-based learning. Available at http://www.ltsn-01.ac.uk/resources/features/pbl. LTSN Medicine, Dentistry and Veterinary Medicine. Accessed 27/02/07.

[No author] (1946) *A College Program in Action: A Review of Working Principles at Columbia College* (New York, Columbia University Press).

[No author] No Education Patents! Available at http://noedupatents.org/. Accessed 16/03/07.

[No author] Nolo Podcasts. Available at http://www.nolo.com/podcasts.cfm. Accessed 19/03/07.

Nolte, J., Eller, P. and Ringel, S.P. (1988) Shifting toward problem based learning in a medical school neurobiology course, *Proceedings of the Annual Conference on Research in Medical Education*, 27, pp. 66–71.

Norman, G. and Schmidt, H. (2000) Effectiveness of problem-based learning curricula: theory, practice, and paper darts, *Medical Education*, 34(9), pp. 721,728.

Norrie, A. (2005) *Law and the Beautiful Soul* (London, The Glasshouse Press).

Noveck, B.S. (2005) A democracy of groups. Available at http://www.firstmonday. org/issues/issue10_11/noveck/index.html. Accessed 27/02/07.

Noveck, B.S. (2006) Democracy – the video game. Virtual worlds and the future of collective action in: J. Balkin and B.S. Noveck (eds) *The State of Play. Law, Games, and Virtual Worlds* (New York, New York University Press).

Oates, L.C. (1997) Beating the odds: reading strategies of law students admitted through alternative admissions programs, *Iowa Law Review*, 83(1), pp. 139–60.

Oliver, D.W. and Shaver, J.P. (1966) *Teaching Public Issues in the High School* (Boston, MA, Houghton Mifflin).

Olson, D.R. (1994) *The World on Paper* (Cambridge and New York, Cambridge University Press).

Ondrejka, C. (2006a) Escaping the gilded cage: user-created content and building the metaverse, in: J.M. Balkin and B.S. Noveck (eds) *The State of Play. Law, Games and Virtual Worlds* (New York, New York University Press).

Ondrejka, C. (2006b) Finding common ground in new worlds, *Games and Culture*, 1(1), pp. 111–15.

[No author] Onewisdom Social Software. Available at http://www.onewisdom. pbwiki.com/SocialSoftware. Accessed 19/03/07.

Ong, W. (1976) *The Presence of the Word* (New Haven, CT, Yale University Press).

Ong, W. (1982) *Orality and Literacy* (London, Methuen).

Ong, W. (1986) Writing is a technology that restructures thought, in: G. Baumann (ed.) *The Written Word: Literacy in Transition* (Wolfstone College Lectures) (Oxford, Oxford University Press).

Open University, [no date] OpenLearn Initiative Available at http://openlearn. open.ac.uk/. Accessed 27/02/07.

Otis, L. (1994) *Organic Memory: History and the Body in the Late Nineteenth and Early Twentieth Centuries* (Lincoln, NE, University of Nebraska Press).

Oz-Salzberger, F. (ed.) (1996), *A. Ferguson, An Essay on the History of Civil Society* (Cambridge, Cambridge University Press).

Packer, C. and Goldsmith, A. (1998) 'Failed sociologists' in the market place: law schools in Australia, *Journal of Law and Society*, 25(1), pp. 33–50.

Padovani, S. and Lansdale, M. (2003) Balancing search and retrieval in hypertext: context-specific trade-offs in navigational tool use, *Journal of Human-Computer Studies*, 57(1), pp. 125–49.

Paivio, A. (1986) *Mental Representation: A Dual Coding Approach (Dual-Code Theory)* (Oxford, Oxford University Press).

Paliwala, A. (2001) Learning in cyberspace, Journal of Information, Law and Technology, 1. Available at http://www2.warwick.ac.uk/fac/soc/law/elj/jilt/2001_1/paliwala/. Accessed 27/02/07.

Paliwala, A. (2005) Changing paradigms of the e: communication, governance and learning, *Journal of Information, Law and Technology*, 2–3. Available at http://www2.warwick.ac.uk/fac/soc/law/elj/jilt/2005_2-3/paliwala/. Accessed 01/03/07.

Papadakis, M.A., Loeser, H. and Healy, K. (2004a) Early detection and evaluation of professionalism deficiencies in medical students, *Academic Medicine*, 76(11), pp. 1100–6.

Papadakis, M.A., Hodgson, C.S., Teherani, A.P.D. and Kohatsu, N.D. (2004b) Unprofessional behavior in medical school is associated with subsequent disciplinary action by a state medical board, *Academic Medicine*, 79(3), pp. 244–79.

Papert, S. (1980) *Mindstorms: Children, Computers and Powerful Ideas* (Brighton, Harvester Press).

Parkes, M.B. (1991) *Scribes, Scripts and Readers: Studies in the Communication, Presentation and Dissemination of Medieval Texts* (London, The Hambledon Press).

Parkes, M.B. (1992) *Pause and Effect: An Introduction to the History of Punctuation in the West* (Aldershot, Scolar Press).

Patch, K. (2004) Conversational engagement tracked, TRNmag.com. Available at http://www.trnmag.com/Stories/2004/120104/Conversational_engagement_tracked_120104.html. Accessed 27/02/07.

Patel, V. and Kaufman, D.R. (2000) Clinical reasoning and biomedical knowledge: implications for teaching, in: J. Higgs and M. Jones (eds) *Clinical Reasoning in the Health Professions* (London, Butterworth Heinemann).

Patterson, E.W. (1950) John Dewey and the law: theories of legal reasoning and valuation, *American Bar Association Journal*, 5(36), pp. 619–34.

Pea, R.D. (1993) Practices of distributed intelligence and designs for education in: G. Salomon (ed.) *Distributed Cognitions: Psychological and Educational Considerations* (Cambridge, Cambridge University Press).

Pearson, R. and van Schaik, P. (2003) The effect of spatial layout of and link colour in web pages on performance in a visual search task and an interactive search task, *Journal of Human-Computer Studies*, 59(3), pp. 327–53.

Peters, R.S. (1959) *Authority, Responsibility and Education* (London, Allen and Unwin).

Petrovic, J.E. (1998) Dewey is a philistine and other grave misreadings, *Oxford Review of Education*, 24(4), pp. 513–20.

Petrucci, A. (1995) *Writers and Readers in Medieval Italy: Studies in the History of Written Culture*, trans. C.M. Radding (New Haven, CT, Yale University Press).

Phillips, M. (1996) *All Must Have Prizes* (London, Little, Brown and Co).

Piaget, J. (1932) *The Moral Judgment of the Child* (London, Kegan Paul).

Pilke, E.M. (2004) Flow experiences in information technology use, *International Journal of Human-Computer Studies*, 61(3), pp. 347–57.

Pleasantville (1998) Internet movie database. Available at http://www.imdb.com/title/tt0120789/quotes. Accessed 27/02/07.

Pocock, J.G.A. (1975) *The Machiavellian Moment. Florentine Political Thought and the Atlantic Republican Tradition* (Princeton, NJ, Princeton University Press).

Poirer, M.K., Clark, M.M., Cerhan, J.H., Pruthri, S., Geda, Y.E. and Dale, L.C. (2004) Teaching motivational interviewing to first year medical students to improve counseling skills in health behaviour changes, *Clinical Procedure*, 79(3), pp. 327–31.

Power, F.C., Higgins, A. and Kohlberg, L. (1989) *'Just Community' Schools Created in the 1970s. Lawrence Kohlberg's Approach to Moral Education* (New York, Columbia University Press).

Prawat, R.S. (2005) Dewey and Vygotsky viewed through the rear-view mirror – and dimly at that, *Educational Researcher*, 31(5), pp. 16–20.

Prislin, M.D., Lie, D., Shapiro, J., Boker, J. and Radecki, S. (2001) Using standardized patients to assess medical students' professionalism, *Academic Medicine*, 76(10 Supplement), pp. S90–92.

Pruijt, H. (2002) Neo-Tayloristic and anti-Tayloristic models of teamworking. Available at http://www.eur.nl/fsw/english/staff/homepages/pruijt/papers/working/. Accessed 27/02/07.

[No author] RAE (2006) RAE 2008 Panel criteria and working methods. Available at http://www.rae.ac.uk/pubs/2006/01/. Accessed 27/02/07.

Rall, M. (2000) Key elements of debriefing for simulator training. ASME Conference 2000. Available at http://www.uni-mainz.de/FB/Medizin/Anaesthesie/SESAM/Downloads/Abstracts%202000.pdf. Accessed 27/02/07.

Rammert, W. (1997) New rules of sociological method: rethinking technology studies, *British Journal of Sociology*, 48(2), pp. 171–91.

Ramsden, P. (1992) *Learning to Teach in Higher Education* (London, Routledge).

Ránki, G. (1987) *Bartok and Kodály Revisited. Indiana University Studies on Hungary*, vol. 2 (Bloomington, IN, Indiana University Press).

Raz, J. (1979) *The Authority of Law* (Oxford, Clarendon Press).

Reed, A.Z. (1928) *Present-Day Law Schools in the United States and Canada* (New York, Carnegie Foundation for the Advancement of Teaching).

[No author] Research Resource on Action Research. Available at http://www.bath.ac.uk/~edsajw/. Accessed 27/02/07.

Rest, J., Narváez, D., Bebeau, M.J. and Thoma, S.J. (1999) *Postconventional Moral Thinking: A Neo-Kohlbergian Approach* (Mahwah, NJ, Erlbaum).

Rest, R. and Deemer, D. (1986) *Life Experiences and Developmental Pathways* (New York, Praeger).

Reynolds, R. (2002) Playing a 'good' game: a philosophical approach to understanding the morality of games. Available at http://www.igda.org/articles/rreynolds_ethics.php. Accessed 27/02/07.

Reynolds, R. (2005) The four worlds theory. Available at http://terranova.blogs.com/terra_nova/2005/08/the_four_worlds.html. Accessed 16/03/07.

Rheingold, H. (1992) A slice of my life in my virtual community. Available at http://interact.uoregon.edu/medialit/MLR/home/index.html. Accessed 01/03/07.

Rheingold, H. (2003) *Smart Mobs. The Next Social Revolution* (New York, Perseus Books).

Rhem, J. (2002) Of diagrams and models: learning as a game of pinball, *National Teaching and Learning Forum*, 11(4), pp. 104–22.

Rhode, D. (2000) Legal education: professional interests and public values, *Indiana Law Review*, 34(1), pp. 23–46.

Riva, G. (2005) Virtual reality in psychotherapy: review, *CyberPsychology and Behavior*, 8(3), pp. 200–30.

Roberts, G. (2003) Review of research assessment. Available at http://www.ra-review.ac.uk/reports/roberts.asp. Accessed 27/02/07.

Rogers, C. (1980) *A Way of Being* (Boston, Houghton Mifflin).

Rose, G. (1984) *A Dialectic of Nihilism: Poststructuralism and Law* (Oxford, Blackwell Publishing).

Rose, G. (1992) *The Broken Middle. Out of Our Ancient Society* (Oxford, Blackwell Publishing).

Rose, G. (1995) *Love's Work. A Reckoning with Life* (New York, Schocken Books).

Rose, G. (1996) *Mourning Becomes the Law* (Cambridge, Cambridge University Press).

Rosenblatt, L. (1978) *The Reader, the Text, the Poem: The Transactional Theory of the Literary Work* (Carbondale, IL, Southern Illinois University Press).

Rothenberg, M. (2003) Weblogs and the semantic web, Broadening the Blog (Part 1), Internet Research 4.0. Available at http://www.ecommons.net/aoir/aoir2003/index.php?p=1. Accessed 27/02/07.

Rourke, L., Anderson, T., Garrison, D.R. and Archer, W. (2001) Assessing social presence in asynchronous text-based computer conferencing, *Journal of Distance Education*, 14(2). Available at http://cade.athabascau.ca/vol14.2/rourke_et_al.html. Accessed 27/02/07.

Rouse, M.A. and Rouse, R.H. (1992) *Authentic Witnesses: Approaches to Medieval Texts and Manuscripts* (Notre Dame, IN, University of Notre Dame Press).

Royal Society, Transport and the Environment Committee (1996) *Interdisciplinarity – Transport and the Environment* (London, Royal Society).

Rubin, E., Knight, W.H. and Bartlett, K. (2006) A conversation among deans from: 'Results: Legal Education, Institutional Change, and a Decade of Gender Studies', *Harvard Journal of Law and Gender* Conference, 2006, *Harvard Journal of Law and Gender*, 29(2), pp. 465–84.

Ryan, A. (1995) *John Dewey and the High Tide of American Liberalism* (New York and London, W.W. Norton and Co).

Saenger, P. (1991) The separation of words and the physiology of reading, in: D.R. Olsen and N. Torrance (eds) *Literacy and Orality* (Cambridge, Cambridge University Press).

Salen, K. and Zimmerman, E. (2004) *Rules of Play. Game Design Fundamentals* (Cambridge, MA, MIT Press).

Salen, K. and Zimmerman, E. (2006) *The Game Design Reader. A Rules of Play Anthology* (Cambridge, MA, MIT Press).

Santos, B. de Sousa (1995) *Toward a New Common Sense. Law, Science and Politics in the Paradigmatic Transition* (New York, Routledge).

Scaife, M. and Rodgers, Y. (1996) External cognition: how do graphical representations work? *International Journal of Human-Computer Studies*, 45(2), pp. 185–213.

Scardamalia, M. and Bereiter, C. (1986) Research on written composition, in: M. Wittrock (ed.) *Handbook of Research on Teaching*, 3rd edn (Skokie, IL, Rand McNally).

Scardamalia, M., Bereiter, C. and Goelman, H. (1982) The role of production factors in writing ability, in: M. Nystrand (ed.) *What Writers Know: The Language, Process, and Structure of Written Discourse* (London, Academic Press).

Schama, S. (1989) *Citizens: A Chronicle of the French Revolution* (London, Penguin).

Schatzki, T.R., Knorr-Cetina, K. and Savigny, E., von (2001) Introduction: practice theory, in: T.R. Schatzki (ed.) *The Practice Turn in Contemporary Theory* (New York, Routledge).

Schlegel, J.H. (1995) *American Legal Realism and Empirical Social Science* (Chapel Hill, NC, University of North Caroline Press).

Schmidt, H.G. (1983) Problem-based learning: rationale and description, *Medical Education*, 17(1), pp. 11–16.

Schmidt, H.G. (1993) Foundations of problem-based learning; some explanatory notes, *Medical Education*, 27(422), pp. 422–32.

Schneuwly, B. and Dolz, J. (1997) Les genres scolaires. Des pratiques langagières aux objets d'enseignement, *Repères*, 15, pp. 27–41.

Schön, D. (1987) *Educating the Reflective Practitioner* (San Francisco, CA, Jossey-Bass).

Schwab, J. (1970) *The Practical: A Language for Curriculum* (Washington, DC, National Education Association).

Schwarcz, S.L. (2006) Explaining the value of transactional lawyering, *Stanford Journal of Law, Business and Finance* forthcoming (2007) 12. Available at Duke

Law School Legal Studies Research Paper Series, No. 108, 29, http://eprints. law.duke.edu/archive/00001563/. Accessed 27/02/07.

Schweber, H. (1998) Before Langdell. The roots of American legal science, in: S. Sheppard (ed.) *The History of Legal Education in the United States. Commentaries and Primary Sources*, vol. II (Pasadena, CA, Salem Press).

Shweder, R.A., Goodnow, J., Hatano, G., Levine, R.A., Markus, H. and Miller, P. (1998) The cultural psychology of development: one mind, many mentalities, in: W. Damon and R.M. Lerner (eds) *Handbook of Child Psychology*, Vol. I. *Theoretical Models of Human Development*, 5th. edn (New York, John Wiley).

Scott, A. (no date) PBL Resources, UKCLE Problem-based Learning Working Group. Available at http://www.ukcle.ac.uk/resources/pbl/group.html. Accessed 15/03/07.

Scottish Arts Council [no date] Arts Across the Curriculum. Available at http://www.scottisharts.org.uk/1/artsinscotland/education.aspx. Accessed 27/02/07.

Scribner, S. and Cole, M. (1981) *The Psychology of Literacy* (Cambridge, MA, Harvard University Press).

Senge, P. (1994) *The Fifth Discipline Fieldbook: Strategies for Building a Learning Organization* (London, Nicholas Brealey Publishing).

Sennett, R. (1978) *The Fall of Public Man. On the Social Psychology of Capitalism* (New York, Vintage Books).

Sennett, R. (1998) *The Corrosion of Character: The Personal Consequences of Work in the New Capitalism* (London, W.W. Norton and Co).

Sfard, A. (1998) On two metaphors for learning and the dangers of choosing just one, *Educational Researcher*, 27(2), pp. 4–13.

Shaffer, D.W. and Squire, K.D. (2006) *The Pasteurization of Education*, International Conference of the Learning Sciences (Bloomington, ICLS). Available at http://epistemicgames.org/cv/papers/pasteurization_for_ICLS. pdf. Accessed 27/02/07.

Shane, P.M. (2004) *Democracy Online. The Prospects for Political Renewal Through the Internet* (New York and London, Routledge).

Shannon, B. (1993) *The Representational and the Presentational: An Essay on Cognition and the Study of Mind* (Hemel Hempstead, Harvester).

Sher, R.B. (1990) Professors of virtue: the social history of the Edinburgh Moral Philosophy Chair, in: M.A. Stewart (ed.) *Eighteenth Century Studies in the Philosophy of the Scottish Enlightenment* (Oxford, Clarendon Press).

Sherr, A. (1986) Lawyers and clients: the first meeting, *Modern Law Review*, 49(3), pp. 323–57.

Sherr, A. (2000) Professional work, professional careers and legal education: educating the lawyer for 2010, *International Journal of the Legal Profession*, 7(3), pp. 325–42.

Sherwin, R.K., Feigenson, N. and Spiesel, C. (2006) Law in the digital age: how visual communication technologies are transforming the practice, theory, and teaching of law, *Boston University Journal of Science and Technology Law*, 12(2), pp. 227–73.

Shirky, C. (2002) In-room chat as a social tool, O'Reilly, P2P.com. Available at http://tinyurl.com/md4bp. Accessed 27/02/07.

Shirky, C. (2003) Social software and the politics of groups. Available at http://www.shirky.com/writings/group_politics.html. Accessed 27/02/07.

Short, J., Williams, E. and Christie, B. (1976) *The Social Psychology of Telecommunications* (New York, Wiley).

Shulman, L. (1998) Course anatomy: the dissection and analysis of knowledge through teaching, in: P. Hutchings (ed.) *The Course Portfolio: How Faculty Can Examine Their Teaching to Advance Practice and Improve Student Learning* (Alexandria, VA, American Association for Higher Education).

Shulman, L. (2002) Making differences: a table of learning, *Change*, 34(6), pp. 36–44. Available at The Carnegie Foundation for the Advancement of Teaching, http://tinyurl.com/39xt2v. Accessed 01/03/07.

Shulman, L., Golde, C.M., Bueschel, A.C. and Garabedian, K.J. (2006) Reclaiming education's doctorates: a critique and a proposal, *Educational Researcher*, 35(3), pp. 25–32.

Shweder, R.A., Goodnow, J., Hatano, G., LeVine, R.A., Markus, H. and Miller, P. (1998) The cultural psychology of development: one mind, many mentalities, in: W. Damon (ed.) *Handbook of Child Psychology*, 5th edn, Vol. 1: R.M. Lerner (ed.) *Theoretical Models of Human Development* (New York, Wiley).

Siemens, G. [no date] elearnspace blog. Available at http://www.elearnspace.org/. Accessed 19/03/07.

Skaalid, B. (2003) Constructivist tools for learning. Available at http://www.usask.ca/education/coursework/802papers/Skaalid/tools.html. Accessed 27/02/07.

Sleeper, R. (1986) *The Necessity of Pragmatism. John Dewey's Conception of Philosophy* (New Haven, CT and London, Yale University Press).

Slevin, J. (2000) *The Internet and Society* (Malden, MA, Polity Press).

Smith, J. (1996) What's all this hype about hypertext?: Teaching literature with George P. Landow's 'The Dickens Web', *Computers and the Humanities*, 30(2), pp. 121–9.

Smith, L.F. (1995) Interviewing clients: a linguistic comparison of the 'traditional' interview and the 'client centered' interview, *Clinical Law Review*, 1(3), pp. 541–92.

Smith, L.F. (1998) Medical paradigms for counseling: giving clients bad news, *Clinical Law Review*, 4(1), pp. 391–431.

Smith, M.M. (1994) The design relationship between the manuscript and the incunable, in: R. Myers, and M. Harris (eds) *A Millennium of the Book: Production, Design and Illustration in Manuscript and Print 900–1900* (Winchester, St Paul's Bibliographies).

Smith, P.E., Fuller, G.N., Kinnersley, P., Brigley, S. and Elwyn, G. (2002) Using simulated consultations to develop communication skills for neurology trainees, *European Journal of Neurology*, 9(1), pp. 83–7.

Snow, M. (1999) *The Nightfisherman. Selected Letters of W.S. Graham* (London, Carcanet).

Southern, R.W. (1963) *St Anselm and his Biographer* (Cambridge, Cambridge University Press).

Spickard III, J.M.D., Alrajeh, N., Cordray, D. and Gigante, J. (2002) Learning about screening using an online or live lecture: does it matter?, *Journal of General Internal Medicine*, 17(7), pp. 540–45.

Spickard III, J.M.D., Smithers, J., Dordrav, D., Gigante, J. and Wofford, J.L. (2004) A randomised trial of an online lecture with and without audio, *Medical Education*, 38(7), pp. 787–90.

Spool, J. (Spool) Evolution Trumps Usability Guidelines, User Interface Engineering. Available at http://www.uie.com/articles/evolution_trumps_ usability. Accessed 01/03/07.

Sproull, L. and Keisler, S. (1991) *Connections: New Ways of Working in the Networked Organization* (Cambridge, MA, MIT Press).

Sraffa, P. (1961) *Production of Commodities by Means of Commodities* (Cambridge, Cambridge University Press).

Stafford, F.J. (1994) *The Last of the Race: the Growth of a Myth from Milton to Darwin* (Oxford, Clarendon Press).

Staudt, R.W. (1991) Legal mindstorms: lawyers, computers and powerful ideas, *Jurimetrics Journal*, 31(2), pp. 171–85.

Stedeford, J. (2003) Evaluation of the care of critically ill patients (COCIP) course. A nurse oriented, simulation based course ASME Conference 2003. Available at http://tinyurl.com/2o5cuy. Accessed 27/02/007.

Steffey, C.S. (2001) The effects of visual and verbal cues in multimedia instruction (unpublished thesis, Virginia Polytechnic Institute and State University). Available at http://tinyurl.com/2rckdx. Accessed 27/02/07.

Steinkuehler, C. (2005) Cognition and learning in massively multiplayer online games: a critical approach (unpublished thesis, University of Wisconsin-Madison). Available at http://website.education.wisc.edu/steinkuehler/thesis. html. Accessed 27/02/07.

Steinkuehler, C. and Williams, D. (2006) Where everybody knows your (screen) name: online games as 'third places', *Journal of Computer-Mediated Communication*, 11(4). Available at http://jcmc.indiana.edu/vol11/issue4/ steinkuehler.html. Accessed 27/02/07.

Stenhouse, L. (1983) *Authority, Education and Emancipation* (London, Heinemann Educational Books).

Stern, D. (2006) *Measuring Medical Professionalism* (New York, Oxford University Press).

Stevens, W. (1978) *The Collected Poems of Wallace Stevens* (New York, Alfred A. Knopf).

Stock, B. (1983) *The Implications of Literacy: Written Language and Models of Interpretation in the Eleventh and Twelfth Centuries* (Princeton, NJ, Princeton University Press).

Stokes, D. (1997) *Pasteur's Quadrant: Basic Science and Technological Innovation* (Washington, DC, Brookings Institution Press).

Stone, A. (1995) *The War of Desire and Technology at the Close of the Mechanical Age* (Cambridge, MA, MIT Press).

Stone, H.F. (1921) Legal education and democratic principle, *American Bar Association Journal*, 7(12), pp. 639–46.

Stone, H.F. (1923) Some aspects of the problem of law simplification, *Columbia Law Review*, 23(4), pp. 319–37.

Stone, H.F. and Mason, A.T. (1953) *Harlan Fiske Stone: Pillar of the Law* (New York, Viking Press).

Stratman, J.F. (2002) When law students read cases: exploring relations between professional legal reasoning roles and problem detection, *Discourse Processes*, 34(1), pp. 57–90.

Strauss, P. (2006) Transsystemia – are we approaching a new Langdellian moment? Is McGill leading the way?, *Journal of Legal Education*, 56(2). Available at http://ssrn.com/abstract=879767. Accessed 27/02/07.

Suchman, L. (1987) *Plans and Situated Actions. The Problem of Human Machine Communication* (Cambridge, Cambridge University Press).

Sullivan, S. (2000) Reconfiguring gender with John Dewey: habit, bodies, and cultural change, *Hypatia*, 15(1), pp. 23–42.

Sullivan, W.M., Colby, A., Wegner, J.W., Bond, L. and Shulman, L. (2007) *Educating Lawyers. Preparation for the Profession of Law* (Stanford, CA, The Carnegie Foundation for the Advancement of Teaching). Summary available at http://www.carnegiefoundation.org/files/elibrary/EducatingLawyers_summary.pdf. Accessed 27/02/07.

Summers, R. (1983) *Instrumentalism and American Legal Theory* (Ithaca, NY, Cornell University Press).

Swaak, J. and de Jong, T. (2001) Discovery simulations and the assessment of intuitive knowledge, *Journal of Computer-Assisted Learning*, 17(3), pp. 284–94.

Swales, J. (1990) *Genre Analysis: English in Academic and Research Settings* (Cambridge, Cambridge University Press).

Swanson-Owens, D. (1994) Using intervention protocols to study the effects of instructional scaffolding on writing and learning, in: P. Smagorinsky (ed.) *Speaking About Writing: Reflections on Research Methodology* (Thousand Oaks, CA, Sage).

Sweller, J. (1988) Cognitive load during problem solving: effects on learning, *Cognitive Science*, 12(1), pp. 257–85.

Sweller, J. (1994) Cognitive load theory, learning difficulty and instructional design, *Learning and Instruction*, 4(2), pp. 295–312.

Sweller, J., van Merrienboer, J.J.G. and Pass, F.G.W.C. (2001) Cognitive architecture and instructional design, *Educational Psychological Review*, 10(3), pp. 251–96.

Tanner, L. (1997) *Dewey's Laboratory School: Lessons for Today* (New York, Columbia University, Teacher's College Press).

Taylor, T. (2007) *Conference on College Composition and Communication Bibliography of Composition and Rhetoric 1984–1999*. Available at http://www.ibiblio.org/cccc/. Accessed 19/03/07.

[No author] Technorati. [no date] Available at http://www.technorati.com/. Accessed 19/03/07.

Terwilliger, J. (1997) Semantics, psychometrics, and assessment reform: a close look at 'authentic' assessment, *Educational Researcher*, 26(8), pp. 24–7.

Thalheimer, W. (2004) Bells, whistles, neon, and purple prose: when interesting words, sounds, and visuals hurt learning and performance— a review of the seductive-augmentation research. Available at http://www.work-learning.com/catalog. Accessed 01/03/07.

Thalheimer, W. (2005) Are wiki's [sic] inherently flawed? Will at Work Learning blog. Available at http://www.willatworklearning.com/2005/12/are_wikis_inher.html. Accessed 19/03/07.

Thomas, D.A. (2003) Predicting law school academic performance from LSAT scores and undergraduate grade point averages: A comprehensive study, *Arizona State Law Journal*, 28(3), pp. 1007–10.

Thompson, E.P. (1971) The moral economy of the crowd in the eighteenth century, *Past and Present*, 50, pp. 76–136.

Thompson, E.P. (1991) *Customs in Common* (London, Penguin).

Thorndike, E.L. (1931) Value of research in education, *Teachers College Record*, 33(2), pp. 96–9.

Thornton, M. (2001) The demise of diversity in legal education: globalisation and the new knowledge economy, *International Journal of the Legal Profession*, 8(1), pp. 37–56.

Timmermans, S. and Berg, M. (2003) *The Gold Standard. The Challenge of Evidence-Based Medicine and Standardization in Health Care* (Philadelphia, PA, Temple University Press).

Tochon, F.V. (2000) When authentic experiences are 'enminded' into disciplinary genres: crossing biographic and situated knowledge, *Learning and Instruction*, 10(4), pp. 331–59.

Toddington, S. (1996) The emperor's new skills: the academy, the profession and the idea of legal education, in: P.B.H. Birks (ed.) *What are Law Schools for? Pressing Problems in the Law*, vol. 2 (Oxford, Oxford University Press).

Todorov, T. (1978) *Genres in Discourse*, trans. C. Porter (Cambridge, Cambridge University Press).

Tomlinson, S. (1997) Edward Lee Thorndike and John Dewey on the science of education, *Oxford Review of Education*, 23(3), pp. 365–83.

Trigwell, K. and Ashwin, P. (2006) An exploratory study of situated conceptions of learning and learning environments, *Higher Education*, 51(2), pp. 243–58.

Trowler, P., Fanghanel, J. and Wareham, T. (2005) Freeing the chi of change: the Higher Education Academy and enhancing teaching and learning in higher education, *Studies in Higher Education*, 30(4), pp. 247–444.

Trubek, L.G. (2005) Crossing boundaries: legal education and the challenge of the new public interest law, in: N*ew Legal Realism Symposium: Is It Time for a New Legal Realism?*, *Wisconsin Law Review*, 2005(2), pp. 455–78.

Tsui, M.F. (2004) *Classroom Discourse and the Space of Learning* (Mahwah, NJ, Lawrence Erlbaum Associates).

Tu, C. (2002) The measurement of social presence in an online learning environment, *International Journal on E-Learning*, 1(2), pp. 34–45.

Tubbs, N. (1997) *Contradiction of Enlightenment. Hegel and the Broken Middle* (Aldershot, Ashgate).

Tulving, E. (1972) Episodic and semantic memory, in: E. Tulving and W. Donaldson (eds) *Organisation of Memory* (New York, Academic Press).

Tulving, E. (1985) Memory and consciousness, *Canadian Psychology*, 26(2), pp. 1–12.

Turkle, S. [no date] MIT Initiative on Technology and Self. Available at http://web.mit.edu/sturkle/techself/. Accessed 27/02/07.

Turkle, S. (1995) *Life on the Screen: Identity in the Age of the Internet* (New York, Simon and Schuster).

Turkle, S. (1996) Virtuality and its discontents, *The American Prospect*, 24 (Winter), pp. 50–57.

Turkle, S. (2005) *The Second Self: Computers and the Human Spirit* (Cambridge, MA, MIT Press).

Turkle, S. (2007) *Evocative Objects: Things We Think With* (Cambridge, MA, MIT Press).

Thurmond, V. and Wambach, K. (2004) Understanding interactions in distance education: a review of the literature, *International Journal of Instructional Technology and Distance Learning*, 1(1). Available at http://www.itdl.org/journal/Jan_04/article02.htm. Accessed 27/02/07.

Turow, S. (1997) *One L* (New York, Warner Books).

Twigger, D., Byard, M., Draper, S., Driver, R., Hartley, J.R., Hennessy, S., Mallen, C., Mohammed, R., O'Malley, C., O'Shea, T. and Scanlon, E. (1991) The 'conceptual change in science' project, *Journal of Computer Assisted Learning*, 7(2), pp. 144–55.

Twining, W. (1967) Pericles and the plumber, *Law Quarterly Review*, 83, pp. 396–426.

Twining, W. (1973) *Karl Llewellyn and the Realist Movement* (London, Weidenfeld and Nicolson).

Twining, W. (1982) The Benson Report and legal education: a personal view, in: P.A. Thomas (ed.) *Law in the Balance: Legal Services in the 1980s* (Oxford, Robertson).

Twining, W. (1985) Talk about realism, *New York University Law Review*, 60(3), pp. 329–84.

Twining, W. (1995) What are law schools for?, *Northern Ireland Legal Quarterly*, 46(3/4), pp. 291–304.

Twining, W. (1997) *Law in Context: Enlarging a Discipline* (Oxford, Oxford University Press).

Twining, W. (2002) *The Great Juristic Bazaar. Jurists' Texts and Lawyers' Stories* (Aldershot, Dartmouth).

[No author] UK Legal Education and Training Group. [no date] Available at www.letg.org.uk. Accessed 27/02/07.

UNESCO Institute for Statistics (2004) Global education digest 2006. Comparing education statistics across the world. Available at http://www.uis.unesco.org/TEMPLATE/pdf/ged/2006/GED2006.pdf. Accessed 27/02/07.

Unger, R. (1983) The Critical Legal Studies movement, *Harvard Law Review*, 96(3), pp. 561–675.

[No author] University of Sydney Multimedia Research Bibliography. Available at http://www.iml.uts.edu.au/learnteach/resources/pubs/mmpubs.html. Accessed 27/02/07.

Vanderstraeten, R. (2002) Dewey's transactional constructivism, *Journal of Philosophy of Education*, 36(2), pp. 233–46.

[No author] Virtual Air Traffic Simulation Network (VATSIM) [no date]. Available at http://www.vatsim.net. Accessed 27/02/07.

Veenman, M.V.M., Prins, F.J. and Elshout, J.J. (2002) Initial inductive learning in a complex computer simulated environment: the role of metacognitive skills and intellectual ability, *Computers in Human Behavior*, 18(3), pp. 327–41.

Vernon, D.T. and Blake, R.L. (1993) Does problem-based learning work? A meta-analysis of evaluative research, *Academic Medicine*, 68(7), pp. 550–63.

Veser, H.A. (ed.) (1989) *The New Historicism* (New York, Routledge).

Vickers, B. (1989) *In Defence of Rhetoric* (Oxford, Clarendon Press).

[No author] (2006) Virtual Hospital Archive: a digital library of health information (Iowa, University of Iowa). Available at http://www.vh.org/welcome/tour/patientsimulations.html. Accessed 27/02/07.

Vrasidas, C. and Glaass, G.V. (2002) A conceptual framework for studying distance education, in: C. Vrasidas and G.V. Glass (eds) *Current Perspectives on Applied Information Technologies*, Vol. I: *Distance Education and Distributed Learning* (Greenwich, CT, Information Age Publishing Inc.).

Vries, de, M., Schmidt, H.G. and de Graaf, E. (1989) Dutch Comparisons: cognitive and motivational effects of problem based learning on medical students, in: H.G. Schmidt, M. Lipkin, M.W. de Vries and J.M. Greep (eds) *New Directions for Medical Education: Problem based Learning and Community Oriented Medical Education* (New York, Springer Verlag).

Wallace, P. (1997) Following the threads of an innovation: the history of standardized patients in medical education, *Caduceus, A Humanities Journal for Medicine and the Health Sciences*, 13(2), pp. 5–28.

Ward, I. (1995) *Law and Literature: Possibilities and Perspectives* (Cambridge, Cambridge University Press).

Watters, C., Duffy, J. and Duffy, K. (2003) Using large tables on small display devices, *Journal of Human-Computer Studies*, 58(3), pp. 21–37.

Weaver, R.L. (1991) Some reflections on the case method, *Legal Studies*, 11(2), pp. 155–71.

Webb, J. (1998) Ethics for lawyers or ethics for citizens? New directions for legal education, *Journal of Law and Society*, 25(1), pp. 134–50.

Webb, J. (1999) Developing ethical lawyers: can legal education enhance access to justice?, *The Law Teacher*, 33(3), pp. 284–97.

Weinstein, I. (2001) Testing multiple intelligences: Comparing evaluation by simulation and written exam, *Clinical Law Review*, 8(1), pp. 247–86.

Wells, G. (1999) *Dialogic Inquiry* (Cambridge, Cambridge University Press).

Welschinger (1884) *Les Almanachs de la Révolution* (Paris, Librairie des Bibliophiles).

Wendel, B. (2005) Moral character and legal (ethics) education. Available at Legal Ethics Forum blog, http://legalethicsforum.typepad.com/blog/2005/06/moral_character.html. Accessed 27/02/07.

Wenger, E. (1998) *Communities of Practice. Learning, Meaning and Identity* (Cambridge, Cambridge University Press).

West, L. (1996) *Beyond Fragments. Adults, Motivation and Higher Education: A Biographical Analysis* (London, Taylor and Francis).

Westwood, F. (2000) *Achieving Best Practice: Shaping Professionals for Success* (London, McGraw-Hill Publishing).

Westwood, F. (2004) *Accelerated Best Practice: Implementing Success in Professional Firms* (London, Palgrave Macmillan).

White, G.E. (1978) *Patterns of American Legal Thought* (Indianapolis, IN, Babs Merrill).

White, M. (1947) *Social Thought in America* (New York, The Viking Press).

Wiegand, S.A. (1997) Deception and artifice: Thelma, Louise and the legal hermeneutic, *Oklahoma City University Law Review*, 22(1), pp. 25–49.

[No author] Wikipedia. [No date] Available at http://en.wikipedia.org/wiki/Main_Page. Accessed 19/03/07.

Wiley, J. (1993) Expertise as mental set: the effects of domain knowledge in creative problem solving, *Memory and Cognition*, 26(4), pp. 716–18.

Williams, C., Aubin, S., Harkin, P. and Cottrell, D. (2001) A randomised, controlled, single-blind trial of teaching provided by a computer-based multimedia package versus lecture, *Medical Education*, 35(9), pp. 847–54.

Williams, E. (1997) Experimental comparisons of face-to-face and mediated communication: a review, *Psychological Bulletin*, 84(5), pp. 963–76.

Winston, B. (1998) *Media Technology and Society: A History. From the Telegraph to the Internet* (New York, Routledge).

Winter, S. (1989) The cognitive dimension of the agon between legal power and narrative meaning, *Michigan Law Review*, 87(8), pp. 2225–79.

Wofford, M.M., Anderson, W., Spickard III, M.D. and Wofford, M.D. (2001) The computer-based lecture, *Journal of General Internal Medicine*, 16(7), pp. 464–7.

Wood, B.D. (1925) The measurement of law school work, *Columbia Law Review*, 25(1), pp. 316–54.

Wood, J. and Cox, R. (1993) Rethinking critical voice: materiality and situated knowledges, *Western Journal of Communication*, 57, pp. 278–87.

Woodcock, B. (2006) MMORPG Statistics. Available at http://www.mmorpgchart.com/. Accessed 16/03/07.

[No author] *World of Warcraft* (2007) Peer-to-Peer Combat. Available at http://www.worldofwarcraft.com/pvp/pvp-article.html. Accessed 16/03/07.

Yee, N. [no date] Daedalus Portal. Available at http://nickyee.com/daedalus/archives/001535.php. Accessed 27/02/07.

Yee, N. (2001) The Norrathian scrolls: a study of EverQuest (version 2.5). Available at http://www.nickyee.com/eqt/report.html. Accessed 27/02/07.

Yee, N. (2006a) The demographics, motivations and derived experiences of users of massively-multiuser online graphical environments, *PRESENCE: Teleoperators and Virtual Environments*, 15(3), pp. 309–29.

Yee, N. (2006b) Motivations of play in online games, CyberPschology and Behavior. Available at http://tinyurl.com/kpfbx).pdf. Accessed 27/02/07.

Yee, N. (2006) Time spent in the meta-game, *The Daedalus Project*, 4/5. Available at http://www.nickyee.com/daedalus/archives/001535.php. Accessed 27/02/07.

York, G. (2002) In South Korea it's the mouse that roars, *The Globe and Mail*. Available athttp://tinyurl.com/373obq. Accessed 27/02/07.

Yu, C., Aoki, P.M. and Woodruff, A. (2004) Detecting user engagement in everyday conversations, in: *8th International Conference on Spoken Language Processing 2* (Jeju Island, Korea), pp. 1329–32.

Zittrain, J. and Edelman, B. (2003) Empirical analysis of internet filtering in China (Berkman Centre for Internet and Society, Harvard Law School). Available at http://cyber.law.harvard.edu/filtering/china/. Accessed 27/02/07.

Zittrain, J. and Palfrey, J. (2005) Internet filtering in China, 2004–5: a country study. Available at http://www.opennetinitiative.net/studies/china/ONI_China_Country_Study.pdf. Accessed 27/02/07.

Index